AGING AND THE INDIAN DIASPORA

AGING
AND THE
INDIAN
DIASPORA

COSMOPOLITAN FAMILIES
IN INDIA AND ABROAD

SARAH LAMB

Indiana University Press
Bloomington and Indianapolis

This book is a publication of

Indiana University Press
601 North Morton Street
Bloomington, IN 47404–3797 USA

www.iupress.indiana.edu

Telephone orders   800–842–6796
Fax orders   812–855–7931
Orders by e-mail   iuporder@indiana.edu

Manufactured in the United States of America

Library of Congress Cataloging-in-Publication Data

Lamb, Sarah, date
    Aging and the Indian diaspora : cosmopolitan families in India and abroad /
Sarah Lamb.
    p.   cm. — (Tracking globalization)
    Includes bibliographical references and index.
    ISBN 978-0-253-35343-6 (cloth : alk. paper) — ISBN 978-0-253-22100-1
(pbk. : alk. paper) 1. Aging—India. 2. Older people—India—Social conditions.
3. East Indians—United States—Social conditions. 4. East Indian diaspora. I. Title.
    HQ1064.I4L35   2009
    306.3'808991411—dc22

                                                        2008054189

        1   2   3   4   5   14   13   12   11   10   09

On the seashore of endless worlds children meet. Tempest roams in the pathless sky, ships get wrecked in the trackless water, death is abroad and children play. On the seashore of endless worlds is the great meeting of children.

—RABINDRANATH TAGORE,
Gitanjali (Song Offerings), 1913

CONTENTS

PREFACE

This book uses aging as a lens to examine and reflect upon profound processes of social change under way in India and the world today. It focuses on older middle-class Indians and their communities in both India and the United States, concentrating on the proliferation of old age homes (a startlingly new phenomenon in India), the growing prevalence of living alone, and the transnational dispersal of families amidst global labor markets. Based on intensive ethnographic fieldwork in several U.S. and Indian cities extending over nearly fifteen years, the book investigates the unique and complex ways that older persons themselves are actively involved in the making and remaking of a society.

The book's epigraph comprises the final lines from "On the shore of endless worlds," a prose poem of the beloved Bengali author and Nobel Prize winner Rabindranath Tagore, from his 1913 collection, *Gitanjali,* or "Song Offerings." The poem depicts children meeting on "the seashore of endless worlds," unaware that death is abroad in the vast deep as they frolic delightedly in the waves. Three of my older Bengali informants— one couple and one single man—invoked the poem to me when reflecting on how their children, and the Indian public at large, are frolicking exultantly in the new opportunities of the present, unaware of the angst and sacrifice involved in entering these new worlds. But the older couple was not so terribly pessimistic, offering that this is a beautiful poem, and that perhaps we all are delightedly playing on the shore. Here is the poem in Tagore's own English translation:

> On the seashore of endless worlds children meet. The infinite sky is motionless overhead and the restless water is boisterous. On the seashore of endless worlds the children meet with shouts and dances.
>
> They build their houses with sand and they play with empty shells. With withered leaves they weave their boats and smilingly float them on the vast deep. Children have their play on the seashore of worlds.
>
> They know not how to swim, they know not how to cast nets. Pearl fishers dive for pearls, merchants sail in their ships, while children gather pebbles and scatter them again. They seek not for hidden treasures, they know not how to cast nets.
>
> The sea surges up with laughter and pale gleams the smile of the sea beach. Death-dealing waves sing meaningless ballads to the

children, even as a mother while rocking her baby's cradle. The sea plays with children, and pale gleams the smile of the sea beach.

On the seashore of endless worlds children meet. Tempest roams in the pathless sky, ships get wrecked in the trackless water, death is abroad and children play. On the seashore of endless worlds is the great meeting of children. (Tagore 1913: poem #60, pp. 54–55)

As poems do, this one has many possible meanings, and not all readers interpret it as I have here. One other interpretation I have heard Bengalis offer is that it is about how people are ignorant of God's presence. Another is that human existence is inherently ephemeral (in contrast to the endlessness of the divine), although at the same time alluring and wonderful. The image of standing on the shore also brings to mind the experience of aging itself, as a life phase of many transitions. I have chosen the poem's lines as an epigraph because they evoke several of the book's core themes: the sense of being on the shore of unknown new worlds during a period of striking social change; the ephemerality of the human condition itself, which is highlighted (Bengalis say) in old age; and the paradoxical mixture of delight and angst, promise and sacrifice that many elder Indians, and their families and communities, experience as they negotiate the new social-cultural worlds of the present.

One of my central arguments is that the significance of aging is not limited to the customary question of how to care for increasing numbers of dependent elderly as the world faces dramatic population maturation. Rather, beliefs and practices surrounding aging illuminate much broader social-cultural phenomena, including global cultural and economic flows; the relationship between persons, families, and states; the nature of gender; and compelling moral visions of how best to live. Further, the book maintains that older persons are not best thought of as devoid of agency (as prevailing popular and scholarly models tend to imply), but can rather be significant and innovative agents of social change. Additionally, the book makes the case that processes of globalization and modernity are produced and experienced not merely through large-scale, universalizing forces, but also—crucially—through the daily life practices and intimate relationships of people.

Although the book focuses on Indians, and in particular Bengalis, it also probes related current debates and assumptions in the United States over how best to age, what shape(s) the family should take, and the proper relationship among individuals, families, the market, and the state. My

Indian informants provide an illuminating lens here as they find them-selves self-consciously grappling with U.S. ideologies and policies, both within India and as they migrate to the United States.

In country after country around the world, there has been a dramatic transformation, from the multigenerational family to the individual, the market, and the state, as the key sites of aging and elder care. Such transi-tions in modes of aging entail quite remarkable shifts in understandings of the human condition, and what it is to be a person. As we will see over the following pages, the United States witnessed in the late 1800s and early 1900s some of the same extraordinary transitions that Indians are going through at present—such as the rise of the notion of the old age home, a decline in multigenerational co-residence, and an increase in state sup-port of the aged. Yet, although they share some intriguing parallels, such transitions carry profoundly different meanings across cultural, political-economic, and historical contexts. The ways Indians are grappling with—both embracing and critiquing—such profound social changes in their lives are what I explore in this ethnography.

ACKNOWLEDGMENTS

Many people and institutions have contributed to this project, in ways more profound than I can express here, over the years that it has been in the making. This book would not have been possible without the generosity of the many people in India and the United States who valued my fieldwork, offered me hours of interviews, imparted their wisdom, and welcomed me into their homes and lives. In California, I am especially grateful to Vasant Gujar, Harikrishna Majmundar, Matra Majmundar, and the other members of the Indo-American Community Center who taught me so much. In Kolkata, I have a debt I can never repay to the women and men living in old age homes whose words and insights animate this book. Their names are too numerous to provide here, but I would like to offer especially my heartfelt thanks, love, and admiration to Kalyani Chowdhury, who taught me a great deal and who wished to have her real name (rather than a pseudonym) printed in my book. The directors and caretakers of numerous old age homes also generously supported my fieldwork by welcoming me into their midst. I would like to thank in particular the directors of the following admirable homes: Ashaniketan, Atithya, Loknath Briddhabas, Mahadevi Birla Niketan, Milan Tirtha, and Swami Mahadevananda Giri Briddhashram. The members of the Laughing Club of Udita, the Dignity Foundation, and Jana Hitaya also welcomed, cheered, and enlightened me. I am especially grateful to Purnima Banerjee and Dipak Nag, who offered me much hospitality and many insights, continuing even over email. In Saptaparni, Satyabrata and Swapna Bhattacharyya (Jethu and Jethima), and Kalyan and Dipti Mitra (Meshomoshai and Mashima), have offered me decades of hospitality and wisdom, as have N. N. Chakraborty and "Boudi" of Cornfield Road. Indrani Chakravarty, of the Calcutta Metropolitan Institute of Gerontology, and Saumitra Basu helped teach me about aging in the city of Kolkata, especially among the poor. Dr. Ranjana Ray and the Anthropology Department of Calcutta University provided me an academic home. S. K. Mitra and his family furnished me and my daughters a lovely place to stay in Udita. Our driver, Sharfuddin Ahmad, faithfully escorted me to far-flung and often difficult-to-find old age homes, and took my daughters to and from the Calcutta International School daily. In his quiet, respectfully reserved manner, he taught me so much about Muslim society in India and the perspectives of the working class. When we left, my younger daughter said that she would miss our driver more than anyone else.

My research assistant, Hena Basu, was a true collaborator on this project. She accompanied me on many field visits to old age homes, assisted me with numerous interviews, sent me notebook after notebook of newspaper clippings, and offered her sensitive interpretations and warm friendship. Without her contributions this book truly would never have emerged as it has.[1] I am grateful to Rachana Agarwal and Mrinalini Tankha for their skilled help in procuring and analyzing research materials pertaining to India for this book. Naomi Schiesel, with great care and shrewd acuity, gathered and analyzed comparative materials pertaining to the United States. Nehraz Mahmood provided valuable assistance with Bengali translations and transliterations.

I am also deeply grateful to my numerous colleagues, friends, and mentors who have offered time, insight, close readings, and illuminating conversations (in person and by email) at various stages of the book's gestation. I am especially indebted to my regular writing partners: Diane Mines, Elizabeth Ferry, Caitrin Lynch, and (most recently) Smitha Radhakrishnan. Others whose contributions I deeply appreciate include Mark Auslander, Amy Borovoy, Lawrence Cohen, Jennifer Cole, Jean Comaroff, Uma Das Gupta, Sanjukta Dasgupta, Deborah Durham, Ann Grodzins Gold, Robert Hunt, Nita Kumar, Sydney Lamb, Tarun Mitra, Linda Mitteness, Kirin Narayan, Ralph Nicholas, Dhooleka Raj, Baccu Roy, Marshall Sahlins, Aditi Nath Sarkar, Ellen Schattschneider, Clinton Seely, Harleen Singh, Jay Sokolovsky, Tulasi Srinivas, Khachig Tololyan, Sylvia Vatuk, and Susan Wadley. I owe an especially profound debt to my mentor, McKim Marriott, who has over decades challenged and encouraged me through his penetrating marginalia and wisdom. My colleagues at Brandeis University in the Anthropology Department and the Women's and Gender Studies Program have provided a sustaining abode, fostering me and my writing through their friendship, collegiality, and intellectual engagement. I also take this opportunity to thank the editors at Indiana University Press for their support of this work and their editorial acumen—in particular Miki Bird, Robert Foster, Rebecca Tolen, and Candace McNulty. Several anonymous reviewers for the press also provided very useful suggestions.

My fieldwork in India was generously funded by a Fulbright-Hays Faculty Research Abroad fellowship, the Theodore and Jane Norman Fund for Faculty Research, and a Mazer Award for Faculty Research at Brandeis

University. The American Institute of Indian Studies offered a generous fellowship, which I had to decline, but I nonetheless greatly enjoyed the hospitality of the AIIS guest house on numerous occasions in Kolkata. Fieldwork among Indian Americans in the San Francisco Bay Area was supported by the National Institute of Aging (grant #T3200045 in Sociocultural Gerontology, Linda Mitteness, director) through a postdoctoral fellowship in the Medical Anthropology Program at the University of California at San Francisco, with additional support from the Louis, Frances, and Jeffrey Sachar Fund of Brandeis University. A tremendous opportunity to write uninterruptedly was provided by a Laurie Faculty Scholar Research Leave through the Women's and Gender Studies Program and the Women's Studies Research Center at Brandeis University.

In addition, I really could not have completed the book without the assistance of all the women who helped me take care of my children and domestic duties while I worked. Too often domestic labor in the United States remains invisible (Hondagneu-Sotelo 2001, Rivas 2002), but the increased employment of professional women in the United States over the past several decades has to an important degree rested on the hired domestic labor performed by others. I am truly grateful for this support and am very fortunate that the women who have helped me and our family have been such exceptional people. They include our nannies, Sonia De La Torre and Leandra DeMello; terrific Brandeis student sitters Lily Adams and Haley Collazo; our au pair and house-sitter Maria Kozlova; our faithful dog walker of six years, Allison Breziner; and in India, Bharati Naskar, who cooked, cleaned, and offered countless marvelous, warming tales.

Finally, I would like to offer profound thanks to members of my family. I acknowledge my parents and parents-in-law—Sydney and Susan Lamb, Sharon Rowell, Doris Black and Robert Black—whose love, blessings, help with child care, and interest in my work have sustained and inspired me. (And, hearing so many tales of mother-in-law—daughter-in-law strife, I have always felt particularly fortunate that my own *śāśurī* Doris is so wonderful.) I cannot express in words the joy and value I have received from my two daughters, Rachel and Lauren, who accompanied me to India for five months when they were thirteen and ten. After listening to so many stories of loneliness in my fieldwork, I appreciated immensely coming home each day to their gregarious companionship (all the more because my old-age-home lady friends told me accurately that even my own days of living intimately with my daughters at home are short-lived). I have also learned a great deal from the astute interpretations and questions both girls have offered me regarding my research, while in India and back at home. I cannot begin to acknowledge the role of my husband Ed Black, my best friend and life companion. He has been enormously patient and supportive of my work—emotionally, intellectually, and materially—over my long, nomadic, and sometimes arduous journey as an anthropologist. My work and my life would not be the same without him.

Parts of chapter 7 originally appeared in "Intimacy in a Transnational Era: The Remaking of Aging among Indian Americans," *Diaspora* 11(3):299–330, © 2002 University of Toronto Press; and "Aging across Worlds: Modern Seniors in an Indian Diaspora," in Jennifer Cole and Deborah Durham, eds., *Generations and Globalization: Youth, Age, and Family in the New World Economy,* pp. 132–163, © 2007 Indiana University Press.

NOTE ON TRANSLATION
AND TRANSLITERATION

Unless otherwise noted, all statements and conversations reported over the following pages came from interviews and conversations that I either tape-recorded or jotted down in field notes during or several hours after the discussions. All translations of conversations, stories, and printed materials are my own, unless otherwise noted. Fieldwork was conducted in both Bengali and English.

For italicized Bengali terms, I have employed the standard system of diacritics most commonly used to transliterate Sanskrit-derived modern languages such as Bengali. I do this so that scholars familiar with diverse South Asian languages may more easily recognize the Bengali terms. However, readers should keep in mind that Bengali pronunciations frequently differ from the standard diacritics. For instance, in Bengali, the short *a* is generally pronounced much closer to a long *ō*. The *s, ṣ,* and *ś* are all generally pronounced as *sh*. So, *śvaśur bāṛi* (father-in-law's or marital house) is pronounced more like *shōshur bāṛi,* and *sevā* (respectful service toward elders) like *shevā,* and *jhagṛā* (argument) like *jhōgṛā.* When English terms were used in an otherwise Bengali conversation, I indicate the original English using 'single quotation marks.'

AGING AND THE INDIAN DIASPORA

1 INTRODUCTION: THE REMAKING OF AGING

Dr. Ranjan Banerjee is a retired psychiatrist living in an exclusive old age home in the Kolkata (Calcutta) suburbs. At seventy-five, he is in good health and shares with his wife a spacious room with a simple kitchenette, attached bath, and modest balcony overlooking radiant green rice fields and a small grove of coconut palm trees. He reflected to me one humid summer morning, as we sat under a quietly whirring ceiling fan in the home's library:

> *RB:* 'Old age homes'[1] are not a concept of *our* country. These days, we are throwing away our 'culture.' The U.S. is the richest nation in the world and therefore has won us over. Now we, too, are only after material wealth as a nation and have become very unhappy. Some are here because their families dumped them here, and there are others whose children are living abroad and can easily afford the money [to pay the old-age-home bills]. But 'old age homes' are not *our* way of life. My parents died *right with us.* . . .
>
> I have a granddaughter and my world revolves around her. I miss her so much when I don't see her for a few days [he paused, with glistening eyes]. Here [in the old age home], there is a little hardship regarding food and all, but that's OK. I have time to read and such. The real hardship comes from missing family, like my granddaughter. . . .
>
> We as a nation have become very unhappy. Material wealth [*artha*] used not to be the prime value in life; rather, family and social closeness were. But now it has become so. I myself am against the 'old age home concept'—but 'old age homes' will stay and increase in India.

Residences for elders are in fact a strikingly new phenomenon emerging rapidly in India's middle-class cosmopolitan centers, replacing for those who live in them the more conventional multigenerational co-residential family that many have long viewed as central to a proper way of aging and society in India. To Dr. Banerjee, old age homes signify not merely a new form of aging, but also much broader social, cultural, and national transformations.

In Palo Alto, California, Matilal Majmundar lives with his wife in a small guesthouse on the grounds of his daughter's spacious home, having come from Gujarat, India, to be with his U.S.-settled children after retiring as a Government of India railroad official. He himself is delighted, almost exuberant, about his life in the United States where, while living right near his wider family, he has actively cultivated what he sees as certain American forms of aging based around individualism, independence, and lifelong productivity. He resides in a separate house, receives financial support not only from his children but also from the U.S. government,[2] takes a class on Shakespeare at a nearby senior center, and writes a regular newspaper column on aging. He is well aware, however, that not all Indians who have followed their children to the United States find the situation unambiguously easy or desirable. In his witty and incisive reflections to me about the pros and cons of "Indian" versus "American" modes of aging, Majmundar opened with a telling anecdote about giving advice to a newly arrived friend:

> One gentleman came from India, old man, just to find out whether he would be comfortable here with his children. I met him. I said, "How are you?"
>
> [He replied,] "Oh, I'm not happy." . . .
>
> He gets up at six o'clock, he requires a cup of tea, he is moving here and there, waiting for a cup of tea. The children, they get up at 8:00, or 7:30, busy with all their activities. . . . At 9:00 or at 8:00–8:30 there will be a breakfast table, so many cups of tea and all these things.
>
> "But what is the use of all this?" [my friend complained.] "Early in the morning I don't get it." I told him that it's very bad of your children, huh?, to lock up the tea and the sugar material!
>
> He said, "No, no, they're not locking."
>
> I [*MM*] said, "Then why don't you prepare?"
>
> He said, "No, I don't like."
>
> Then I [*MM*] said, "You better go to India. You better go

back to India. In India, if you take a second cup, or a third cup of tea, they will object, they will object. Here, you can take even *ten* cups of tea, prepare yourself, any material you use, your children will never object. But, if you want their *time,* they will object. They will object if you want their time. So, better go to India. Here is not the place for you."

Where is it best to age? The United States in this narrative is the land of material prosperity and independence; India is the site of family intimacy and plentiful time.[3] Yet, Dr. Ranjan Banerjee would not so readily agree that India itself is today so assuredly replete with intergenerational intimacy and time.

These two vignettes speak vividly to the variety and intensity of meanings accruing to aging for cosmopolitan middle-class Indians. Many in India are participating in a public moment of reflection. How will they work out aging, and with it a valued society, in a terrain where family members are dispersed across the country and world, and values such as materialism and individualism seem to have taken center stage? Television serials, newspaper stories, films, and everyday conversations abound with this question, many of them concerned with the proliferation of old age homes in India, a new and exceptional phenomenon in the nation; and with the scattering of families around the globe in response to labor markets. Emerging novel modes of aging are taken by many Indians, at home and abroad, to represent a profound transformation—a transformation involving not only aging per se, but principles underlying the foundation of society and the very identity of India as a nation and culture.

The majority of older Indians, however, still live with adult children in multigenerational homes—an arrangement long widely considered to be the most "normal" and "proper" form of aging and family in India.[4] And the majority is not part of the burgeoning urban middle class (of English-speaking, email-using, refrigerator-purchasing, world-traveling, financially comfortable persons),[5] among whom contemporary alternatives to joint family living such as old age homes are most on the rise. Nonetheless, the middle class has a very palpable, influential presence in India's urban centers and India's public culture, as do middle-class discourses surrounding new modes of aging.

This book explores such transitions and discourses, focusing on the ways older persons among the urban middle classes themselves craft and experience novel forms of aging, as they confront—both embracing and challenging—processes they associate with "modern," "Western," and "global" living. It is a book about broad, macro processes—global labor markets, the transnational dissemination of ideas, and the making of modern nations. At the same time, the book is about intimate human relations—the life stories of individual persons, the intricate working out of gender and kinship, and abiding human questions about how best to live.

The book takes off from a few earlier studies of aging in India, perhaps especially Lawrence Cohen's *No Aging in India: Alzheimer's, the Bad Family and Other Modern Things* (1998). In that book, Cohen also examines how debates over aging are tied to visions of modernity and the nation in India. Cohen finds that, in the 1980s and 1990s, the dominant narrative used by Indian gerontologists and others to explain the contemporary predicaments of aging was that of the "decline of the joint family" under the force of the "four horsemen of the contemporary apocalypse"—modernization, industrialization, urbanization, and Westernization (p. 17)—a still familiar theme. Such a view, Cohen finds, interprets serious travails of aging, in particular senility, as pointing to a "bad family" and as transpiring when an old person does not receive familial support, service (*sevā*), and respect. Although I focused my earlier book, *White Saris and Sweet Mangoes* (Lamb 2000), on the kinds of multigenerational rural families that many urban Indians would consider quite traditional, I was also struck then by the villagers' discourses of the decline of the joint family as a salient trope through which they interpreted the past, present, and future.[6]

What is new, however, over the past fifteen years or so since Cohen and I conducted the bulk of our field research in the late 1980s and early 1990s, are the markedly unique forms that certain alternatives to joint-family-based modes of aging are taking in contemporary India, especially the surge of *formal institutions of extra-family aging,* such as old age homes and organizations offering surrogate sons "for hire." Most dramatic has been the rise of old age homes for the middle and upper middle classes. Understood to be largely Western-style and Western-inspired institutions, elder residences barely existed in India until recently; and Cohen (1998:113–120) and I (Lamb 2000:136–137) could only uncover a few fledgling ones after searching. Old age homes now number near one thousand across India's urban centers, most of them having been established over just the past one to fifteen years.[7]

Another new development is the salience of transnational living among the urban middle and upper classes in India. During the British colonial era, it was relatively common for the very bright youth of the elite to travel abroad for education, most often to the United Kingdom; but then it was typical for these youth to return to India to reside and establish their careers. Beginning around the late 1960s, however, it became increasingly common for elite urban youth not only to study abroad for a few years, but also to *settle permanently abroad,* pursuing professional careers in places like the United States, Canada, England, Australia, Singapore, and Dubai. Time has passed, and the parents of these youth, originally instrumental in fostering their children's journeys, are becoming older. The widespread belief now, in fact, is that most older persons among the middle and upper classes in cities like Kolkata have children (often all of them) living abroad—resulting for these persons in very novel ways of organizing life in old age. The fact that so many women are entering the local and international work force also has an impact: many believe that working women are not only less able but also less inclined to care for their elders—especially their husbands' kin—in the home.

Finally, important to this project is the fact that not all tales of extra-family aging center only or even primarily on the "bad family"—that is, on modern *degeneration.* In earlier works, both Cohen (1998) and I (Lamb 2000) concentrated rather exclusively on negative stories of modernity, as loss. For instance, Cohen paints compellingly the modern and Western as the central villains in the dominant middle-class and gerontological narratives of modernity, which repeatedly portray a fall from a state of moral superiority and traditional Indianness, represented quintessentially by the joint family and reverence for elders, to a contemporary state of bad, lost families and elder disregard (pp. 104–106 passim). However, perhaps because some of the dominant narratives have changed, and because my own fieldwork shifted from primarily rural to urban settings, and because I may have listened differently this time,[8] I found that in my more recent fieldwork, I encountered much more complex and multivalent narratives of modernity, which vertiginously intertwined celebration with denunciation.

True, much of the prevailing public discourse in India, in the media and daily conversations, is indeed (still) that contemporary forms of non-family-based aging are signs of a deplorable societal degeneracy. "Old Age Homes Against Our Culture," reads one representative newspaper headline (*The Hindu* Staff Reporter 2004). "Used to joint family structures, the elderly these days do not have even their children to talk to, leading lonely lives fraught with anguish," another journalist opens his story. "In our hurry to scale individual heights, is young India using the elderly as a stepladder before leaving them to fend for themselves?" (Bag 2003:3). The neglected old person serves here as an easy shorthand for the perceived collapse of traditional Indian values and lifeways in the face of a creeping global modernity.

Yet, the perspectives of older Indians themselves are much more richly complex and nuanced, as is some media discourse. Although many older Indians, such as retired psychiatrist Dr. Ranjan Banerjee, do roundly condemn the arrival of old age homes in India and the waning of joint family living, others are optimistic and resourcefully agentive in dealing with social changes. Many feel that they would have liked to have retained much of what they imagine to be the past; but since this past is not attainable, they work creatively to carve out a new life and mode of aging in the present. Quite a few living in old age homes, for instance, were the ones to decide firmly on their own that they would be moving in—clipping out newspaper advertisements (which some still carefully save and pull out with pride), making enquiries, and then making the move (often while their families protest, they say),[9] adjusting to the new way of life, making friends among peers, speaking of each other as their new families, and (for some) viewing the move as a positive opportunity to cultivate a spiritual detachment from worldly affairs. Many see living apart from offspring, further, as better than other options, such as keeping their children from following successful careers, or residing with children amid vast generation gaps, or following their children to alien lands such as the United States. Others who do accompany offspring to the United States find themselves actively embracing many features of American life, even while condemning others. And not all believe that the past was as wonderful and all-sustaining as current nostalgic narratives dictate. Some gerontologists and journalists argue, further, that depending on the family is "backward"; and feminist discourse in India often depicts the joint family system as patriarchal, a way of life that can be particularly hard on daughters-in-law and young women.

This book examines such competing, varied perspectives, while focusing on particular individuals' stories, as a means of pointing (more fully than can be done through unifying generalizations) to the varied, complex, ambivalent, and deeply felt ways that persons are forging lives across nations such as India and the United States and what they perceive to be an evolving global social-cultural milieu. I focus on the paradoxical experience of living simultaneously in and across diverse spatial, temporal, and ideological worlds—perceived by my informants to be those of locality and globality, India and the West, tradition and modernity, those days and now. Elders and their families creatively intermix and co-construct these worlds, as they strive to craft meaningful lives and forms of aging in a present characterized by a profound sense of both exhilarating and unsettling social-cultural change.

The book probes, too, not only discourses in India but also related current debates and assumptions in the United States over how best to age, what shape(s) the family should take, what the proper relationship is among individuals, families, and the state, and what visions of gender fit into all this. My Indian informants themselves provide one of the key lenses into "American culture"[10] here, as they find themselves grappling with American ideologies, images, and policies, both within India and as they come to the United States.

In certain respects, the book also contributes to the current world-wide discourse on the "global crisis of aging," as the world faces dramatic population maturation. Population aging is the process by which older individuals (conventionally defined as those over age sixty-five) become a proportionally larger part of the population. Initially experienced over the past half century by the most developed countries, population aging is now a near universal process (though occurring at different rates and degrees of intensity), caused by declines in fertility and, to a lesser extent, increases in life expectancy.[11] The United Nations describes the process as: "unprecedented, without parallel in human history, . . . a global phenomenon affecting every man, woman and child";[12] and another report characterizes it as "a revolution—with few parallels in humanity's past."[13] Strikingly, population aging is framed very frequently, in the media, by policy makers, the United Nations and national governments, as an impending social and economic "crisis"—caused by increasing numbers of older persons with decreasing amounts of funds and persons to care for them. (The premise is that old persons cost money rather than produce income, and need care rather than provide care.) States are wondering how to deal with this impending problem. China, for instance, is promoting old age homes and late-life romance and remarriage (so widowed persons who remarry can support each other), to ease the burden of caring for the aged on both shrinking numbers of junior kin and a state with limited resources;[14] and many nations of Europe as well as the United States are grappling over restructuring old-age pensions and retirement policies.[15]

Although current discourses about the contemporary "problems" of aging in India do not highlight population maturation as much as the more general image of the declining joint family in the face of "modernity," many Indians are nonetheless engaging quite self-consciously in debates relevant to the broader international discourse spurred by population aging, probing: Where is the best site of elder care: the individual, the family, the market, or the state? And: What kinds of social, cultural, moral and economic principles are entailed by the competing answers to this abiding question?[16]

This book also seeks in part to reframe the dominant discourse on aging prevalent within academic, media, and policy circles internationally. For one of the book's central arguments is that the significance of aging is not limited to the customary question of how to care for increasing numbers of dependent elderly (assumed to be passive victims, being acted upon rather than acting) as the world faces dramatic population maturation. Rather, beliefs and practices surrounding aging illuminate much broader social-cultural phenomena, including the relationships among persons, families, and states; the nature of gender; global cultural and economic flows; and compelling moral visions of the good and the bad. Further, the book moves on to argue that older persons (like the younger) are not best thought of as devoid of agency, but can rather be significant and complex agents of social change.

In examining aging in these ways, this book builds on several bodies of earlier work, interrogating and contributing to the ways we study and conceptualize modernity, social change, globalization, and gender, along with aging and, of course, social-cultural life in India—concerns that I will turn to now.

Grappling with Modernities and Aging: Making Worlds in the Present

One of this book's central concerns is the making of modernity. I am interested in modernity both as a scholarly, analytic category and even more as a local category employed by my informants, who use terms such as "modern" (in English or the closest Bengali equivalent, *ādhunik*), "these days" (*ājkāl*), "now" and "nowadays" (*ekhan, ekhankār*), to refer broadly to the present, one characterized by perceived profound social change.

There are two major ways of understanding the rise of modernity at large in academic and popular discourses. One—dominant in much social theory and in daily popular and political talk in the United States, as well as to some extent in India—is that modernity is a uniform, culture-neutral destination to which all paths of development lead. This model is what Charles Taylor (2001) labels the "*acultural* theory" of modernity. According to this perspective, the project of modernity, first formulated in eighteenth-century Europe by philosophers of the Enlightenment, gradually spreads and takes hold around the world, bringing with it such characteristic social, intellectual, institutional, and political-economic forms as secular reason, individualistic understandings of the self, efficiency, market-driven industrial economies, bureaucratically administered states, and economic materialism.[17] This vision of a movement toward a uniform modernity is based on the premise that the past was significantly different from the present and characterized by traditional (or superstitious, religious, backward) beliefs and allegiances. As Charles Taylor reflects, the "traditional pasts" of diverse societies may have once looked very culturally different from one another, but from the perspective of the acultural theory of modernity, once these pasts are shucked off, "the march of modernity will end up making all cultures look the same. . . . This means, of course, that we expect that they will end up looking Western" (2001:181).

The second major way of understanding modernity emphasizes that modernit*ies* are multiple: persons and nations engage in often passionate projects of negotiating and fashioning *particular forms of modernity* that are historically and culturally contingent.[18] To think in terms of such "alternative modernities" has become a pivotal trend in anthropology and cultural studies, one this study takes off from. The focus on alternative modernities highlights culture, particularity, human agency, creative adaptation, and the complicated blurring of distinctions between the traditional and modern, local and global.

To emphasize alternatives and cultural and historical specificity, however, does not mean that there is no convergence. Taylor asserts that "a viable theory of alternative modernities has to be able to relate both the pull of sameness and the forces making for difference" (2001:182). James Ferguson cautions as well against celebrating "alternatives" as a means of masking global inequalities (2006:176–193). (For instance, the children of North American elders are not traveling in droves to "developing" nations such as India.) As the following pages reveal, the practices and reflections of my informants—older persons and their communities in cosmopolitan India—reveal a complex interplay and dialectic between both:

1) convergence (modernity as a shared, globally emerging, strongly Western-originating set of common social-cultural and political-economic forms such as individualism, efficiency, scientific rationalism, capitalism, etc.), and 2) divergence: the negotiating and fashioning of particular forms and appropriations of modernity that are profoundly historically and culturally specific (see Gaonkar 2001:23).[19] In his introduction to *Alternative Modernities,* Dilip Gaonkar writes first of the common roots and global spread of modernity:

> Born in and of the West some centuries ago under relatively specific sociohistorical conditions, modernity is now everywhere. It has arrived not suddenly, but slowly, bit by bit, over the long durée— awakened by contact; transported through commerce; administered by empires, bearing colonial inscriptions; propelled by nationalism; and now increasingly shared by global media, migration and capital. . . . [It is] no longer from the West alone, although the West remains the major clearinghouse of global modernity. (2001:1)

Yet, as Gaonkar, Taylor, and anthropologists such as Stacy Pigg assert, although modernity can "appear ubiquitous and enduring, it is not the same everywhere and at all times." Rather, people "adopt, deploy, modify and question" the discourses and forms of modernity (Pigg 1996:164), as they fashion, "creatively adapt" (Gaonkar 2001:18) and "engage critically" "their own hybrid modernities" (Gaonkar 2001:14). Clifford Geertz asserted as far back as the 1960s, while examining modernities in Indonesia and Morocco, that "whatever its outside provocations, and whatever foreign borrowing may be involved, modernity, like capital, is largely made at home" (1968:21).[20]

Along these lines, I seek to examine the ways older persons and their communities are producing and conceptualizing a meaningful, Indian modernity through working out new modes of aging. The key question here is an age-old one for anthropology, and that is: how do people make their worlds, make sense of and make themselves at home in the world, *in the present?*[21] As I examine further in the following chapters, the working out of the present very often also entails reimagining the past and charting out visions of the future. These are insistent questions that my informants are themselves quite self-consciously and articulately and passionately grappling with: When the present is characterized by perceived vast social transformations, by living simultaneously in juxtaposed worlds, by paradox and contradiction—how can this present be made livable, comfortable, meaningful, one's own?

In fact, many others have explored in various ways the fashioning and conceptualizing of modernity or modernization in India and elsewhere in South Asia,[22] several of these recently focusing revealingly on gender.[23] Strikingly, however, very little work has been produced on aging,[24] although aging and elders loom large in the ways many in India are working out what is involved in making life in the present, or being modern (as a person, family, society, and nation) in India today.

In his ethnography of middle-class life in Kathmandu, Nepal, Mark Liechty writes of "one of the paradoxes of global modernity at the turn of the millennium, a paradox whereby a 'Western' model or image of modernity is simultaneously the object of intense local desire and always out of reach, seemingly by definition an unachievable condition for those in the 'non-West'" (2002:xi). Though undoubtedly true for many, this stance is not a dominant one held by the largely elite, middle- and upper-middle-class older Indians on whom this ethnography focuses. The persons I grew to know were not engaged centrally in a project of striving to attain (even if redefining) a state that the "Western" and "developed" nations had attained already, from which they were left behind, yearning to catch up. Rather, it was more that my informants accepted that many features of the "modern" "West" *had arrived* in India and in diasporic Indians' lives, partly through their own doing. What they needed to work on now was to make sense of these, to critique and evaluate them, to contend with them—embracing some, rejecting others, reshaping and interpreting yet others, and, when possible and desirable, integrating the more "Western" forms with certain more "Indian" (often represented as "traditional" or "older") principles, institutions, lifeways, and conceptualizations of personhood, family, and the life course.

At the forefront of this ethnography, then, lies a tension and critical interplay between globality and particularity, Western hegemony and local specificity, and creative human agency and structural constraints. My informants themselves are asking: *Are* we participating, for better and/or for worse, in some sort of shared, global modernizing project? *Are* we taking on the culture of the Americans or of the West? Is that the consequence of adopting institutions and practices that, at least at first glance, seem quintessentially Western, including old age homes, nuclear families and market-based elder care? Or can such practices and ideologies be translated, critiqued, only partially adopted, and intertwined with older and more local Indian lifeways and values? My informants are striving very purposefully to create a modernity that is simultaneously both cosmopolitan/Western/ global *and* uniquely Indian—in an effort to make meaningful lives for themselves in the present.

So I examine, for example: in what ways are old age homes not merely globally ubiquitous organizations for making families and societies modern, or practical responses to changes in family structure accompanying political-economic and social shifts, but rather unique local institutions creatively forged and interpreted, critiqued and expanded, by local actors? There is a widespread perception among Indian residents of old age homes, for instance, that these homes—commonly referred to as "ashrams" (or *bṛiddhāśrams,* "[spiritual] shelters for the old")—are a contemporary version of the classical Hindu third and fourth life stages, in which persons purposefully leave their households of reproduction on a path of late-life spiritual cultivation. Old age homes are also viewed as appreciated sites of *sevā,* respectful service toward elders—a key component of perceived Hindu modes of aging; although in the elder homes this *sevā* is offered by paid proprietors and staff rather than kin, a not insignificant distinction.

I also critically examine with my informants the individualizing processes evident in the emerging forms of aging among middle-class Indians. Several scholars have queried whether modernity elicits and accentuates individualistic modes of personhood.[25] This is a keenly relevant question for some of my informants as well, for to many of them, "modern individualism" is not the most familiar form of personhood. Rather, they have accentuated in more contexts of their lives what scholars have termed dividual, relational, socio-centric, and/or family-centered ways of being.[26] Yet, the elders I did fieldwork with are encountering and practicing many novel forms of organizing old age that can be considered quite individualizing. Some quick examples include: 1) living "alone" (with either a spouse or entirely singly, but in either case without children); 2) participating in peer-oriented seniors' clubs that promote self-developing activities and hobbies; 3) market-based elder care (which does not entail the kinds of intimate exchanging of bodily and emotional substances that family-based care and co-residence do); and 4) ideals of individual egalitarianism (in contrast to, for instance, aged and gendered hierarchy), and so the inappropriateness of expecting that a daughter-in-law will serve her parents-in-law. We will see over the following pages, however, that these forms of individualism are not simply accepted and practiced by the older Indians I grew to know, as part of their familiar habitus[27] or ordinary, unremarked culture (as they would be for many in the United States). Rather, they are practiced with great critical reflection, dialogue, and debate.

One simple example: living singly or with a spouse is the most dominant form, currently at about 76 percent of the sixty-five-and-over population, of residence for elders in the United States, where the practice is widely considered not only normal but even ideal (as compared, for instance, to institutionalization or having to depend on children).[28] In India, in contrast, my informants speak with astonishment of the growing trend of living "alone"—which for elders can mean residing either entirely singly or with a spouse, but without children—constructing it as something "impossible," "unthinkable" and even "not fully human" (see chapter 6). This does not mean that living alone is regarded as unequivocally bad. Some have chosen the arrangement for complex reasons. However, to many in India the old age home, no less than living alone, is a radically new idea; and yet, living there intimately among others—especially in crowded dormitory-style accommodations of three to six to a room, the arrangement often preferred by residents—feels much more familiar and normal than living alone.

Another quick example: the sense of declining relationality and burgeoning individualism at large in India recently spurred a body of Indian legislators to make into law what they contend was once simply ordinary practice—that children (if they possess any means to do so) must support their parents, or risk being fined or thrown into jail. This is a decree similar to U.S. child support but not elder support laws, thus revealing in the two contexts very different notions of personhood, in/dependence and in/dividualism over the life course (chapter 8).

Charles Taylor writes that "perhaps the most important task of social sciences in our day [is] understanding the full gamut of alternative modernities which are in the making in different parts of the world." Not to do so, to rely on acultural theory, "locks us into an ethnocentric prison, condemned to project our own forms onto everyone else, . . . and blinds us to the diversity in our world" (2001:185). Examining the diverse and complex ways older Indians and their communities are critically reflecting upon aging in the present helps free us from such an ethnocentric prison.

Elder Agency: Rethinking the Generation Gap

This book also strives to rethink the ways we have viewed aging and generation in relation to social change and the fashioning of modernities. Scholars have long thought of social change in generational terms, although generation is still a rather under-theorized concept in anthropology. Karl Mannheim, in his classic essay "The Problem of Generations," speculated that cultural transformation comes about through the continuous emergence of new generations: as each generation comes into "fresh contact" with its social and cultural heritage, it remodels what it finds (1952[1927]:293). Meyer Fortes mused that a generational model is an "apt imagery by means of which to depict continuities and discontinuities in a community's social and cultural life over a stretch of time" (1984:106). Pierre Bourdieu writes of how the habituses of people born of different generations will often be in conflict, because their habituses have been produced under different circumstances:

> This is why generation conflicts oppose not age-classes separated by natural properties, but habitus which have been produced by different *modes of generation,* that is, by conditions of existence which, in imposing different definitions of the impossible, the possible, and the probable, cause one group to experience as natural or reasonable practices or aspirations which another group finds unthinkable or scandalous, and vice versa. (1977:78)

Several scholars have more recently claimed that generations are a key site through which to understand the social processes and social changes associated with modernity and globalization (e.g., Cole and Durham 2007, LiPuma 2000). Edward LiPuma argues, for instance, that "there can be no theory of transformation without a theory and ethnography of generations, a concept often presupposed in anthropological discourse but rarely spoken about" (2000:xiii). His ethnography focuses on the process of encompassment of the Maring of Highland New Guinea by colonialism, capitalism, and Christianity—"what is known as modernity" (p. xi). He examines the period from roughly 1955 to 1980, when the oldest generation (those generally over about age sixty) could recall a life unfettered by foreign interventions; when the middle generation in power (aged thirty to mid-fifties) had been brought up in a traditional world but lived now wholly in the modern; and when the younger generation had never known a world untouched by missions and government and capitalism (p. 16). LiPuma argues that by examining the changing categories of knowledge and structures of desire across these generations, he is able to illuminate the broader dynamics of social-cultural transformation in Melanesia and beyond (p. 63), arguing that "an understanding of generations is essential to an account of . . . the creation of the modern" (p. 64).

Interestingly, the implication in these studies is that social change happens primarily because youth move forward, while the old remain fixed in time and culture. To Karl Mannheim, for instance, "cultural creation and cultural accumulation are not accomplished by the same individuals" (1952[1927]:293). It is the *young* who are engaged in cultural *creation,* by coming into "fresh contact" with inherited traditions. True, on an individual level, persons of any age or generation can engage in some "fresh contact" if they, for instance, move, change jobs, or climb up the social ladder (p. 293). But in general, to Mannheim, it is "the continuous emergence of new human beings . . . [which] alone makes a fresh selection possible" (p. 294). The fact that youth lack past experience "means a lightening of the ballast for the young; it facilitates their living on in a changing world" (p. 296). That he conceives of change primarily in terms of the young is implied as well by his use of the metaphor "social rejuvenation" to refer to the process of social change (pp. 296–297; see also Cole and Durham 2007:18). Several decades earlier, Auguste Comte also located the impetus for social change in the younger generation, suggesting that increases in life span would slow down the tempo of social progress, because the conservative, restrictive influence of the older generation would operate for a longer time, should they live longer, thus thwarting the "innovating instinct which distinguishes the young" (1974[1855]:518; cf. Mannheim 1952:277; Berger 1960:13).[29]

Because youth figures so prominently in how social change is imagined in both scholarly and colloquial discourses, it is perhaps not surprising that youth, more than any other age group, has been the subject of recent studies addressing the relationship between age, modernity, and processes of globalization (cf. Cole and Durham 2007:18, Wulff 1995:10). There has been a recent surge of work emphasizing the transformative impact of "youth cultures" and "youth agency" in the contemporary global era.[30] Youth are readily described as "cultural agents" (e.g., Wulff 1995:8) and as "agents of change [who] *produce* the new conditions for their lives" (Dolby and

Rizvi 2008:5, emphasis original). In contrast, searches in AnthroSource, Amazon.com, and library databases for "elder agency," "senior agency," "old people AND agency," or "senior culture," "elder culture," etc., do not turn up anything—as if to join "elder" or "old people" with "agency" is an oxymoron. The popular and scholarly "generation gap" idiom likewise carries an image of change occurring because the young move forward, leaving behind the static, staid old. Ann Gold and Bhoju Ram Gujar express prevalent assumptions when they describe their own positions in the "middle" between two generations—"our seniors more sure of the terms on which life should be led; our juniors bred to swim in floods of change" (2002:4). In her *Television, Ethnicity and Cultural Change,* Marie Gillespie (1995) conveys a familiar portrait in which the elder generations of South Asians in Britain signify and foster "tradition," while the young embrace change. Such perspectives are, in fact, common in the literature on the South Asian diaspora, which 1) concentrates on youth and frequently youths' middle-generation adult parents (e.g., Bacon 1996; Gillespie 1995; Hall 2002; Maira 2002, 2005; Narayan 2002; Raj 2003; Shukla 2003); and 2) in the brief discussions of elders (those above around age sixty, often having moved abroad to follow their adult children), portrays them largely in simple terms as old-fashioned, having difficulty adjusting to new circumstances, and tied to "tradition" (e.g., Gillespie 1995:80, Rangaswamy 2000:193–211).[31]

Such models emphasizing the young as the key vectors of change, and the conflicting habituses of newer and older generations, are in many ways compelling, at both analytical and folk levels. This is certainly a model familiar in many respects to my older middle-class Indian informants, who frequently highlight in daily conversations their powerful sense that they grew up in a world vastly different from that they are now experiencing —that their taken-for-granted assumptions, aspirations, and ways of organizing daily life are poles apart from those of their children and grandchildren. They almost all grew up in joint families, for instance, but do not live in them now.[32] "We couldn't have even dreamed earlier that people would be living like this!" a widowed math professor exclaimed ambivalently, her two children settled in the United States. "We had no 'concept' at all even that a person could live alone!" They speak of the huge amounts of money available now, compared to previously: the idea that a parent could buy a whole Cadbury chocolate bar for 25 rupees for one child would have been unthinkable; they and their mothers and aunts used to save carefully, to make a special dish, even the vegetable peelings, which are now discarded with ease. "We couldn't even so much as glance at our husbands if our mothers-in-law were present. . . . When we were young girls, we had no independence at all," a group of lady elder-abode residents reflected. And on and on.

Yet: One of the central arguments of this book is that it is inadequate to think of the young as the only or perhaps even primary locus of social-cultural change. One reason so many of our scholarly studies focus so narrowly on youth as instigators of change is likely our broader cultural notion of old people as old-fashioned and unchanging (popular culture frequently informs scholarly models)—the familiar presumption that "you can't teach an old dog new tricks." Yet, this ethnography aims to refute dominant assumptions that older persons are simply passive objects—being acted upon and left behind rather than acting—incapable of creative agency, critical self-reflection, and change. I aim to demonstrate through an ethnography focusing on older people that prevalent models of generation and social change do not capture well the complexity of the lives and perspectives of the older generation, and thus of the workings and experience of social-cultural transformation.

My data show that, even though they tend to be viewed by others and to view themselves as in many ways emblematic of "tradition," those of the senior generation are *at the same time* very often actively involved in fashioning new modes of life for themselves and their descendants. My research concentrated on persons considered in their communities to be of the senior or very senior (in Bengali, "increased" or *briddha*) generations, ranging in chronological age from about their late fifties to their nineties. What defined persons as "senior" was most importantly their position in relation to family and work cycles. So, old age or seniority begins, most notably, when one's children are grown and married, and in addition (if one has worked out of the home), when one retires. (Those with government jobs in India face a mandatory retirement age of either fifty-eight or sixty.[33] Among the working classes, who are not the focus of this study, most have jobs without retirement policies and so retire only if and when they can, after amassing some savings or establishing sons and daughters-in-law to support them.) Some of my informants on the younger end of seniority were still caring for their own parent/s or parent/s-in-law, often in their own homes (or, in a few cases, co-residing in an old age home), although they were still locally defined as "old" or "senior" themselves, according to family cycle, work, and chronological age criteria.

Many of these older informants saw themselves as the ones in their society experiencing and grappling with the most cultural change, as both older and newer (to put it simply) models of living were very real, live, and present for them. Those of the senior generation grew up with the older model, and in many ways were upholding it, bringing it into the present, reconstructing and interpreting it. (Just as older persons do not remain fixed and unchanging, the "past" and "tradition" which they supposedly embody are also emergent phenomena [chapter 2].) However, the older persons I grew to know had in many cases *not* simply been passively left behind by children who were (or would be) the only forward-moving ones. The seniors were very often the ones who, in their earlier lives as in the present, purposefully instigated new models for living and instilled them in their children. They did so, for instance, by sending their children to elite English-medium schools, funding initial sojourns abroad, and moving out of extended family homes to nuclear units and elder residences. True, some elders were passively "thrown away" by children to places like old age homes, as I explore in chapter 4. Agency, or the capacity to act, is always socially, culturally, and linguistically constrained, and there were indeed powerful constraints operating upon elders' lives.[34] Nonetheless, even those who were "thrown away" or otherwise constrained by the exigencies of families, mores, money, and health experienced "fresh contact" (in Mannheim's sense) via residing in places like elder residences, compelling them to rethink in creative and interesting ways received ideas and practices.

This older generation is, then, simultaneously holding two competing models of what makes a successful life, experiencing quite a profound sense of disruption, questioning, uncertainty, ambivalence—juggling constantly in their minds, weighing pros and cons. They are caring for their own elders even while relinquishing their kids. They are pushing their kids forward and away, even while yearning to pull them back. They are wondering which lifeway is better, not only for themselves (for most are willing to try to quell their more self-focused desires), but also for their children, their society, their nation at large. Have they been swept up in something that seemed alluring but that actually, they now realize, has only limited value? Or, is the whole project of globalized modernity something really worth pursuing?

They see their children as having it much more simply. And much simpler but inadequate, also, is a theoretical model where old and new worlds are neatly mapped onto a binary of divergent old and new generations.

Some of what I explore here is surely unique to this group of older cosmopolitan Indians; but some, I suggest, has broader theoretical implications—for how we study and conceptualize the relationship between age, generation, social change, and the fashioning of modernities. I use this ethnography in part, then, to make the case that our theoretical understandings can be moved productively forward if we pay more attention to, and do close ethnographic research with, older persons as key research subjects and potential agents.

Studies that assume, explicitly or implicitly, that the old cannot be vitally involved in processes of social-cultural change have limitations. First, they do not capture well the ways social change works as part of broad processes of intergenerational transformation—as Cole and Durham put it, "the fact that transformations in the practices associated with one generation necessarily affect either the ascending or descending generation" (2007:18). Second, they do not capture well how conflicting habituses tied to changing eras can transpire within the *same* person and generation. Competing models of the possible and impossible, normal and abnormal, valued and disparaged—what makes a "successful" life, society, and nation—can be juxtaposed and intertwined within the same individual and generation, rather than simply across a binary divide of old and young.[35] Third, they ignore the way a whole category of persons may be involved in the making and remaking of society.

Gender and Care Work: "Family Crises" in India and the United States

The book's focus on aging and on India, finally, aims to contribute to academic and popular debates on gender and care work that have been spurred by two trends: the massive entry of women into the labor force in the United States and other nations;[36] and the dramatic increase in the transnational migration from developing countries of women, many of whom must leave their own families of origin and children behind to do so (Ehrenreich and Hochschild 2002; Gamburd 2000; George 2005; Hondagneu-Sotelo 2001; Parrenas 2002, 2005). In U.S. academic and public discourses, concerns over care work have centered on the child, and in particular anxieties and ambivalence regarding locating child care outside the family and apart from the mother. In contrast, anxieties surrounding care work in India and its diasporas currently center much more on *elder* care than on child care, and especially the locating of parental care outside

the family. These contrasts are consistent with deep, not always acknowledged and scrutinized, cultural assumptions. For Euro-Americans, it is
normative for children to be dependent on and cared for by their parents,
especially the mother, but not for elderly parents to be strongly dependent
on their adult children. A prevalent cultural model for Indians is that both
parents and children will care for each other reciprocally in turn: just as
children are naturally and appropriately dependent on their parents when
young, so are parents naturally and appropriately dependent on their children when old. In India as in the United States, it is women who typically
provide the most care for children and elders, although Indian male sons,
along with daughters-in-law, are expected to care for senior parents. In the
United States, to the extent that adult children do engage in care work for
elderly parents, it is more often daughters rather than sons who do so (a
point evident in prevailing discourses about the "sandwich generation,"
which I examine below).

Let me here examine just a bit further U.S. and Indian discourses surrounding care work, gender and the shape of the family, to set the stage for
what more is to come in the book. In prominent U.S. discourses, women's
work outside the home has resulted in a crisis of child care and thus of the
family (see Hochschild 2001, Hansen 2005). Although many argue alter-
natively that it is best for society, including fathers, children, and mothers,
if the "natural" association of women with domesticity and child care is
deconstructed (e.g., Williams 2000), and that there is little data to suggest
that maternal employment is damaging to children or families (Hoffman
1998), others express deep anxiety about child care arrangements that do
not rely squarely on the mother. Joan Williams cites, for instance, a recent
survey finding that "fully two-thirds of Americans believe it would be best
for women to stay home and care for their families and children" (2000:2).
Mary Eberstadt's *Home-Alone America* (2004) portrays alarmingly the
empty homes of dual-career families and the rise of day care as at the root
of the problems facing today's youth. *The Economist* reports on Eberstadt's
book: "In that loneliness, and in children's resentment of it, lie the roots
of most of the ills that beset America's youngsters. The loneliness . . . starts
in day care. Deposited, by working mothers, too soon and too long in the
care of strangers, small children suffer . . ." (*The Economist* 2004:1). Boston
pediatrician, professor, and author T. Berry Brazelton proclaims that the
conflict between mother love and work is "tearing women to bits in this
country" (Krucoff 1985:12). News media, popular literature and academic

texts continue to stream forth with stories expressing the dangers and anxieties surrounding maternal employment.[37]

The growing trend of *transnational* motherhood has also awakened scholarly and public narratives of anxiety. The increased employment of women in wealthy nations such as the United States has been subsidized by the work performed by Latina, Caribbean, Filipina and other immigrant domestic workers from developing countries, many of whom must rely on someone else to care for their own children in their homelands.[38] This is an arrangement that Rhacel Parrenas (2005) has termed "the international division of reproductive labor" and Pierrette Hondagneu-Sotelo (2001) "the new world domestic order." Hondagneu-Sotelo finds that Latina nannies in Los Angeles tend to "endorse motherhood as a full-time vocation for those able to afford it," and thus are frequently critical of the well-to-do mothers they work for. However, for those suffering financial hardships they advocate "more elastic definitions of motherhood—including forms of transnational motherhood that may force long separations of space and time on a mother and her children," if through such separations a mother can better economically support her family (2001:26). Still, researchers suggest that these women and their children can suffer tremendously. Parrenas finds, for instance, that children in mother-away transnational families express "a lack of intimacy, feelings of abandonment, and a commodification of mother-child bonds" (2005:120). Barbara Ehrenreich and Arlie Hochschild open their introduction to *Global Woman* with the heart-rending narrative of a Sri Lankan nanny caring for her plump two-year-old charge in Athens, Greece, as her own three children in Sri Lanka receive a monthly remittance check but board in a grim orphanage, attempt suicide, and fail to reply to their mother's letters (2002:1–2).[39]

It is striking that in such scholarly, media, and daily discourses on gender and care work, there is so much ambivalence and anxiety regarding locating child care outside the family, but very little concern regarding extra-family care arrangements for the elderly.[40] This is because primary dependence on kin has not been the dominant way that Euro-Americans have defined and organized aging and elder care.[41] (Scholarly as well as popular works tend to reflect broader cultural models.) Forms of extra-family elder care that people in India see ambivalently as at once puzzling, disturbing, and innovative—such as independent living, retirement communities, old-age homes, hired live-in companions and nurses, and state-funded senior escort services and bus passes—have long been established and viewed as natural in the United States. Although of course many U.S. children do spend much time and effort caring for senior parents (escorting to the doctor, preparing meals, offering love and companionship), most U.S. parents and children would be equally uncomfortable if the child were called upon to provide intimate bodily care or full material support for a parent. Further, it is common for both older Americans and their adult children to desire to live independently. Andrei Simic observes: "What the American elderly seem to fear most is 'demeaning dependence' on their children or other kin. Rather, the ideal is to remain 'one's own person'" (1990:94).

Interestingly, however, as we have already begun to see, visions of a "crisis" in families in contemporary India and its diasporas center much more on aging and elder care than on the child. This "crisis" is spurred by daughters-in-law working out of the home, the transnational migration of both male and female children, and a sort of general de-gendered blaming of the younger generation for failing to care adequately for its elders. As the narratives go, the problem regarding working women is not so much that work makes a woman *unable to* provide care for her parents or parents-in-law in her home, but rather that she (because of the independence and agency she derives from employment) will be less likely to *agree to* serving her parents-in-law. "Broken" families refer most often not to those separated by divorce as in the United States, but to multigenerational, joint families that have fractured into nuclear units. One reason there does not seem to be a great deal of anxiety currently in India surrounding the impact of maternal employment on the child is that the child almost always remains living at home with the parents,[42] even if maternal care is supplemented by that provided by a servant, nanny, or crèche. As I discuss in chapter 6, most in India have long considered it normal and appropriate for families who can afford it to hire servants to help provide care for a child or elder within a multigenerational home; the "crisis" occurs when elders and juniors no longer co-reside.

A "crisis" also occurs if the two generations co-reside but the juniors are perceived as extremely inattentive. During my fieldwork period in Kolkata, a recently retired elder man in his sixties committed suicide by hanging. In his suicide note, he blamed his son and daughter-in-law, with whom he lived along with his wife, for causing his death due to their acts of mental and physical torture. The son and daughter-in-law were imprisoned for two months. When I interviewed the district Officer in Charge about the case and asked what kind of filial "torture" had transpired, he replied in a matter-of-fact tone, "Oh, they didn't feed him. They didn't maintain him properly—giving him tea and water, serving and attending to him—You know, all that is required for the proper caring of old men." The Officer in Charge interpreted this and other similar cases in terms of a framework of modernity: "These days" the younger generation has become "materialistic" and "self-centered" and no longer wishes to care for its elders. His comments also reveal how taken-for-granted is the assumption that it is normal and appropriate, even if these days not always assured, that adult children care for their elders.[43]

In the United States, to the extent problems surrounding elder care and the family come up in daily and media discourses, it is often in terms of the stresses of the "sandwich generation"—an idiom that focuses not on problems faced by elders as subjects or as deserving recipients of care, but on adult women pressed like sandwich meat between two generations, struggling arduously to care simultaneously for both children and aging parents (though generally not by co-residing with the parents), while also pursuing careers. There is a sense in some of this discourse that the adult woman's primary responsibility is to her children and perhaps her work; that one should not let the "burdens" and "sacrifices" of parental care interfere too drastically with motherly or professional duties. (For representative newspaper stories read: "Curse of the Sandwich Generation," "Juggling Family, Job and Aged Dependent," "Parent Care: Caregiver Between a Rock and a Hard Case," "Surviving the Push and Pull of the Sandwich Generation," and "Don't Quit Work to Care for Mom.")[44] A strong implicit sense of the inappropriateness of caring for parental elders pervades family studies historian Stephanie Coontz's comments on the sandwich generation: "Elder care takes a tremendous toll on families. . . . Marital relations fray; aging caregivers find that their own health suffers; and the children of the 'sandwich generation' caregivers get reduced time and attention. Corporations report that elder-care problems are at least as great a cause of absenteeism and employee stress as child-care ones. And the financial burden is stunning" (1992:191). Caring for elder parents is quite pronouncedly represented as a bad idea—bad for children, marriages, the individual adult child's health, productivity at work, *and* the economy.

What similar and different models are being debated in India? This book scrutinizes changing gendered and generational arrangements among the Indian middle classes, in order to push forward understandings of the complex and varying ways family, care giving, and intimacy can be worked out in the face of competing cultural mores and the global flows of persons and ideologies. By having the Indian and North American materials speak to each other (at times explicitly, and at times as an implicit backdrop), the project supports the feminist aim to make care work—and the assumptions, values, and models of family and gender embedded in it—more visible, by "de-naturalizing" it. It is also in keeping with one of the long-term aims of cross-cultural research in anthropology, to "make the strange familiar and the familiar strange," illuminating one's own often taken-for-granted ideologies by looking at them in new light from outside.

Fieldwork in India and the United States

Fieldwork for this project extended over nearly fifteen years and several U.S. and Indian cities. Concentrating on the Kolkata (formerly Calcutta) and San Francisco metropolitan regions, I focused on three groups of older middle- and upper-middle-class Indians: those living in elder residences in India, those living in India "alone" apart from children, and those who follow adult children to the United States. Persons of each of these groups were living what could be considered unconventional lives—outside of an India-based joint family setting—and so provided an illuminating lens through which to study the ways older persons and their communities are reconfiguring aging, gender, and family—remaking the end of life—as they strive to fashion meaningful modernities.

In India, my fieldwork concentrated on Bengalis, those living in the Indian state of West Bengal, which boasts Kolkata, India's third largest city, as its capital.[45] Kolkata's cosmopolitan circles are now comprised of persons from all over India, however, and so I also engaged with elders from Tamil Nadu, Bangalore, Delhi, Gujarat, and Bihar, especially when doing fieldwork in the more elite, cosmopolitan senior citizens' organizations and old age homes. Although many of my informants felt tied to their more local ethnic identities as Bengalis or Gujaratis or Tamilians, in the context of my research focusing on transnational families, cosmopolitan circles, and broad global trends, people very often spoke of themselves as "Indian." So in this book, I also frequently write of "Indians" and "India," although the terms can veil often deeply perceived differences of language, ethnicity, and religion. Almost all of my research subjects were also Hindu. Muslims form the largest non-majority group in Kolkata, but because the Hindu and Muslim communities are so highly segregated, I did not encounter any

Muslims in the Hindu-majority apartment complexes or neighborhoods in which I lived, nor in the senior citizens organizations or old age homes I studied. I also could not locate any Muslim-only old age homes or seniors' organizations (a fact I comment on in chapter 3). My driver, however, was Muslim, and I incorporate his insights and those of his family members when relevant into my discussions.

From 2003 to 2007 I made annual fieldwork visits to Kolkata and two short trips to New Delhi, interviewing and spending time with residents of old age homes, elders living independently apart from children, and members and directors of aging-related NGOs. In 2005–2006, I was extraordinarily pleased to be able to take my ten and thirteen-year-old daughters with me, which enabled me to stay for a relatively longer period of five months. The girls attended the Calcutta International School as we set up house in a recently established middle-class apartment complex, where quite a few elders living apart from transnational offspring had also settled. Through striving to construct a life for and with my daughters there, I learned much about middle-class family life that would have otherwise remained distant and abstract.

Over these research trips, I ended up studying 100 elder-abode residents and 34 persons who were living, according to local conceptualizations, "alone" (that is, apart from children)—with a spouse, with a live-in servant, or completely singly. I was able to locate 71 old age homes in the Kolkata environs, visiting 32 personally, and gathering more minimal information about the others through phone calls, a mailed survey, newspaper advertisements, and word of mouth. Some of the 32 homes I visited only once, staying for just about an hour, chatting primarily with a director or manager and then only briefly touring the home. At others, I stayed for several hours and interviewed privately both directors and a few residents. At still others, I made numerous visits spanning my four different trips to India over the five-year period, during which time I not only interviewed residents and directors but also engaged in more informal participant observation fieldwork. This entailed "hanging out," chatting one-on-one and in small social groups, having tea together and sharing meals, poring over each others' family photographs, exchanging letters and email messages, going to cultural functions and prayer sessions, and occasionally meeting a few kin. I attended two funerals of old-age-home residents; and at one home, I spent the night with my two daughters in its welcoming guest quarters. I also journeyed with several residents as they made trips to relatives' homes, their own former residences (which several maintained and returned to periodically), and social events. In addition, I made four revealing visits to old age homes with senior Bengali friends who were considering perhaps one day residing in one, learning by witnessing the homes through these women's eyes as they contemplated such a profound move.

There were six elder residences that I grew to know most intimately. Two of these were among the largest and most elegant homes in the region, housing 40–50 residents each in private and double rooms, and managed by prominent business corporations.[46] One other more modest 40-resident home was run by a Hindu spiritual organization and organized around a central temple, combining dormitory-style living with a set of private rooms. The other three were smaller (5–16-resident) institutions established in ordinary middle-class residences by proprietors who—though often genuinely wishing as well to provide respectful and loving service or *sevā* to elders—also frankly admitted to operating the homes as a means to support themselves and their families. In all, I formally gathered data from 100 old-age-home residents and came into more casual contact with at least about 50 others. I aimed to speak not only with residents but also with directors and staff, although I regrettably found few opportunities to have private conversations with staff.

I was also very eager, each time the scant opportunities arose to meet kin, to complement and complexify the stories I gathered from senior residents. Altogether, though, I ended up meeting with just two sons, four daughters, one daughter-in-law, one grandchild, and one sister. Among the reasons opportunities to meet kin seemed scant: first, some elder-abode residents actually have very few kin living nearby, and second, some living in elder residences do not get along well with their kin. (These first two are in fact frequently the major factors behind why an elder is in a home in the first place.) Third, some kin, especially sons and daughters-in-law, are reportedly embarrassed to be seen visiting, as old-age-home living carries a stigma for the families; and fourth, most kin visit on Sundays, a day that I myself was often absent, as it was the day that (during my longest fieldwork period in 2006) my daughters were out of school and my driver had off.

To study those living independently apart from children, I interviewed persons in their apartments and homes, and hung out with elders at several of the new senior citizens' organizations springing up around Kolkata, especially the Laughing Club of Udita, the Dignity Foundation, and Jana

Hitaya ("For the Welfare of People"). I also sought out founders of the evolving, market-based service organizations offering elder care for hire.

In the United States, research with older Indian immigrants and their families took place over an eighteen-month period in 1994 and 1995 (while I was a postdoctoral fellow in sociocultural gerontology at the University of California at San Francisco), and during annual summer visits since that time. I spent time with Indian American[47] families in the San Francisco South Bay near Silicon Valley, where I accompanied older immigrants to local seniors' meetings; volunteered (as a member of the board and chauffeur) in an Indian American community senior center; attended family gatherings, religious ceremonies, and late-morning tea breaks; and interviewed people about their life stories, hopes, dreams, losses and struggles. From 1996 on I continued to do much of the same in the Boston region. In both the San Francisco and Boston areas, Indian Americans live largely in mixed-ethnic (often primarily white) urban and suburban neighborhoods, in comfortable middle-class and upper-middle-class homes.[48] My Indian American informants were mostly Hindu (though with some Sikhs and Jains), and largely Bengali and Gujarati (though with some Punjabis, other North Indians, and South Indians). Most of the people I have grown to know have been associated in some way, as members or friends of members, with the Indo-American community center where I volunteered, or with an organization for Bengalis overseas, Prabasi. Others are simply neighbors, colleagues, or friends of friends.

I wish to note, finally, that although this research focused on the middle and upper-middle classes in India and the United States, not all of those I studied were tremendously elite. For instance, the first time many had experienced having a refrigerator and enjoying cold drinks in their residences was when they moved into an old age home. And the majority of elder-abode residents I met were more comfortable speaking Bengali than English. Steve Derné (2005), E. Sridharan (2004) and others distinguish between an "elite" or "transnational" middle class (about 3 percent of Indians and 10 percent of the urban population) and a less elite, more locally oriented broader middle class (about 20 percent of Indians and 40 percent of the urban population) who cannot speak English well and can barely imagine buying a car, but who see themselves as well above the poor living in slums and surviving day-to-day in laboring jobs. Both groups are commonly described as "middle class" in India, and I conducted research among both groups.

In both the United States and India, I conversed primarily in Bengali with Bengali seniors, and primarily in English with younger Bengalis and non-Bengali Indians. My research assistant, Hena Basu, accompanied me on scores of visits to elder residences, sent me notebooks full of media clippings by mail when I was absent from Kolkata, and shared insights with me as we mulled over the remarkable stories we heard. I sometimes tape-recorded conversations, and at other times Hena and I took notes, scribbling away on our pads, I trying hard to capture verbatim statements and the particular ways people expressed things, and Hena excellent at seizing all the facts and chronologies of events.

Because much of this ethnography is so very personal and deals with familial tensions and pain, and because of the stigma involved for many in India regarding living in an old age home, I have had to be particularly careful in protecting identities. Except in cases of professionals speaking about their own public or published positions, I have modified when necessary certain identifying characteristics and changed the names of informants, while selecting pseudonyms that match the caste, gender, and ethnic status of the original. In most cases, I have also changed the names of the old age homes in which I conducted research. I have used photographs only when those portrayed have given me permission to do so.

This book is my best attempt at conveying the lives, stories, dreams, and predicaments of those I came to know. It is an ethnography of the ways particular persons were involved in the extraordinary project of making and remaking their forms of aging and being, as they worked out how to be at home in a present characterized by perceived profound processes of social and cultural change.

Chapter 2 places contemporary concerns over aging and social change in India in the context of a burgeoning new middle-class, exploring the ways my informants and the public media fashion both tradition and modernity, "what was" and "what is," through debating new ways of aging. The book then turns to the three main ethnographic situations it examines: making lives in old age homes (chapters 3–5), living independently (chapter 6), and following adult children to the United States (chapter 7). The final ethnographic chapter, chapter 8, examines U.S. and Indian state policies regarding whether elder care should be the responsibility of families or the government, and my informants' interpretations of and interactions with such state programs.

2 THE PRODUCTION OF TRADITION, MODERNITY, AND A NEW MIDDLE CLASS

To be modern is to find ourselves in an environment that promises us adventure, power, joy, growth, transformation of ourselves and the world—and, at the same time, that threatens to destroy everything we have, everything we know, everything we are. . . . It pours us all into a maelstrom of perpetual disintegration and renewal, of struggle and contradiction, of ambiguity and anguish. To be modern is to be part of a universe in which, as Marx said, "all that is solid melts into air."

—MARSHALL BERMAN, *All That Is Solid Melts into Air* (1988:15)

Modernity is more often perceived as lure than as threat, and people (not just the elite) everywhere, at every national or cultural site, rise to meet it, negotiate it, and appropriate it in their own fashion.

—DILIP PARAMESHWAR GAONKAR, *Alternative Modernities* (2001:21)

Perceived as both a lure and a threat, modernity was experienced by many I grew to know in India in the early 2000s as a time, indeed, when "all that is solid melts into air." Such perceptions of modernity were intimately tied as well to visions of the past; for as scholars have long pointed out, the project of fashioning modernity is always also one of fashioning a past that is now lost or pushed away.

As we were winding our way through heavy traffic one warm Kolkata evening, I mentioned to my driver Sharfuddin Ahmad that the next day I was pleased to be visiting the daughter of a married couple living in an old age home whom I had come to know well. I remarked that I was very interested in meeting the daughter, as I had barely ever seen any sign of

the children of old-age-home residents. The daughter has a brother, I mentioned, so maybe I'll be able to find out from her why her brother doesn't
look after his parents? My driver, a middle-aged man of four children
approaching their marriageable years, promptly and pensively replied:

> Oh, madam, these days children (*chelerā*)[1] have become such
> a way that they just don't (*emni*, for no particular reason) look
> after their parents. This age (*yug*) is very bad, you know? If old
> parents have some money, *then* the children will stay with them
> and look after them, as long as the parents are advantageous
> to them financially. But if they don't have money, after they
> retire, the children will just push them aside. After you give a
> son's marriage, you never know—What will the wife-daughter-
> in-law (*boumā*) be like? Will she or will she not want to look
> after her mother-in-law? Both those who have love marriages,
> and those whose parents arrange their marriages—in either
> case, there's no certainty what the wife will be like. And the
> younger generation these days prefers to live separately. I've
> seen movies and things about the youth of these days—what
> has gotten into their heads, I just can't understand! Those who
> have money put their parents into some kind of an old age
> home, and those who don't just push their parents out some-
> where into the street.

Kerala film director Jayaraj's award-winning movie, *Pathos* (*Karunam*),
portrays an aging Kerala couple, abandoned by their children who have
settled in America. The couple eagerly plans for a visit from their sons,
cleaning the house, preparing food, and putting up a swing in the garden
for the grandchildren. Then the news comes: the children have canceled
in favor of a trip to the Niagara Falls. Worse yet: the sons arrange to
sell the ancestral property and place their parents in an old age home.
Director Jayaraj comments on his motivations in making the film: "In
Europe, it may be normal that children leave home. But in our society, we
have roots, and suddenly, all these families have started sending their children abroad; the children lose contact with their past; they forget to come
home." Critiquing the contemporary materialism that has supplanted
family intimacy, he adds: "These children who have settled in America
are not poor. They make a lot of money and they just want to make more

money" (in Dupont 2000). The director reflects in another interview: "Even in a small province such as the one I live in, the number of old age homes are increasing every day. Glorified mortuaries with dead bodies of parents wait indefinitely for their children, settled abroad. These real-life situations motivated me to make this film" (in Chatterji 2004).

On the occasion of the International Day of Older Persons on October 1, 2004, Government of India ministers published messages in newspapers around India. "We, the Indians, belonging to a glorious cultural tradition, have the inbuilt quality of respecting all the elders," begins a statement by the Minister of State for Social Justice and Empowerment. "We are the pioneers in the field of civilization and the rays of civilization have radiated throughout the world from the heart of India," the letter goes on. Yet, the Minister cautions that "recent times" have witnessed an "erosion in the value system" that may "lead to a colossal disaster." The letter closes: "Let us make the light of love ever-shine in the evening of the lives of our elders. Let there not be any sunset in their lives." Prime Minister Manmohan Singh proclaims in his accompanying message: "We must . . . work to harness our traditional values of respect and reverence for the elders with existing policies."[2]

As is clear from these three brief vignettes, many frame their talk of contemporary aging against the backdrop of a contrast with a traditional Indian past. The ways people conceive of their past, experience the present and imagine the future are intricately wrapped together. I turn, then, to look more closely at my informants' and public media constructions of the past, as an important context for understanding the ways people are working out modes of aging in the present.

Fashioning the Past

As I analyze narratives of aging in a traditional past, my aim is neither to claim nor to disclaim that this past "really was." When people speak about the past, they are always selecting certain elements from their recollections or perceptions, while neglecting to invoke others. What people construct or experience as past "tradition" *now*, only also becomes tradition in contrast to and in the present context of modernity. So, tradition itself, like modernity, is not something that is fixed and outside history and contemporary human agency, but rather something that is being actively constructed, interpreted and used in the present.[3]

Aging in the Joint Family:
Intergenerational Reciprocity and Sevā

In contemporary narratives, it is the multigenerational joint family more than anything else that represents tradition in contrast to an emerging modernity. Although a "joint family" technically refers to a family consisting of two or more brothers living together along with their parents, spouses and children, the phrase is more loosely and popularly used in India to refer to any multigenerational household including at least one senior parent and one married adult child (generally a son) with spouse. In a joint family system, old age itself is essentially a family matter, and adult children, in particular sons and daughters-in-law, live with and care for their aging parents—out of love, a deep respect for elders, and a profound sense of moral, even spiritual, duty to attempt to repay the inerasable debts (*ṛṇ*) they owe their parents for all the effort, expense and affection the parents expended to produce and raise them. Such joint family living pertains in contemporary narratives not only to care in old age, but also to a much wider host of social values and meanings, including supportive interdependence, fellow-feeling, a time when kinship was more important than material success, warm rambling households, connection to village lands, moral-spiritual order, patriarchy, tradition, and "Indianness."

At the heart of the joint family is a system of intergenerational reciprocity. Significantly, people indicate that it is precisely what parents once gave their children—such as a body in birth, food, material goods, money, a home, forms of love, the cleaning of urine and bowel movements—that children are expected to provide in return for their parents, years later in old age and by reconstructing and venerating them as ancestors after death (see table 2.1). Although the common discourse is that *children* provide for and co-reside with their senior parents in these ways, in practice it is *sons* and daughters-in-law who are expected to fill this role. Upon marriage, daughters formally relinquish obligations to their own parents, taking on responsibility for their in-laws (though Indians commonly describe daughters as more "loving" than sons, and many married daughters offer their parents visits, gifts, and practical assistance throughout life).

The providing of care for seniors in the family is often termed (in many Indian languages) *sevā*, service to and respect for the aged. *Sevā* can be offered to deities as well as elders. When provided to elders, *sevā* entails acts such as serving food and tea, massaging tired limbs, combing hair,

TABLE 2.1.
"Traditional" Indian Intergenerational Reciprocity

Media of Transaction	PHASE 1: Initial giving (parents → children)	PHASE 2: Reciprocated giving; the repaying of debts (adult children → elderly parents)
Material support	Food, clothing, money, shelter, education	Food, clothing, money, shelter
Services	Daily care, serving food, cleaning bodily wastes (all requiring a great deal of effort)	Daily care, serving food and tea, cleaning bodily wastes (if parent becomes incontinent)
Emotional Support	Love, affection	Love, respect
Body	Given via birth	Children reconstruct for parents as ancestors via funeral rites

Note: This table is adapted from Lamb 2000:49.

bringing warm bath water, and offering loving respect—in short, striving to fulfill all of the elder's bodily and emotional needs.[4] Related to *sevā* is the familiar gesture of *praṇām* practiced by many Indians, when a junior bows down to touch an elder's feet in a sign of respect, and in turn the elder places his or her hands affectionately on the junior's head and offers blessings, such as "May you live well," "May your children be well." Juniors perform *sevā* not simply as a gift in the present, but in exchange for the elders' earlier tremendous labors in giving birth to and fostering them.

Such long-term reciprocal transactions create and sustain intimate bodily and emotional ties, what Bengalis often term *māyā*. *Māyā* means attachment, affection, compassion, and love, and Bengalis think of the ties of *māyā* as entailing both bodily and emotional bindings (*bandhan*). A range of studies has explored how, in many contexts, Indians think of persons as relatively fluid and open, that is "dividual"[5] or divisible in nature, in contrast to the prevalent Western notion of the relatively self-contained and bounded *in*dividual.[6] Through transactions of food, touch, objects, words, and bodily fluids (such as via sexual relations, breast-feeding, and reproduction), family members give and receive parts of themselves, forging not only emotional but also bodily ties. According to such conceptualizations, by co-residing in the same household, and by giving and receiving food, material goods, bodily care, and affection, parents and descendants not only meet each other's survival needs, but also sustain intimate ties of kinship. (Thus, if a child were merely to pay for an elder's care but not to co-reside with the elder, this would constitute a very different—and much more individuated—type of relationship.)

Property and inheritance play a somewhat complicated, ambiguous role in representations of the traditional Indian intergenerational system. Descendants are supposed to serve and provide for their elders in exchange for sacrifices their elders have already made for them. That is, elders have already earned the right to be served by their juniors, because of their tremendous earlier gifts. However, it is widely recognized that, in practice, even in the past, the expectation of an inheritance frequently serves and served as a major motivator of filial service. Such an expectation— that those who stand to receive an inheritance from an elder are specifically obligated to provide care—becomes legally concretized in the 2007 "Maintenance and Welfare of Parents and Senior Citizens Bill" (chapter 8). Relatedly, one reason daughters are *not* normally expected to care for their elder parents is because daughters frequently do not stand to inherit a significant degree of their parents' property at death. (Rather, the dowry parents give a daughter and her marital family at the time of marriage serves, many say, as the daughter's inheritance.) Yet, even for sons, to exchange parental care for inheritance is not the "proper" way of doing things, neither in the past nor in the present.

Many tales, both old and new, feature such a theme. In one classic tale, a wealthy old man preparing for his death divides his property among his sons. The sons, having inherited all they expect to inherit, promptly begin to maltreat and neglect their father. The aged man encounters an old friend and tells him of his woes. The friend promises to help. He calls all the sons and daughters-in-law together and before them bestows to their father a large, locked, heavy chest, announcing that he is returning a long-standing debt with interest, which has now amounted to thousands of rupees. When the sons learn of their father's new wealth, they begin to be more attentive to him than ever before! The old man carefully guards the key and is well served for the rest of his days. When he passes away, the sons and daughters-in-law greedily unlock the chest only to find it filled with stones.[7] Importantly, the moral of such stories is never to celebrate an exchange of elder care for property, but rather to condemn the ungrateful and selfish sons and daughters-in-law who fail to recognize their normal moral obligations to care for their parents unconditionally.

In addition to intergenerational reciprocity and *sevā,* "respect for elders" is also regularly presented in daily conversations and media discourse as a vital part of Indian "tradition," as conveyed in the Minister of State's message on the International Day of Older Persons cited above: "We, the Indians, belonging to a glorious cultural tradition, have the inbuilt quality of respecting all the elders." According to such discourses, all elders, not merely one's own senior kin, are to be respected, simply because of their seniority. Thus the director of a New Delhi–based NGO, Agewell Foundation, commented to me that if given the choice between the junior Bush and the senior Bush, Indians would never have selected the junior Bush; they would have unquestionably gone with the senior. Referring to the election of George W. Bush in 2000, he wondered why Americans had preferred the son when his father was still alive and well. He went on, speaking in English:

> If there is a seventy-eight-year-old person within an Indian family, most likely that person would be respected, although perhaps now relegated to the side due to modern pressures. In traditional India, the older person's opinions were sought before any family decisions were made, such as marriage or spending money. The senior-most person—of whatever age or medical condition—would be asked for his or her opinion and counsel.

This system of intergenerational reciprocity and elder respect is widely described in daily conversations and the public media as not only a culturally Indian, but also a natural, practical, and morally proper way of doing things. Narayan Sarkar, a retired engineer who at age seventy lived with his wife in their south Kolkata home, their two children settled in the United States, contemplated pensively: "In our families, we raised our children—why? Our idea, our dream was that when we grew old, our sons and daughters-in-law would serve us (*sevā karbe*). And it is our dream, and a natural thing, to hope for this, to want this. We did this for our parents, and they for theirs." A middle-aged man from rural West Bengal, who lived with and cared for his incontinent and bedridden mother, spoke similarly of the system of reciprocal parent-child care as a natural and proper one, as I came upon him one morning while he was assiduously cleaning his mother's sheets:

> Caring for parents is the children's duty; it is *dharma* [moral-religious order; right way of living]. As parents raised their children, children will also care for their parents during their sick years, when they get old. For example, if I am old and I have a bowel movement, my son will clean it and he won't ask, "Why did you do it there?" This is what we did for him when he was young. When I am old and dying, who will take me to go pee and defecate? My children will have to do it.[8]

The Indian press as well makes much of the "traditional Indian joint family" in almost every story it presents on contemporary aging, often contrasting the imagined past with an imperfect present: "India's grandparents were once revered and cared for by the extended families that they headed . . ."; "Famous for its culture of respect for the elderly, India is taking this tradition . . ."; "Earlier, the joint family system guaranteed care, concern and attention for the elderly . . ."; "The Great Indian Joint Family—our good old support system . . ."—narratives that I will complete shortly when turning to depictions of modernity.[9] Deborah Moggach, in her 2004 novel *These Foolish Things,* floated the idea of outsourcing elderly populations from the developed world to India. In this playful novel, British pensioners can enjoy warm weather, mango juice with their gin, inexpensive pricing, and the Indian culture of elder care in a Bangalore retirement home. "Her idea has a basis. Elderly care is part of our cultural values," an Indian government official is reported as remarking (Jayaswal 2006).

It is striking how contemporary representations so often highlight a very simple, idealized model of the joint family, one in which elders seamlessly receive loving respectful care, and no conflict, injustice, or economic hardship prevails. However, ethnographic research has long portrayed complex tensions in the workings of joint family relations, including conflicts between mothers-in-law and daughters-in-law, elders abandoned by children in the face of poverty, youth who ridicule the old, and disjoined nuclear-style households.[10] Moreover, although not the most dominant narrative, some of my middle-class Kolkata and U.S-based informants did describe the Indian joint family to me in more complex and ambivalent terms, as a patriarchal, restrictive, and/or conflict-prone institution, one that could be difficult especially for daughters-in-law and even young sons. It is notable that most of the ethnographic examples I found of statements extolling the joint family come from men, while the more ambivalent statements in my field notes were often made by women. This is not surprising, given that men have conventionally stayed within the same family from birth through death, while the position of women in both their natal and marital families is more shifting and precarious,[11] and the difficult position of the daughter-in-law in the Indian joint family has long been a prevalent theme in public discourse.

Gayatri Prasad, a middle-aged woman journalist who now lived independently in Kolkata with only her husband, her two daughters grown and married out, described the large joint family in which she had grown up. She was the youngest of six children of her immediate parents, and they had lived with her senior uncle and his wife and children, along with her paternal grandparents. She described nostalgically how at weddings, the whole extended family would gather together for one entire month, basking in time and company, the children all having fun playing together on freshly watered lawns surrounded by flowers. In the joint family setting, she continued approvingly, she and her siblings all learned the "core Indian values"—of family closeness, spirituality, respect for elders, the merit of taking the time to help grandfather up and down the stairs without being asked. And she herself had learned to navigate the joint family, too, getting what she wanted, such as an education, by bypassing her own parents and going straight to her elder uncle. But she told also of how her sisters' lives had been "ruined" in the joint family, their personal desires and ambitions squelched. "Elders sometimes had *too* much power," Gayatri reflected. "They were absolute dictators. They could be just and benevolent but not necessarily so."

Two elder-abode residents and roommates, Kalyani-di and Uma-di,[12] were chatting with me one evening about the changes under way in their society, notably the move from a joint family system to a system of nuclear families and old age homes. "Some people say that these changes are good," Kalyani-di reflected, "because a lot of arguing (*jhagṛā*) used to happen in large joint families." "When we were young girls, our mothers-in-law would give us so much trouble! *Bāpre bāp!*"[13] Uma-di interjected, and both women gasped and laughed for a moment as they recollected how they had suffered at the hands of their mothers-in-law. Then Kalyani added contemplatively, with a tone of more praise than criticism, "But, people need other people to live. Before, no matter *how bad* relations were at home, people *had* to live together." Although in this and other conversations these women seemed to express a preference for what they perceived to be the joint family system of the past, they did not paint joint family living in simple harmonious terms.

Whether viewed as glorious or fraught with tensions and inequalities, enduring or a waning relic of the past, it is difficult to stress enough how salient the "Indian joint family" is as a trope with which Indians interpret contemporary aging. Throughout my fieldwork period, I found that a whole range of people—the old and young, male and female, those living in joint families and without, journalists and filmmakers—repeatedly expressed taken-for-granted assumptions that the most normal, familiar, and "traditional," even if not ubiquitous, way of aging and elder care for Indians is within a multi-generational or joint family.

Interestingly, although so many present the joint family as a quintessentially *Indian* institution, they very often use the English "joint family" rather than an Indian-language equivalent (such as the Bengali *ekānnabartī paribār*),[14] even when engaging in an otherwise Indian-language conversation. In fact, other English terms frequently interjected into Bengali conversations —such as "culture" and "Indian culture"—are also, like "joint family," intended specifically to convey tradition or Indianness; but the use of English highlights how these concepts *become* specifically "traditional" and "Indian" in the context of and in contrast to the modern and foreign. So, as we will see over the following pages, "Indian culture" is frequently juxtaposed to "Western culture," and "joint family" to "nuclear family" and "old age home." Stacy Pigg (2001) notes how English terms are frequently used in Nepal to discuss taboo topics and mark them as modern (which can be seen in West Bengal, too, with phrases like "old age home"). But, in a related move, Bengalis also use English terms to signal concepts that have come to be viewed as quintessentially traditional or Indian precisely when they come into contrast with perceived alternative modern or Western forms.

Aging and the Forest:
Late-Life Spirituality and Human Transience

In addition to using the trope of the joint family, many Indians think of traditional ways of Indian aging in terms of the Hindu textual formulation of the four stages or *āśramas* of life. According to the classical Hindu ethical-legal texts, persons move through a series of four life stages or "shelters" (*āśramas*)—as a student, a married householder, a disengaged forest dweller (*vānaprastha*), and finally a wandering renouncer (*sannyāsī*).[15] In the Hindu texts, this schema in fact applies specifically to upper-caste males, while Manu devotes little attention to defining the appropriate stages of a woman's life, which are determined by her relationships to the men upon whom she depends for support and guidance: her father in youth, her husband in marriage, and her sons in old age (*The Laws of Manu* V.148; Manu 1886:195, 1991:115). But I found that both women and men, especially among the more well-educated, frequently invoked a model of the four Hindu life stages when discussing the experiences of aging.

In the *āśrama* schema, two life phases constitute older age. When a man sees the sons of his sons and white hair on his head, he knows it is time to enter the forest-dweller or *vānaprastha* phase—departing from his home to live as a hermit, either with or without his wife, or remaining in the household but with a mind focused on God. The final life stage is conceptualized as a time of complete renunciation of the phenomenal world and its pleasures and ties. As a *sannyāsī* or renouncer, a man strives to become free from all worldly attachments, through taking leave of family members, abnegating caste identity, giving up all possessions, performing his own funeral rites, begging, and constantly moving from place to place so that no new attachments will develop. If a person is able to free himself from all binding attachments in this way, he may be able to attain ultimate "release" (*moksha*) from the cycle of rebirths, redeaths, and reattachments to worldly life, or *saṃsār* (this is also the word commonly used for "family, household"; its core or literal meaning is "flowing or moving together"). Few Hindus actually move to the forest or become wandering renouncers in old age, but many do view late life as an appropriate and valuable time for focusing increasingly on God and spiritual awareness. They find compelling a model of the life course in which one concentrates on worldly matters—

marriage, reproduction, and material gains and pleasures—during one's adult householder years, and then turns in later life toward spirituality and consciousness of human transience.

In some ways, though, the two models of old age explored thus far in this chapter—being served within an intimate joint family, and moving to the forest to focus on God—are in conflict, because in one a person receives care precisely within the family, and in the other the person purposefully renounces ties to the family and world. Many of the spiritually minded older Indians I know claim to find it perfectly acceptable and possible to concentrate on spirituality in late life even while living within the family. However, as I explore in *White Saris and Sweet Mangoes,* others feel conflicted and torn. They feel that their bindings of *māyā*—their bodily and emotional ties to the persons, places, and things of their lived worlds—*should* decline as they grow older, but that, instead, the natural tendency is for the ties of *māyā* to grow stronger and more numerous as life goes on. They *should* be loosening ties to their families and homes, developing a readiness for death and a greater awareness of God; and yet they still experience a strong yearning to see one more granddaughter's wedding, to drink one more cup of tea from a beloved grandson's hand, to eat one more sweet mango.

This theme of literal or metaphorical spiritual forest-dwelling in late life is not as salient in narratives of modernity as is the theme of the joint family, possibly because the spirituality of the aged is not so widely perceived to be threatened by contemporary social changes in India. Narratives in which the "materialist" West is encroaching into "spiritual" India—with valuable as well as injurious results—do abound; yet many feel that Western materialism exerts even more of a pull on the young than the old. Further, some of my older informants suggest that the waning family ties of modernity and globalization may in fact facilitate late-life forest-dwelling; that several features of modern social life—such as dispersed families and even old age homes (as a contemporary version of the ancient Hindu "forest" away from the family)—thus might actually complement certain Indian or Hindu "traditions" of aging.

Imagining the Present

As those I grew to know in Kolkata and the diaspora represented what they perceived to be traditional forms of Indian aging, they also produced meanings and images about a Bengali or Indian modernity.

In Kolkata, modernity is perceived as entailing a cluster of concepts and terms, including the English "modern," or *ādhunik* in Bengali, and other terms conveying the temporal present, such as "these days" (*ājkāl*) and "nowadays" or "now" (*ekhankār, ekhan*). To those in Kolkata, what I gloss as "modernity" is essentially the present itself, as different from the past—"these days" as opposed to "those days," "now" as opposed to "before." As such, modernity is regularly associated with *Western* values, lifeways and processes, and in fact, in the nineteenth century, the Bengali term most commonly employed to describe the modern or new (*nabya*) was explicitly linked to Western education and thought, the civilization inaugurated under English rule (Chatterjee 1997). Modernity today is also regularly associated with features of "globalization" (a term commonly used in English), such as the global spread of Western values and lifeways, a (Western-dominated) global economy and media, and transnational or diasporic living. Modernity entails as well a host of other facets of contemporary life, frequently including urban residence, nuclear families, small flats, individualism, consumerism, materialism, careerism, a persistent lack of time, weak family ties, waning patriarchy, and old age homes.

Much of what Bengalis conceive as the present was inaugurated first under foreign colonial rule and then under Western-dominated globalization; this may be one reason Bengali conceptualizations of modernity cannot but be deeply ambivalent, Partha Chatterjee argues. In contrast to the "these days" felt to be not entirely of their own making, Bengalis often construct a "'those days' when there was beauty, prosperity and a healthy sociability, and which was, above all, our own creation" (1997:210). Amartya Sen, though, disagrees with Chatterjee's and other scholars' attempts to neatly distinguish and celebrate "our culture" as opposed to "their culture" prevalent in contemporary India.[16] Instead, Sen argues that "In our heterogeneity and in our openness lies our pride, not our disgrace. Satyajit Ray taught us this, and that lesson is profoundly important for India. And for Asia, and for the world" (p. 138).

Let us here look first at some of the stories of decline indeed so prevalent in India today. As we have already begun to see, visions of modernity are often intertwined with images of aging, in which the most dominant theme is the decline of the joint family. One representative English-language newspaper story, reporting on the new Government of India legislation that could send children to jail for failing to look after their elderly parents (a law I examine in chapter 8), reads: "The Indian family scenario seems to be crumbling in the nuclear age, . . . with an alarming increase in the number of senior citizens taking refuge in old age homes, . . . city parents . . . hit by the empty-nest syndrome, . . . [and a] parallel decline in respect for the elderly" (Salvadore and Mukherjee 2007). Another news story, detailing the suicide of an eighty-year-old retired Kolkata engineer whose only son lived abroad, opens: "Used to joint family structures, the elderly these days do not have even their children to talk to, leading lonely lives fraught with anguish" (Bag 2003:3). One Bengali gentleman reflects in a letter to the editor titled, "To Age is Now a Curse" (*Bṛddha Hoyāṭā Ekhan Abhiśāp*):

> During our adolescence, most Bengali households consisted of joint families. . . . [Yet,] the joint families or family units with one common kitchen have disappeared like dinosaurs. . . . Hence now all are nuclear families. . . . Aged parents are neglected and ignored in the family. I am now 71 plus. Most of my relatives now live in various parts of West Bengal. I have seen the miserable condition that those of my age, and even older than me, have been thrown into![17]

Acclaimed Bengali film director and actress Aparna Sen, introducing a special issue titled "Problems of Aged Parents" for the popular women's magazine *Sananda,* highlights the failed reciprocity in today's intergenerational relationships: "It takes a lot of care to bring up a human baby. What kind of a human quality is it to throw into a neglected and uncared-for state those aged parents of ours without whose care it would have been impossible for us to grow up!"[18]

The blockbuster Bollywood film, *Baghban,* one of the biggest cinematic hits in India in 2003, features the failed intergenerational reciprocity, dissolving joint family system, and chasm between the past and present envisioned as distinguishing the contemporary era. Just like a gardener (*bāghbān*) who plants trees and nourishes them in the hopes that he will be able to rest in their shade when he grows old, the movie's hero, Raj Malhotra (played by the legendary Amitabh Bachchan), and his wife Pooja raise a family of four sons who are all now nicely settled in their professions. Against his banker's and former employer's advice, the father upon retirement invests all of his income, including his provident fund, in his sons who, he believes, are the assets who will secure his future. "I am not worried about life after retirement at all," Raj Malhotra declares toward the film's opening. "With God's grace we have four children. That means we have four invaluable fixed deposits. Eight hands are enough to support me."[19] Once their father's bank account is empty, however, the sons and daughters-in-law treat the parents with contempt and refuse to care for them properly. In the end, the hero publishes a best-selling novel (titled *Baghban,* like the movie) based on the mistreatment received from the hands of his sons; overnight he becomes millionaire, and the sons come groveling back, but he does not forgive them. The film closes as the father addresses a captive audience gathered to celebrate the book, his sons and daughters-in-law listening meekly:

> I am not a writer. . . . I have only written what life has shown me. *Baghban* is not about me or any one person. This book is about the silence that exists between the past and the future. This book is about every bridge that has broken between two successive generations. This book is about those bent shoulders on which some children sat and enjoyed the carnivals of the world. This book is about those shivering, empty hands that once held the hands of their young children and taught them how to walk. . . . The world has changed. Life has changed. People of my age please remember—

The father-author continues in a sarcastic tone, describing how the ways of the past have disappeared into the contemptible present:

> What unworthy relationships we used to be entangled in! We saw the lord's face in our father's faces. We found heaven in the feet of our mothers. But now people have smartened up. Today's generation has become very intelligent and practical. For them every relationship is like a ladder which they step on to move up in life. And when that ladder [like a relationship with an old parent] loses its worth, then like broken furniture, broken utensils, torn clothes, yesterday's newspaper, it is discarded into a storage area.

He takes on the resonant tone of an eloquent orator:

> But life does not move up like a ladder. Life grows like a tree. Parents are *not* like the first rung in a ladder. Parents are the *roots* of the tree of life. No matter how tall the tree might grow, how healthy and green it might be, cutting the roots will not allow it to remain healthy and green.
>
> That is why, today, I ask with great politeness and respect, that the children for whose joy a father happily spends every penny he has earned, why do these children hesitate to shine a little light for the parents when their eyes become weak? If a father can help his son to

take the first step in his life, then why can't that son help his father take the last step of his life? Why are the parents, who spend their entire lives bestowing pleasures on their children, punished with tears and loneliness?

Similar images abound in my informants' own narratives, many of whom, of diverse ages and circumstances, viewed the film *Baghban* and declared it to be highly moving, truthful, and compelling. One morning I spoke with Benu, the younger son and hard-working professional of a middle-class Kolkata family, a family still arranged jointly, housing two married brothers, their wives, children, and parents. "Today, the younger people have become very materialistic and selfish," Benu reflected. "They only think of advancing their own careers, working hard, making money, being able to buy more things. Perhaps today they are finally able to buy a car, and then they think: Why not another? It's like that." He went on to tell of how, because of the younger generation's career orientation, shortage of time, materialism, and selfishness, "Many people don't want to care for their parents any more. They think: I'll just put them in an old age home, or live separately. Perhaps they might even get offered an apartment as a perk through their job, and they want to accept it so they can move ahead. But perhaps their parents aren't allowed in the apartment, or there's no space for them there." He asserted that he himself, however, was totally against people "abandoning" their parents in this way and plans to live permanently as a joint family, echoing the strains of *Baghban* as he avowed: "Could a tree live without its roots? No, it would die. My parents are my *roots*. They are the ones who raised me and nourished me and still sustain me. If they were gone, I couldn't exist—right?"

I earlier introduced Kalyani-di and Uma-di, residents of a modest ten-person elder abode just a short cycle-rickshaw ride or walk from the apartment complex in which I lived with my two daughters. One evening, as the sun was setting and we were lighting mosquito coils on the small front verandah, the conversation turned, as it so often did, to how things are so different now than in the past. Kalyani-di exclaimed: "There are *huge* transformations now in our society! Everyone has become hugely selfish! No one wants to live closely any longer. Everyone wants to live alone. You'll see—as many new homes are being built, all of them are the same kind—just for two people, two people." Uma-di interjected with a mocking smile: "Soon they'll be for just one person! Even husbands and wives will live separately!" Kalyani-di had reflected on an earlier occasion:

"If we had grown up with the idea that we might live separately from our children, then it might not be so hard to get used to now. But with our own eyes we had never seen or known anything like this. We never could have even *dreamed* that an abode for elders (*bṛiddhābās*) existed, that we would be here, in a place like this!"

Many of the older generation comment that such dramatic modern transformations are occurring with extraordinary rapidity right in their time, so that they find themselves in the unique position of having grown up in one world and now making their lives in a radically different one. "The changes have been *sudden* (*haṭhāt*)! Right in *our* generation!" a Dignity Foundation member exclaimed at one of their monthly gatherings. The Dignity Foundation is a "Senior Citizens Life Enrichment" association, founded in Mumbai in 1995 with branches in Kolkata, Chennai, and several other major Indian cities, its members mostly upper-middle-class seniors living independently from their children. Another gentleman jumped into the conversation, grinning, as he loudly voiced a lament: "We, of *this* generation, we suffered from our parents—how they rebuked us! And *now*, we suffer from our *children*—how *they* rebuke us!"

However, as I have noted, visions of modernity or the present are richly multivalent. Not all are tales of unremitting disaster. A more upbeat *Sunday Times of India* story claims that the joint family—essential to Indian culture—will not disappear but is rather making a resurgence, while incorporating contemporary values: "We are finally realizing the wisdom of our conventional ways. While nuclear families in the West go sub-nuclear in quest of the I-me-myself ideal, the Great Indian Joint Family (GIJF) is being reinvented. . . . Why can't we be without it? Because unlike our western counterparts, each one of us is already more than an individual: we're a network of relationships" (Baruah 2004:11). The newly "made-over" GIJF combines older and newer elements: members have their own space (sometimes in separate adjoining flats), but they are there for each other, too; one can call on friends as well as family for emotional fulfillment; and one can be a working woman along with a wife, mom, daughter-in-law, and aunt. An optimistic letter to the editor from a Kolkata gentleman asserts, "A pragmatic answer to the concerns voiced [in a recent newspaper story on the rise of old age homes] would be for our society to accept and encourage the concept of old age homes as a viable replacement for the joint family of yore."[20] Another upbeat Sunday news story cheerfully titled "Hello! Old Age," features a group of lady friends "well into their seventies" who meet up regularly at the most modern and hip Kolkata joints, like KFC and Barista coffee. "Increasingly in Kolkata," the reporter narrates, "many senior citizens are taking charge of their own lives, wishing away dependency and redefining the conventional rules of old age."[21]

The Social Contexts of "Modern Aging" in a New Middle Class

No single cause, but a whole complex of social changes, explains the emergence of novel ways of thinking about aging in India. Why *now* have old age homes suddenly burgeoned in the nation? Why now has there been a swell of institutions geared toward producing independent, non-family-based elder living? Why now has aging taken such a hold in the public imagination as a sign of the paradoxes and complexities of the contemporary age? Several interrelated factors are at work, connected to the complex reforms of the 1990s collectively known as economic liberalization; an upwelling of money from a booming economy, outsourcing jobs, and expatriate remittances; the mounting trend of transnational migration; the substantial entry of women into the professional workforce; and the intensity of India's participation in a global circulation of ideologies. All these processes are tied to what policy makers, academics, journalists, and the public have deemed the growth of a significant new form of middle-class life in India.[22] The processes have clustered together to create a situation where, among the urban middle classes in particular, there is more desire (among many but not all) to create new opportunities for managing aging other than multigenerational family residence; there is more money to pay for these new options; and yet there is anxiety (among many but not all) about what these transformations mean—for self, family, and nation.

On the level of political economy, several forces have come together to help create a burgeoning new urban middle class with noticeably more disposable income to spend and, many believe, an array of new values and lifestyles. The early 1990s in India marked a period of pronounced economic liberalization under the government led by Prime Minister Narasimha Rao. Since achieving status as an independent nation in 1947, India had pursued economic development with limited global entanglements; but in 1991, the economy was opened significantly to foreign investment and trade. Within five years, imports doubled, exports tripled, and foreign capital investment quintupled (Derné 2005:178). Opportunities for both consumption and employment were now shaped by global markets;

many professionals experienced a sharp rise in salaries; and the number of persons considered to be part of the fast-growing category of the middle class rose to somewhere between 100 and 250 million (depending on the criteria used to define middle class), from figures two to five times lower, over just ten years from 1989 to 1999 (Sridharan 2004:412–413).[23]

In addition to bringing more disposable income into many people's hands, the new global economic climate fostered the dispersal of families across the nation and world. With the establishment of large multinational corporations in India and booming IT, biotech, and real estate industries, many young professionals were pulled from smaller or less cosmopolitan cities such as Patna and even Kolkata[24] to careers in global economic hubs like Bangalore, New Delhi, and Mumbai—frequently leaving behind larger multigenerational homes for nuclear-family-style flats.

The past several decades have also been a period of intense transnational migration. Although people have emigrated from India for centuries, it has only been over the past few decades that it has become commonplace, even expected, for young adults of India's cosmopolitan middle classes to migrate abroad for higher education and professional opportunities, frequently ending up settling permanently overseas. In 2006, annual NRI (non-resident Indian) remittances to India totaled over $24 billion (with 44 percent coming from the United States).[25] Indians emigrate to nations such as Australia, Canada, England, Singapore, the United Arab Emirates, and very notably the United States—where the Indian American population has risen from just about 5,000 in 1960 to over 1.5 million in 2000, a three-hundred-fold increase in just forty years. In 2002 the Government of India, recognizing the cultural and economic significance of expatriate Indians, launched a Persons of Indian Origin card scheme allowing holders visa-free entry and rights to buy property and invest in the nation, aiming as well to "reinforce their emotional bonds . . . to their original country."[26] The comings and goings of NRIs play a significant role in urban middle-class Indian culture, and many of the new institutions of aging are targeted specifically at the parents of Indians living abroad. One of these is the Rosedale Gardens apartment complex constructed in 2007 on Kolkata's outskirts, with 60 of the 504 apartments designed especially for the elderly living alone, and 46 of these 60 reserved in particular for senior citizens with NRI offspring—a plan conceived by two U.S.-settled NRIs who had left parents behind in Kolkata.[27]

Media globalization has accompanied economic liberalization in India, fostering as well a powerful climate of social-cultural change and heady intermingling of local and global images and ideologies. Transnational satellite broadcasting made its Indian debut in January 1991—cable television offerings suddenly competing with state-run television, at the same time that the slackening of foreign-exchange restrictions allowed Hollywood films to vie with Bollywood productions. Steve Derné notes the radical transformation of India's media:

> Fueled by advertisers trying to reach the new Indian market, the number of television channels grew from one state-run channel in 1991 to seventy cable channels in 1999. Access to television increased from less than 10 percent of the urban population in 1990 to nearly 75 percent by 1999. In 1991, cable television reached 300,000 homes; by 1999 it reached 24 million homes. With the easing of foreign-exchange restrictions, previously unavailable Hollywood films were dubbed into Hindi and screened widely. (2005:178)

Elaborate shopping malls, multiplex cinemas, high-rise apartment complexes with private swimming pools, restaurants, and gyms, and international food chains like McDonalds and Pizza Hut are also mushrooming across India's metropolises, almost as one watches, where nothing like that existed even just a few years earlier.[28] India's first global-consumer-oriented shopping mall opened in Mumbai in 1999, and within just five years according to one estimate, three hundred malls were under construction countrywide[29]—replete with air conditioning, escalators, piped music, multiplex cinema theaters, food courts, and stores selling the leading Indian and international brands. "Earlier, a large majority of Indians believed in the Spartan asceticism of the Father of the Nation, Mahatma Gandhi," one journalist comments on the fast-budding Indian consumer culture. "But the new generation of shoppers—like their contemporaries worldwide—believe in living for today and splurging at the mushrooming malls over the weekends" (Bist 2004). Although it is only the elite who can afford to shop regularly at chic malls, many less-well-to-do within the broad category of the middle class throng to gaze, watch a film, or indulge in snacks.

A recent Kolkata *Telegraph* newspaper story reflects rather glibly on such changes in Bengali middle-class consumptive practices, linking them to even more pervasive transformations in value systems and ways of life:

> Call it a brand new attitude or a 21st century class struggle, but the Bengali Middle Class (BMC) is morphing. Just the other day, the

quintessential 'Bong' [Bengali] was cocooned in his middle-class values, safely ensconced in tradition. Today, as a *Telegraph-MODE* survey reveals, the Bengali in Calcutta is all set for a dramatic metamorphosis.

In almost every field—from clothes to food to social habits—the city's Bengali middle class is changing. Gone are the days when a BMC would subscribe to a life of restraint and modesty. Family axioms such as no late night parties, no alcohol, no impulsive decisions and no luxuries are being obliterated with remarkable ease.

The statistics say it all. About 95 per cent of those surveyed agree that the BMC today is more modern and less conservative in outlook than it once was, while 42 per cent in the 20–50 age group care little about issues pertaining to morality. Eighty-two per cent feel it is important to be trendy and confident, and one out of every four polled loves to eat out.

A casual visit to Pizza Hut or a Kentucky Fried Chicken (KFC) outlet on any given day would back the statistics. The swelling BMC crowd—which couldn't think beyond *machher jhol aar bhaat* (fish curry and rice) till the other day—can be spotted tucking into crispy drums of heaven or smacking their lips after a spicy chicken and mushroom pizza. (T. Ray 2006)

Middle-class people in Kolkata of various ages, genders and backgrounds are talking about these matters, many finding it rather fun, new and exciting to participate in it all. At the same time, many, and not only among the older generation, engage in critical reflection, wondering if these trends are all completely desirable and if much of the Kolkata they have known and loved is fading away. The *Telegraph* story goes on to report that a significant number of young middle-class adults has to seek mental health counseling, for as one psychiatrist explains, "When your core values receive a jolt you feel neither here nor there." And the *Telegraph* survey revealed that 91 percent in the 60–75 age group feel that the Bengali Middle Class is "going wild and losing its family values" (T. Ray 2006).

Finally, changing gender mores form another critical dimension of contemporary middle-class culture with an impact on aging and family life. Compared to those a generation earlier, urban middle-class women are more highly educated, older at marriage, and entering the workforce in the hundreds of thousands (Radhakrishnan 2006). Such well-educated, professional women have significantly more agency in the family than had their mothers and mothers-in-law, creating an environment—as both older and younger persons, both women and men, concur—in which many women are simultaneously less inclined to and less able to co-reside with and care for their parents-in-law. Although I encountered some persons who lamented such changes, the more pervasive sentiment at large was that the traditional position of the daughter-in-law had always left something to be desired, and that perhaps it is not so beneficial for younger women to devote their lives toward submissively serving their in-laws in the home.

It is striking that there seems today to be less public anxiety over the movement of women from the domestic to the public sphere than over the parallel movement of elders. The figures of old people and women are similar in that both can powerfully signify the family, upon which the "core values" of the nation hinge. In the nineteenth and early twentieth centuries, during the era of British colonialism and anti-colonial national-ism, the family was held up as essential to Indianness; yet the focus then was on women.[30] Partha Chatterjee (1990, 1993) examines how middle-class Bengali women in particular served to uphold a "traditional," Indian spiritual domain, located in the domestic sphere, distinguished from an increasingly "Western" materialist outer world that progressively engaged Indian men. Debates linking women with family, tradition, and Indianness have also been salient within the contemporary Indian diaspora, where Indian women are widely expected to be the critical maintainers of "Indian family values," through such practices as performing culturally attuned childrearing and community service, and preparing Indian food in the home (Radhakrishnan 2008, T. Srinivas 2006, Das Gupta 2006:63).[31]

Contemporary public anxieties, however, seem to center even more on the figure of the old person than on the woman.[32] This shift has transpired as middle-class women are entering the professional workforce at a dramatic rate, taking a pivotal place in the public sphere. In fact, some current dis-courses represent contemporary Indian women not merely as maintainers of "Indian family values," but also as significant producers of India's new global economic success. Smitha Radhakrishnan has observed, for instance, how recent "media representations of India's booming IT industry have often carried a woman's face, suggesting that the tech revolution in India has signaled a gender revolution as well" (2008:11). As the roles of women are shifting, anxieties over maintaining "core Indian values" in the home are placed increasingly onto old people and intergenerational relations.

So, a cluster of events and processes have come together to foster a new kind of urban middle-class society conducive to novel ways of orga-nizing aging and anxieties over such transitions. Some children, following career paths, have moved far from parents, across the nation or world. Some younger women are asserting preferences not to co-reside with their husband's parents. Many parents and children feel that there is simply a different kind of "culture" at large, allowing for new lifestyles and family arrangements. There is a widespread sense, too, that a "generation gap" is increasing, partly because the pace and scope of contemporary social change seems so intense. Although of course I argued in chapter 1 that it is misleading to think that the old cannot change, partaking in new trends such as mall culture, email, and gendered egalitarianism, many of my older informants do feel that the young are moving culturally forward or away from "traditional ways" faster than they are. That many of the younger generation engage in practices such as parties with alcohol, conspicuous consumption, fast food on the go instead of a sit-down rice meal, a busy lifestyle with little time for home, makes some elders uncomfortable. So, if another option is now available, some elders conclude that they may actually prefer to live separately from their children—to keep relations easier—while still hopefully visiting and remaining emotionally close. One of the key reasons more people live outside of the conventional joint family today is also, simply, that they can afford to. (This is also an important reason behind the growth in single-person households in the United States (Francese 2003).) That is, the establishing of separate residences and the "outsourcing" of elder care from the family to, for instance, old age homes requires economic resources that earlier generations even among the fairly well-off middle classes did not readily possess.

A Brief Interlude: The Spheres of Class

This chapter has emphasized the perspectives and experiences of the middle classes in India, the focus of my fieldwork for this project and of recent media attention on aging. One gets a sense from this material of a very cosmopolitan India, where people, ideas, goods, money and communications flow easily to and from a wider world.

But I also spent some time with urban poor elders in Kolkata, especially through the Calcutta Metropolitan Institute of Gerontology (CMIG). CMIG sought out the very poorest of the poor elderly in the city—those living in slums, on the streets, inside pipes, with or without their families— and invited them to come to the institute daily from noon to four, to sit under a ceiling fan, chat with each other, watch television, prepare paper packets for sale in the market, and receive food. The institute was near my rented flat, and I would go when I could in the afternoons to hang out.

The elderly women and men at CMIG interpreted their abject condition in old age not in terms of the changing ways of a global modernity but rather in terms of timeless poverty. Sons don't care for their parents because or when sons don't have money. These seniors were not participating in the complex mobilities and global interconnections that so engage their middle- and upper-class neighbors. They went to and from CMIG by foot, often stooped over while carrying a small cloth bundle of meager belongings. The CMIG set on which they watched their daily hour of television was tuned to a local Bengali station. They had no kin or acquaintances living abroad.

One sultry afternoon after we had eaten a snack of *muṛi* (puffed rice) and tea, one among the group of ladies I was sitting with asked eagerly, "Say, is it true, tell me, that in the U.S., people go around wearing leaves and are otherwise naked?"

"No, no. That's not actually true," I replied.

"OK, another thing I heard!" she continued keenly, proposing a story that seemed to her equally far-fetched. "Is it true?—that when here it's day, there it's night?"

"Yes, that is true."

Another woman joined the conversation, from her spot on the floor where she rested on a piece of burlap sack. "We've seen airplanes in the sky. They're so small! Really, can people fit in them?"

A third woman interjected to explain that when planes are on the ground, you can see that they are very large. "Have you ever been to Dum Dum [Airport]?" she asked. "If you go there, you can see how big airplanes are!"

The other ladies were interested and asked how one gets to Kolkata's airport. I explained that, in fact, a local bus goes right from the new bypass running in front of the Calcutta Metropolitan Institute of Gerontology to the airport. (I had noticed the buses going by.) It would be, I thought, less than an hour's ride.

"How much would it cost?" one of the ladies wanted to know.

"I think about five or ten rupees," I surmised. That would be about ten or twenty cents, or the price of a half kilo of inexpensive rice.

"See! No wonder we can't go. Where would we get money to spend like that?"

This simple exchange brings home just how dramatically the spatial, cultural, and economic spheres of class diverge in scale.

3 THE RISE OF OLD AGE HOMES IN INDIA

One late morning in the winter of 2006, my research assistant, Hena, and I were chatting with Sri Ashok Bose, a warm, articulate man in his early eighties, who had been living in the Ramakrishna Mission Home for Aged People since its inauguration twenty-two years earlier. We sat in his simply furnished private room framed by two large windows open to a pleasant winter breeze and tree-filtered sunlight. In the room was a single bed covered with a pleasing yellow and orange cotton spread, a small wooden desk with chair, an additional chair next to the bed, and a tall metal wardrobe. Dressed in a blue plaid lungi,[1] tan button-down shirt, and richly colored maroon wool vest, Sri Ashok spoke with us animatedly about the disciplined routines of his daily life and how he had come to live in the home.

Sri Ashok was a bachelor who had long been devoted to a spiritual life, an aim in keeping with this home's mission, as described by one of its directors, to provide "a life away from the din of family, spent in solitary religious practices," "a site to pursue the *vānaprastha āśrama*," or the third and "forest-dwelling" phase of the Hindu householder's life.[2] Sri Ashok had gradually begun to lose his eyesight in his mid-fifties, but he had been able to serve out a full career as a Government of West Bengal Home Department employee, and he now drew a pension with which he could fund his expenses. But before retirement, he had worried about how to care for himself in old age, being then almost blind and having no children of his own to depend on. He tells the story: "Then one day, I came across a notice in the newspaper that the Ramakrishna Mission was planning to start an old age home! As *soon* as I read that, I went to [the Mission headquarters]." He recalls his application letter with detail and emotion: "I wrote, 'If I am accepted here, then that is very good.'" He paused and continued with a full voice: "'But if I am not selected, then please don't write that news in a letter. Because since I am blind, someone else will have to read the letter to me, and—I won't be able to bear that.'" He then narrated, brimming with pleasure and pride, "But they wrote back in a letter, saying: 'So long you have served us. Now let us serve you.'" He repeated, smiling broadly: "'So long you have served us. Now let us serve you!' And so I received admission!"

"About this ashram," Sri Ashok went on, referring to the institution throughout as an ashram or spiritual shelter/abode, "there's something you should know: we are living here *completely* without worry. *Everything* we need, we receive: the giving of food, tea [though he had earlier explained that he had never drunk tea much in his life; but that others take tea, and that he enjoys biscuits during tea time], warm bath water—*whatever* we need, we receive. *Truly,* there are no worries! At *precisely* the right time, the tea comes, the food comes! Be there a strike, or a storm, whatever there is, *still* the food comes at just the right time." And, indeed, just as he was speaking, his midday meal arrived, a few minutes before noon, placed quietly on the desk-cum-eating table next to his window, as some other residents chose instead to make their way through the halls to the common dining room, several pausing in his doorway to greet him as they passed.

When Hena and I got up to leave shortly after, we offered *praṇām* and he blessed us—in the ordinary junior-elder reciprocal exchange that so many Indians practice, where the junior bows down and touches the elder's feet as a sign of respect, and in turn the elder places his or her hands affectionately on the junior's head and offers blessings. Then he held onto my hands warmly as he spoke briefly of his fondness for Americans (who had welcomed Swami Vivekananda to New York and Chicago a hundred years earlier) and invited us to visit again.

A few days later I had a very different encounter: I visited Aram ("Comfort"), a small elder residence just a short walk or cycle-rickshaw ride from the apartment complex where I was living with my two daughters. It was the home that I probably visited the most often, and I gradually became quite close to three of the ladies who lived there, who were room-mates and widows, two of whom had sons and daughters-in-law living right in Kolkata and one whose only daughter resided in Delhi. We had had especially poignant conversations that day, as they had mourned their plights in the old age home, after a lifetime of living intimately with family and sacrificing for their children. As I got up to leave, I bent down to offer them *praṇām*. Uma-di and Kavika-di blessed me in return; but Kalyani-di —the most elegant of the three, a very beautiful, poised woman at age eighty-one—stopped me, her tender smile laced with chagrin, "Why are you offering so much *praṇām* to us—we, who are so full of sadness, who can't give you proper blessings?" It was as if living in an old age home had stripped Kalyani-di of the capacity to be a fruitful, potent elder.[3] She had just been telling me of how she goes over and over, in her mind, begging her son and daughter-in-law, with whom she almost never actually speaks, to give her "release" from the old age home. "They have so much!—gold, things," she scolded, speaking of her son and his wife, "Can you imagine? Anyone with that many things giving someone to an old age home?"

The place where she and her roommates lived was just a small, ordinary four-room flat that a young man, recently married and without other gainful employment, had rented to make into an old age home as his source of income. He dropped by once each morning to deliver food supplies, and otherwise two ayahs, or caregivers, and the ten residents, of whom seven were largely bedridden, composed the home. Purportedly for security reasons, a padlock generally remained on the front gate, and it took some time and effort each time I dropped by to have one of the residents call one of the busy ayahs to bring the key to let me in. As there was no telephone on the premises, Kalyani-di had borrowed my mobile phone that morning to call one of her kin, a daughter's son: "I'm still alive! Have you forgotten me? Please tell your mother to visit!" Kalyani-di and her roommates had reflected (as I reported briefly in chapter 2), "If we had grown up with the idea that we might live separately from our children, then it might not be so hard to get used to now. But with our own eyes we had never seen or known anything like this. We never could have even *dreamed* that a *bṛiddhābās* [abode for elders] existed, that we would be here, in a place like this!" It was not the particular conditions of their elder residence that shocked and disturbed these women; the flat where the elder home was established was an ordinary, fine, middle-class residence. It was the whole notion that elders could live in a separate institution established just for them, apart from their families, that still stunned these three women.

These brief vignettes speak to the variety and intensity of meanings attached to the rise of what in English are most commonly termed "old age homes" in India today.[4] Until the past few decades, old age homes almost did not exist in India, save for a handful established by Christian missionaries during the British colonial era, largely catering to Anglo Indians and the very poor. Now, residences for elders are rapidly springing up throughout India's urban and suburban neighborhoods, primarily for the Hindu middle and upper-middle classes. Although such institutions still house only a small minority of persons, they are receiving an enormous amount of media and public attention: journalists, filmmakers, residents, residents' kin, proprietors, social workers, gerontologists, NGOs, and those on the streets are all deliberating over what the surge of old age homes means for Indian persons, families, and society.

The predominant public discourse, in keeping with that of many of the old-age-home residents I have come to know, is substantially negative, and often scathingly so: old age homes signify the falling apart of society, a deplorable Westernization, children "throwing away" their parents, bitter alienation, rampant materialism, a loss of Indian traditions and values.

Yet, some public and media discourse is much more positive, as are the views of many of the old-age-home proprietors and indeed a sizable number of the homes' residents. More optimistic assessments profess that old age homes offer a valuable, welcome alternative to family-based living, sustain those who have no kin readily to depend on, liberate both older and younger generations to live independently and freely, foster gendered and aged egalitarianism, and in fact are perhaps not so radically "new" or fundamentally "Western" after all. For instance, some, like Ashok Bose, expressly perceive old-age-home living as akin to the forest-dwelling or *vānaprastha* life phase long presented in Hindu texts as appropriate for older age, where one purposefully loosens ties to family and the world in order to pursue spiritual realization. Further, in old age homes, elders are often the recipients of quite a bit of sustained *sevā,* or respectful service given to superiors—a key component of perceived traditional Indian ways of aging.[5] The residents of most homes do enjoy the receipt of *sevā*—in the form of the faithful arrival of daily 5:00 AM bed tea, meals served, oil massaged into hair, bath water warmed and delivered—even though this *sevā* is offered by hired staff and proprietors rather than one's own junior kin (a not insignificant distinction, which I explore below).

This and the following two chapters concentrate on the intensely ambivalent, richly varied meanings and values that residents, proprietors, kin, and the public have tied to these emerging institutions. What does the rise of old age homes mean for the ways Indians are (re)working aging, personhood, family, gender, and cultural-moral values in the contemporary era? In what ways does old-age-home living entail profoundly new ways of being? At the same time, in what important ways are older Indian and Bengali values and lifeways incorporated into the homes, making them intriguingly local instantiations of an increasingly globally ubiquitous institution?

An Overview of the Homes

Perhaps the single most striking dimension of the emergence of new modes of aging and family in India is the near flood of old age homes that has risen in India's major urban centers. During the British colonial era in the nineteenth and early twentieth centuries, a few early old age homes were established. Christian organizations such as The Little Sisters of the Poor were primarily the founders of these initial homes, inhabited almost exclusively by Anglo Indians and by the destitute. The Little Sisters of the Poor, a Roman Catholic religious order for women, was instituted in the mid-nineteenth century to care for the impoverished elderly lining the streets of France. The organization gradually expanded to establish old age homes for the poor in thirty-one countries, opening its first Indian old age home in Kolkata in 1882 and later adding six more across the nation. During the late 1800s and early 1900s, several old age homes for the Anglo Indian community also emerged. The Anglo Indians are a distinct minority community in India consisting of persons of mixed English and Indian ancestry and practicing an Anglo-centric culture based around English as the native language, European-style dress and cuisine, and the Christian religion. Thus the earliest old age homes in the nation were regarded by the wider Indian public as distinctly Western-originating, Western-style institutions.

Many of these oldest homes are still thriving today, such as the first Little Sisters of the Poor home established in central Kolkata in 1882. Recently remodeled, it is now an impressive-looking, grand white building, housing 150 older residents from any faith, free of charge—the only criteria being that the residents must be destitute, have no kin to support them, and be willing to perform daily chores, as able, in the home. Those older homes that have expressly maintained their Christian Anglo identities, however, such Kolkata's 150-year-old St. Lawrence de Souza home, are gradually fading away as the community gets smaller and smaller, housing merely a handful of white-haired ladies dressed in knee-length printed cotton frocks fashionable fifty or so years ago among the British.[6] People in Kolkata now still view such old Christian institutions as appropriate and even valuable for the two groups they serve: the very poor who have no kin to rely on, and the aging community of Anglo Indians—many of whom, in fact, have no remaining descendants in India upon whom they could depend, and who are viewed in any event as culturally very Western.

What is strikingly new over recent years is the rush of old age homes appearing for middle- and upper-middle-class Indians who are largely Hindu. This phenomenon began gradually in the 1980s and took off quite intensely in the late 1990s and early 2000s. In 1995, HelpAge India began to publish a *Directory of Old Age Homes in India,* and its (soon-to-be-updated) 2002 edition lists eight hundred across India's urban centers (HelpAge India 2002; see also Sawhney 2003:187). From 2003–2006, I was able to locate seventy-one old age homes in the Kolkata environs alone, the vast majority having been founded over the last one to fifteen years.[7] In about 2004, regular columns began to appear in the Classifieds sections of Kolkata's Bengali newspapers under "*Briddhābās*" (abodes for elders), advertising homes with vacancies.

These newer old age homes are almost entirely a middle-class phenomenon, mostly possible only for those with retirement pensions, professional children, and/or considerable savings. Run by both established non-governmental organizations (NGOs) and also private entrepreneurs, the for-pay home rates range from about 1,000 to 6,000 Indian rupees per month (a little over 20 to 120 USD), and often require a sizable joining fee or security deposit of anywhere from about 5,000 to 500,000 rupees (or about $100 to $10,000). An ordinary retirement pension for a middle-class professional might range from 3,000 to 15,000 rupees per month and thus could cover the monthly expenses. A full-time domestic servant (for six to seven days a week at about twelve hours per day), which many middle- and upper-class urban Indian families employ, would be paid about 1,500 to 3,000 rupees per month, roughly equivalent to the monthly fees of a modestly priced old age home. To come up with the security deposit, some sell a house or flat, or dip into savings accounts. This deposit is usually refundable, without interest, to the resident or a nominee, should the resident withdraw from the institution or pass away.

Few among the very wealthy at this point are turning to old age homes; they have more other options open to them, such as the financial capacity to maintain their own private homes with plentiful servants, even in the absence of children.

For the poor, there are a very limited number of old-age-home options, and within the urban poor communities where I have done fieldwork, the clear sentiment is that old age homes are distinctly for big/rich people (*baṛa lok*). Their own elders, say the poor, must still count on their own kin, or else beg on the streets, or scrape out some kind of meager living by rolling cigarettes, making paper grocery packets, selling fruit on the street, or the like. A few Christian charity homes surviving from the British era and several newer homes founded by Indian philanthropic organizations do offer free or subsidized accommodations at low rates for the relatively or very poor (table 3.1). Such charitable institutions receive some limited financial assistance from HelpAge India and the central Indian government. The Government of West Bengal maintains just one old age home for the poor, in the southern suburbs of Kolkata, originally established in 1968 as a Home for Old and Infirm Political Sufferers, to shelter Freedom Fighters who had battled the British during the Independence movement and those who had resisted various Congress Party policies in the 1950s and 1960s (see chapter 8). Now this institution is open even to those without a political background, sixty-eight residents in all, if they are destitute, aged, and can demonstrate that they have no kin upon whom they could rely.

My and others' research has at yet uncovered no Muslim homes for the aged in India (e.g., Liebig 2003:166). Nor have I personally encountered any individual Muslims living in the old age homes of Kolkata, although the Mother Superior of the Little Sisters of the Poor home in Kolkata told me that they housed a few Muslim residents. Most of the Kolkata elder homes do not label themselves as Hindu; however, ordinarily Hindus and Muslims in the region do not share intimate living spaces with one another.[8] My Muslim driver in 2006 and 2007 was curious about my research as he took me to and observed numerous old age homes, but he commented on several occasions that Muslims would never consider putting their elders into such a home. Of course, as I continue to explore, many Hindus say the same, and a few old age homes are slowly emerging in neighboring Muslim-dominated Bangladesh.[9] In terms of caste membership, in the for-pay elder residences in and around Kolkata, I encountered only persons of the highest Bengali Hindu caste groups, Brahmans and Kayasthas.

The philanthropic organization homes listed in table 3.1 fall into two types: those offering free or reduced-rate accommodations to the poor (a limited number), and those that charge going rates while still subsidizing the homes (the majority). I should note that the line between the "private (for-profit) business" and the "philanthropic organization" categorizations is somewhat fuzzy. As I explore further below, many proprietors and others are uncomfortable classifying old age homes as for-profit businesses, preferring rather to present their enterprises as "no-profit/no-loss" or benevolent "serving others"–type projects. However (going beyond strictly informant-supplied categorizations in this case), I have classified those institutions as private (for-profit) businesses if they have not registered with the government as a non-profit charitable organization for tax purposes, and (from what I can gather) generate at least some income that the proprietors can use, generally to support themselves and their households. This does not mean that the sole or even primary motivation of those involved in the "for-profit" business enterprises is necessarily that of financial gain.

Regarded widely as a distinctly modern and Western mode of managing aging, the institutions are referred to most commonly using the English designation "old age home." In Kolkata, Bengali alternatives such as *briddhābās*—abode (*ābās*) for elders (*briddha*, literally "increased" or "senior")—are also gradually becoming more prevalent. A second term, *briddhāśram*—"shelter" or "ashram" for elders (*briddha*)—carries distinct connotations of both spirituality (where elders can purposefully cultivate freedom from worldly ties) and refuge (for those who have no place else to go). One of the most sophisticated elder institutions in Kolkata calls itself a "Home for Senior Citizens," and the cosmopolitan residents there, who also partake in cocktail parties and jaunts to the neighborhood espresso café and movie theater, explicitly rejected (in keeping with current American trends) what they felt to be the rather pejorative and pitying label of "old."

Accommodations can come in the form of single, double, or dormitory-style rooms; and in some a husband and wife (or mother and daughter, or two siblings) can opt to live together.[10] The homes range in size mostly from about five to fifty residents.[11] These residents are commonly referred to, within media, public, and even institutional discourses, as "inmates" (though without explicitly intending to convey the negative prison-related connotations the term carries in American English) or "boarders." More familiarly in Bengali, proprietors and staff frequently call the residents by respectful and affectionate kin terms such as *māsīmā* (mother's sister), *ṭhākurmā* (grandmother), or *mesomaśāe* (mother's sister's husband).[12] The residents come from a wide range of family situations: some are childless, others have only daughters, others' children are all abroad, and others (of those I interviewed, the largest number) have sons and daughters-in-law living right nearby (see table 3.2). It is significant to note that most

TABLE 3.1.
Old Age Homes in Greater Kolkata by Type of Organization

Private (For-Profit) Business	46
Philanthropic Organization	20
(# offering free or reduced-rate accommodations for the poor: 5)	
Christian Charity (free or reduced rates)	4
Government of West Bengal (free)	1

Note: (N = 71 located, 2003–2006)

Indians feel it strongly inappropriate to live in a married daughter's home, although such attitudes are changing somewhat due to various factors, probably the most significant being that more daughters are earning their own incomes.[13] Some homes are for one gender only (in Kolkata, I found one for men only, and several more for only women); and while most are mixed-gender residences, they generally house considerably more women than men, a fact I reflect on further below.

In terms of degrees of comfort and amenities offered, I encountered two primary kinds of institutions. The larger and fancier homes are situated in institutions built especially for the purpose, resembling other modern apartment complexes rising around the city. These have been founded primarily by philanthropic non-governmental organizations, or by the "corporate social responsibility" or "social projects" wings of large business corporations such as the Aditya Birla Group (which runs the

TABLE 3.2.
Old-Age-Home Resident Profiles: Status of Children

Sons and daughters-in-law in Kolkata region	33
No children	30
Only daughters	18
(Local: 15; outside Kolkata: 2; overseas: 1)	
Son(s all) abroad	18
(Outside Kolkata: 9; overseas: 9)	
Unmarried son	1

Note: Based on 100 subjects—75 female, 25 male

Mahadevi Birla Niketan old age home) and the Peerless General Finance and Investment Company (which runs Milan Tirtha). Such organizations previously devoted themselves to initiatives such as healthcare, education for the poor, and sustainable livelihoods, and have recently turned as well to founding, and partly subsidizing, old age homes. Because of these subsidies, the homes run by the large, well-established NGOs or corporations tend to be the finest around, offering generally many more facilities—such as separate dining and function rooms, elevators, small libraries and temples—than do most of the purely private institutions. Over the past several years, a few large (40-50-room), upmarket old age homes have also been established in Kolkata by private parties. In all, about ten of the seventy-one homes I located were of this relatively luxurious nature. In addition to the larger facilities and more spacious common rooms, such upscale institutions generally offer residents private bedrooms, attached baths replete with showers, the possibility of air conditioning and small personal refrigerators, sometimes a small kitchenette, and the like. Such homes tend to cost more and appeal to those who have maintained relatively affluent lifestyles earlier.

The more numerous smaller homes, run by both more minor NGOs and private entrepreneurs, have been launched in donated schools, former medical clinics, and most frequently private households—owned or rented flats in ordinary middle-class neighborhoods. These homes are set up by and large very like the kinds of ordinary middle-class households that the residents tend to come from, with similar living, eating, sleeping, bathing, and cooking arrangements. Many of these arrangements would strike many Americans as quite austere and cramped. For instance, private bathrooms are not the norm. Most homes do not have showers or baths; instead, residents bathe using buckets of water, heated over a stove in winter. People tend more often to share bedrooms (in groups of about two to six) rather than have a private room. But to most residents (and to me, having spent a lot of time in similar Indian households), all this is quite normal, familiar, and even often very welcome. For instance, many residents much prefer to share a room rather than to maintain a private bedroom in an arrangement that would strike most of their generation as unusually isolated and lonely.[14]

When I first began doing this research in 2003, the majority of old age homes I encountered required that residents, at least when joining the facilities, be in fairly good mental and physical health, able to walk, talk, and perform basic activities of daily living, such as eating, dressing, and bathing. Many required an interview and often a medical examination to determine eligibility. Then, in the event that a resident later became seriously ill or incapacitated, the policy of many institutions was that the resident must be sent home. "Home," I would wonder, in discussing such policies with various managers, "is just *where* for many of these residents?" This incongruous policy had also struck an active member of a senior citizens club, who at a gathering to discuss the emergence of old age homes, commented, "You are given an umbrella, and then just when it starts to rain, the umbrella is taken away!" By 2006, however, I observed that an increasing number of homes were harboring physically and mentally disabled elders, who simply had to pay additionally for a private nurse's care, which the home would arrange and supervise if such care were necessary. The homes do also provide weekly or biweekly doctor's visits.

In India, "nursing homes" (called by that name in English) are not thought of as institutions devoted in particular to the long-term care of the elderly as they are in the United States. Rather, birthing mothers, those recovering from surgeries, and some older people requiring medical care use nursing homes for relatively contained periods of time. Most old age homes in India, then, are more similar to U.S. assisted living residences. Cosmopolitan communities in the increasingly sophisticated cities of Chennai and Bangalore have also witnessed the opening of a few posh retirement communities modeled after those in Western Europe and the United States, where senior citizens may purchase small independent apartments on maintained grounds while also partaking, when they wish to, of provided meals, medical attention, housekeeping, maintenance staff, and social activities.

The minimum age requirement observed by most residences for elders in India is sixty, a common age of retirement in India. I encountered several residents who were younger still, however, such as an older resident's wife still in her fifties and a divorced and childless woman in her forties who found the old age home a safe and comfortable place to live. (India's cities offer few other non-family living options, especially for single women.) Very many residents whom I encountered, at any chronological age, would be considered quite "young" by U.S. standards—fit and sharp—and (again, by U.S. estimations) well able to get by on their own.

The homes provide all meals, served either in common dining rooms or at bedside for those less mobile and in homes lacking space. Bed tea (at dawn), morning tea with breakfast, and afternoon tea are also punctually served. Numerous institutions offer a choice between vegetarian and non-vegetarian diets, appealing especially to many upper-caste widows who, in Bengal, are widely expected to observe strict vegetarianism (avoiding not only meat, fish, and eggs, but also garlic and onions).[15] However, not all homes prepare separate vegetarian meals, so quite a few widowed residents tell (some complaining, others accepting, still others seemingly pleased) of how they have had to forgo all such order and rules. In some of the fancier homes, residents have set up small kitchenettes in their rooms, with refrigerator, hot plate, and a few supplies for making tea and snacks for themselves and guests.

Residents' clothes are washed and rooms cleaned; and in fact one of the distinct advantages of old-age-home living, many say, is that older people no longer have to manage their own servants. Even most ordinary middle-class households in India maintain servants to help with household chores, something that requires money, just as residing in an old age home does. Peppering Indian newspapers over recent years are also stories of aged persons being tricked, robbed, and even murdered by domestic work-ers, contributing to a widespread sense that it is inappropriate and even dangerous for elders to live on their own (chapter 6). Some old-age-home residents also tell of how bored and irritated they had become listening to their servants' monotonous stories over and over again, as they had become increasingly homebound in their older years.

In India's old age homes to date, strikingly minimal formal activi-ties are planned, and residents spend their time reading, chatting, simply sitting, playing cards, knitting, writing journals and letters, having tea, watching television, going on morning walks, taking a stroll to a nearby market, and (in the fancier ones) attending occasional cultural programs and functions. Female residents might also help with some light cooking, such as peeling vegetables, cleaning small stones from dried lentils, or tasting a dish to see if it has turned out right. The larger homes generally house a *mandir* or temple, where residents can pray, make offerings to dei-ties and sing hymns. Most women boarders and some men also maintain their own small shrines in their rooms, where they perform daily *pūjās*, serving and honoring both deities and deceased kin such as husbands and parents. Especially if in a private room, residents tend to decorate their spaces elaborately, with photographs, wall hangings, small furnishings from home, a television—making their spaces their own new homes. The larger, more posh homes have established one or two common areas for congregating, watching television or playing games, or to use as a library or computer room with internet access. Some more elaborate homes also maintain quite lovely gardens with flowers, vegetables, sometimes a cow or dog or two, walkways, benches, and perhaps a small fish and lily pond.

The government does not consistently regulate old age homes in India to date, although it does provide minimal financial support to some institutions serving the relatively poor, through the organization HelpAge India; and some Indian gerontologists and newspaper editorials are calling for increasing regulation (e.g., Narasimhan 2004, Sengupta 2005, *The Hindu* Special Correspondent 2004). The lack of regulation presents a potentially precarious scenario. The homes run by the larger philanthropic organizations *are* regulated and scrutinized at least by their own committees—by boards of directors, presidents, donors, and members who volunteer and visit—providing a somewhat public eye. In the small business, private old age homes, which make up the majority of the homes in Kolkata (table 3.1), residents and their families are completely dependent on the goodness, knowledge, and skills, or lack thereof, of the proprietors. By far the majority of the thirteen private homes I spent a good deal of time in seemed to me to be decently run, fine places—that is, clean, the residents' basic needs met, with generally respectful staff and pleasant living conditions—arranged, by and large, very like the kinds of ordinary, familiar, middle-class households that the residents tend to come from. But a few disturbing cases stand out. In one small private home, a toilet stands right in the midst of the sleeping and eating quarters of three roommates, not even separated by a protective curtain—an arrangement that profoundly upsets ordinary Indian sensibilities regarding pollution, purity, and propriety. In another home, the proprietor simply took for himself and his wife a radio-cassette player that my ten-year-old daughter and I had lovingly donated to the home's residents. In a third home, according to the daughter of a resident, the nurse that the home had arranged to provide care for her bedridden mother was completely unsupervised and unskilled, and so the daughter returned from Delhi, where she lived and worked, to find her mother covered in bedsores and requiring hospitalization.

However, as I have noted, by far the majority of the private-business homes I visited struck me, and my research assistant Hena, as quite pleasant, loving, clean, adequate—run, as were the larger more formal institutions, by well-meaning and hard-working proprietors. The smaller,

FIGURE 3.1. Dhara Roy in her elaborately decorated room with Hena, my research assistant (left). Dhara-di shares two adjoining rooms with her husband and mother.

FIGURE 3.2. Two lady residents chat and knit as their morning goes by.

FIGURE 3.3. A winter day in the gardens of the Swami Mahadevananda Giri Briddhashram.

FIGURE 3.4. Residents chat in the open-air corridor in front of their rooms.

private homes also tended to be the most "homey" (in Bengali, *gharoyā*), rather than institutional, a quality that many residents said had originally attracted them and that they appreciated.[16] So, for instance, in Atithiseva ("Hospitality"), the six lady residents would spend a good part of each day with the two proprietors hanging out in the central kitchen and common room, chatting, helping to plan meals and do light cooking, speaking of the proprietors as being like their own sons or nephews, and often with one or two of the proprietors' children hanging around—sitting on their "grandmothers'" laps or leaning on their chairs—and occasionally with the proprietors' wives dropping by. The residents affectionately described one of the proprietors, Shiven, as a particularly good cook: he had learned from his mother, who was around their age, and in fact each day before leaving home on his way to work, he would ask his mother (with whom he lived, until she passed away during my period of fieldwork) what he should pick up from the market and cook that day for all of his "aunts."

Everyday Narratives: Why Old Age Homes *Now*?

Chapter 2 offered an analysis of the complex social changes helping to explain the rise of non-family based modes of aging in contemporary India. Here, I delve more closely into my informants' daily narratives and musings about the emergence of, in particular, old age homes in their nation.

"Why old age homes now?" was one of the questions I repeatedly asked. Many residents and directors also spontaneously broke into discussions of this relevant topic.

There would be the usual shared catalog of common responses: the joint family system is breaking down (this single response surfaced in almost any discussion); families are becoming small; nuclear families are taking over; people are living now in small flats; children are moving abroad; those of the younger generation have become very busy—with their jobs, the push for material prosperity, parties, and their own children; people have no time now (to care for aged relatives, for instance); selfishness and individualism are on the rise; the ways of "Western" societies (including old age homes, a feature of the West) are exerting their force globally; daughters-in-law are becoming older (at marriage), more educated, more career-bound and thus more assertive; the older generation is unable to adjust to newer ways; generation gaps are increasing; there is now a looser sense of family and social-moral obligations; patriarchy is on the decline; more people have more money and so can afford to live separately; there are more options now for ways to live one's life.

Presented very much as features of "today's times" (*ājkāl*) and "modern society" (*ādhunik samāj*), some people would describe such contemporary changes in very disparaging terms, others more matter-of-factly, and still others with some degree of celebration.

Mukund Gangopadhyay, who lived with his wife in the Swami Paramananda Baba Ashram for Elders, was one who viewed the emergence of old age homes in India in highly disparaging terms, and he invoked the classical Hindu devolutionary model of the four *yugas* or ages to make sense of the contemporary social changes that have allowed their rise. According to this well-known theory, things get progressively worse over time rather than better, as humankind gradually moves through four ages to reach the most degenerate of all times, the contemporary Kali Yuga. Mukund-babu, one of his good friends in the home Bimal Mitra, a few other residents, the home's manager, my research assistant, Hena, and I were chatting outdoors, sitting on the benches arranged in the home's spacious gardens on a pleasant winter morning in 2004, a year after my first visit to this elder abode. The frequently voiced topic—Why are there old age homes now?—came up. Mukund-babu's co-resident friend Bimal-da commented matter-of-factly, "When people get old, their kids kick them out, disown them (*bātil kare dāe*)—this happens in all countries." Mukund-babu took immediate exception, interjecting forcefully, "*Before,* that didn't happen *here!* There was no kicking out of houses! People lived with their families— with their sons if they had them; if not, with other relatives.[17] Everyone is saying that 'progress'[18] is happening," he went on. "But is this progress [*agragati*]? or stagnation [*jaṛatā*]?!"

He went on to explain, for my benefit, the Hindu theory of the four *yugas* as laid out in the Bhagavad Gita—how, with each age, society dete- riorates more and more, until, "in my individual opinion, all this will be destroyed—completely smashed. We are seeing it before our very eyes right now." Hena chided Mukund-babu for being so very negative: "How can you say that everything has rotted? . . . Your mind has withdrawn since coming here. . . . If individuals make the world around them good, then gradually we can create a good society. . . ." They argued, as I tried to take notes, making a note to myself, too, to tell Hena that I'm actually inter- ested in Mukund-babu's negative theories and that perhaps she shouldn't attempt to silence them, trying to cheer him up. Some standing around got bored and wandered off, and Hena, Mukund-babu, and his friend Bimal-da ended up agreeing that at least some good *āḍḍā*—a particularly Bengali term for fulfilling, intense, argumentative conversation—had transpired.

Mukund Gangopadhyay was not alone in viewing old age homes as the result of radical global apocalyptic change, but more of those involved in the homes tied their emergence to three more specific interrelated trends, trends that were not always regarded as negative: 1) multifaceted processes of "Westernization," the rise of a new middle class, and a general loss of or change in "traditional" lifeways; 2) a transformation of gendered and generational relationships, specifically a waning of patriarchy; and 3) a relaxing of powerful social-moral obligations surrounding the family—the opening up of more options regarding ways of organizing intergenerational relationships, which have always been fraught with difficulty. These kinds of social trends, introduced in earlier chapters, merit a bit more examination here in the specific context of people's efforts to make sense of old age homes. Through fashioning narratives to answer the pressing question of "Why old age homes now?" elders, old-age-home proprietors and the public construct and reflect upon understandings of modernity in India.

"Westernization," New Middle-Class Lifeways, and a Loss of/ Change in "Traditional" Values

"Westernization" figures as a major trope in current discourse about the emergence of old age homes in India, along with the rise of a new kind of middle-class culture. Recall, for instance, Dr. Ranjan Banerjee's reflections, cited in opening the book:

> 'Old age homes' are not a concept of *our* country. These days, we are throwing away our 'culture.' The U.S. is the richest nation in the world and therefore has won us over. Now we, too, are only after material wealth as a nation and have become very unhappy. . . . 'Old age homes' are not *our* way of life. . . . Material wealth [*artha*] used not to be the prime value in life; rather, family and social closeness were. But now it has become so. I myself am against the 'old age home concept'—but, 'old age homes' will stay and increase in India.

People also commonly spoke to me of old age homes as "my" (i.e., the United States') country's or culture's "system." Even my research assistant

Hena on several occasions replied to residents who asked me if there were old age homes in my country, "Yes, of course! Old age homes are *from* her culture, and we are learning from them!"

To some extent one could say that this straightforward explanation of the origin of old age homes in India is simply true—that they came originally from the West. For instance, as described above, the first old age homes in India were built under British rule, mostly by Christian groups such as the Little Sisters of the Poor. Several Indian founders of contemporary old age homes also told me specifically of how they were first inspired to establish their homes after traveling to Western nations such as England and encountering such institutions there. However, the institutions themselves would not have thrived in India in the absence of broader social trends, which many people link explicitly to a broader influence of "Western" ways, especially among the new middle class.

It is interesting to scrutinize what images of the West figure in such discourses. The following often get grouped together: nuclear families, small flats, transnational living, consumerism, lack of time, efficiency, rationality, materialism and individualism. These are placed in contrast to more "traditionally" Indian characteristics: family bonds, intimacy, plentiful time, spirituality, large houses and families, care and respect for elders, material frugality. A Bengali Catholic sister working at Kolkata's oldest old age home, the newly remodeled Little Sisters of the Poor institution, responded to my query about why old age homes now: "Like Americans, people don't have *time* anymore." (I was struck. I know that I, an American, do indeed feel *terribly* pressed by a shortage of time while in the United States, but—are we known so internationally to be singularly characterized by this irritating feature of contemporary life?)[19] She went on to explain how today's Indian children are extremely busy with their jobs and such, and they also frequently live abroad, pursuing professional careers while leaving their parents behind. Even those who remain in India choose to live now in small, modern flats, she remarked. "So, they send their parents to paying homes. At least they are paying. They have money but they can't or don't want to look after their parents themselves." She added, "There are so many [old age] homes now, but there is still such a rush! We have so many on the waiting list. If anyone dies, we fill the spot immediately."

One afternoon, I was sitting in the central courtyard of Ashaniketan, a pleasantly designed home that houses twelve women in dormitory-style accommodations. We were all gathered together in the outdoor courtyard, where the ladies usually congregate in the afternoons, enjoying tea. When I raised the topic, "Why old age homes now?" a lively discussion ensued about familiar themes—busy children, independent living, the decline in joint families—as they spoke almost in unison, though not un-cheerfully: "'Joint families' are all breaking up." "Before, we all lived in one *saṃsār* [family, household]." "Before, people had big, big houses. Now they all live in small, small flats." "The chief point is that families are getting small. Before they had seven to eight children; now they have one to two children only." "Children are very busy now." "The children are all going outside [Kolkata] and to foreign countries to work." "These days in the flats, everyone wants to have a bathroom attached to each bedroom, and each person wants their own room—They're not all sleeping together like they used to. But, you can't find such flats for lots of people: the flats come in sizes of two to three bedrooms. So now there is no room for the old people." The new living arrangements nurture modern values of privacy and individualism.

To illustrate these points, several spoke of their families of youth. One described how hers had been *such* a large family, of three brothers and three sisters, aunts, uncles and grandparents, all living together on their family land in East Bengal. Another woman described her natal home: "Five sisters and three brothers, and such a large house! This kind of family doesn't exist any more."

"There are those of us without kids," one woman added, "and also those *with* kids. But even those with kids are left alone; the kids are very busy, or they move abroad to work. So, we are left alone all day. We felt very lonely before coming here." "Old age homes are new here," another volunteered. "They have begun with our 'generation.'" I asked, "Will your *children* live in old age homes?" And several laughed, replying, "Yes, certainly!" "Ashrams for elders are increasing *so* much, that *wherever* you go, you hear that a new one is starting!"

As discussed in chapter 2, a major impetus behind such transformations is the upwelling of money that has entered the middle and upper middle classes following India's economic liberalization policies of the early 1990s. The new trend of for-pay old age homes is specifically for the middle classes, and can rightly be considered a part of a new, broader consumerism: the buying or consuming of care. Sanjita Sen, society lady[20] and co-founder of Ananda Ashram, a brand new abode and one of the more posh old age homes of Kolkata, defined their targeted clientele: "For those who have adjusted with their kids abroad, and who have children who are eager to pay, *more* than eager to pay for their parents' happiness— we arrange for mental peace, and also physical peace." Momentarily she added as well that many elder parents themselves are also able to pay, and choose to pay, in a sense buying their comfort, convenience, security, and independence.

A recent newspaper story titled "Old, But Free" explores the motivations of a well-off older woman who had just driven out with a group of friends to investigate an old people's complex that was being built on the outskirts of the city of Bangalore. The reporter wondered what motivated her to plan for this kind of living. The story concludes:

> There was a time when there was a distinct stigma attached to being in an old folks' home. The homes that existed were dismal and shoddy. To live in one of them implied a lack of anywhere else to live and a lack of caring on the part of one's children. But all that has now changed, not least of which are attitudes. Increasingly, the old are now reluctant to move in with their children. They are loath to give up their independence, yet . . . they seek comfort. . . .
>
> The response to this demand is a spate of senior citizens' complexes that are mushrooming all over the country. They consist of well-designed, attractive homes . . . where the residents have all their needs attended to. They live independently, yet, where food, medical attention, housekeeping, and companionship are concerned, free of all cares and worries. On the face of it, what could be better! (Vasudeva 2006)

Here, moving to an elder residence is part of a whole new consumerist way of middle-class life, one that entails reorganizing and reconceptualizing not only old age and family, but also much broader visions of personhood, social-moral values, and the very aims of life.

Gendered and Generational Changes, and a Waning Patriarchy

Gender and especially the changing position of women also figure centrally in many narratives explaining the rise of old age homes today. Some speak in favor of gendered social changes, viewing them as liberatory, especially for younger women; while others blame women for what they regard as the degenerations of a modern era.[21]

Sadanand Chatterjee, the director of a rather large forty-resident old age home for paying and a few free residents, claimed that changes regarding gender were the main force behind the rise of India's old age homes, although the idea for the homes also "came from Western culture," he argued. "Traditionally, India had no such system; it was part of India's ancient *dharma* [moral-religious conduct] to care for one's elders." In addition to being the founder and director of this home, he was also a Brahman priest, and he spoke to Hena and me with his sacred thread[22] showing prominently outside his thin T-shirt, as he relaxed in an armchair in his living quarters adjoining the elder residence, his eyes straying periodically to a television blaring a Bengali matinee behind us. As a young man assisting his father with his priestly duties at the thronging Kalighat Kali temple, he had seen families simply casting aside their elder kin, leaving them to beg in the streets around the temple. The main force behind such changes in Indian society, he asserted, is the changing role of women, who are marrying at older ages and increasingly entering the paid work force:

> Daughters-in-law used to marry at young ages and then could easily become one [*ek*] with the family. But now they are not marrying until after twenty-five or thirty, and so they are not so flexible. And the parents-in-law are also not able to adjust. When their daughter-in-law came as just a little girl, it was easy to learn to adore her. . . .
>
> Further, daughters-in-law who have jobs can assert themselves and say that they want to live independently. And another related thing: mothers are going out to work and so are not properly giving milk to their children. The children are being raised by ayahs. So, children are crying, and old people are crying.

This man's comments irritated my research assistant Hena, who later told me that she felt he was being sexist, too easily blaming all of society's current ills on women. I concurred that there was something about his tone and manner, a kind of arrogant indifference, that could rub one the wrong way. However, many others, including many women of various ages, backgrounds, and feminist sensibilities, made not-dissimilar observations to me, viewing the increasing agency of women and waning patriarchy as at the root, for worse and better, of social changes that have allowed old age homes.

One evening I went with a mentor and friend, retired professor Aparna Das Gupta, to visit one of her distant relatives, Mrs. R. N. Roy, the ninety-year-old widowed wife of a founder of one of the more well-regarded old age homes in Kolkata. Mrs. Roy had once remarked to Aparna-di that it had been her husband's dearest dream over the final decade of his life, in post retirement, to establish the old age home. I was curious as to how he had developed such a dream, so Aparna-di took me to meet the aged widow. Mrs. Roy recalled:

> My husband had been thinking of starting an old age home for many years. We been abroad ten to twelve times and seen the old age homes there, but at first, at that time, the idea didn't enter his head. Then later he came to perceive that in this generation, sons and daughters-in-law don't like to live with their mothers-in-law and fathers-in-law, the way we used to look after our parents and grandparents in the past. . . . And in this generation, the parents also have become very educated, and they, too, do not want to put up with or accept [*mene neoyā*] their children's demands. Thinking about all this, my husband began to dream about starting an old age home.

She later elaborated: "Sons and daughters-in-law don't want to live with their parents, and the parents also feel hurt by the children; they feel bound to move out, for the sake of peace." "Did it used to be like this?" "No," she and Aparna-di replied in unison. Aparna-di, reflecting, tried to explain, speaking in English: "Earlier—forgive me for using the word, but I mean it just descriptively [she gave a slight apologetic laugh]—we lived in a very *patriarchal* society. The husband dominated. I'm not using the term in a bad sense, just a factual sense," she clarified. "And his wife wouldn't want to disturb her husband or his parents. Now, we no longer have such a patriarchal society. Women have a lot of say in the younger generation."

"Take my case, for instance," Aparna-di was now a woman in her sixties, who had been widowed for the past several years, and still a very active and accomplished academic. She had lived for many years in a multigenerational household with her parents-in-law, although her own recently married only son and wife lived abroad, with Aparna-di's blessings. "My mother-in-law used to be quite harsh, but I couldn't say anything. If I did say anything to my husband, then he would tell me quietly to just accept it—he couldn't fight with his parents. Now, a *bou* [wife-daughter-in-law] *will* tell her husband, and her husband will tell his parents. Now, if adjustments are to be made, they will be made by the *older* generation." Mrs. Roy nodded in agreement. "If the *older* generation adjusts," Aparna-di went on, "both generations can live together. Otherwise, they can't live as a joint family. The older generation will have to move out on its own." Many old-age-home resident ladies offered similar narratives and commented that it is even with their blessings that they and their daughters-in-law are branching out on their own.

Age-Old Tensions, the Relaxing of Social-Moral Obligations, and the Creation of New Possibilities for Living

A third related cluster of reasons emerging from my informants' attempts to provide answers to the question, "Why old age homes now?" surrounds an acknowledgement that intergenerational living has never been unfettered by problems. Many founders and proprietors of old age homes speak of their task as to provide a welcome alternative living arrangement, to help open up in India other options besides family—which doesn't always work—as a site for aging. Some residents voice similar visions. This new model, of old age home living as a viable alternative to the family, is one that tends to be based on a view of the positive value (to a degree, at least) of individual independence and of gendered and aged egalitarianism.

In making such arguments about the positive value of old-age-home living, most proprietors speak of the elders they serve in quite reverential terms, and some in fact dedicate the homes to their own *gurujan* (literally, "respected persons"; another term for elders) such as their parents, framing large garlanded portraits of a mother and/or father in a front office, or naming the home after the beloved forebear.

I came across, however, one highly disgruntled proprietor of an old age home nestled in a peripheral suburban region of Kolkata—who poured forth a diatribe against the *irritating* (*biraktakar*) seniors of his home (while continually ordering more cups of tea for us both, so greatly was he enjoying the opportunity finally to have an interested, listening ear for his complaints). To this director, Dr. Roy, true, old age homes are indeed a valuable tool or solution opening up new options in modern society. But, importantly, this is not because modern *children* are flawed (the more prominent discourse). It is that Indian society has finally come to a place where elder respect is no longer compulsory when the elders are not deserving of respect. "Why old age homes now?" he responded to my query. "Because before, no matter *how* much quarrelling and inconvenience [*jhagṛā, asubiddhā*] there was at home, the children could not kick their parents out." He told a story of one mother who had three sons. She lamented to everyone, "Oh, my sons are all bad, and that's why I've had to come to the home." "Now," the director narrated animatedly, "*One* son could be bad; maybe *two* sons could be bad. But, how could *three* sons be bad? So, who is bad—tell me? . . . These old people are *so* irritating [*eta biraktakar, nā?*]; you *wouldn't* be able to understand!" "These days old age homes are necessary," he went on, "because if we didn't have them, where else could they [the old people] go? There's nowhere else . . . We *have* to put up with them, but the families no longer do."

Although it was rare in my fieldwork to encounter people so comfortable being openly critical of elders in this way, many older and younger people in more gentle terms did offer that contemporary mores and old-age-home living allowed junior and senior generations to coexist with more freedom, egalitarianism and ease than previously. Such discussions often highlighted the looser and less hierarchical gender arrangements of today's families, most notably the relative liberation of the daughter-in-law (in this these analyses were similar to those of priest and proprietor Sadanand Chatterjee, but expressed in more celebratory terms). Many elder residents, most notably women, reminisced about the intense difficulties they had experienced—both as younger daughters-in-law struggling under their mothers-in-law, and as mothers-in-law struggling with their daughters-in-law—living in multi-generational households. Several women felt that *they* of their generation had especially felt the brunt of such struggles, as they had been under the stern rule of their mothers-in-law when young, and now—if they wished to coexist with their daughters-in-law—had to submit to the daughter-in-law's rule, in these changing times of strong younger women. Several expressed then feeling great relief and even joy at having an alternative living arrangement to turn to in the form of the old age home. "It's because of this home that we are saved," a group of four women roommates told me after spending a good hour or so complaining about their daughters-in-law.

Mrs. Aarti DasGupta and Mrs. Sanjita Sen, two society ladies in their fifties, devoted a great deal of their own time and funds, while also amassing support from several charitable organizations, in order to establish a modestly sized yet posh old age home bordering the vast, lovely guava orchards of an old zamindar[23] community south of Kolkata where Aarti had inherited some land. They reflected on their motivations: "We are trying to start to wipe out the stigma of living in an old age home," Aarti asserted, referring to the prevailing powerful public sentiment that to live in an old age home carries a terrible stigma of moral deterioration, for both the elder and elder's family. "'Come and *happily* stay with us' is our motto." "It's not that the children are throwing away their parents; it's not *always* that," Sanjita went on. "These are just the circumstances of modern society. We are just taking one step in solving this problem, in opening up another kind of option for living in old age."

Elaborating upon the "circumstances of modern society," the women portrayed a contemporary scene of adult children living abroad, and of parents and children enjoying separate, independent living arrangements. The children of both Aarti and Sanjita, in fact, lived abroad in Los Angeles, Sydney, London, and Delhi. "Children today are not precisely neglecting their parents. But often they have no option of having their parents stay with them. The parents are also not eager to stay with their children abroad. But old age is advancing, and whether rich or poor, the old need attention and care." Among their peers, very few are staying with children, they commented. "We have just our husbands, and our friends," the two close friends laughed; and they reflected that they themselves would look forward to residing in an elder residence, if they could find a good, comfortable, modern one like the kind they are building—with internet access, a library, a proper phone system, hot and cold running water, and lively and intellectual peers. One of their prospective boarders is a retired, widowed Harvard professor with no children in India, planning to keep up his Kolkata apartment with servants, but wanting to supplement that with an additional living option, to break up what was coming to seem like a monotonous daily routine of post-retirement and post-family independent old age.

Such a novel non-family-based living option is regarded by some as especially appealing and significant for those who have no sons, a sizable proportion of old-age-home residents and almost half of those in my study (see table 3.2). One woman resident, Inu Ghosh, who had never married and was childless, reflected upon how, in older times, unmarried aunts used to always find a place to live in their relatives' households, with brothers, nephews, and such. "Relatives" (*ātmīya*), or one's "own people," is a term generally used to refer to those who are kin but not those who would ordinarily make up one's immediate household. The fact that old, son-less aunts used to be able to live with "relatives" was a fact that many others brought up to me as a sign of the *better,* more admirable, socially and morally committed, family-binding earlier times. But this elder-abode resident had a different, compelling perspective: "If living in a relative's house, I wouldn't be able to ask for anything." She gave some examples: like a glass of water delivered, help tying up a mosquito net, an extra serving of a good dish, fetching something from the market. "I would have to lie on my bed and wait quietly, hoping that it would arrive. Here at the old age home, I can hold my head up high and ask for what I need. They are here to serve *me*. I am *paying* for this service, so I can ask for whatever I want, with dignity."

Another resident, mother of only daughters, voiced almost precisely the same narrative. Most Indians, including Bengalis, feel strongly that parents should not live with their married daughters but rather only with sons, and so the old age home provided son-less women like her the opportunity to live "independently" (*svādhīn-bhābe*), with "head held high." "I didn't want to be like the old aunt in *Pather Panchali*," Inu Ghosh went on to add with a wry smile. Interestingly, quite a few others mentioned this aunt, old Indir Thakrun from Satyajit Ray's debut film, as an example of how, in earlier times, elder relatives were always cared for by their extended kin. There used to always be elderly childless widows in every family, people would say, and they would find a place to live among kin; there would be no thought of turning them away. However, old Indir Thakrun's position in both the film and household is ambiguous. Although one reviewer describes her as "the most lovable character in the film, . . . an old, cynical, loving and storytelling aunt,"[24] her place in her cousin's household is precarious. Another reviewer calls her "the most comic and tragic figure in the film, subsisting on whatever handouts she can get from the family, who mostly find her a nuisance to be around."[25] Anthropologist Lawrence Cohen, who visited in the 1990s one of Kolkata's earliest old age homes, Nava Nir ("New Nest"), found the majority of residents to be old women without sons, and commented that "the rise of homes like Nava Nir suggests less a sloughing off of parents than the emergence of a different response to old people with weak claims upon family support" (1998:119). This "different response" is much more individual-centered, independent, egalitarian, and market-based: one finds and pays for one's own housing and care, living among peers away from the family.

A New Kind of Commercial Enterprise?

Finally, any discussion of the reasons for the emergence of old age homes in India must consider what Dr. Indrani Chakravarty, Director of the Calcutta Metropolitan Institute of Gerontology, asserted plainly: "The reason old age homes have been springing up like crazy is that they can produce some income: people pay to stay."[26]

I found it interesting that most people I spoke with were decidedly uncomfortable referring to old age homes as commercial enterprises or "businesses" (in Bengali, *byabsā*). It was as if it was strongly inappropriate to think of making money off something as rightly family-based as elder care. A person aiming to earn money by opening an old age home seemed to me to be viewed, in many people's eyes, as akin to the morally disconcerting state of a mercenary—someone motivated by profit only, rather than loyalty that would spring from being a true part of a nation, in the case of a (mercenary) soldier, or a family, in the case of an old-age-home proprietor. Or worse still, perhaps a profit-based old-age-home proprietor could be viewed as being something like a pimp, gaining by offering something for sale so intimate and personal that it shouldn't be on the market, thus providing an example of the worst features of profit-driven capitalism.

While living in Kolkata in 2006, I was invited to present on my research at a local academic conference titled "Senescence." At the end of my session, the chair of the panel, a distinguished senior professor from the University of Delhi, stood up to make an impromptu impassioned speech:

> Some of this discussion has seemed to be advocating that we adopt old age homes. But we should *not!* . . . The very data, provided by Sarah here, shows that the *majority* of old age homes in Kolkata are *businesses* [said scathingly]. There is only one government old age home, a few run by Christian missionaries, a few by NGOs; the rest are private *businesses!* [again, the word uttered dripping with revulsion]. They are making *money!*—they are making *money!*—by having people in old age homes. Let's not get persuaded by the idea that old age homes are the answer. They are not! *Family* is the answer. We need to strengthen the *family!*

My research assistant Hena also admitted to having been taken aback when I first used the English term "business" and the Bengali "*byabsā*" to classify the for-profit old age homes (those founded by private entrepreneurs rather than charitable organizations, and serving as the proprietors' source of living); but she later concurred that it was probably an appropriate categorization. Even if "business" and "*byabsā*" are rarely uttered terms, clearly the central motivation of many of the old-age-home proprietors I met was to make a living. Significantly, however, this did not necessarily mean that such proprietors were also not sincerely caring, respectful, and motivated to establish a "good" home.

The two co-proprietors of Atithiseva (Hospitality), Shiven Chowdhury and Ratan Ghosh, had been close friends since childhood; both were married, with young children, and living, like traditional good sons, with their own parents in their family homes; and, holding no other jobs, they needed sources of income. With the idea of opening a ladies' hostel for students, they rented a flat in their neighborhood and put an ad in the newspaper; but no ladies came. Then a neighbor suggested that there was a lot of hassle involved in running a ladies' hostel: why not advertise under the new "*Briddhābās*" or old-age-home column instead? The neighbor mentioned that he himself had a sister-in-law who might even like to stay; she was a widow with no children who had fallen a few times. "So, the thought entered our heads," Shiven recalled. "We decided to put in two ads: one for ladies, and one for old people. A few ladies came to look, but none were really staying. Then finally one old woman (*briddhā*) came, and gradually only old people came to look, and slowly all six 'seats' were filled." The small four-bedroom flat now houses all women, two in double and two in single rooms. Hena asked Ratan one day if he found the work fulfilling, if he received an inner sense of satisfaction that he was doing important work, and Ratan answered, "I'll speak very frankly. Everyone looks after his own self first. We have to fill our stomachs with a little rice and *ḍāl*. But," he went on, "I feel very happy, very proud, when you say that we have built a good old age home." I had just recently complimented him sincerely on the home; I had visited a few times by then and had always found the home to be extremely welcoming and "homey" (*gharoyā*), a quality they had been striving for. "It's a huge responsibility," Ratan reflected. "We sometimes have thoughts of expanding up to twelve 'seats,' because we aren't really able to meet all our expenses with just six; but we're worried that with twelve, we wouldn't be able to give everyone the same kind of individual attention. Everyone needs attention."

The industrious proprietor of Seva—a cluster of seven modest old age homes housing altogether ninety male and female residents, in rented houses scattered around a pleasant middle-class residential neighborhood—admitted candidly and cheerfully when Hena and I asked him about how he likes his work and how he had the idea to start these homes, "One has to do something to support one's household. But I am really enjoying it. From morning to evening I'm running after all of them; I eat my noon meals with them. I'm really receiving a lot of joy [*ānanda-i pācchi*]."

Another young entrepreneur, Rakesh Laskar of Aram ("Comfort"), was first set up as an old-age-home proprietor by his father-in-law. When I mentioned this to Hena, she mused that he must have had a "love marriage," because ordinarily a man of his (middle-) class background would not be married unless he had a good, regular job (running an old age home does not quite have this status).[27] Sure enough, when I brought up the topic with the three lady residents I was close to (Kalyani-di, Kavika-di, and Uma-di, introduced in opening this chapter), they smiled and validated Hena's surmise: indeed, their proprietor and a girl in the neighborhood had met, fallen in love, and had a "love marriage," even though the young man ("very handsome and charming," they observed, "don't you agree?") was in fact at the time unemployed. His parents disowned him in anger, disapproving of the sudden marriage, so the young man moved into his in-law's home with his wife, an arrangement that generally entails some embarrassment and loss of respect. The father-in-law was the one to orchestrate the rental of the four-room flat, on the ground floor of a two-story home in an ordinary middle-class residential neighborhood, for his new son-in-law to manage as an old age home for his source of living.

A Brief Comparison to the Origins of Elder Housing in the United States

Interestingly, the emergence of old age homes in the United States and Western Europe occurred under some similar social and economic circumstances, in the late nineteenth and early twentieth centuries (one point worth noting is that old age homes are not an ancient and timeless Western "tradition"). Although in the United States it was never the case that a majority of parents would continue to live with and gradually be supported by their adult children after the children were married,[28] when people lived in farming communities (as did 95 percent of Americans before 1800),[29] it was usual for extended family members to reside in close proximity (where they could engage in various forms of mutual assistance),[30] and for an elderly parent who became frail or widowed to then move in with his or her married children.[31] Then, in the 1800s and continuing into the 1900s, Americans began to move increasingly away from family farming communities to cities, often finding themselves in small apartments or tenements. In the early- and mid-1800s, many younger people also traveled west for economic opportunity, pursuing the free homesteading land that the government was offering and more often than not leaving older family members behind.

Henry Seager, in his 1910 classic book, *Social Insurance: A Program of Social Reform,* reflects on the impact such changing social-economic conditions had on provisions for old age:

> Old-age poverty is, of course, not a new problem. There is every evidence, however, that it is a problem of growing seriousness. In the country household there is a place for the aged parent or grandparent. The family has a settled abode, and economic interest re-enforces filial regard in securing to old people proper care and consideration. So long as any strength remains, there is useful work about the house or farm which they may do. Moreover, the cost of maintaining an aged relative in the country is so small as to seem an insignificant burden. In the crowded tenement houses of modern cities the situation is very different. Here [in the cities], as industry is now organized, there is little for an aged person to do. . . . Furthermore, the cost of maintaining an aged relative in the city is an appreciable item in a wage earner's budget. . . . Changing economic conditions are rendering the dependence of old people on their descendants for support increasingly precarious. (Seager 1910:116–117)[32]

It was under such changing social-economic conditions, including urbanization and the increasing dispersal of families, that the first homes for the aged in the United States arose. One important distinction between the rise of old age homes in the United States and in India is that the original impetus behind the establishment of elder residential facilities in the United States was clearly to alleviate *old-age poverty*—which was also the central aim of the first, British-era old age homes in India but not of the homes that have really taken off in the contemporary period. The "poorhouses" of the eighteenth and nineteenth centuries in the United States (modeled after those in England) consistently housed large concentrations of both orphaned children and indigent elderly. The first residential facilities built specifically for the aged began to emerge in the mid-1800s, founded by the non-profit "benevolent societies" and "fraternal organizations" associated with nearly every ethnic, religious, social, and professional group of the time (such as the Irish Benevolent Society, German Benevolent Society,

Masons, Knights of Columbus, Ladies' Relief Society, Home for Aged and Infirm Colored Persons, and Sailors' Snug Harbor). These were built in response to what were widely viewed as the terrible and degrading conditions in the poorhouses, to give the "respectable" once-middle-class old people of one's community a decent place to live. By the early 1900s, hundreds of such voluntary and non-profit old age homes had been built.[33]

By the 1930s and 1940s, spurred by the Social Security Act of 1935, the U.S. government began to regulate and financially support some "nursing" homes devoted to the long-term medical care of the elderly, and began in addition to build some government-owned nursing homes. The greatest incentive to the private nursing home industry came with the passage of Medicare in 1965. Carole Haber reports: "According to the legislation, aged individuals were eligible for support for up to 100 days of nursing home residency, following a three-day hospital stay. As a consequence, the nursing home industry, which had grown steadily in the years following Social Security, increased dramatically. Between 1960 and 1976, the number of homes grew by 140%, the nursing beds increased 302%, and, most significantly, the revenues received by the industry rose 2000%" (1993:109).

Now, in the contemporary United States, several kinds of both government-funded and private elder residential facilities are common, for those of a range of social classes. 1) "Care facilities" include both a) "assisted living" residences, where residents receive supervision and assistance with daily non-medical needs; and b) "nursing homes" or state-licensed health-care facilities, where residents can receive around-the-clock nursing care and extensive medical supervision. 2) "Retirement housing" (often termed "retirement communities," "active adult communities," or "independent living communities") refers to planned communities designed exclusively for seniors, in which the residents do not need daily assistance with medical or personal care. Generally residents live in private apartments or cottages, with access to common social, dining, and activity areas. 3) "Continuing care retirement communities" offer in a campus-like setting a continuum of living options, from independent living to assisted living to skilled nursing care.[34] Still, the majority of older Americans do not live in elder residential facilities (in 1999, roughly 7.2 percent of all people age sixty-five or older resided in some form of elder housing).[35] For many, the "ideal" is to live independently, in neither an institution or with children, as I explore further in chapters 6 and 7.

As in India, not everyone was comfortable in early America with the notion of elders living in institutions apart from or "abandoned by" their children and families. In a 1879 song, "Out from the Poorhouse," an old man laments the fact that he gave all of his property—his farm and years of savings—to his children, only to find himself pushed into a poorhouse rather than being cared for by those "lov'd ones" for whom he worked so hard to give a start:

> *Oh! How my children have wrung my poor heart*
> *God knows I have worked hard to give them a start*
> *But they drove me at last—when I would I'd ne'er been born—*
> *Off to the Poorhouse, alone and forlorn.*
>
> . . .
>
> *A poor broken-hearted old man am I,*
> *Betray'd by my lov'd ones, and left here to die.*
> *Oh! how the boys could have gladden'd my life!*
> *Oh! how I've missed them, the girls, and my wife.* (Chadsey 1879)

Interestingly enough, the long-standing fear that the elderly would end up in the almshouse has also a definite parallel in the contemporary rhetoric surrounding the fear of ending up in a nursing home. Carole Haber observes that by the late 1970s, the outcry against nursing homes rivaled the early-twentieth-century outrage over the almshouses (1993:110).[36]

"Shunned by Those Whom They Breastfed": Public Horror Stories

I close this chapter by briefly reflecting upon the overwhelmingly scathing narratives surrounding the rise of old age homes in everyday public—media and conversational—discourse in India today. Although some positive examples can be found (for instance, a Bengali teleserial called "Santiniketan" depicting the lives of several lady residents in an old age home was described to me by a few as beautifully done and even uplifting), the majority of public discourse is strikingly negative. There is (still) a powerful stigma attached to old-age-home living, accruing to both residents and the families viewed as sending or "throwing away" (*phele dāoyā*) their kin there. The "horror story" narratives speak to this stigma, and to the unease people are experiencing contemplating profound processes of social change.[37] Old-age-home living evokes pressing questions about the way things should be and are, pertaining to the very nature and organization of families, relationships, daily lives, human values, and even the identity of India as a nation and culture. People also perhaps gain some pleasure or relief in telling and listening to tales of the plights of others?

One of the most lurid accounts appeared in a Sunday magazine cover story for *The Hindu* national newspaper, called "Homes of the Future?":

> Shunned by those whom they breastfed, whose midnight tantrums they endured, whose mess they cleaned without ever covering the nose with eau de cologne–swabbed towel, whom they perched on their shoulders and with whom they played and sang, . . . the ignored aged have no choice now but to exist in the cages of old age homes. The decision of their children or kin to dump them in an old age home is replayed again and again in their head, like a squealing track on a damaged disk. . . . The homes across the nation, where the aged are dumped, are often worse than a sty where overcrowding and grunts are common. (G. Ghosh 1998)

We are confronted here with chaos, disarray, a terrible failed reciprocity, a sinking into an amoral animalistic state. "No one is allowed to go in or out" of old age homes, envisions another newspaper story,[38] and the cost is exorbitant. "[The aged] are actually paying to be in a prison!" (Sharma and Menon 2000).

Sakuntala Narasimhan, in a 24 August 2004 *Deccan Herald* news story titled "Old Age Home Horrors," tells the story of four elderly sisters who admit their seventy-three-year-old bachelor brother to an old age home in good health and are dismayed to find just two weeks later that he is not only deceased but that his body has been sewn into a sack and that the sisters must pay the remaining portion of the 25,000 rupee deposit, or else the body will not be released. "A deposit is, by definition, something that is supposed to be returned—but institutions like this gobble it up (and make money)," Narasimhan condemns. She quotes another family "which has also rued its decision to opt for an old people's home for an elderly relative: 'It is not just the money, it is the criminality of taking advantage of helpless, elderly people entrusted to their care.'"

Introduced briefly in chapter 2, the award-winning movie *Karunam* (Pathos) is a film of quiet devastation, depicting an aged couple waiting futilely for their children's and grandchildren's visit from abroad. They plan favorite dishes, set up a swing set in the garden, and reminisce about their sons' childhoods. But the children never come, instead making a summer trip to see the Niagara Falls. In fact, the sons have arranged through a local priest to sell off the plantation and house assiduously built by their father, and to send their parents off to an old age home. The father dies from the shock of it all, and the film closes with the mother escaping to a nearby residence for mentally disabled children, where she caresses and is caressed by them. These children, innocent and untouched by modernity, are the only ones who still know how to give and receive affection. "My film unfolds the insecurity of the aged, visible everywhere," comments director Jayaraaj. "Even in a small province such as the one I live in, the number of old age homes is increasing every day—glorified mortuaries with dead bodies of parents wait indefinitely for their children, settled abroad" (quoted in Chatterji 2004).

Bengali poet Subho Das Gupta's verse titled "Janmadin" (Birthday)[39] paints a mother silently speaking to her son desolately alone from an old age home on the first of the Bengali month of Sravana, the son's birthday. My narration of this poignant tale is interspersed with my own occasional interpretations and comments in parentheses:

The mother begins by telling her son all about his birth and how much his father and mother sacrificed for him to raise and love him. His parents were poor and did not buy new clothes or milk for themselves, instead giving all they could to their one son. They educated him, and he did well on his exams. His father proudly said, "Higher education is for achieving high respect." The young son found employment in a big office, received a large salary, and moved himself and his two parents into a two-bedroom flat provided by the office. (From the tale thus far, it seems that both intergenerational intimacy and modern professional success can be achieved.) Then the father dies and the son is sobbing on his chest, which makes the mother, who just lost her own husband, feel even more shaken. (Yet the son's tears properly signify filial love.)

Then suddenly the story shifts to the lonely present. The readers find that the old mother is in an old age home, for she says to her son, Khokan: "Far, far away from Kolkata, in the old age home of this suburb, I am absolutely alone, Khokan. I desperately desire to meet you—you, my daughter-in-law and tiny Billu. You are all now so far away, in the shining marble-floored house of Salt Lake." (So, the son is well off, for he lives in a marble-floored house in one of the more newly constructed, well-to-do communities of Kolkata.) The mother goes on: "Today, on your birthday, I am sure there is a grand party, isn't there, Khokan? Full of guests, lots of celebration, lavish food. That's very good. That's very good." The old mother then recalls again the boy's childhood, and the mother's protective love, in their "broken room" in an older part of Kolkata (poor materially, yet rich in family intimacy): "You, while lying by my side, off and on, would suddenly get scared. And throw your arms around me. I would say, what's the fear for? Here I am. Khokan has his mother, and one who has a mother, does he ever get caught by ghosts? You would go off to sleep fully assured, hugging my chest.

"In your modern family [*ādhunik saṃsāre*], couldn't you find a little space to accommodate this old woman? Pratima [my daughter-in-law], too, is a mother. She too has, like my Khokan, a piece of moon illuminating her lap! But what a strange change of time! Khokan! You perhaps no longer eat *payas* now [the traditional Bengali birthday dish, rice pudding], do you? You have no idea, Khokan. I have cooked *payas* for you this morning. Yes, from the money sent by you. (So, continuing to sacrifice for her son, the mother doesn't spend the money on herself.) The whole day I am seated keeping that vessel [of birthday pudding] in front of me. Here in this Home for the Aged. In my lonely room. No one else is there. Khokan, would you visit for once? Once. Only once."

Family intimacy and love, material simplicity, and tradition (symbolized by the beloved birthday pudding, *payas*) are sharply juxtaposed against material success, loneliness, alienation between generations, modern foods and parties, and a selfish disregard for others, seniors, and the past.

Similar stances predominated in the everyday conversations I had with people I met on the streets, in the markets, and at social gatherings. Everyone had something to say on the topic, although almost no one I met actually knew anyone—a relative, friend or acquaintance—*in* an old age home, these being still so new and housing only a small minority of the population. A common response would be, when people heard what I was studying: "That's such an important topic. People these days are throwing away [*phele dāoyā*] their parents. It's so deplorable, despicable, immoral, degrading. . . ." If I asked whether anyone in their family was in an old age home, I would get a response akin to this one I received while standing in the crowded check-in line at the New Delhi airport, chatting with a Bengali family: "No! We would *never* do that! We believe that to throw one's parents away in an old age home is criminal!" My friend and colleague in the United States, an Indian-born professor, commented similarly and emphatically that it would be "absolutely out of the question," "morally and culturally unthinkable" for her or her family to consider an old age home. One acquaintance in Kolkata replied, when I asked whether he knew anyone in an old age home:

> No, I don't. But someone I know told me about a case: there was a son who lived in their neighborhood where an old age home had sprung up, and so he put his mother there. Every day the mother could be seen sitting on her balcony crying and moaning that her son didn't visit. After a few months (or was it a year?) went by, the son began to feel bad, and he wanted to visit; but by that time he was too embarrassed. What if people saw him visiting with the old woman on the balcony and then realized that *he* was the negligent son?

So, the modern son is selfish, disregards his parent, and is more concerned about public image than moral behavior.

Most such sensationally negative narratives I encountered, both in the media and on the streets, seemed in fact to me to be more urban legend than fact, presented by those who had not spent time in and did not personally know people living in old age homes. The moral panic in such narratives is tied to a widespread sense that emerging novel forms of aging in India represent a profound transformation—a transformation involving not only aging per se, but principles underlying the very foundation of society and the identity of India as a nation and culture. The most salient theme in such horror story tales portrays a vision of the limits of materialism. Modern consumerism, professional success, and the self-centeredness of the "me" generation are alluring, yet ultimately void of real social, moral and spiritual value.

However, the perspectives and experiences of those making their lives in the new residences for elders are much more complex and varied, and they often give evidence of agency. It is to these perspectives and lives that I turn in the following chapter.

4 BECOMING AN ELDER-ABODE MEMBER

One early afternoon I was greeted in the front lobby of an elegant old Kolkata club by Monisha Mashi ("Aunt" Monisha). She was dressed in a fine embroidered blue-and-white cotton summer sari with matching blouse that complemented her jet-black hair, cut stylishly short in a fashion popular among modern professional women. With her usual breezy energy, she led me to the club's verandah. Although the early spring weather was already beginning to turn too hot, we chose to sit outside, and Monisha Mashi promptly ordered two beers and *maśalā* (spiced) peanuts for us both. I was surprised and delighted: this would be my first beer on this five-month fieldwork trip, and it seemed particularly fun and unanticipated to share it with an old-age-home resident who had invited me to join her at one of her favorite clubs.[1] After our beer and peanuts came a very British-style lunch of fish and chips followed by custard. Monisha Mashi talked animatedly about the philosophy surrounding her choice to move into a residence for elders. "People ask me, 'Huh?! Staying in an old age home? No! Don't joke! You are so happy-go-lucky!'" alluding to the prevailing public sentiment that old-age-home living is for the despondent and rejected. "But I say, 'I have everything.' We sold our house and car: I came there [to the home] in the midst of full health. I don't own anything any more. But I received everything: everything out of nothing. The idea of *vānaprastha* ["forest-dwelling," the third life phase and the beginnings of older age][2] is to forsake everything, and *then* to enjoy—to enjoy your life *through* abandonment [*tyāg*]. I have everything I need living there!"

It had been Monisha Mashi's inspiration to move into Milan Tirtha, one of the finest old age homes in the region, run by the prominent, well-respected Peerless business corporation as one of their corporate social responsibility projects, and situated appealingly on the banks of a branch of the holy Ganges River in north Kolkata. She had persuaded her husband to make the move with her several years earlier while he was still alive. Their two daughters were grown and had moved abroad, he had retired, and she no longer wanted to be burdened with house, car, driver, servants, and all the trappings of upper-middle-class domestic and society life. Such an attitude of rejecting worldly goods toward the end of life is one with long roots in India.[3] When going to look at the home, she had found a studio apartment, then unused, in a separate, free-standing building on the home's grounds, above the guest quarters set up for the residents' visiting kin. The apartment boasted beautiful, large southwest-facing windows overlooking the river through which the afternoon and evening sunlight poured. Monisha Mashi persuaded the management to let her and her husband move in there, paying extra fees, for she found the ordinary residents' quarters less appealing—smaller single and double rooms without kitchen facilities, arranged in three stories along open-air corridors. I had first met Monisha Mashi in her elder-abode apartment when I was on an overnight stay at the home with my two daughters. We were just about to settle in for the evening when the night manager knocked on our door to announce that there was someone upstairs who wanted to meet me. I climbed the stairs curiously, having been unaware that anyone lived up there, and I opened the door to Monisha Mashi's apartment, tastefully decorated with the kinds of colorful ethnic Indian embroidered fabrics and mirrored pillows popular among the educated elite, with books scattered everywhere and the computer on. And now about a week later we were enjoying lunch and conversation together.

"People say, 'Oh, you must feel so lonely,'" Monisha Mashi related. "But I never feel alone or lonely. I say, 'I am living with *myself*. *You* are the best person to cure your own woes, through introspection. . . .' The other Milan Tirtha residents say, 'Oh, we are all obsolete—forsaken by our families.' I say, 'Alone perhaps, not lonely. If you want, you can keep *yourself* busy.'" At age seventy, Monisha Mashi herself was an impressively active woman, not only through introspection. She spent several full days a week volunteering at an NGO that helped to ameliorate the lives of underprivileged widows and girls, directing their computer vocational training program. She also tutored English to neighborhood youths, maintained a close circle of friends and membership in two of Kolkata's major social clubs, and visited her two daughters generally for a month or two each year—one in Mumbai, and one in South Africa, both of whom led interesting professional lives and with whom Mashi maintained warm, close relationships. But Monisha Mashi said that even while remaining busy, involved in the world, she aimed to do so with detachment. "Vedanta[4] says that one should try to reside in the world keeping *māyā* [attachments, ties] at bay, like a drop of water on a lotus leaf. Even if a lotus leaf is growing right in the water, not a drop sticks to it!—it just runs off. This is how we should try to be, living fully in the world, but not attached to any of it."

"But that is not an easy thing to do!" she added later. "*Vānaprastha* [or "forest-dwelling," the third life phase, which she compared to old-age-home living] is not a 'jungle'[5] exactly, but it *is* a harsh life. But if one abandons [*tyāg karā*] and cuts *māyā* [attachments], *then* one can be ready for *sannyās*"—true liberation and spiritual realization, at the end of life.[6]

Monisha Mashi's stance is very different from the dominant "throwing away one's parents" discourse that surrounds old-age-home living in India today. Some persons do seem to be very much "thrown away" as passive objects by their children; yet others, like Monisha Mashi, are decisively agentive and sanguine about this new option for living.

This chapter concentrates on the complex diversity of residents' perspectives and lives, focusing on the process by which persons become members of elder abodes. I explore the complicated and diverse paths that lead them there, and begin to consider what significant transformations of self, family, gender, and aging are entailed by the move to a residence for elders.

A focus on residents' own diverse, intricate, and moving narratives is strikingly absent from both the public discourse and the scant academic literature produced thus far on India's old age homes, which predominantly seem to take the perspective of the outsider looking in, striving merely to imagine or guess what might be transpiring within the lives and minds of the residents.[7] I know as yet of no other anthropological or sociological—ethnographic fieldwork based—studies of India's old age homes. One of the key aims of social-cultural anthropology is to come as close as possible to understanding the perspectives, experiences, stories, and world views of those whom we study—to learn, through actually listening to and hanging out with others, how they make sense of their worlds. As I mentioned in the introduction, this is what I aimed to accomplish through intensive fieldwork in old age homes, and what I attempt to begin to convey here—as I examine how those whom I came to know, as they moved into elder abodes, are grappling strategically with what they see as the changing conditions of their contemporary society and lives.

Making the Move

All the people I met living in residences for elders had a particular narrative about how they came to be there. For some, this was a rather canned and practiced response. Since in general people regarded the old age home as such an unusual place to be, it demanded explanation. "Oh, *that* question again," some uttered in annoyance, or irritated boredom, when I ventured to ask. So, I ended up not always explicitly asking. Sometimes I would simply wait for the story to emerge (which it did not always do). The question seemed to imply a critique, along the lines of "What's wrong with you that you are *here?*"

One director of one of the more elite old age homes spoke astutely of the ways residents packaged their stories, reinforcing the prevailing assumption that elder residences are sites of pain and rejection:

> Some had lived in joint families. Others had worked far from their families before retiring. For others, their sons now work far away. But whatever the case, pain [*bedanā*] will always be there. Everyone will *say,* "My sons are good, my daughters are good." They will never say, "I came here upon receiving a blow from my son" [*āmār chele theke āghāṭ peye esechi*], but nonetheless . . .

In Indian society it is excruciatingly painful and embarrassing to admit that one's son does not want one.

Phele dāoyā is the term most commonly used in Bengali public discourse to refer to the act by which a family, son, or son and daughter-in-law place an elder in an old age home. Meaning literally to "throw out," "throw away," or "abandon," it is the same verb used to refer to the "throwing away" of garbage. Residents and their kin almost never employ this term when speaking of their own situations, instead using more neutral and gentle terminology such as *rākhā,* "to place." In both phrasings, the elder is a passive object, being acted upon rather than acting.

The majority of residents I met, however, played quite a significant, often highly strategic, role in making the decision to move into the elder residence. Although in many cases it is difficult and to some degree inaccurate to pin down just one primary agent in the decision-making process, I attempted to do so to illustrate in broad strokes some key trends; table

4.1 represents this best attempt. Since I was not always comfortable probing far enough to be confident that I had the full story of how a resident came to be in the home, I have placed quite a few of my research subjects into the "unsure" category. The "self" category is therefore likely somewhat over-represented here, because those stories are not generally the ones that are so terribly painful and awkward to disclose. The "unsure" group contains those who did not share detailed stories with me as to how they came to be in an elder home, as this sensitive subject ended up being a topic I did not always push. It is important to be aware, as I discuss further below, that even the "self" category can contain those who experienced pain or turmoil or rejection within their families; facing such turmoil, some choose to find an alternative living arrangement in one of the new old age homes.

Although, as noted, the "self" categories in these tables may be somewhat over-represented, it is nonetheless significant that a striking majority of both female and especially male residents I encountered appeared to have played an active, agentive role in coming to reside in an elder abode— contrary to the prevalent public assumption that elder abode residents are "thrown away" by their kin. I turn now to explore in more depth what I found to be the three major modes of becoming an elder-abode member, examining also the gendered dimensions of these three positions as I go: being "thrown away"; choosing, but amid anguish and family turmoil; and actively pursuing a new way of living.

Being "Placed" or "Thrown Away"

At the beginning of the previous chapter I briefly introduced Kalyani Chatterjee, the elegant eighty-one-year-old resident of Aram ("Comfort") who had borrowed my mobile phone to call her grandson, and who had exclaimed that earlier in her life she could never even have dreamed that she would be living in a place such as a residence for elders. Kalyani-di one day told Hena and me her life story. She had asked us to come on a late morning around 10:00 AM to hear it, a time when she is generally free, after having completed her breakfast, morning prayers, and daily bath. We sat on stools and the staircase in the narrow open-air front hall of the small flat that had become the old age home. Her friend and roommate, Uma-di, came and went, hearing most of the story. Kalyani-di was eager to have her narrative appear in my book. I tell it at some length here, to give her ultimate placement in the old age home by her son a fuller context.

Kalyani was born in East Bengal, what is now Bangladesh, as were so

TABLE **4.1.**
Decision Impetus for Residence in an Elder Abode: Primary Agent

I. Female residents (N=75)

Self	30
Son(s)	9
Other male kin (nephew, 3; brother, 2; son-in-law, 2; grandson, 1)	8
Self with male kin (son, nephew, male cousin)	3
Husband (wife moved in with/followed him)	2
Daughter	5
Sister	2
Employer	1
Unsure	15

II. Male residents (N=25)

Self	17
Son (with father's counsel)	1
Older brother (resident younger brother has been intellectually disabled since birth)	1
Wife (resident husband has dementia)	1
Unsure	5

Note: In each of the "self-with-male-kin" cases, the female resident reported that she herself had initially broached the idea of moving into an elder abode, typically after coming across an advertisement in the paper, and then had asked a male kin for advice and assistance in making the arrangements.

many who now inhabit Kolkata's southern, more newly settled neighborhoods. She was a much loved daughter of her father, a schoolmaster, who lavished on her affection and care. She described her childhood home as an educated middle-class household, which had plenty of members in a large joint family—including eight brothers and sisters, an uncle and his family—rice fields, ponds, cows, fruit trees—"everything." She reminisced, "It was such a good life. I stayed there with my parents until I was nineteen years old, until after I passed [the grade ten] matriculation exams, and *then* only was I married." She told of how there had been no school for girls after grade four, but her father arranged it so that even all of his daughters

FIGURE 4.1. Kalyani-di.

were educated at home. She studied not only literature, English, and math, but also musical instruments, singing, and dancing. She told of how her mother sometimes complained that she was not learning the cooking and household management skills that would be required after marriage, "but my father simply ignored it. . . . I was a much-loved daughter [*khub ādarer meye chilām*]. In this way, I was raised. In this way—receiving so much love—I grew up, and my marriage happened."[8]

Kalyani-di's husband's family lived in a village close to her father's, and her husband worked in a government position in Dhaka, the Dhaka Collectorate. Kalyani would stay at her in-laws' place for a few days, where she would "cry and cry." Then she would rush back to her father's home, and then back to her in-laws' home. "Like this one year went by, and within one year, my first child—a daughter—was born."

Just two years later, in 1947, India received independence from Britain, and Bengal was partitioned into West Bengal and East Pakistan (later Bangladesh), severely disrupting Kalyani's and so many other Bengali families. Bengali Hindus, like Kalyani's family, fled to West Bengal, India;

and many Bengali Muslims living in India fled to East Pakistan. Because Kalyani-di's husband was working for the government in Dhaka, though, he chose to remain there, and so he and his family became Pakistani citizens. "But we were Hindu," Kalyani-di recounted. "So we went into hiding. We were Brahmans [the highest Hindu caste], so the men of our family had to tear off and hide their sacred threads [a sign of Hindu upper caste status]. And I had to take off my iron wedding bangle, and wipe the vermilion from my forehead," signs of a Hindu married woman. This was a period of intense Hindu-Muslim communal violence.

Not long after, when things began to grow very bad for Hindus in Pakistan with huge riots breaking out, Kalyani-di's husband decided that he must send the family to India. "We fled just wearing the one piece of clothing on our backs, and nothing else." At that time, her oldest daughter was only three years old, and she had had two more sons. Her father and a few other natal kin also fled to the city then known as Calcutta—the capital Bengali city in India—but Kalyani-di's husband and his brother stayed in Dhaka where they had jobs.

In Calcutta (now Kolkata), Kalyani-di raised her children with great difficulty and exertion (*kaṣṭa*), but she tells of those years with a sense of real pride in her strength and accomplishments. Her husband sent money when he could, but it was very difficult to get money from Dhaka to Calcutta at that time. Her father also offered some assistance. But Kalyani-di soon realized that she would have to earn money herself if she was to raise her children well. She worked as a schoolteacher for many years, receiving a meager salary, and then added a job tailoring uniforms for the staff of a tuberculosis hospital. She later secured a more lucrative and prestigious position as an X-ray technician at the hospital, after being trained by the hospital director who had been impressed by her hard work and character. At that time, no other women held such jobs, and at first when she would report to work at the X-ray department, the guards would stop her and say, "Women don't come in here." During her noon break and in the evenings, Kalyani-di did private tutoring to add on to her income. She kept a kitchen garden, cooked, cleaned the house, sent her children to school, and supervised their studying. "Truly, I worked so hard," she recalled. "I would get up at 4:00 AM and catch the bus and work at this and that job, and then return home at night. I would worry—how can anyone work like this, and manage a household? But I had to raise and educate my children. I knew I *had* to educate my children."[9]

Meanwhile, when her younger son was just five and a half years old, he died. He had wanted so badly to see his father in Dhaka, so Kalyani-di took him with her and made the journey. They were there for just fifteen days, and within fifteen days, her son died. She narrated, "I returned back here [to Kolkata] like a crazy person, insane with grief. My oldest son was then seven or eight years old. I came back from there, and I hadn't realized, but my conception had happened right then when I was in Dhaka. And so my youngest daughter was born. And with them—the three children—I made our family [*saṃsār karechi*]." Within several years, she received news that her husband had also died suddenly in Dhaka, and so Kalyani-di became a widow.

Kalyani-di's final job was as a secretary for the Rotary Club, where she worked from 1970 to 1992. "My salary was not large, but they loved me very much. They gave me *so much* love, respect, courteousness," her voice choked as she recalled. "I worked there for twenty-two years, and I didn't even take one day's vacation during that time. I was dear to all of them, and I loved them. I received a first prize once—a small table clock; and I once received a wall clock. And then two years later, I received a silver platter, with my name and years of service engraved on it. When I left that job, I cried hard."

Kalyani-di ceased her working life when she was sixty-seven, after she had educated all three children, arranged and paid for the marriages of her two daughters, and brought a daughter-in-law into her household. For sixteen years, both her daughter-in-law and Kalyani-di worked to earn money, while sharing the household duties. Kalyani-di would spend most of each Sunday cooking. Two grandchildren were born. Then one day her son approached her and said, "Ma, why don't you leave your job? I'm here, and your daughter-in-law is here." So Kalyani-di went to tell her employer, "My son won't let me work any more." The employer replied, "*Bāh!*[10] What a good son you have! Well, still, any time—please come visit us." Kalyani-di began to weep as she narrated: "In this way, my working life ended [*āmār cākri jiban śes hae gelo*]. And from then on I have suffered greatly, received so much pain [*kaṣṭa*]." She paused to collect herself, and then went on: "Leaving this work, and just sitting at home—And, please don't mind me saying this, but: I didn't receive peace at home. And so like this, I came to the ashram for old people [*briddhāśram*]."

Kalyani-di had managed to save some money over her long working life, and after she retired, she turned what she had over to her son to help him establish a textile business. Such practices have long been common in India: as persons move into their post-householder life in older age, many have felt it appropriate to turn over any assets (such as a savings account or the deed to a house) to their children. Many told me, however, that this is absolutely not a good idea, as children will love their parents only as long as the parents have property. Much recent media discourse also speaks to this theme.[11] The textile business failed, and so Kalyani-di's daughter-in-law became the only real earning member of the household. That is when her son suddenly said to his mother one day that he didn't feel comfortable having her reside with them, when they were living off of his wife's money.[12] Without consulting with his sisters, he gave his mother just a day's notice and asked her to be prepared to go to a home for the aged. Kalyani-di complied. That was four years before I met her in 2006.

Whenever Kalyani-di's son comes to visit the home, Kalyani-di begs him to get her released (*mukti*). She pleads, "Take me anywhere you like— just out of this prison." At the same time, she is anxious over how her expenses in the home will continue to be met, as the fees are currently paid by her daughter-in-law, and her son says that he doesn't know how long this arrangement can be sustained. In reply, Kalyani-di insisted, "You arrange for my release from this place and I am confident that I can find ways and means of supporting myself!"

Hena and I asked if Kalyani-di's daughters could do anything about all this. Kalyani-di excused them by saying that her elder daughter had practically no financial resources, and that her younger daughter's husband did step in to offer to pay 600 rupees a month toward the home's fees (of 2000 rupees a month). But Kalyani-di's son demanded that his brother-in-law should pay 50 percent of the expenses, which the man rejected, saying that Kalyani-di's son had never consulted them before admitting his mother to the home. "How much can daughters do in this society," Kalyani-di's roommate, Uma-di, added sympathetically, "after they are married?"

To make matters even worse, it seems that Kalyani-di's son has a very controlling and possibly paranoid personality. He has forbidden his sisters to meet with his wife, fearful that they will influence and persuade her to step in to release the mother. He now visits Kalyani-di only very rarely, and once when Kalyani-di phoned her daughter-in-law at work to find out how her son was, the son got angry and left instructions with the home's proprietor, Rakesh Laskar, not to let his mother phone his wife again, "disturbing everyone at work." (Kalyani-di has no ordinary access to a phone, so she must borrow the proprietor's mobile phone if she wishes to make a call.) Uma-di added, "She called her daughter-in-law, and then her son told Rakesh not to let his mother call there again—It's a *humiliating* matter [*lajjār byāpār*], isn't it?"

Kalyani-di closed her narrative:

> That this thing would happen I couldn't have even imagined. That I would have to leave my home [*āmār bāṛi*]. Of course, even while living at home [*bāṛi*], people experience all sorts of situations and are not always perfectly happy.[13] But I could never have even imagined living like this [in an ashram for old people]. That is what gets to me the most now. I had established my own independence [*nije svādhīn bhābe rayechi*]. I had worked and done everything. I had run a household. It was *I* who had made the family [*saṃsār tairi karechi āmi*]. And now this imprisoned life [*bandī jiban*] is mine. Seeing that lock and key [placed on the front gate of the home]—how it makes me feel. All the time the lock and key. . . . Now my fear is, how many more days will I have to live? If I get like this—

Kalyani-di gestured to another resident, shriveled and bedridden, with a catheter extending from her cot to a container on the ground. "Oh my!" Uma-di gasped, and they both shuddered.

Then Kalyani-di apologized for taking so long with her narrative, saying that we should also listen to her roommate Uma-di's story, for Uma-di had led an important life and had once owned so much gold, even though she now also found herself here in the home. Uma-di protested modestly, "No, my life really wasn't exciting or important at all. I didn't work like you did. I just led an ordinary household life." Hena and I told Kalyani-di how eloquently she spoke and how moved we were by her story. The home's two ayahs—nurses-housekeepers-cooks—were almost done preparing the noon meal, and it had grown very hot and still outside, with the scorching April sun high in the air. Hena and I left with full hearts, promising to return within a few days.

There are a few striking features of Kalyani-di's narrative. One is the palpable way she contrasts her earlier adult life of actively making, doing, and accomplishing, with the extreme passivity, powerlessness, and subjection of her current life in the ashram for elders. In not only this narrative, but also other conversations, Kalyani-di repeatedly articulated how agentive she had been in her adult life, employing the active verbs "to do" (*kara*) and "to cause to do" or "make happen" (*kariyā*), as in:

> I caused my three children to 'graduate,' exerting much effort, much effort.
> *Āmi ei tinte chelemeyeke 'graduate' kariyechi anek kaṣṭa kare, anek kaṣṭa.*

> With my own 'service' [work] I gave the marriages of all three children.
> *Āmār ei 'service' theke āmi ei tinte chelemeyeke biye diyechi.*

> I established my own independence.
> *Nije svādhīn bhābe rayechi.*

> I worked, I did everything.
> *Cākri karechi, sab kichu karechi.*

> I made our family.
> *Saṃsār karechi.*

> It was *I* who made/built our family.
> *Saṃsār tairi karechi āmi.*

Kalyani-di's keen sense of the strong, active agency she had realized during her adult life was particularly striking given that many Bengali women (especially of her era) commonly convey a sense in ordinary talk of being passive recipients of action rather than active agents, of having life events happen *to* them (as in *āmār hayeche*)[14]—as indeed Kalyani-di also did when she spoke of her own marriage as a young woman as something that had "happened to" her at age nineteen, but not when she spoke of her later adult life as head of household without her husband. At the end of her life, though, Kalyani-di's displacement to the old age home is something over which she feels utterly powerless, explicitly comparing her condition to that of a prisoner, behind lock and key. Indeed, the front metal gate of her old age home was generally kept locked, ostensibly to keep away any potential burglars, as well as to guard against any unsafe wandering on the part of some of the more disabled residents (one was blind and another had mild dementia). Only the ayahs and the proprietor held the keys.[15] In addition, since Kalyani-di had been placed into the home by her son, the son was treated (by the proprietor, and even by Kalyani-di herself) as her guardian, and so she and those around her seemed to accept that she could no longer make major life decisions on her own. It was this utter sense of incapacity and inactivity that she seemed most unable to bear.

It is notable also how Kalyani-di's son, now the senior male of the family, seems so unquestioningly to reign over his mother, wife, and sisters, at least regarding the matter of his mother's care. According to her narrative, Kalyani-di simply complied with her son's resolution to place her in the home, escorted silently there just a day after he told her of the plan. Her daughters and daughter-in-law likewise went along submissively with the son's decision although, according to Kalyani-di, it was not their idea. In fact, Kalyani-di explicitly absolves her daughter-in-law from responsibility, saying that she and her *boumā*[16] had always gotten along fine and that, "My daughter-in-law does not have that kind of independence that she can just do what she wants. She has to heed my son's wishes."

Now that I am sitting in the United States writing this, I find myself wondering: Why didn't Kalyani-di simply resist? Tell her son that she didn't agree to go? Or find a way to move out on her own? But during the time of the fieldwork, neither Hena or I thought to ask these questions directly of her, presumably because we were so accustomed to hearing similar accounts from other older widowed mothers who deferred to their sons.

In the Laws of Manu[17] is found a well-known set of lines which many Indians pronounce in daily conversation: a woman should never be independent, but should be guided and controlled by her father in childhood, her husband in youth, and her sons in old age (Laws of Manu V.147–148, Manu 1886:195, 1991:115).[18] Some who bring up this axiom in daily conversation are critical of it; that is, not all pronounce it with endorsement. However, all Indians are familiar with the adage. Although Kalyani-di broke free from this axiom for many years when she was forced to, or perhaps one could say given the opportunity to, live apart from her husband, she ended accepting a position of dependence on her son. For a period and in certain important ways, it seems, those around Kalyani-di and perhaps even Kalyani-di herself found such a position to be very appropriate and even gratifying. She tells her boss that she is leaving her beloved job of twenty-two years because her son doesn't want her to work anymore, and the employer replies with pleasure and praise, "*Bāh!* What a good son you have!" By far the majority of those I met living in residences for elders who were "placed" there by their sons or other male kin were women (see table 4.1), and most in such circumstances seemed not to question their position of submission to their sons (or nephews, grandsons, brothers, husbands).

Uma-di, Kalyani's roommate, for instance, remarked when explaining how she had come to be in the home, after she had broken her leg and her care caused her daughter-in-law and a female servant great exertion, "What can I say? Whatever my son says, that's what happens" (*Ki balbo? Chele jā bale, tāi*).

In contrast, table 4.1 indicates that, among those I interviewed, almost all men were the primary agents in control of the decision to move into their elder abodes. One man who described his son making the arrangements for him discussed how the son had taken his father's counsel in the process. The only two men who clearly seemed to have not been involved in the decision were mentally disabled. Although the prevailing media and public discourse about modern children "throwing away" their parents into old age homes is not gender specific, clearly there is a very important gendered dimension to the process.

Another important theme in Kalyani-di's narrative is her profound sense of failed reciprocity and alienation. As in many other similar narratives I heard, Kalyani-di emphasized how much she had sacrificed and exerted—how much *kaṣṭa* (exertion, pain, suffering) she had extended—to raise her children; but then, in the end, they give nothing back to her.[19]

Some who are "placed" or "thrown away" into old age homes experience this at the hands of kin other than sons. Maya Mukherjee of Loknath had only one beloved child, a daughter. She had been a widow for many years and, supported largely by her husband's pension, had raised her daughter on her own, "with so much care and exertion [*jatna-kaṣṭa*], giving her everything—jewelry, an education, marriage." After the daughter was married, the girl pleaded successfully with her husband to let her mother move in with them, telling him, "My mother has no one else," even though most Indians feel keenly that it is highly inappropriate for parents to live with and depend on married daughters.[20] Maya-di offered that her daughter *could* invite her to move in, since her daughter worked (as a schoolteacher), and thus could financially contribute to the household. But after several years, when her daughter was expecting their first child, the *jāmāi* or son-in-law decided that he had had enough of the situation and "threw out" his mother-in-law. Maya-di's roommates in the home continually commented about how "bad" the son-in-law is! and how very "good" the daughter is!—"She is *so* good. She loves her mother *so* much—you don't see that in a daughter these days!" In general, in fact, when a daughter "places" her mother into an old age home, people do not consider this "throwing away." Rather, since a daughter has no cultural-moral obligation to reside with and support her parents, a daughter who helps establish a parent in an elder residence is viewed as stepping in with affection and generosity to help sustain her mother in a time of need. Maya-di's daughter continues secretly to pay for her mother's expenses, a fact that makes Maya-di feel very proud and loved. Since having a baby, though, the daughter had not been able to make it to the home to visit her mother or show her the child (who was about nine months old when I was having these conversations). Maya-di rationalized, explaining that her daughter was just too busy from the pressures of both job and motherhood. And the home's proprietor himself discreetly went to visit the daughter once each month to bring back the fees.

In quite a few cases, the impetus behind placing a kin member in a residence for elders was that the elder had become highly frail, senile, or otherwise incapacitated, making the household members feel that it was very difficult, or even dangerous, for the person to remain at home. This was especially true when the other household members, including daughters-in-law, were away working all day. That is what happened in the case of the bedridden woman with the catheter whom Kalyani-di and Uma-di shuddered to think of becoming. She had lived with her son, daughter-in-law (who worked), and grandchildren until she became very frail and bedridden several years earlier. Her son placed her in the old age home, but he visited every single evening, spending an hour or two with his mother, tenderly massaging her legs with oil, sitting by her side, and holding her hand.

Another man with an advanced case of what may have been Alzheimer's disease was placed in an old age home by his wife, while she went to live with her only son and grandchildren in the United States. According to the home's proprietor, many hearing of the man's condition were shocked that a wife could put her husband in an institution and go off, but this proprietor (herself a forceful, articulate, and highly independent woman, divorced, and with several years of medical school training) firmly supported the wife, saying, "Those who criticize her are wrong! Why shouldn't she try to live her life? [Her husband] doesn't recognize her at all. He doesn't even recall that he is married."

"Everyone Has Come Here out of Pain":
Choosing between Bad and Worse

A good proportion of the residents I met whom I placed into the "self" category in table 4.1—that is, those whom I considered to have been the primary agent in "choosing" to move into an elder residence—made the choice only under very painful and constrained circumstances. One thoughtful woman, Gauri Chattopadhyay, had made the decision to move to an old age home with her husband just days after their only (unmarried) son had died of cancer, thinking, "If I have to cook another meal for just him [my husband] and me, I just can't bear it." She commented quietly, "Everyone has come here out of pain." The pain was sometimes the death of children or spouses, and often family disagreements and struggles.

Some women divulged to me the details of their household struggles, which most often concerned tensions between them and their daughters-in-law and/or sons. Rani Mukherjee, at sixty-nine, told nostalgically of how she had been born into a joint family and married into a joint family. But then, shortly after she and her husband had arranged their son's marriage, her son began misbehaving with his parents, taking sides with his wife and parents-in-law, and demanding that his parents turn over the family house to his name. Rani-di's husband could not bear this shock and died of heart failure. Rani-di then took a tough decision, selling their home and giving some money to her son while keeping the rest in savings and moving into the elder abode.

Seeming to wish to justify her difficult decision to maintain control over her property and sever ties with her son, Rani-di told a (perhaps partly apocryphal?) story of a woman from her neighborhood. This widowed woman lived with her two grown sons. Telling her that they needed to avoid the harassment of paying municipal taxes or some such, they persuaded her to turn her property over to them. Soon one of the sons sold off his share to the other brother and moved out. The old mother was then pushed into the space beneath the staircase. Every day this mother had to move from one son to another to collect her day's meal, carrying her begging bowl. As Rani finished the story, her eyes filled with tears, and she wondered aloud what was happening with her son, who had been out of a job for some months after his firm closed down. She spoke of living in the ashram for elders as a valuable alternative to enduring deep injustice in the family but clearly had not gotten over the blow of witnessing the shattering of her own household.

Women residents often complained to each other about their daughters-in-law. This, in fact, is a common theme across India, both within and outside of old age homes. Between a mother-in-law and daughter-in-law festers a natural tension, as the senior woman must bring in a girl from an "other" family, and both compete for the son/husband's loyalty and affection and for control over the household and hearth (see, e.g., Lamb 2000:71–74). On one occasion when I was visiting the Loknath elder ashram as a group of women were chatting over afternoon tea, one mentioned to her friend Chobi-di that Chobi-di's daughter-in-law had looked very nice last Sunday when she came visiting wearing the traditional white conch shell (*śaṅkhā*) and red (*palā*) bangles of a married Bengali woman, and a becoming red sari. (Red is a traditional color for a young wife-daughter-in-law or *boumā*, signifying marital status, auspiciousness, and fertility.) The widowed mother-in-law Chobi-di replied cuttingly, "You see how cunning [*cālāk*] my daughter-in-law is! She knew that everyone in this old-age-home environment would admire her for wearing *śaṅkhā-palā* and a red sari, so she put those on when coming here. But I'm sure she ripped them off the minute she left!" and went on to describe how her daughter-in-law in fact has no traditional family values whatsoever.

No men fully opened up to me to reveal the details of their household struggles, which other Bengalis with whom I spoke explained in two ways: men do not talk as easily about private emotional problems as women do (a premise familiar also in the United States); and men, in general (both as fathers and fathers-in-law), do not tend to struggle as much with junior kin as do women; the biggest source of tension within families is that between mothers-in-law and daughters-in-law.[21] In Kolkata in 2006, I spoke with quite a few women around my age who were of the age of daughters-in-law whose parents-in-law were entering "old age"—retired and/or widowed, in the process of moving aside from the position of head of household. Several spoke readily of how, in general, it is harder to live with and care for mothers-in-law than fathers-in-law, because the older men are not as involved in internal household affairs, such as the kitchen. Older men also seemed to be, several women commented, in general less demanding and more self-sufficient, perhaps more self-confident, needing less attention and respectful service from their *boumās*. There is, however, of course, a great deal of variety in families, including certainly fathers and fathers-in-law who struggle with junior kin.

Psychiatrist and old-age-home resident Dr. Ranjan Banerjee, whom I introduced in opening the book, was clearly deeply pained by his rift with his son, and only made the decision to move to the elder residence under great duress and angst, all the while feeling passionately that the earlier ways were far better, when parents lived and died "right with" their sons. Mukund Gangopadhyay, whom I visited over a period of several years (from 2003 to 2006), would especially at first speak very bitterly, though vaguely, about how "these days" "children kick their parents out."[22] He was still married and lived in the old age home with his wife. They had three children, all married, one son and two daughters. He hinted once or twice about not getting along well especially with his daughter-in-law, and seemed to be bitter that his son perhaps sided more with her than with him. His bitterness faded a bit over the years, though, and by 2006 he admitted to feeling calmer and more accepting of the whole situation, in part because he had come to realize that his son didn't have it very easy either. The son's wife, in fact, now spent most of the year working in a different city, so the younger couple did not even live together much any longer. Although Mukund-babu spoke in general terms about elders being "kicked out," he had been the one to make the arrangements to live in the old age home, and he funded the residence with his pension.

One elder-home male resident, R. N. Datta, said to Hena and me, in very surly and exacting tones, that he would agree to speak with us *only* if we did not inquire about his family. We promised and got to chatting about this and that. He was in his sixties, recently retired, fit, and an avid reader. His roommate was also present and at one point let slip that Mr. Datta had a wife and sons living right nearby. R. N. Datta was furious: "Who said that you could bring that up?!" he snapped at his roommate. And to us, "Don't write that down! That is nobody's business but mine!" I, in fact, held my pen still, yet I could not help but remember the exchange in sharp detail. Clearly the senior man found it highly painful and humiliating to acknowledge living apart from his wife and sons in an old age home.

Several men and women who had ultimately made the decision to move into a residence for elders commented that squabbles and hard words between co-residents, and between residents and staff, hurt far less than those between kin—and for that reason they were able more easily to endure living in the elder abodes than with their families.

Actively Pursuing a New Way of Living

In addition to those "thrown away" into homes and those who choose them under duress as only one of two undesirable options, there is another important category of residents: those who actively and even eagerly pursue such a mode of living. Media and public discourse in India focuses on crises and transgressions, and the quite common world-wide image of the old person as passive "victim" needing care. Although the public discourse does not highlight the resourceful and innovative old-age-home resident, I have estimated that a good third of those I interviewed had strategically pursued their new way of living and aging in the world.

Of the one hundred residents I interviewed, I have considered that thirty-six were actively pursuing this new way of living, for the kinds of reasons I describe below. It is likely, however, that I ended up interviewing a higher, somewhat unrepresentative, proportion of "happy" residents with positive, active outlooks; I imagine such people would more probably be eager to speak with an outside visitor than those who are more depressed about their situations. In several smaller homes, however, I did manage to gather information from each resident.

There are a few main factors that seem to inspire people to *wish to* join residences for elders, which turned up as recurring themes in diverse residents' narratives:

FIRST, HAVING NO SONS

I have already introduced Monisha Mashi (at the beginning of this chapter) and Ashok Bose (at the opening of chapter 3), both of whom actively pursued and seemed truly to appreciate their new living options. Neither had sons, and in fact Sri Ashok was altogether childless, which surely helped to make the old age home seem like a viable and welcome choice. Although this fact does not seem to be at the forefront of consciousness in public critiques of the emerging institutions, a very sizable proportion of old-age-home residents (in fact, nearly half or 48 percent of my subjects) do not actually have the ideal "traditional" multigenerational family option available to them—that is, they have no sons (see table 3.2 in chapter 3). Many appear to be truly delighted to find an alternative other than scraping by on their own, or living like a maidservant in the corners of houses of distant kin.

Sri Nimai Sarkar, for instance, told of how he had come to his old age home: on the very day of his retirement, while eating his last lunch at the canteen, he found an advertisement for an old age home in the newspaper. He saw it as *such* a fortuitous event! He, who had been living the canteen life—a lifelong bachelor—who hadn't known *what* he was going to do after retirement. He still keeps the ad with him, carrying it in his front pocket. "Why are there so many old age homes now?" he responded to my query. "Because joint families are breaking up—that's the reason, nothing else. And people are preferring smaller flats." He added lightheartedly, "I think it's just fine!" He has three brothers living nearby but describes himself as very "independent" (*svādhīn*). "I lived alone before, and I can live here alone. With old age homes now in India, there are more 'choices' for old people."

It is important to note that living alone is not viewed at all as an attractive or viable option for the majority in India (as it is for many in the United States, where single-person households are currently the second most common type).[23] As I explore further in chapter 6, people in India commonly speak of living alone in such terms as "unnatural," "unthinkable," "not human," or "impossible." Peppering Indian newspapers over recent years are also stories of aged persons being tricked, robbed, and even murdered by domestic workers and burglars, contributing to a widespread sense that it is inappropriate and even dangerous for elders to live on their own.

SECOND, SEEKING A "FOREST-DWELLING" LIFE

Both Monisha Mashi and Ashok Bose were keenly spiritual people and saw old-age-home living, as did many others, as offering a unique, modern opportunity to pursue a valued and traditional "forest-dwelling" (*vānaprastha*) lifestyle—breaking free from binding family and worldly ties, in order to cultivate spiritual awareness and readiness for the passages of death. In the following chapter, I explore in much more depth the intriguing "forest-dwelling" qualities of Indian old age homes.

THIRD, CULTIVATING AN INDEPENDENT AND NUCLEAR-FAMILY LIFESTYLE

Some who had actively chosen to move into a residence for elders were people who had for many years cultivated what could be described as an independent, egalitarian, nuclear-family-oriented (sometimes labeled "modern" or "Western") lifestyle, and who had come to see elder residences as fitting in appropriately with such plans. Those who most directly articulated such positions tended to be among the more elite and highly educated, and often those (both men and women) who had had quite distinguished careers and who had spent some or a lot of time abroad or in major cosmopolitan Indian cities such as Delhi. "Let them [our children] live independently; let us live independently. Let them be happy; let us be happy," was the kind of proclamation several among this class declared. I would also hear statements (that sounded very "American" to me, and expressed in English) such as, "We don't wish to be *burdens* on our children"[24] or "It wouldn't be *fair* to them to ask them to care for us." They would explain how they had in fact raised their children to pursue independent, professional careers and lifestyles, sending them to elite English-medium schools, funding educational opportunities abroad, allowing them to choose their own marriage partners, and encouraging them to set up households of their own after marriage. For various reasons, often due to their own careers, these seniors as adults had also often not lived (full time, at least) in multigenerational households with their parents or parents-in-law. Some (more women, but also men) also remarked that independent living is especially better for daughters-in-law, who in fact, they generalized, have never liked to live with and care for their parents-in-law.

FOURTH, WELCOMING THE TREMENDOUS CONVENIENCE AND SECURITY

In old age homes, food and tea are served, rooms are cleaned, the building is maintained, night guards are (almost always) present; and, importantly, one does not need to manage one's own servants. Even ordinary middle-class households in India maintain servants; yet people complain that it can be difficult to find trustworthy and capable ones. S. N. Bhusan told of how he and his older sister came to live with each other after each had become widowed, but by the end it had become such a hassle for the two to manage their household. "You can't get good maidservants these days, and so we were depending on home delivery food. That gets very boring after a while. I was disgusted. So, one day, just after having my dinner, I was watching TV . . . , and I saw an advertisement about this place!" It was the kind of strip advertisement, in English, that runs beneath a program. "I immediately wrote down the phone number, and the next day in the morning I rang up. I asked, 'When can I see the place?' They said, 'Anytime.' So, I went later that day and liked the place, and a few days later my sister and I moved in!" Many residents also tell of how bored and irritated they had become listening to their servants' monotonous stories, as they had grown increasingly homebound in later life.

FIFTH, ENJOYING COMPANIONSHIP

Finally, some residents are attracted to what they expect will be the constant companionship and sociality in a residence for elders. Even those living in large families can feel very isolated the way middle-class life is organized these days in Kolkata—with junior members out all day and busy with jobs, school, marketing, cafes, social events, movies. "Why not move to a place where I will always be surrounded by people?" some told me. The retired Harvard professor, a Bengali man who had moved back to Kolkata, said that he could of course easily afford a single room in the elder residence he had selected, but that he had had enough of living alone, and was looking forward to the company in a shared double.

Deep Ambivalence Even amid Active Pursuit

I close this section on "Actively Pursuing a New Way of Living" by reflecting on how people's lives and perspectives are much more complex and ambiguous than are simple categories. So I turn to Soumil Chowdhury, whom I consider in many ways to be a quintessential example of someone who had actively pursued, strategically *chosen,* life in a residence for elders. I met him—a very forthcoming, energetic, and articulate man—as he was making the final arrangements to move into the residence of his choice, after having visited twenty-five homes and met some 150 old-age-home residents over a period of four years while searching for the perfect elder abode. He was seventy-two, in good health, and he had retired twelve years earlier from his profession at the Calcutta Port Trust. He explained that he was not exactly abandoning *saṃsār* (worldly-household-family life); for instance, he was planning to keep and return periodically to his two-story Ballygunge, Kolkata, home, where he and his wife currently lived in the flat right above his married son. "But I need a second place, somewhere that is peaceful, good for meditation, an empty, tranquil space [*phākā, niribili jāegā*]. It's good to live a little 'alone' from *saṃsār*," he went on. "In *saṃsār,* there are so many bindings." He also commented, smiling somewhat slyly, that he "wishes to be in hiding a bit," since several members of his very large extended family seem to feel that now, as he has retired and receives a pension, he should be in the position to contribute generously to them on request. He had come to see the elder residence once alone, then once with his wife, then again with his wife and wife's brother, and now again by himself to make the final arrangements. "The rooms are beautiful upstairs! That's why I like it so much. We have chosen room #5. There are open windows on both sides, front to back. It opens onto a beautiful roof verandah filled with flower pots—it reminds me of Santiniketan," the beloved country retreat of well-off Kolkatans. Soumil-babu was also pleased that the home has a temple.

Living separately from his kin (other than his wife, who would be coming with him) would not be a radically new arrangement for him. Within two years of his marriage, he and his wife had moved out from the large joint-family village home, where his landed zamindar ancestors had resided for many generations, and he set up a separate flat in Kolkata near where he worked. Later he built a two-story house in the city. After his son's marriage, Soumil-babu and his wife moved into the upper flat of the home, while his son, daughter-in-law, and granddaughter occupied the ground floor. His son now works for the Delhi branch of a U.S. firm, and his daughter-in-law and granddaughter (still full time in Kolkata) manage their own small computer company. For his whole adult life, Soumil-babu had cultivated a type of "modern" nuclear-family independence, both for himself and his for descendants.

However, at the same time that he told me compellingly of the reasons he had actively sought living in an elder abode, he also had a lot of critical things to say about his nation's new trend of old-age-home living. As I had with me my driver and leased car, I offered Soumil-babu a ride back to Kolkata from the elder abode, about an hour's drive from the city. Toward the end of the journey, he voiced an eloquent and nostalgic commentary on how people were much happier before, living in large joint families, which were especially wonderful for children and for old people—everyone eating all together, the same food, seated in long lines on the floor, by lantern-light, in the village. To make sense of the social changes that he perceived to have occurred during his lifetime, he invoked the familiar contrast between "traditional India" and the "modern West." I quote at some length:

> I've seen that most 'boarders' in old age homes are unhappy. We are experiencing a clash between the 'Indian era' and the 'Western era.' We [that is, Indians] want to live 'jointly,' amid our relatives [ātmīya svajan, or "own people"], not alone [ekā]. We don't want to live alone. In 'European culture,' everyone

does want to live separately [*ālādā, ālādā*]. We [Indians] love to chat, to have intimate conversations [*āḍḍā*]. We like to have everyone living together [*eksange*]. We don't want old age homes [*bṛiddhābās*]. We want 'joint families'—sisters and brothers, daughters and sons, granddaughters and grandsons, all together. When I die, I will want them all by my side. Will I want there to be old-age-home people by my side? No, I will not. However much people say in the old age homes that they are fine, they are not. They would all prefer to be with their relatives. This is 'Indian culture.'

But 'modern culture,' 'European culture' will enter our children's lives. It is *harming* our 'culture.' So, our young persons will care only about themselves, and their spouses. They won't even want their own children for long—they will send them to 'hostels' after eighteen years.

I'm a person with an 'old [-fashioned] temperament.' Why? Because I grew up in a huge 'joint family.' Twenty-five to thirty people together would sit down to eat. We had no electricity so we would eat by lantern light. In the 'modern age,' people dislike this. But I was very happy as a child. We ate in long lines and whatever there was we divided among us. The cooking was done over a wooden fire in an earthen pot. . . . There were uncles and aunts, brothers and sisters, ponds, cows, servants. Now this kind of thing is no longer.

Old-age-home living is probably not a simple proposition, without ambivalence, for anyone, for it entails for most such a radically new way of living and thinking about self, family, culture, and old age. Soumilbabu, almost more than any resident I met, had so actively, purposefully and meticulously chosen the path of old-age-home living, and yet even he faced it with deep ambivalence and misgivings.

A Daughter's Tale

I close this larger section on how people come to be in old age homes with a long, revealing story from a daughter's perspective, which beautifully illuminates the complex family and individual, gendered and generational processes that are at play in the movement from family to a "home." I visited with the daughter of Bankim and Karabi Ganguly, a married couple who had moved six years earlier into the Vanaprastha Briddhasram, situated in a moderately sized town about an hour's drive from central Kolkata. I had known the senior couple for four of those years, visiting with them each time I was in India and corresponding occasionally via letters during my absences. I should note before moving on to his daughter's quite critical narrative that I have always really enjoyed and respected both Bankim-babu and his wife. They share a modest double room with attached bath and a small kitchenette arranged in one corner. An open-air verandah extends past their room and the long line of about fourteen other private rooms. The verandah itself looks out over the spacious walled grounds of the ashram. The setting resembles a semi-rural extended family compound. There are fruit trees, a kitchen garden, a large stone well, a few milk cows and an earthen barn, saris drying on clothes lines, a central building with a vast kitchen and elaborate temple, and another dwelling housing several rooms of women living dormitory style. Bankim-babu and his wife appear to have a tender, mutually affectionate relationship. He walks to the nearby center of town every morning to pick up a few extra food items—fruit, biscuits, Bengali sweets—for them to share. They both enjoy reading and they selectively watch a few television programs on the set in their room. Karabi is often on the phone with her daughter when I visit; the daughter had bought them a mobile phone to use, since the ashram itself had only one phone inconveniently located in the central office. One day the daughter told her parents that she would really like to meet me, and shortly afterward she phoned to invite me to her home one Sunday.

Bulbul Chatterjee, the daughter, lives with her husband and two near-grown sons in a small middle-class home in north Kolkata, down a lane too narrow for cars. She is the oldest of four siblings, including two other married sisters and one married brother. She was exceptionally warm, lively, articulate, and forthcoming, and reminded me of my former dear research assistant Hena from my earlier eighteen months of fieldwork living in the village of Mangaldihi. Like that Hena, Bulbul was very generous with her affection: she fed me a sweet from a spoon, for instance, and then ate the other half herself; she helped me to wash my hands after eating the rice that she had prepared and insisted I eat, rubbing my hands for me with one hand while pouring water from the other. Both acts are signs of affection and openness, as they entail the quite intimate sharing of substances.[25] Our very interesting conversation follows:

> SL: I am so happy to meet you, because I like your parents
> so much, and also—I've been meeting so many people who

live in old age homes, but I never yet have met or seen any of their children! [I later did meet several more children, but throughout most of my fieldwork, they seemed to be strikingly scarce.]

BC: One thing you should understand for your research is that those who live in old age homes—many of them, probably the *majority* of them—are *not* there because they absolutely *have* to be—that is, because their sons and *boumās*[26] really threw them out of the house, or because they have no relatives.

People *make* [*tairi karā*] their own lives. There really *is* no one with no relatives [*ātmīya*]. If people say that they have no relatives, this means that earlier in their life, they weren't good to their relatives. When people would get together, they wouldn't mix with them well, or give to them, or enjoy their company. So, the kin didn't end up *liking* the person—and that's how people get to a state in old age when there is no one to look after them. If you don't have any good relations with your kin now, then you certainly were not a very good person before. You are that kind of person that you 'created' this 'situation.'

Let me tell you the story of what happened with my parents:

My father had a very hot temper all of his life—he was a very angry [*rāgī*] man.[27] No one—none of us—could stand being around him. When my sisters, brother, and I were home during the day with our mother, we all had a very good time together, studying and chatting; but when my father came home, it was 'pin drop silent.' None of us would say anything, we were so frightened of his temper. Because of my father, I really couldn't stand the atmosphere at home, and I wanted to do anything to get out of there; but I didn't know how to leave. So, that's why at only age sixteen, I ended up getting married.

My *mother*, on the other hand, was *such* a good woman. She loved us *so* much—*such* a good [*bhālo*] woman you can't find anywhere. For instance, when we were young and all the other parents were hiring private tutors for their children, our mother taught everything to us herself. She would help us with math, with English—everything. She was always by our side.

And she cooked for us, and cared for us, loved us—there was nothing she wouldn't do for us. But my father was a different matter. He was such an angry man, and he always thought that whatever decision *he* came to, thinking on his own without deliberating with anyone, was *the* correct decision. Once he made up his mind, he would never change.

And he didn't know how to raise us properly; he threw so much money at his son, trying to educate him and get him established, but really the son didn't turn out so well. It was my younger sister who really had the brains. She was an excellent student, but when she wanted to go on for her MA, my father said that he wouldn't spend that much money. So he spent it all on my brother, which was a waste, and my sister lost her opportunity to really make something of herself. And it was because of my father's ways that I, too, just to get away from the household, ended up getting married at such a young age [implying that this was a "love marriage,"[28] in the neighborhood], thus ruining my own opportunities for education. I got married after passing my [tenth-grade] exams, but because of getting married I was not able to study further and pursue a career.

Later Bulbul explained how, after her sons started school, she studied on her own at home and passed the secondary high school exam; and now she and her husband have established quite a successful business together. She went on:

BC: Then, another important factor: You know that in Bengali families, the *boumā* comes from a different household. Now, that means that of course she will have very different ways—a different culture [*saṃskār*], in fact. Each household/family [*saṃsār*] has its own *saṃskār* [rituals, tendencies]. And it takes some *time* for both parties to come to share the same culture. You know—if one person's family has the routine that when they get up they eat rice first thing in the morning, and another person's family has the routine of eating *ruṭi* [flat bread] first thing in the morning, and then the person who eats rice comes into the *ruṭi* household and still eats rice for several days—what's the fault in that? It takes some time, and compromise on both sides, to adjust. But my parents couldn't understand that.

Here, it may seem that Bulbul blames her mother a little, too. But she later suggests that the problems were still more her father's, largely because he didn't deal with them properly and, as the senior household male, he had more responsibility. She continued:

> BC: My parents and our *boumā* couldn't adjust well at all with each other. They were only in the house together for one and a half or two years before my parents left. One other factor was that our *boumā* married at quite an older age—she was about twenty-five or twenty-six.

> SL: It's much harder when the *boumā* is older, right?

> BC: Yes, indeed! I was only sixteen at marriage, but she was twenty-five or twenty-six. Just like with a plant—it's much easier to transplant a young plant; it can adjust to the new soil. But if a mature plant is transplanted, it has a much more difficult time adjusting to the new environment and in fact may never adjust well.[29]

> So—I don't want to say anything against our *boumā;* she came from another family and all. But, she wouldn't do any work around the house at all. My mother continued to do *everything* after she arrived: cooking, managing the marketing, everything. The *boumā* would sleep late, getting up at around 8:00 AM every day, and her husband, my brother, had to leave for work at 8:30 AM. So, who would make his breakfast and everything, to get him ready to leave? Naturally my mother would do it. Then my mother would cook all morning. But if a little before noon, she said to her *boumā,* "Look, I've been cooking all morning, and now I want to go take my bath. Can you look after this rice?" the *boumā* would get angry. Perhaps my mother would say this to her in a loud and angry voice herself. She was such a quiet and calm [*ṭhāṇḍā,* cool] woman usually, but that meant that the worries and thoughts would pile up inside of her, and her pressure would rise, and then if she finally spoke, it might come out angrily.

> So, things weren't good at all in the house.

> But my father really loved his *boumā* at that time, and he wouldn't listen to my mother's complaints at all, or give her any support. So, that was his fault [*doṣ*]. A woman—what kind of support does she have in life? When she's young, she

is supposed to get it from her father, and then after marriage from her husband, and then late in life, from her son.[30] But my mother didn't have any support from anyone. And then our *boumā* thought, "Well, if I get along so well with my father-in-law, then why do I have to worry about my mother-in-law?"

It got to be such a state that my mother ended up thinking of suicide; and finally, she even tried to commit suicide one day, by taking some sleeping pills. She ended up in the hospital. Then my father called my sister, who also lived nearby in Durgapur [the city where their family home was, several hours from Kolkata] and asked her to take my mother home with her. I also went to Durgapur right away then, and helped my mom get settled in my sister's home. When I went to my parents' house to get my mom's things, my dad told me to be quiet and not speak to my brother or his wife about what was happening, just to sneak in there and get my mother's things and leave. I also thought that that was wrong—Why couldn't we all talk together about what was happening and try to work things out?

So, my mother stayed at my sister's house, and my father was still in his house with his son and *boumā*. But, he only lasted there a few days. Since his *boumā* wasn't used to doing household work at all, my father wasn't getting his meals properly in time at all, or tea, or anything. So he, too, became very angry and left for my sister's house. After a few days there, though, he also wasn't happy there. And my sister had her hands full, with three small children under six years. So, she called me and begged me to come get our parents right away, to bring them to live here with us in Kolkata. But at that time it was the rainy season, and there were great floods and the trains weren't running. I said, "Listen, I can't come until the trains start running, but as soon as they do, I'll be there."

I'm the oldest in the family, and people listen to me and treat me with respect. They know I can manage things and get things done. My husband really loves my mother, his mother-in-law, and he said that of course she can stay with us, for the rest of her life. He loves her even more than his own mother. For she used to do things for us, helping us secretly, after we were married, and he hasn't forgotten all those things.

So I went to get my parents and I brought them back to live with us in our flat in Kolkata. It wasn't a large place, but there was enough room. We thought then that they would stay with us for the rest of their lives, and that was fine with us. We were never the types to be concerned about what others in society [*samāj*] might say—that it's not appropriate for parents to live with their son-in-law.

It was a *very* busy and difficult time for me; though. My oldest son was just about to take his class eleven exams, which are very important exams—and not something that can be repeated again sometime later, if they don't work out well now. They *had* to be done well *this* time, or else he would lose all his chances. I was also working then. So, somehow or other, I managed to do the cooking, get everyone fed, go to work, help my son with his studies, and look after my parents. My father, though, often wasn't happy with things, and he would interfere. For instance, he didn't like the way I was forcing my son to study all the time. My mother understood, though, and she would say to my father, "Of course, she has to force her son to study. If the mother doesn't do so, who will?" Nonetheless, even amid these disagreements, we were managing.

Then one day, without telling anyone where he was going, my father went out to look at a *briddhāśram* [ashram for elders]. It got to be noon, and then afternoon, and he still wasn't coming home, and we began to get really worried about him. An older man, out in the streets—where could he be? But he was out looking at the *briddhāśram,* and by the time he came back, he had decided to move in.

SL: How did he know or hear about it?

BC: Through the newspaper! Ads and things had been appearing for some time then. So, he came back and said to us that he had come to realize that he really wasn't the kind of person who could live with others, and so he was going to go live in a *briddhāśram.* My mother said, "Fine, you go live there. But I am going to stay here with my daughter." My father wouldn't let her stay, though. He had made up his mind, and once he does so, he won't budge at all, listen to others, or stop to consider that he might be making a mistake.

We in the family were so opposed, though! And we also worried—what would people think? They would be going right to the *briddhāśram* from *our* home, and surely people would think that something had gone wrong in our home, or that we had thrown them out. That would be a great disgrace [*apamān*] and bring disrespect [*asammān*]. But they went nonetheless, and there you have it. That was in 2000.

Bulbul's long narrative seemed partly motivated, in fact, as a means to restore respect. She then went on to conclude that "my father made four big 'mistakes' in his life," the fourth being moving to the old age home. (In my notes later that evening, I mused: "It's interesting/significant that she does view living in an old age home ultimately as a 'mistake,' in keeping with prevailing societal images (even though her father chose it). This is probably also due to the fact that neither parent actually professes (to her or to me) to be liking life in the home, though again, her father chose it, and he is not seeking alternative arrangements.")

These were the "four mistakes," building up to the decision to move into the old age home. (I summarize her explanations in brackets.)

1) The first mistake was the way he raised us [angry, with no real understanding of how to properly raise kids].

2) The second mistake was building a house and signing it over to his son right then. [Her parents had had a new house built several years back, and although she had advised her father to keep it in his and her mother's name, her father hadn't listened, and put the home right away in his son's name, shortly before the son's marriage. Then when the son was married, the *boumā* realized: "Oh, the house is in my *husband's* name." So, then, she didn't need to worry about her relationship with her parents-in-law at all.]

3) The third mistake was not siding with his wife at all and getting his relatives' advice about their problems. [There were plenty of aunts and other relatives nearby in their city, Bulbul claimed, who could have stepped in to help forge decent relationships in the household between the parents-in-law and daughter-in-law.]

4) The fourth mistake: going to the old age home without consulting anyone.

Bulbul went on to tell how she wished that her mother could stay with her more often, but, she added:

> My mother sometimes likes to come stay with us, and I *love* having her here. I *love* my mother—whenever she wants to stay, she is welcome. I would love it if she would stay here with us always. But my father—who never much before seemed to care that much about her—now suddenly can't live without her at all. If she's away for just two days, or even one, he starts getting agitated, and he comes to bring her back to him.

We see here the complex layers of a family's poignant story, involving fathers, mothers, daughters, sons, daughters-in-law, and competing values and life aims surrounding work, love, success, family, gender, tradition, and modernity. I will continue to analyze this story's significance in focusing on gender below.

Gender in the Home

As is evident in Bulbul's and many other narratives, gender is an important dimension in the process by which persons move into abodes for elders. How women and men are defined, and the forms of agency they have or lack, play a vital role both in how people enter into old age homes and how they experience them. I close this chapter with a brief examination of a few key features of gender that help illuminate Bulbul's and others' stories.

I have already discussed how agency and independence can be strongly limited for many women, as they and their kin comply with the kinds of expectations expressed in the lines from Manu and in various ways in everyday talk: "A woman should never be independent, but should be given support and guidance by her father in childhood, her husband in youth, and her sons in old age" (Laws of Manu V.147–148). Bulbul's mother, Karabi, played no part in her husband's decision to move them both to the ashram for elders, and she had little control over how often and how long she could stay with her daughter. Such an ideology underlies how and why so many women get to old age homes against their own desires, will, or initiative, and also why so many women feel so trapped and isolated from outer worlds in the homes.

In the era when today's current older women were young wives, and still for many in more conservative families now, a married woman who wishes to visit her natal home must wait for a male kin member, often a brother, to arrive to escort her there. She cannot go on her own. In a similar fashion, many women in abodes for elders wait for sons, sons-in-law, nephews, and grandsons to come invite and escort them on visits to their families. When Bulbul's mother goes to visit her daughter, it is generally her son-in-law who comes to escort her, and then her husband who, a day or two later, arrives to bring her back. Sometimes, though less frequently, daughters can take on the role of escort, especially those who have achieved a high degree of independence through their own earning and/or higher education. Many older women residents I knew would not otherwise leave the elder abodes, although male residents in good health did frequently travel on their own, to the homes of kin, their own former houses, and on journeys for pleasure. Male residents more often than female residents also went out on a daily basis for things like marketing and morning walks, often doing small errands for other less mobile residents, including women who may be perfectly physically fit but who nonetheless experience a felt restricted mobility due to their gender. In most of the homes, there were, in fact, no particular rules restricting the movements of women, but many women had grown up simply unaccustomed to being able to be in charge of their own travels and to venture out alone. I need to emphasize again here, however, the great variety in such practices: the more elite, the more highly educated, those who had had professional careers, and certain women with independent spirits certainly did travel on their own—which I will get to shortly.

Mene Neoyā *or Coming to Accept:*
Ways of Framing the Moves of a Woman's Life

As I listened to certain women's stories of how they had come to be in, and then come to accept life in, an elder abode, it struck me that many of them spoke of this shift in ways similar to how they spoke of other key moves in their lives—in particular the shift to their *śvaśur bāṛi* or "father-in-law's home" after marriage. Women residents commonly say that they have come to accept or have had to accept (*mene neoyā, mene niyechi,* or *mene nite hayeche*) living in an old age home, language that, significantly,

I did not notice men using. When I would ask women to speak of their earlier lives, it struck me that they also described moving to their *śvaśur bāṛi* in a noticeably similar fashion. Then I began to think, too, about how these stories resonate with so many other narratives I had heard from Bengali women over years of doing research in the region, regarding their movements to their *śvaśur bāṛi*.[31] *Mene neoyā*, a phrase that women often use in such contexts, can be translated as "coming to accept," "taking what comes," or even "coming to honor," from the verbs *neoyā* (to take or to bear) and *mānā* (to heed, accept, observe, respect, honor). Women speak of major life transitions that they have "come to accept"—such as marriage, moving to an elder abode, and also widowhood—as also being things that "happen to" them: they are put into situations that are not precisely of their own choosing or making, but that they then have to learn to accept, or even to respect or honor—if they wish to get along smoothly with others, and to feel at peace with themselves, their lives, and their surroundings.

Supriya-di of Milan Tirtha, a very articulate and thoughtful person, with beautiful dyed long black hair and a pleasant, full face, spoke quite explicitly about having had to get adjusted to all three of these somewhat parallel experiences in her life: her *śvaśur bāṛi* (marital home), widowhood (at a young age), and living in an old age home. She remarked sincerely that she had gotten used to and had really adjusted to living in the old age home (though she has a son, daughter-in-law, and grandchildren living right nearby), just as she had had to accept and adjust to those earlier life phases.

> For instance, I became a widow at quite an early age—I was just forty-five. And I had to accept that [*mene nite hayeche*]. It was his [my husband's] job—he had a dangerous job, flying airplanes in the air force, and that's how he died, in fact, in a plane crash. And so that's how it was. I could say that it was just fate. And so I had to accept it. And since then I've been doing all the things that Brahman widows do—a completely vegetarian diet, no fish, no onions, no garlic, nothing; white saris; *ekādośī*—you know? fasting on the eleventh day of the lunar fortnight.

She spoke matter-of-factly of all these features of a traditional Bengali Brahman widow's life,[32] without complaint; they were simply part of marriage and widowhood for her, part of being a Brahman woman, part of her life. "And now I am in the old age home," she went on, "and really, I have adjusted to living here."

Supriya-di also spoke in detail that evening, almost cheerfully enjoying the reminiscing, of how grueling it had been when she was first taken to her *śvaśur bāṛi,* where nothing was familiar, she knew no one, and had to submit to the stern rule of her mother-in-law; but she had borne and come to accept all that as well. She spoke of respecting and honoring her mother-in-law, too, although the senior woman had kept a very tight rule over all her daughters-in-law throughout her life.

When I returned home to our flat that evening after visiting with Supriya-di, I was chatting in the kitchen with our part-time cook, Bharati. She began to speak of her own move to her *śvaśur bāṛi* ten or so years earlier, a very familiar tale: of how it was so far from her *bāper bāṛi* (father's home), how everything was strange and different there, how she didn't know anyone at first, and how she would cry and cry, yearning for her *bāper bāṛi.* Sometimes in the beginning she could return there for even three months at a time, escorted by her brother, but then she would have to return to her *śvaśur bāṛi.* Gradually, however, she came to accept her marital home and to feel comfortable there.

So, I sat at my computer that night composing a list of the ways that moving to an elder abode and to one's *śvaśur bāṛi* are similar, for a woman. Here are some elements from that list:

Moving to an Elder Abode Is Like Moving to a Śvaśur Bāṛi or "Father-in-Law's Home"

1) *At first, at least, both residences feel like an "other" place, made up of "others"* (parer lok), *rather than one's "own people" or "household people"* (nijer lok, bāṛir lok). The English term "home," often used to refer to residences for elders, has a distinctly institutional feel, and people often use the term, implicitly and explicitly, to distinguish the institution from a *bāṛi* or *ghar* (Bengali terms for home), which are "real" homes, as in places of belonging, intimacy, and familiarity. Similarly, a *śvaśur bāṛi* (father-in-law's home, marital home) has, like the English "home," connotations of distance, of being not really "one's own." In both residences, in the early days especially, women experience painful feelings of having been torn away, of loneliness and of yearning for their (real)

home (*bāṛi*) and "own people." Of course, many women gradually come to feel very much a part of their *śvaśur bāṛis*, especially after raising children there and becoming mothers-in-law and female household heads (*ginnī*) in their own right. If that happens, they generally stop referring to that home as their *śvaśur bāṛi*, but rather come simply to call it *bāṛi* or "home."

2) *The decision to go to a residence is very often (especially for this generation of senior women) not fully or really their own at all, but rather something that others arrange for them.* As with a traditional arranged marriage, very often it is kin who make the inquiries, find the home (or groom), and finalize the plans—so that the woman resident is often going to the home sight-unseen, as some of them also set eyes on their husbands for the first time on their wedding day. (For a wedding, kin endeavor carefully to arrange a good match. Notably, however, it seemed to me that often not as much effort went into finding a good "match" between a resident and a particular old age home. Often kin simply made arrangements in the first one or two homes they encountered; many had little idea that a wide selection might exist.)

3) *A woman's capacity to travel out from both types of residence is often limited.* Traditionally, in a *śvaśur bāṛi*, the daughter-in-law needed her mother-in-law's permission to go out at all, and many women stayed confined to their marital households the majority of the time. We have seen, similarly, how female residents commonly treat their elder abodes in like ways. Kalyani-di and her roommates Kavika-di and Uma-di feel utterly shut in, like "prisoners." Even if they wish to go out for just a short walk, they must request the ayahs to unlock the front metal gate. When I broached the possibility one day of taking them out to the movies or for a shopping trip, they seemed highly hesitant, wondering if that would be allowed, without their sons' permission. In a similar fashion, both daughters-in-law and elder-home residents are commonly escorted by male kin from time to time to visit close relatives for periods of a few days to several

months each year. Most of the elder abodes uphold sign-in and sign-out procedures. Male residents generally sign themselves in and out, but many women leave, particularly on longer, overnight trips, only if signed out and escorted by male kin. The brochure for one all-women elder residence, Sraddhanjali, provides a list of rules. Number 18 reads: "If on any occasion the boarder wants to go out of the Home to her relative's house or anywhere else, either her guardian or her recognized relative will have to accompany her."

4) *Women are taught not to, or end up finding it best not to, complain at either residence.* One of the defining features of life in one's *śvaśur bāṛi*, to many of the women of the current senior generation, is that they had to accept what comes without complaint. Women who were close to their husbands could whisper a few words to them late at night when they were finally alone together. They could also protest mildly to their parents on visits home. But they would be told by mothers, fathers, and often husbands just to bear it, that there's nothing that can be done, that a woman must accept what happens in her in-laws' home. Similarly, I found that women residents would gripe mildly to me and each other about things they did not like about their elder abodes, but they often added that these things were not worth complaining about to the management, or that there was nothing that could be done. Some of these gripes were more or less serious than others: they could be that the ceiling fans needed more regular cleaning, or that a particular staff member was not respectful enough, or that the pieces of fish served were too small. The incident that struck and disturbed me perhaps the most was when the proprietor had appropriated for his wife the radio-tape-player that I had given as a gift to Kalyani-di, Uma-di, and their third roommate. When I, bitterly hurt along with them, indignantly asked what could be done, they replied, "Nothing," and in fact they implored me not to address the proprietor, who was their caretaker now and the one in charge; they did not want to disturb their relationship with him.

5) *Life in both a* śvaśur bāṛi *and an elder abode is something that a woman must learn to accept and, if she can, even respect.*
    She must bear the life transitions that come her way, adjust to new settings, forge new relationships, and make peace with her surroundings. This is the way of a woman's life. A piece of proverbial wisdom voices it thus: a woman will fare best if she is malleable like clay, to be cast into a shape of his choice by the potter (ordinarily her husband), able to discard earlier loyalties, attributes, and ties, to become absorbed into her marital home (and by extension, I suggest, an elder abode) (see Dube 1988:18, Lamb 2000:207).

If one accepts this comparative list, one can see how quite traditional features of gender can in fact be carried out through old-age-home living. For a woman, the move to an elder abode, like other transitions of the female life course, can demand a profound dependence, passivity, and pliability.

A Woman's Independence, and How Living in an Elder Abode Can Be Very Different from Living in a Śvaśur Bāṛi

After preparing the above list of potential similarities between moving to elder abodes and moving to in-laws' homes, I decided to try out the analogy with some of my elder-abode resident friends. I quickly discovered that many did not find the analogy terribly compelling, for not all the women I met living in elder abodes were by any means living submissive lives controlled by male kin; and in fact life in an elder abode seemed to help some decisively break free of such traditional patriarchal strictures. I have kept the preceding list in this book, however, for I still believe that it does well convey *some* key dimensions of gender and elder-abode living for *some* women.

So, "Is moving to an old age home at all like moving to a *śvaśur bāṛi?*" I asked a group of women at Loknath Briddhabas. They laughed. "No! We are *friends* [*bandhu*] here. This is like living among *friends!*" Some other women had similar reactions: "No! This is like living in a [college] 'hostel!'"[33] New life in a *śvaśur bāṛi* for almost all of them carried immediate connotations of suffering, powerlessness, being at the bottom in a hierarchy of household ranks, having to be meek and subservient and to serve one's elders, and to be burdened by household work. In contrast, in an elder abode, one is there to be served by the staff and proprietors, rather than to serve. Women in elder abodes are also, usually for the first time in their lives, completely free of household duties.

Further, in an elder abode, the residents are living largely among equals. In Loknath, for instance, the women all addressed each other respectfully and affectionately as *didi* or "older sister." Ordinarily, if one person in a relationship is called *didi,* then the other will be *bon* (younger sister), but by calling everyone *didi,* the Loknath residents cheerfully chose to emphasize their equal rank. So, though they were strangers at first, they could easily come to mix, laugh, commiserate, and share with each other. Several women remarked that they had always heard that living in a hostel was supposed to be really fun (*mojā*), and one told her daughter that she is "having [her] 'hostel' life now." "This maybe is not *as* fun as that," Mina-di reflected, "but actually, we are having a very good time together." She was among a group of six women residents who played cards together every afternoon at five, the winner taking the others out for espresso at one of the fashionable coffee shops that had sprung up in the adjoining mall. The members of Atithiseva decided to celebrate the home's fifth birthday, commemorating the day they first moved in together, and they invited me to the merry celebration (Figure 4.2).

When I asked Uma-di of Aram (Kalyani-di's roommate) if the experience of moving into the ashram for elders was similar to the experience of moving to her *śvaśur bāṛi,* she also did not seem to find the analogy terribly compelling, replying that it had even been harder and more shocking to move to her in-laws' home. "When I went to my in-laws' home, I had been *so* sheltered and hadn't had a lot of experiences. I didn't know anything of the world other than my father's home. . . . In my in-laws' home I didn't even have the key to my *ālmāri* [chest or closet]. My mother-in-law controlled everything." So, although she had been given some gold, saris, and other belongings at her wedding, she had no access to these possessions. "By the time I came to the elder-ashram," she went on, "I had seen and experienced things, and I had lived in several places." And although she did not own much any longer, Uma-di did in the elder ashram have control over the key to the small locked chest that she, like the other residents, kept next to her bed for a few precious possessions.

In fact, quite a few women living in elder abodes experience a high degree of independence and freedom, by managing their own expenses, by

FIGURE 4.2. Enjoying a "hostel life" in an all-female elder home, members celebrate the home's fifth birthday. (Author is second from right.)

going out on their own (not all wait to be escorted), and simply by being released from family life. Of those women who made the decision to move in to an elder residence on their own (about 40 percent of the women in my study; see table 4.1), most all were considerably empowered by having independent financial means. Some were widows receiving their share of their deceased husband's pensions; others had worked themselves and thus had their own pensions; a few had savings in their own names. Not all the women I met living in elder abodes were, by any means, living submissive lives controlled by fathers, husbands, and sons. I will explore these themes further through Renuka-di's story.

At age eighty-four, Renuka-di is a very lively woman, and the most gregarious of the group of five with whom she resides dormitory style in the Swami Paramananda Baba Briddhasram. She claims with conviction to be thoroughly enjoying her independent (*svādhīn*) life in the forty-person elder ashram. She tells of having made the decision herself to move in after becoming a widow, although she has four sons and daughters-in-law and seven grandchildren, with whom she reportedly could have lived. Her husband had been a very domineering man, and while he was alive, she had had no knowledge of money at all and could make no important household decisions. Once when I asked her if she had ever broached with her husband the topic of moving to an elder ashram, she exclaimed, "No! He would have stripped the skin off of my very back!" The "Ashram Mother" (the ashram manager's own sixty-two-year-old mother, who herself spent most of her time at the ashram, helping direct its daily affairs and mingling with the residents) told me that Renuka-di had been a very dramatic lady through most of her life and on several occasions had attempted, or feigned to attempt, suicide by running into a large pond, while protesting her husband's authoritarian attitudes. After she became a widow, she made the decision to come to the elder ashram, speaking of the move as *her* decision while telling of how her sons all love her so much. She now professes to be thoroughly enjoying especially her freedom from household obligations and her ability to control the pension she receives as the widow of her husband, a former government employee. This is the first time in her life that she has had money of her own to spend, and if she had lived with her sons, the pension would not have remained under her control.

In fact, among the generation of women around Renuka-di's age and even younger (those born before around 1960 or so), their husbands would almost never think to teach them how to manage finances, or have access to a bank account. (They might teach such things to a *daughter,* though, and this is one way that female gender roles are changing.) Instead the husbands think, "If I have a son, why should I teach my wife? My son can do it." Thus, even if a widow is nominally the one to receive a pension or other property in her husband's name, if she resides with her son/s, she will ordinarily not control the funds. This means that some of the pension-receiving widowed women in elder abodes are experiencing a kind of financial freedom, autonomy, and independence that they never experienced before.

Renuka-di relishes this financial independence. She goes out often to buy sweets for herself and her roommates, and she gives money to the Ashram Mother, who is in charge of the home's kitchen, to purchase extra large pieces of fish for her, or mutton on a day when otherwise fish would be served and she is craving meat. She travels several times each year to visit various kin, including her sons in the town where she also has to go periodically to withdraw her pension from her husband's former bank.

She is immensely proud of the pension, which she refers to as her "salary" (*māine*).

One day Renuka-di told Hena and me a story with a great deal of pleasure, which seemed to epitomize what still appeared to strike her as her delightfully novel and almost sacrilegious freedom from typical domestic and motherly duties. On a recent visit to one of her sons' homes, where she was staying for a few days while she picked up her pension from the bank, her son asked her to make him the delicious fish dish that she makes so well and that he used to love so much. "Ma, why don't you cook that *kai* fish, the special way that you make it?" the son eagerly requested. Renuka-di said that she replied, "*Ish!* That is expensive, *kai* fish—how much? About 25 rupees per fish? I don't want to get involved. Why don't you buy it yourself, and I will teach your wife how to cook it."

Hena observed later to me that this tale was really quite remarkable. Ordinarily a senior mother would feel compelled to make the fish as requested, as she may also well wish to do so, demonstrating her ongoing affection for and usefulness within her son's household. By asking his mother to cook the fish, the son is both signaling that he knows that she has money and attempting to get her to spend some of it on them, and at the same time trying to please and flatter his mother. But Renuka-di seemed to be savoring her independence, financially as well as practically and emotionally. Telling them to buy and cook the fish themselves is an assertive act of independence and of distancing herself from them.

Further, and tellingly, the freedoms senior women such as Renuka-di achieve by living in elder residences complement the often parallel freedoms of their daughters-in-law, who are then not compelled to serve and be subservient to their mothers-in-law in a co-residential home. Quite a few of the older women I came to know readily acknowledged that the "earlier" system of intergenerational reciprocity—though often sustaining for elders, children, and men—was especially not an easy one for young married women. Many of these older women explicitly voiced (selflessly, it seemed to me) their pleasure in helping to foster a new system of separate and egalitarian living that they saw as ultimately better for their daughters and daughters-in-law.

For most people, then, moving to an abode for elders entails a quite radical transformation of self, from an intensely family-focused to a much more individual-centered way of being (although for certain women, especially, a family focus can remain very strong). Those who live in elder residences experience and interpret this transformation in an important variety of ways. For some, it can be incredibly alienating and distressing, as they are stripped of what they had always imagined as a fundamental way of being and of aging, entailing the daily giving to and receiving from kin in the intimate setting of a multi-generational household (*saṃsār*), made up of those who "flow or move together," the literal meaning of *saṃsār* or family, household, and worldly life. For some of these residents, even while living in an abode for elders, their emotional focus and sense of self remains still very much centered on the family; for instance, one Aram woman lies on her bed and cries out continually for her seven children in turn, calling each by name, "Supriya, come (*āy*)! Ganesh, come! Gopal, come! . . ." But in the context of an old age home, they are deprived of the everyday interactions with kin—the daily receipt of *sevā,* love, and material support—that sustain both the family and self as meaningful and vital parts of each other. Such residents often do not have anything to substitute for the family as a source of fulfillment or identity, not viewing, for instance, alternative values such as the cultivation of individuality, independence (*svādhīnatā*), or gendered and aged egalitarianism as meaningful aspirations.

Others, however, for complex and varying reasons, and often with a vigorous degree of ambivalence, have actively cultivated the much more independent, individualist way of being entailed by living away from the family in an elder abode. This movement can involve significant transformations of gender, especially for women, of both senior and junior generations.

Although I have closed this chapter by emphasizing dramatic changes in forms of self, aging, family, and in certain respects gender that old-age-home living can entail, in the next chapter I will explore how, in important and intriguing ways, Indian elder abodes are not simply modern, individual-making projects.

5 TEA AND THE FOREST: MAKING A WESTERN INSTITUTION INDIAN

One of the most important contributions anthropology has made to the scholarly study of globalization over the past few decades has been its emphasis on the complex and crucial ways that people around the world do not simply passively receive commodities and other phenomena that travel to their nations from the West. Instead, in fundamental and intricate ways, persons in any community always bring local cultural frameworks to bear, actively interpreting, appropriating, rejecting, and resignifying imported commodities, images, ideologies, and institutional forms. Anthropologists have variously termed such processes the "customization of foreign cultural forms," the "indigenization of modernity," and the "localization of the global," arguing against any simple hypothesis that "globalization entails a cultural homogenization of the world."[1] India's old age homes provide a revealing example of such important processes of customization. Those participating in India's new old age homes are innovatively striving to maintain older needs, desires, and values while also producing and fulfilling, and sometimes resisting, new ones, wrestling strategically with what they see as the conditions of their modern society.

When I first began this project, I myself thought of the old age homes in India as largely "Western"-style institutions. Historically, institutional care for the elderly has been predominantly a Western phenomenon, developing in Western Europe and North America beginning in the mid-1800s and gradually coming to be very widespread and normal, although never practiced universally, in these nations.[2] This is also how so many of my informants, and so much of public and media discourse in India, often put it. "Old Age Homes Against Our Culture," reads one representative newspaper headline, with the article moving on to report a government official in the southern state of Tamil Nadu proclaiming to a group of students that "the concept of old age homes reflects the impact of western culture" and asking the students to "take a vow that they would not leave their parents in old age homes" (*The Hindu* Staff Reporter, 2004). Retired psychiatrist and old-age-home resident Dr. Ranjan Banerjee asserted to me: "'Old age homes'[3] are not a concept of *our* country. These days, we are throwing away our 'culture.' The U.S. is the richest nation in the world and therefore has won us over." Gradually, however, after delving further into my fieldwork, learning and thinking more about it all, and preparing several lectures on old age homes for Indian audiences in Kolkata, I began to realize profoundly how very *Indian* are the institutions in India, in really important ways.

To make this judgment, one first needs to understand something about Western residences for elders. Although I have not done the same kind of anthropological fieldwork on elder residences in any Western nation as I have done in India, I have had quite a lot of informal experience in U.S. senior residential facilities. I volunteered for four years on Sunday mornings at one (Jewish Home for the Aged) while in college in Providence, Rhode Island. I then worked as the Activities Director at a nursing home in a small town in Maine for the year between college and graduate school. Now my own mother-in-law, with whom I feel very close, lives in a "retirement community" in northern California (a fact that I would surely be embarrassed to admit in many contexts if I were in an Indian family). I have also long been interested in reading academic literature about and collecting brochures and media stories pertaining to senior residences in the United States.

So, here I first present what I see as a few core aims of U.S. residential facilities for elders. I then move on to elaborate what I have come to understand as key, distinctly Indian values and aims embedded in the rising old age homes in India. The "Indian" cultural forms here, however, like the "Western" forms the Indians are engaging with, are of course not static; rather, both Western and Indian cultural forms take on new, hybrid meanings and shapes in a dialectical process of rich interplay, negotiation, and translation.[4] This chapter's examination thus seeks to counter simplistic arguments about "Westernization" versus "traditional identity" both in India and around the world, moving beyond simple binaries such as tradition and modernity, East and West, the local and the global, that continue to endure in both academic and non-academic spheres.

Senior Residences in the United States: Some Core Cultural Aims

As I mentioned briefly in chapter 3, there are three major categories of senior residences now common in the United States.[5] 1) "Care facilities" include both a) "assisted living" residences, where residents receive supervision and assistance with daily non-medical needs; and b) "nursing homes" or state-licensed healthcare facilities, where residents can receive around-the-clock nursing care and extensive medical supervision. 2) "Retirement housing" (often termed "retirement communities," "active adult communities," or "independent living communities") refers to planned communities designed exclusively for seniors, in which the residents do not need daily assistance with medical or personal care. Generally residents live in private apartments or cottages, with access to common social, dining, and activity areas. 3) "Continuing care retirement communities" offer in a campus-like setting a continuum of living options, from independent living to assisted living to skilled nursing care. These three kinds of senior residential facilities are in certain respects, of course, highly distinct; yet they share important similarities in values and assumptions regarding aging.[6]

Maintaining "Independence"

One of the main aims expressed by many older Americans in a variety of contexts is that they wish to maintain their independence. The living situation widely considered ideal is to reside in one's own independent household, alone or with a spouse. Such independence is also possible in a retirement community where residents live in their own separate quarters (while taking advantage of the social community of age peers and the convenience of amenities like grounds maintenance and optional common meals). Interestingly, moving into an assisted living or nursing facility can also be thought of as facilitating "independence" in certain important respects, because the senior would not be dependent on his or her children or other younger relatives. This is what is anathema to many Americans—depending on children for intimate bodily, personal, and financial care. Americans do generally wish to be emotionally close to their children, to receive from them things like visits, phone calls, love, and escorts to the doctor; but they do not wish to "depend on" them, or to co-reside. This is especially true for native-born and white Euro-Americans. Among more recent immigrant and non-white ethnic groups, forms of intergenerational interdependence are often much more common and valued.[7]

Studies such as those by Margaret Clark (1972), Andrei Simic (1990), and Maria Vesperi (1985) reveal that many Americans think of depending on younger relatives for support in old age destructive to their sense of dignity and value as a responsible person. Furthermore, most Americans expect benefits in parent-child transactions to move in a one-way (and thus nonreciprocal) lifetime flow of resources "down" from senior to junior. It is proper for parents to give to children (even, through gifts of money or inheritances, when their children are adults); but if an adult child gives to an aged parent, then the parent is seen as childlike (cf. Lamb 2000:52–53, Hunt 2002:109–110). Andrei Simic observes: "What the American elderly seem to fear most is 'demeaning dependence' on their children or other kin. Rather, the ideal is to remain 'one's own person'" (1990:94).

It is significant that many older Americans are more comfortable relying on hired aides or nurses for intimate care, such as bathing and other bodily functions, than on their children (although ideally they would hope not to have to depend on anyone in these ways). One reason for this preference may be that if the services are paid for, the elder is engaging in a reciprocal, rather than purely dependent, relationship—the exchange of money for services. Further, the relationship is one of rather impersonal market exchange, potentially shielding the elder from feelings of indignity and embarrassment that would be more likely to arise in a more personal social relationship. If an American elder does end up co-residing with children, most would prefer that an aide be hired to come into the home to provide intimate bodily care, such as helping with incontinence or bathing, should such care be required. This kind of position clearly contrasts with prevalent Indian principles of intergenerational reciprocity, where Indians of both generations frequently cite the handling of incontinence as precisely the kind of service that parents and children each in turn appropriately provide for the other, and where lifelong intergenerational interdependence is a core value (see chapter 2 and Lamb 2000:46–52).

In India as in the United States, institutional living is unmistakably marked by "independence." Yet such a lack of dependence is precisely what many Indian old-age-home residents and the public find most disturbing, as it points to the fact that the old persons have no one to offer them proper *sevā*—service to and respect for aged parents (cf. Cohen 1998:117). Among the most cosmopolitan Indian residents, I did hear what struck me as quite American-sounding declarations, such as that they "don't want to be burdens" on their children and that, indeed, they value their (modern) "independence" or *svādhīnatā*. Yet, these statements came in a clear context where they signified a release of children from ordinary social-moral obligations. When I have informally chatted with Americans about their reasons for joining senior residential facilities, almost none bring up their children as a motivation at all—claiming neither that their children "threw them away," nor that they, for whatever reasons, do not wish to live with them. In contrast, in India, the subject of children *always* comes up. Even if an elder resident does not have any, that fact in itself will need to be explained.

Once after I had recently returned from a research trip to India, I was struck by a conversation held by several members of a California retirement community. They were talking about how the policy whereby residents could have more than one gate pass to enter the premises had recently been rescinded, apparently because several members had not wanted their children (who had formerly held passes) to have such easy, uncontrolled access to the facility. Such a policy to keep members' children out would be unthinkable, I felt, in the Indian context, even among the most independent-minded.

Sustaining an "Active" Life

A second major cultural aim of the U.S. "retirement communities" in particular is to facilitate the sustaining of an "active" lifestyle. Most retirement communities offer a remarkable abundance of activities, including sports, classes, craft and hobby studios, travel, games, dances, and various opportunities to socialize. Many residents believe that they are able to stay *more* active living in a community of age peers than they would if they had remained in their former homes in a mixed-age neighborhood. Even U.S. nursing homes for the more frail elderly are not devoid of the cultural aim of sustaining activity as far as possible throughout life. It is normal for nursing homes, for instance, to employ a full-time "activities director" (my own job for a year right after college), responsible for creating a full calendar of events, including exercise classes for those in wheelchairs, singing, memoir writing, movies, Bible study, visits from local children's groups, ice cream socials, and "lifelong learning" courses.

This aspiration to maintain productive activity in senior residences is in keeping with more general contemporary American attitudes about aging and personhood, which I call "permanent adulthood," "non-aging," or "anti-aging" models (see Lamb 2000:142–143, 2002b:66). In such cultural models, persons strive to *stay the same* as much as possible as they move through later life, in fact denying any changes of age (see Gillick 2006). One motivation behind such an "anti-aging" perspective is that prevalent assumptions in the contemporary United States are that if change *does* occur in late life, such change is predominantly *negative* in character—entailing loss, decline, decay, meaninglessness, and ageism (see Gullette 1997, 2004). If later life processes of change are not viewed as meaningful transformations on the way to something else positive, it is no wonder people would fight against the changes of age. Such perspectives on aging are nowhere as apparent as in the burgeoning commercial anti-aging market in America, offering a surge of "solutions" to aging, ranging from Botox to "rejuvenating" toothpaste,[8] Buddhist meditation[9] to anti-aging hormones, anti-aging vitamins[10] to brain video games and calisthenics.[11] Further, beginning in about the 1970s, it became no longer appropriate in the United States to refer to someone in polite discourse as "old"; the preferred term became rather merely "old*er*." Even potentially more neutral or honorific terms like "senior" make many older people uncomfortable.

Another facet of "permanent adulthood" is an "active" model of aging. North Americans wish to enjoy it all, to keep living life to its fullest, to feel that nothing ever must become out of bounds, that there is no fixed period when one can no longer be productive, romantic, sexual,[12] acquiring new forms of knowledge, and vitally involved in the world. Sociologist Akiko Hashimoto describes such a stance as "the vital notion common in American society that life does not come to a meaningful completion without living it up fully until the last moment" (1996:7). A brochure for an award-winning "senior adult community" in Walnut Creek, California, proclaims: "Rossmoor is a community where recreation is a way of life." Peppering the attractive brochure are photographs of persons playing golf, swimming, hiking, and enjoying gourmet meals together—"a world of choices for today's individuals." Another brochure for an assisted living facility in Massachusetts features on its cover a vibrant photograph of a stylish, sporty silver-haired woman dressed in a jeans jacket, army pants, and a bright red beret, standing while playing an electric guitar with her head thrown back into a wide smile, illustrating a bold caption, "I choose to rock on." Brochures for U.S. retirement communities also regularly feature photographs of silver-haired men and women, smiling at each other, heads leaning together, perhaps with a vibrant red rose held between them—signifying the lifelong potential of romance, the anticipation that one could move into the community and meet a new partner. Nowhere is "old," "elderly," or "aged" mentioned.

Juxtapose these images to those from an attractive, four-page color brochure featuring the Ananda Ashram (or Ashram of Joy), one of the most upscale elder abodes in the Kolkata region. It calls itself "the abode for the aged and the lonely." One sees images of tranquil flower gardens, trees, and pleasantly furnished white-washed bedrooms. The mission of the home is described thus: "Ananda Ashram is a caring, considerate, and comforting home for the lonely elders of our society in this cruel and indifferent world. An irresistibly serene and soothing habitat for the frayed nerves of the anchorless, adrift, and aged people of our society." Under eligibility, the abode is described as "a loving home for retired people, people over 55 years of age. However, people who are over 50 are also welcome." (Note that in India the English term "retired" can refer not only to those largely middle- and upper-middle-class men who are formally retired from professional work, but also those such as housewives who have passed on domestic productive and reproductive duties to sons and daughters-in-law.) The brochure in addition mentions one of the salient features of the ashram: the "promotion of Indian heritage." We will see in more depth shortly how some very culturally distinct models of aging, elder-residence-living, and personhood are cultivated in many such Indian elder residences. This brochure elucidates three important features of Indian visions of aging: elders as properly the recipients of loving and respectful care or *sevā;* late life as an appropriate time of serenity, peacefulness, and detachment; and old age as a distinct and name-able life phase (that is, "aged" and "old" are utterable terms), and one that can begin as early as fifty or fifty-five.

Medicalizing and Prolonging the End of Life

The contemporary U.S. system of biomedicine equally sustains a "permanent persons" mode, with its fundamental aim of prolonging life as long as possible, through ever more advanced medical technology. Although some Americans are decidedly uncomfortable with the notion of dying hooked up to elaborate machines and are promoting "right to die" initiatives, living wills, and alternative forms of community-based end-of-life care,[13] it is still very common for elders to be swept up into medical institutions over the final days, months, and even years of life. In 2005, in the United States, about 4.5 percent of those aged sixty-five and older lived in nursing homes, with the percentage increasing dramatically with age: 18.2 percent of those aged eighty-five years and older resided in nursing homes.[14] Many of those who do not live in nursing homes still end up spending their last days or weeks in hospital intensive care units.[15] Anthropologist Luisa Margolies writes movingly about her own mother's final five months of life in seven different medical institutions, where, without really pausing to question, or to heed her mother's clearly expressed wish to be allowed to die, medical practitioners engaged in an "all-out assault to defeat death" (2004:230).

Such practices come as part of an American deep cultural discomfort with aging and dying. We see medicine as a way to control and even forestall death and bodily decline. Medicalization is the process, very widespread in contemporary U.S. society, whereby phenomena that could well be viewed as a natural part of the life course (such as aging, dying, or menopause), or a social or political-economic problem (such as social deviance[16] or hunger[17]), come to be defined as *medical* problems, requiring the intervention of medicine to be controlled and cured.[18] We tend to medicalize phenomena that make us uncomfortable, because we regard biomedicine as offering a tangible fix—one that often masks the more complex and enduring social, political-economic, spiritual, and/or natural-life-course dimensions of our problems and fears. In the United States, aging and dying are both highly medicalized.

Byron Good reflects on the key soteriological role that biomedicine plays in American culture, where death, finitude, and sickness are found in the human body, and "salvation, or at least some partial representation of it, is present in the technical efficacy of medicine" (1994:86). "[I]n this country, we spend an astounding proportion of our health care dollars on the last several weeks of life," he observes, "so great is our commitment and our technological capacity for extending life" (p. 87). The *New York Times Magazine* reports that U.S. biologists are working furiously to defeat the genetic process of aging, broadcasting on its cover: "Racing Toward Immortality (Or at Least Your 150th Birthday)." The American Academy of Anti-Aging Medicine (A4M), founded in 1993, celebrates A4M's active agenda of anti-aging biomedical research that has, reportedly, brought millions to the realization that "Aging Is Not Inevitable."[19] On its website for the Fourteenth Annual International Conference on Anti-Aging Medicine, the academy went so far as to proclaim that doctors can now "combat aging as a disease."[20]

Although even ancient Indian medical traditions, such as Ayurveda, developed *rasāyana* longevity therapies to combat aging, and in India many relatives rush elderly kin to contemporary biomedical hospitals for treatment, aging is far less medicalized in India than it is in the United States.

Lawrence Cohen, in fact, observes that traditional Indian medical practitioners find the morality of geriatric intervention questionable: longevity therapies can be aimed preventatively at the young or middle-aged, they feel, but seeing the primary task of geriatric medicine as the denial of decline and death is unwise and healthy (1998:112). Nursing homes in India are not focused on the senior population but rather treat persons of all ages, including, often, birthing mothers. The majority of India's old age homes offer minimal medical care, and if a person becomes very ill or frail, he or she is often brought home to kin to die. The majority of older Indians I have spoken with both in India and in the United States testify firmly that they do not wish to artificially prolong their lives by partaking of complicated medical technological interventions. (As I noted above, many Americans do also feel the same way, but the U.S. system makes it difficult for some to avoid intensive medical treatment.) In the "Hindu" or "Indian" way, people say, the body should be discarded when old and used, like used clothing, or like a rice plant that grows, produces seed, then naturally withers and fades away. Matilal Majmundar, a seventy-five-year-old immigrant from Gujarat living in the United States near his U.S.-settled daughter, gave me his strong impressions of the medicalized American nursing home for older people: "The position of nursing home—intolerable. I have visited the nursing home. I have visited, yes, and I have seen people suffering. I tell you, such a bad situation has come over here. That because of medical facilities, we are living too long."

Many Indians in fact consider it appropriate and desirable for older people to express a spiritual and emotional readiness for death.[21] I am continually struck by how casually, readily, and even merrily older Indians chat about their own impending deaths, contrasting U.S. mores where death is often a taboo subject.[22] Eighty-one-year-old elder-abode resident Srimati Bela Bose, gave me the following cheerfully imparted farewell, "If I am here when you return, fine; and if by then I've gone to the cremation ground, then you won't see me." When I asked another resident how she and her companions were doing, seventy-five-year-old Basanti Mukherjee replied casually with a smile, "Age increases but we are not able to go to our destination [by dying]. God is not paying any attention to us." Hindus such as Basanti Mukherjee typically believe that dying can entail movement on to several new "destinations," including, possibly, ultimate release or *moksha* from the cycle of rebirths and redeaths (this is difficult to achieve, however); heaven or *svarga* (which is generally not thought of as an eternal state as it is in Christianity); ancestorhood; and/or rebirth.[23] For those who take for granted the notion of passage on to new forms of life after dying, it is easy to imagine that at the end of one's life it is appropriate to discard the body that has become worn, so that one may move on to new existences.

Making the Homes Indian: *Sevā* and the Family

Several of the key meanings and aims of residences for elders in the United States are not, then, shared seamlessly by those in India. The Indian elder abodes I have come to know are not aimed primarily toward maintaining independence and an active lifestyle, or the medicalization of aging and dying. Instead, those involved with the old age homes in India have tied to these institutions several important and quite distinctly Indian meanings and aims, involving notions surrounding *sevā* (service to and respect for the aged), the joint family, and late-life spirituality or *vānaprastha* ("forest-dwelling").

In both North America and India, the old age home can be a quintessential space of absence of family, a marked alternative to family care and co-residence. Yet the Indian old age homes are at the same time an *instantiation* of family values and of *sevā*—service to and respect for the aged. It took me a while to come to this realization, although later I found that it was staring me in the face, and upon re-reading Lawrence Cohen's analysis of a "retirement ashram" he had visited in India, I remembered that he, too, remarked upon how that old age home fashioned itself as a "locus of *sevā*" and an "equivalent space to the family" (1998:115). But the dominant public discourse in India is of the old age home as an archetypical sign of the dissolution of the family and the discarding of *sevā*.

Recall that receiving *sevā* within the family is a key component of dominant representations of a good, proper, traditional, Indian old age (chapter 2). And, in fact, many of the elder abodes I visited are set up expressly to offer good *sevā*. Indeed, several I encountered are simply *named* Seva.[24] Other similarly evocative names include Sraddhanjali (Offering of Reverence) and Gurujan Kunja (Garden Abode for Respected Elders). The manager of Gurujan Kunja explained the home's name: "It indicates the home's purpose: to serve and honor the old people living here. You see, they are all revered people living here." In advertisements and brochures for old age homes, *sevā* is often underscored, as in this one from the Bengali classifieds: "Placing aged husbands and wives together, we serve with great care and effort" (*sevā-jatna kari*).

Resident Ashok Bose (from the opening of chapter 3) recalled with gratitude and emotion the letter he had received from the Ramakrishna Mission Home for Aged People after applying for admission: "So long you have served us; now let us serve (*sevā karā*) you."[25] Shiven Chowdhury, co-proprietor of Atithiseva ("Hospitality," or serving guests), expressed how an attitude of humble service (*sevā*) is a priority for him, and how he always responds readily when any resident calls. Sri Ram Lahiri, manager of Milan Tirtha, in turn described, with what struck both Hena and me as real sincerity, how the elder residents receive much respect (*sammān*) living there, and how the managers and staff try very hard to care well for the residents by providing *sevā*. The motivation for establishing their old age homes, for some founders, was precisely to provide *sevā*—to elders who (simply by virtue of being elder) deserve to receive it, but who are not able to find it within their families.

Residents, too, frequently spoke with praise of how certain dedicated managers and proprietors "*khub sevā kare*"—"do a lot of *sevā*." (The work of staff members, though, is much less often described by residents as *sevā*, as I will illustrate shortly. And not all managers, proprietors, and institutions are equally described in these ways; some are more highly regarded and appreciated than others.)

Pushpa was a young, very amiable and round-faced woman who had established a modest old age home (called Loknath, after a Bengali Hindu ascetic) with her husband, renting out a spacious ground floor flat in a two-story home in a middle-class residential neighborhood. I visited frequently and felt continually uplifted by the warm, home-like atmosphere, Pushpa's delicious Bengali cooking, and the friendship offered to me by several of the residents as well as Pushpa. One afternoon, as a group of us sat chatting in the middle bedroom shared by five lady residents, Pushpa was describing how she often sleeps there at night and does all the home's cooking, and much of the hair-combing, taking the more frail residents to the bathroom, mosquito net-tying, and the like. "This is my *saṃsār* (household, family)," she added with a smile. Her own only twelve-year-old son had just recently begun to reside at a boarding school, and she otherwise lived only with her husband. A few residents interjected, "She is really performing *sevā* for us (*āmāderke khub sevā karche*)."

Sevā, which I first introduced in chapter 2, is widely regarded in India as one of the key components of proper treatment in old age—something that junior kin, especially sons and daughters-in-law, would ideally provide for their seniors, including such acts as preparing and serving food and tea, massaging tired limbs, combing hair, hanging up a mosquito net before bed, reading aloud, escorting to the doctor, managing incontinence, and offering respectful love—in short, attending to the elder's daily bodily and emotional needs and comforts. *Sevā* can also be used to refer to the ministrations a priest or devotee provides for a temple deity (images of Hindu deities are regularly offered food, water, bathing, dressing, etc.); and the term can likewise be used to refer to the work an employee or servant performs for an employer—but only when the speaker wishes to indicate the worker's unusual degree of respect and devotion, going beyond an ordinary exchange of money for services.[26]

In fact, *sevā* is something that cannot ordinarily be bought or sold. So the desirability of receiving *sevā* in a (paid-for) old age home can be somewhat ambiguous. For this reason, some proprietors specifically strive to separate out the providing of *sevā* from the charging of money. As Dr. Sipra Chowdhury, founder of Sayannya ("Afternoon"), remarked: "If an ashram for elders means a place of *sevā,* then I can't charge a fixed, standard price. That is quite impossible for me." She tells how she publishes a suggested rate, but residents and families may pay what they can, and she cares for one ninety-year-old frail lady resident with no children almost free of charge.

Residents who appreciate the *sevā* they receive in elder abodes routinely list favorably all the amenities and services offered: bed tea every morning at 5:00 or 6:00 AM, breakfast, a full Bengali noon meal, tea in the afternoon, "tiffin" in the early evening, and finally supper. The types of food are listed as well: daily fish (except for vegetarians and in the few very spiritual-minded vegetarian homes), meat once a week, rice, vegetables, milk, yogurt, at least one sweet, and a little fruit. Drinking water and warm bath water (in homes with no hot running water) are delivered. Clothes are washed (unless the resident opts to do this herself) and rooms are cleaned. Attentive and affectionate proprietors and staff, like Pushpa, go around every afternoon to comb and arrange the lady residents' hair.

I opened this book with an anecdote about the tribulations of getting early morning tea in America faced by a newly arrived elder Indian immigrant whose children were too preoccupied with their lives to think of preparing it for him. This gentleman was advised by his friend—a senior Indian man who had become adjusted to American ways—to simply prepare the tea himself; but the newer immigrant felt uncomfortable with such a prospect. In this current chapter's title, I use tea to signify the practice of being served. Seniors and superiors, in "traditional" or "proper" Indian contexts, rarely prepare their own tea, but rather are served by servants, daughters-in-law, or other juniors. Proprietors and the brochures describing old age homes in India always specify how often tea is offered, and residents who like their homes will readily cite being served tea: "bed tea" brought right to their rooms at dawn, tea with breakfast, and tea in the afternoon. In other contexts, according to prevailing talk, it is difficult these days for many seniors to be served tea, in the era of modern egalitarianism, small families, busy-ness, and individuality. (One of my professional acquaintances in Kolkata, however, a young, recently married, female history professor, mentioned to me that providing bed tea to her parents-in-law was one household duty she faithfully performs, although she had been relieved from the responsibility of housework during the day, as she was employed and busy as a professor.)

The majority of the elder-abode residents I encountered, I should remind readers, were by American standards quite "young" in chronological years (in their sixties and seventies, sometimes even fifties) and on the whole quite physically and mentally fit—that is, certainly capable of performing on their own many or all of these daily tasks associated with *sevā,* such as preparing tea. But along with many in their wider communities, most viewed late life as an appropriate period for receiving attentive care from juniors, rather than continuing to exert themselves—a period of retirement not only from external employment but also from household work. Further, most men of this generation and middle and upper-middle class had never performed domestic tasks at all, even in earlier life phases, as they had been readily served by mothers, wives, daughters-in-law, and domestic servants at home.

In these ways, old-age-home living is not unambiguously a life of independence at all. Residents become independent from family, true, but also properly and purposefully dependent on others—the proprietors, managers, and staff who take the place of junior kin by offering the residents *sevā.*

One could also say that some sons and other junior kin actually continue to practice certain forms of *sevā* through the institution of the old age home, by paying the old-age-home bills and purchasing items like medicines and mobile phones—thereby keeping material support located within the multigenerational family, even if daily service and residence are not.

About one-third of my female informants were supported financially in the old age homes by their sons (or, much less often, by other junior kin such as daughters, nephews, grandsons, and sons-in-law). Interestingly, though, only one of my twenty-five male elder-abode-resident informants—a sharp and witty man of ninety-seven—was supported financially by his sons, and this he reported that he regretted, commenting, "I don't like having to depend on my sons, but I do so entirely. . . . I regret that my job didn't come with a pension." All of my other male informants (save one supported by his older brother, and another who resided free of charge) paid their own expenses through their own pensions and savings; so, except for small gifts of items like refrigerators or computers, men living in elder abodes as a whole did not commonly receive financial *sevā* from sons.[27]

However, many women residents of elder abodes were supported financially entirely by their sons, and many of these interpreted this support proudly as an ongoing form of their sons' *sevā* and of filial love. Srimati Mina Das Gupta, for instance, told with real pride and pleasure of how although she receives a pension through her deceased husband, her son won't let her spend a penny of it. Instead, he covers all of her old-age-home expenses himself. He even pays extra to secure his mother a special private suite, set up like a small two-room apartment, on the home's grounds. When he visits once a year from where he lives and works in Delhi, he purchases for her rooms new, colorful curtains, bedspreads, and pillows. "He also gave me a phone and television," she showed me proudly. "He doesn't want me to be lacking anything." She claims not to mind living in the old age home, that it was partly her decision, as she had not enjoyed living far from West Bengal as she had done for several years in her only son's Delhi home after her husband died.

Alpana Bardhan, a sweet and stooped eighty-one-year-old resident of Loknath, cried easily when speaking of how she had to live now in an ashram for elders, after receiving so much happiness earlier in her father's, father-in-law's, and two sons' homes. But she said that she didn't blame her sons for sending her to the ashram, as they had "no other means" (*kono upāe nei*)—in her frail state, she couldn't be left alone; the sons and daughters-in-law had to go out to work; and these days servants are hard to find and can't be trusted. After weeping for a few moments, though, she would begin to smile and tell me how much her sons still love and serve her by paying for all of her expenses in the home as well as visiting. "My sons just came and spent 4,000 rupees on X-rays and blood tests," she exclaimed one morning. "They come to give me medicine—1,000 rupees of medicine!" She showed me proudly various containers lined up on her bedside table—medicines, vitamin pills, and vegetable-and-fruit-juiced-based vitamin drinks. She found there, too, a box of biscuits that her sons had brought, and she offered me two, regretting that she had no more fresh sweets to present, for her sons had brought those as well this past Sunday, but she had eaten them all already.

Of course some residents, like Kalyani-di of chapter 4 (who had fled from what is now Bangladesh, raised her family, and was then pushed into an elder ashram by her son), do not interpret a son's financial support of the old age home as *sevā* at all, but rather as a callous and previously unimaginable form of desertion and imprisonment. However, we can see how many residents and proprietors draw on what they regard as traditional images, practices, and values surrounding the strong family and respectful service to aged parents, and re-employ these in the context of the modern old age home—establishing the old age home as a new locus of *sevā,* and making the homes and their meanings in certain respects distinctly Indian.

The Institution as Joint Family?

A related way that those participating in the emerging old age homes in India are appropriating and interpreting them in their own fashion—viewing and crafting them through a lens of locality—is by constructing them as an alternative form of the traditional joint family (*ekānnabartī paribār*). Such a project goes hand in hand with fashioning the old age home as a site of *sevā,* since the most proper setting for *sevā* is the family. If an old age home can *be* a form of (intimate, sustaining, multigenerational, joint) family, then some of the more familiar meanings and practices surrounding aging—as taking place within the central site of the family—are sustained, even in what strikes many as the radically new and alien context of the elder institution. We witness a complex simultaneity of sharply divergent models: of the old age home both as quintessential signifier of the demise of the joint family under forces of Western corruption and modernity (a salient theme in so many of the narratives explored in earlier chapters), and as a site of strong Indian family values and lifeways.

The joint family analogy came up in many residents' and proprietors' narratives. For instance, when I asked the thoughtful resident Dyuti Basu of Atithiseva if their elder abode was kind of like a (student) hostel, she at first nodded but then changed her mind, "No, a 'hostel' is different—that's

for young people. This is like an *ekānnabartī paribār,* a 'joint family.'"
Several others ladies sitting with us agreed, and on that occasion and on
others explained why. They all ate food or rice from the same hearth (the
literal meaning of *ekānnabartī*—a place of "one rice" or "shared meals"),[28]
they lived together, they had *māyā* and affection for one other, they called
each other and the proprietors by kin terms, and the general atmosphere of
their place was very "homey" or "home-like" (*gharoyā*)—that is, it looked
and felt like an ordinary middle-class household, in a regular flat situated
down a narrow, cobble-stoned lane in a bustling north Kolkata middle-
class neighborhood.

This particular residence, Atithiseva, was not very large, housing only
six lady residents; but one feature of other old age homes that spurred the
joint family comparison was their frequent large size—twenty to twenty-
five people living under the same roof, eating the same food cooked in
large pots in an expansive kitchen, sometimes with not quite generous
enough portions of a special food such as *iliś* fish to completely satiate,
but recognizing that one must simply divide what is there, in crowded
conditions overflowing with people. This crowdedness—the sense of many
people living all together, perhaps never having quite enough, but also
never being alone (*ekā*) or without companionship (*nisanga*), and with
each member's basic needs provided for—was presented by both those
within and outside of old age homes, and largely affectionately, with an
air of both praise and nostalgia, as a quintessential defining characteristic
of the joint family and of the (less elite) old age home. (The few most
elite homes, featuring private single rooms and plentiful space, were not
frequently described to me as like joint families.)

Many residents' stories of coming to live in an elder abode highlighted
how they had earlier become very alone or lonely (*ekā,* from the root *ek*
or "one"—the state of one-ness or singlehood), and without togetherness (*nisanga*), before moving to the elder abode. They spoke of living in
the modern, busy, nuclear, individualized, small-flat-living households of
their junior kin, where not many people co-resided and those who did so
maintained their own single bedrooms and were busy with their separate
activities, including jobs, schooling, hobbies, and social circles. Although
the old age home was not regarded as precisely equivalent to the traditional multigenerational joint family, quite a few seemed to feel that it
came closer to such a family system—one that they had been accustomed
to in their youths—than did the modern nuclear family. Conditions that

many Americans and even the newer generation of middle and upper class Indians might find terribly crowded and lacking in individual privacy were specifically those that were valued by many of the elder-abode residents. When I asked the stooped and sweet-smiling ninety-three-year-old Ushma SenGupta of Loknath how she liked her living arrangements, she replied that she actually was feeling a bit *nisanga,* lacking companionship or togetherness, "because there are only two of us living in this room." The other three bedrooms of the ashram housed three to five ladies each, and two more beds had recently been set up in the common TV-viewing and congregating area.

Sentiments and practices expressing love and emotional closeness are highlighted in both residents' and proprietors' narratives of the close, kin-like ties fostered in the old age home. All of the residents of Loknath spoke of the proprietors of their home, Gautam and Pushpa, a warm and affectionate married couple in their early thirties, with glowing praise, describing their dedication, service (*sevā*), effort (*jatna*), and love (*bhālobāsā*). One morning I sat chatting with Ragini-di and Maya-di in the home's pleasant, many-windowed front room, where three women kept their beds, and where visitors and other residents often congregated. Ragini-di, an articulate and active woman who went out shopping and chatting with neighbors daily, and who was keeping a diary on old-age-home living in case she wished to write a book of her experiences one day, commented with emotion, "Gautam is *very* dutiful, *very* good. Pushpa, too. They 'treat all boarders as my mother.' *This* was my attraction. Gautam is not a son of my own womb (*āmār peter chele nae*), but he cares so much. I have sons, but that a non-blood boy/son (*chele*)[29] could do all this—" Maya-di jumped in, "I looked at only this one ashram. I liked Gautam and Pushpa so much, I came here. It's for *them* that I came." Alpana-di joined in to tell of how although "the girl [a staff member] scolded me for spilling water this morning," and tears came briefly to her eyes, remembering the hurt, "Pushpa and Gautam love me so much."

Not only residents, but some proprietors and managers became emotional telling of the close kin-like ties they had fostered with their residents. Manager Ram Lahiri of Milan Tirtha had held his job for twelve years, since the founding of the home (established by the well-respected Peerless organization, known also for its fine hospitals), situated auspiciously and attractively on the banks of a branch of the holy Ganges river.[30] This manager remarked that even if he were transferred to another job, he would quit that one to return to this one even without pay, since the work means so much to him and the residents have become like his own family. In about his early fifties and never married, he lives nearby with his parents. When necessary, if a resident is ill or suffering, or if a night staff member does not show up, Sri Lahiri spends the night at the home. "This is not an empty life career," he related. "One must be 'fully devoted.'" He told the story of an elderly woman resident who got sick and was dying. "She called me into her room one morning at breakfast, and she gave me a half-eaten sweet, putting it right into my mouth. She didn't think at all that I am unrelated. She just took a bite of that sweet, and then put the other half right into my mouth." Indeed, this is the kind of personal and affectionate transaction, the feeding of half-eaten *ēṭo* or saliva-covered food, that is ordinarily reserved for close kin or "one's own people" (*ātmīya svajan*), and that not only expresses bodily and emotional closeness, but also *creates* it, through the intimate sharing of substances.[31]

Aloka Mitra, founder with the Women's Coordinating Council of two of the first old age homes in Kolkata in the early 1980s, both called Navanir or New Nest, spoke (largely in English) in her typical upbeat and energetic manner of how the ladies of Navanir love her:

> Even more than food and shelter—at this age, they want love: to love and to be loved, a close connection, before they die. They think of me as like a daughter, their *meye* (daughter). I have received so many *Mā*s (mothers). Like a mother would, they do *pūjās* (religious rituals) for me, praying for my health and for my children. They also call *me* 'Ma,' because I care for them. Bengalis can do this: they call their *daughters* 'Ma,' like I call my daughter, since she cares for me so well. . . . The [Navanir ladies] say that if they can't sleep at night, they think of my face, and then they are able to fall asleep.[32]

Several of the Navanir ladies in fact shared their poetry and diary entries with me, in which they extolled Aloka Mitra as their mother, daughter, benefactor, and savior. Most of the Navanir women I spoke with had no sons and were not particularly well off, so they were especially grateful to find a place to stay, one that was rather modestly priced compared to other homes. One of the two Navanirs housed a few men, but Aloka Mitra did not speak of the men sharing the same kind of parent-daughter relationship with her.

It is a normal practice in many contexts of everyday life in India for those involved in social interactions to address each other using kin terms: merchants sell their wares to their "older sisters," "aunts," and "brothers," and household employees and employers call each other "sister," "older brother," "older brother's wife," and "grandfather." This practice keeps ordinary social interactions warm, familial, and respectful.[33] Elder-abode proprietors and staff thus ordinarily call their female residents aunts (most commonly *māsi* or mother's sister), older sisters (*didi*) and, if very advanced in age, *didimā* or *ṭhākurmā* (grandmother).[34] Male residents can be called *dādā* (big brother), *dādu* (grandfather), or *mesomaśāe* (uncle or mother's sister's husband). Interestingly, though, male residents seemed a little less likely than female residents to participate in the constructing of close kin ties in the homes, and so some male residents are also addressed as "sir" or "mister" or their Bengali equivalents such as "*bābu*." Female residents especially often refer to a close, admired, or appreciated male proprietor or manager as both like my or our "son" (*chele*) *and* as "father" (*bābā*), expressing the same kind of inversion and closeness that Aloka Mitra described regarding mother-daughter roles that can be both shared and reversed. Residents commonly addressed each other affectionately, respectfully, and familially as *didi* (elder sister) and *dādā* (elder brother), although some highlighted the peer *friendship* qualities of their relationship, simply calling each other by name.

Notably, although staff and residents also frequently employed kin terms in addressing one another (especially when a junior addressed a senior), it seemed that staff members were regarded as more like servants (also an ordinary part of a joint-family household) than kin members. So, proprietors and managers could be equivalent to sons and daughters, but staff only to servants. This was due likely to the different class and caste positions of the various groups: residents, managers and proprietors tended to share high caste and middle or higher class backgrounds, whereas the staff came from varying caste positions and usually the lower or working classes. Still, co-proprietor Ratan Ghosh of Atithiseva (Hospitality) described the staff members of their old age home as "not just workers": "Those who work here, they are very rare, *really* good; they are interested in everyone; they really try. . . . We don't look at them as just *kājer lok* (work persons or servants). If someone soils the bed, they wash it out without complaining at all. You can't find this anywhere." The performing of such intimate work involving the handling of another's bodily substances is the very kind of act that is often offered as the paradigm of what sons do for their own parents, and parents for their own children—and so this example signaled the potential of real family-type intimacy possible between some staff and residents.[35]

Several of the old age homes where I spent time possessed one quality that made these homes, at least, feel similar to an Indian "joint family" household. This was the multigenerational array of kin members, especially of the managers and staff, who came and went to and from the homes and sometimes even resided there for periods of time. This open quality of the homes made them seem very unlike the "total institutions" described by Erving Goffman—the "closed worlds" of certain of the West's asylums—homes for the aged, mental hospitals, TB sanatoriums, jails, work camps, etc.—characterized by an "encompassing or total character . . . symbolized by the barrier to social intercourse with the outside" (1961:3). Kalyani-di's and Uma-di's elder ashram, Aram (Comfort) described in chapters 3 and 4, however, did indeed fit Goffman's vision of the total institution, with its locked front gate and infrequent visitors; but most I encountered were considerably more fluid.

At the Swami Paramananda Baba Briddhashram, an ashram for forty elders organized around a central Hindu temple (the one where Renuka-di of chapter 4 resides), the woman called by residents and staff the "Ashram Mata" or "Ashram Mother" was the mother of the home's manager. She herself was widowed and similar in age to many of the home's residents, in her mid-sixties. A robust and energetic woman, she led the prayers and hymn-singing at the ashram temple every morning, oversaw the kitchen, and spent most of each day talking with and supervising the residents and staff. The manager's school-aged son and niece, a boy and a girl of ten and fourteen, also spent much of their non-school time at the ashram, doing their studying, chatting with residents (whom they called *didimā* and *dādu*—maternal grandmother and grandfather) and helping to tend the ashram's two cows, German shepherd, and vegetable and flower gardens. The manager's sister had been widowed at a young age, and she now lived most of the time at the elder ashram, although she was only in her mid-thirties The widowed sister helped out in the ashram, spending time with residents and performing other useful tasks. The staff also sometimes brought in their families. Two staff members were married to each other, and they had a baby while I was there in 2006, which they brought to the ashram daily. The residents held the baby and watched her learn to lift up her head and roll over.

In the winter of 2006, the manager's other sister, who lived nearby with her children, husband, and parents-in-law, was struck with breast cancer. Her immediate family, brother, and mother spent thousands of rupees taking her to various hospitals for surgery, radiation, and chemotherapy, but she remained in dire condition. The Ashram Mother decided to bring her ailing daughter to live at the elder residence, where she and her other widowed daughter could attend to her daily. They set her up in one of the spare rooms and continually took turns by her side oiling her skin, gently massaging her, trying in vain to encourage her to eat, and stroking her now-bald head. The residents prayed for her recovery, saying that they had lived full lives and were ready to go: "Please, God, take me and not this girl." But she died at the ashram several months later.[36] The residents participated in the family's mourning.

To really probe the ways that India's old age homes might be considered like (and unlike) joint families, it is useful to scrutinize the various local terms that refer to what may be called in English "family" and "home." *Saṃsār* and *ekānnabartī paribār* can be used in both contexts, to refer to an ordinary household or joint family (organized ordinarily around the blood ties of a male *baṃśa* or lineage), or to the domestic group of an old age home. I have already introduced the term *ekānnabartī paribār*, generally glossed as joint family and literally meaning a "one rice" or "shared meal" (*ekānnabartī*) "family" (*paribār*). The two central acts that constitute the joint family in these usages are the sharing of food cooked from the same hearth, and co-residing. Though residents of an old age home might claim that the institution is "*like* an *ekānnabartī paribār*" rather than that it *is* one, the fact that they participate daily in the two central acts that constitute an *ekānnabartī paribār* is significant. Inden and Nicholas write, in their analysis of Bengali kinship: "Of all symbolic activities, the sharing of food (*ekānna*) most clearly and concretely expresses and sustains the shared body relationships of the persons of the same *parivāra* (or family)" (1977:18). They also observe that "sharing the same house is, for most Bengalis, of secondary importance to the sharing of food in sustaining the family" (p. 18).

Saṃsār, also widely used in Bengali and other north Indian languages to refer to what in English might be called "family," is quite commonly used in the context of old age homes. Both residents and involved proprietors will readily refer to the institutions as "my *saṃsār*" or "my *saṃsār* now." Meaning literally "that which flows together" (from the roots *saṃ*, "together, with" and *sr̥*, "to flow, move"), in its most comprehensive sense, *saṃsār* refers to the whole material world and to the flux of births and deaths that all living beings and things go through together. More mundanely, the term designates one's own family or household, including not only the persons with whom one lives, but also the physical space of the house, any animals, a household's deities, and the material goods of a household, including kitchen utensils, bedding, clothing, and other belongings. All this collectively makes up what Bengalis call their *saṃsār*— the assembly of persons and things that "flow with" persons as they move through their lives.

A *saṃsār,* then, is not at all necessarily limited to a family based on blood ties. For instance, when I have resided in India for a period of just a few months or a year, if I set up a household, buying kitchen utensils and bedspreads, cooking meals and the like, people will refer to my abode as my *saṃsār.* A *saṃsār* is something that can be constructed through daily practice. However, some elder-abode residents do use "*saṃsār*" to refer to the earlier home or family that they left behind, uttering with pain and nostalgia statements like, "I still feel the pull (*ṭān*) of *saṃsār*," meaning that they miss terribly their (own, earlier, "real") families and homes. Or: "I feel bad when I don't hear any news from my kids for a few days—After all, I came here after doing *saṃsār* (living a family life) for so many years."

This usage illuminates another meaning of *saṃsār* for Bengalis, one I write about in Lamb 2000: "The *Samsad Bengali-English Dictionary,* like some of my human informants, also lists 'the bindings of *māyā*' (*māy-ābandhan*) as one of the overlapping meanings of *saṃsār*—that is, the bodily and emotional attachments or bindings that connect people with the persons and things that make up their households and wider inhabited worlds" (p. 42). According to this meaning, *saṃsār* is the locus of one's *māyā*—love, affection, attachment, bodily and emotional ties. Only some are able to cultivate such *māyā* in and for an old age home.

Two further terms that are probably the most commonly used by Bengalis to refer to one's home and family are *bāṛi* (house, home) and *bāṛir lok* (the people of [my] home). Interestingly, I never heard these terms employed to refer to the people or place of an old age home.[37] Instead, they are very commonly used to distinguish the old age home from the *real* home and kin (though a term such as "real" is not used; rather, the concept seems to be embedded or implied within the term *bāṛi*). Elder-abode residents speak of visits to and from their *bāṛir lok,* or how they miss terribly their *bāṛi* or *bāṛir lok,* or how they will have to return to their *bāṛir lok* if they become very ill. There are other more formal terms to refer to relatives, such as "one's own people" or *ātmīya svajan* (also not used to denote co-residents of an old age home), but *bāṛir lok* (people of one's house) is the term that is most commonly used to refer to one's closest kin. If asked where their *bāṛi* (home) is, residents will discuss some place other than the old age home. For most women, several important *bāṛis* can be distinguished: their *bāper bāṛi* (father's or childhood home), *śvaśur bāṛi* (father-in-law's or marital home), and perhaps simply *bāṛi* (if the woman and her husband had lived and raised children in a home of their own, or if the marital home had become and felt like theirs or hers after her parents-in-law had passed away).

The primary acts that create the very close kin ties of "the people of my house" involve the intimate sharing and exchanging of bodily substances through practices such as reproduction and marriage. A Bengali wife is considered to develop a shared-body or *sapiṇḍa* relationship with her husband and the members of his *bāṛi* and lineage (*baṃśa*); that is, she is not simply an "in-law" or relative by (legal) marriage, as she would be generally considered to be in the United States. Through various ritual acts during the marriage ceremony that involve the bride ingesting the groom's substances, by receiving her husband's seed through intercourse, by residing in his home, and by eating the food from his family's hearth, a wife comes to absorb the bodily substances that make her a substantial, bodily, part of her husband's family (Lamb 1997, 2000:207–212). Those living together in an elder abode do share food from the same hearth and reside in the same dwelling, but they do not ordinarily engage in the other kinds of intimate bodily exchanges that could transform them to become each other's *bāṛir lok.* It may be worth noting here, however, that it is perhaps the relative flexibility that women (compared to men) are regarded as possessing—a flexibility that allows them to leave one home at marriage to become part of another—that in part explains why women in Bengali elder abodes seem to be more able and inclined to forge close kin-like ties with co-residents and proprietors than do men.[38]

So, in important and revealing ways, an old age home can be one's household and joint family: a *saṃsār* (that which flows with one) and an *ekānnabartī paribār* (a shared-rice family). But it cannot be one's *bāṛi* or true home.

Here is where it might, then, be illuminating to consider a few people's narratives that highlight how an old age home is *un*like a real family, narratives rejecting the family-like models that others, both purposefully and instinctively, strive to forge as they work to make elder institutions meaningful and familiar. Ninety-seven-year-old Sri Ramesh Sinha, for instance, described his life in the Milan Tirtha old age home on the banks of the Ganges: "Here we get tea, food, everything we need. . . . But how much better it would be even to get tea from a *bāṛir lok* (someone at home)?— maybe a grandchild, who would say, 'Here, *dādu* (grandfather), I've had this half cup of tea, and now half is left—will you drink it?'" His words echo back to those of Matilal Majmundar in the book's opening: in a good Indian family, one may possibly receive less materially—perhaps only a half cup rather than a full cup of tea—but whatever there is will be offered by and shared with close kin, expressing and forging love, or *māyā*. Sri Ramesh had grown up in a large joint family comprising his father and seven of his father's brothers, all living together in the same house. He now has two married sons and several grandsons of his own, but they each live in separate households.

I first introduced Soumil Chowdhury in chapter 4, an articulate and thoughtful retired official of the Calcutta Port Trust. Although he had actively pursued his move to an elder residence, scrupulously visiting twenty-five over a period of four years while selecting the best one for himself and his wife, he expressed reservations about the move, focusing on the sharp contrast between an elder residence and the life in a joint family that he and his age-mates had grown up with. I repeat some of his earlier narrative:

> We [Indians] want to live 'jointly,' amid our relatives (*ātmīya svajan*, "own people"), not alone (*ekā*). We don't want to live alone. In 'European culture,' everyone does want to live separately (*ālādā, ālādā*). We [Indians] love to chat, to have intimate conversations (*āḍḍā*). We like to have everyone living together (*eksange*). We don't want old age homes. We want 'joint families'—sisters and brothers, daughters and sons, granddaughters and grandsons, all together. When I die, I will want them all by my side. Will I want there to be old-age-home people by my side? No, I will not. However much people say in the old age

homes that they are fine, they are not. They would all prefer to
be with their relatives. This is 'Indian culture.'

To Soumil-babu, Indian families are characterized by plentiful true kin,
talking, eating, living and even dying all together; whereas "old-age-home
people" (*briddhābās lok*) are an unmistakably distinct breed forming almost
the antithesis of the joint family, portrayed here as not unlike strangers,
with whom one lives "alone," "separately," in the imagined alien style of
Europeans.

Elder-abode resident and psychiatrist Dr. Ranjan Banerjee's reflections
(introduced earlier) echo similar thoughts: "'Old age homes' are not a concept of *our* country. These days, we are throwing away our 'culture.' . . . My
parents died *right with us.* . . . I have a granddaughter and my world revolves
around her. I miss her so much when I don't see her for a few days." He and
his wife had lived with their son, daughter-in-law, and granddaughter in the
senior man's family home, until they had departed due to some unspoken
family conflict a few years earlier. He disclosed that, whatever the minor
discomforts of living in an old age home, the real hardship they experienced
derived from missing loved family. Generalizing this form of unhappiness
to the nation as a whole, he explained that material wealth (*artha*) was
replacing family and social closeness as the prime value of the society, under
the influence of U.S. culture. He pronounced himself "against the 'old age
home concept,'" but regretfully predicted that "'old age homes' will stay
and increase in India."

Resident Bimal Mitra of the Swami Paramananda Baba Briddhashram
also rejected, light-heartedly, the family model of an elder ashram when he
jokingly remarked that, "We have all become numbers here!" referring to
the numbers painted above the doorways to their rooms, which were lined
up along an extended covered verandah. He and his co-resident friends
often referred to each other by the numbers of their rooms, seeming to be
making affectionate fun of what struck them as their bizarre institutional
setting. "Has number 23 come out yet?" "I hear that number 9 is not feeling well today." The same man also chuckled about how he was aware
that the English term "inmates," commonly used to refer to the residents
of old age homes in India, was reserved in the United States and United
Kingdom primarily for the occupants of prisons.

Gauri Chattopadhyay was another resident, a thoughtful, soft-spoken married woman in her mid-sixties, whose astute reflections on old-age-home living conveyed her keen sense that most relationships in the institution were much emptier and less appealing than were those among true kin. One day Hena and I were making our way back from a visit to a large, well-established elder residence in the southern suburbs of Kolkata when it occurred to Hena that she knew someone living in an old age home that must be somewhere nearby. Gauri-boudi was a close family friend who had moved to an elder residence with her seriously ailing physician husband, shortly after their only son had tragically died of cancer in his young adulthood. We stopped to ask shopkeepers and passers-by for directions, and came upon the Sarat Chandra Niketan home, situated on a pleasant, quiet, winding upper-middle-class residential road, lined by two- and three-story private homes with colorful clothes drying on balconies and rooftops. There were lovely large flowering trees and coconut palms in small gated front yards, and people occasionally walked by. It happened to be right during the afternoon eating and resting hours, though, so when we knocked on the locked front gate we were met with quite a deal of harsh suspicion and resistance by the guard, who said that we absolutely could not visit at that time. Hena persisted, asking him to at least let her "*dādā* and *boudi*" (older brother and brother's wife)[39] know that she had called; he went off and after some time came back to ask again what Hena's name was, and after another long wait he slowly opened the gate to let us in. We stepped into a pleasant, spacious inner courtyard surrounded by trees and potted flowers. Hena's *boudi* was leaning out and waving warmly from her second story window. We passed through a few spotless pale yellow halls and up some stairs to get to her room; it was very quiet inside; all the doors to the residents' rooms were closed; but the place struck both of us as refreshingly new, peaceful, pleasant.

Gauri-*boudi* shared a large balconied room with her bedridden husband. An assistant or ayah was there with them, a slim woman in about her thirties, who smiled amiably and curiously at us and hung out mostly on the verandah while we visited. The husband lay curled and slight under a thin gray blanket on the edge of the bed. He moaned a few times when Hena went to try to greet him. Gauri-boudi spoke of her husband frankly as no longer a human or a man (*mānus*), and said that he doesn't recognize anyone, understand anything, or get up or move on his own. Even with the aide, how difficult it is to get him to the bathroom and to bathe him and care for him! How heavy he is! "I tell him," she related frankly, with her quiet air of sage acceptance, "You should quickly try now to die. It's time for you to go. Don't take any more medicines." She struck me as a thoughtful, wise, self-respecting person, who was facing and had faced a lot of difficulty in her life, and who admitted clearly to not enjoying much of it, but who did not seem to be either truly depressed or overly self-pitying. Their room was quite sizable, with a double bed plenty large enough for her curled-up husband, herself, and a quantity of reading materials laid out between them. They had a small refrigerator and a television, a few chairs, a cabinet for clothes, shelves for their things, an attached bath, two large windows, and a pleasant balcony. Past the balcony, my eyes rested on lovely coconut, banana, and papaya trees, and a gate covered with magenta and white bougainvillea.

Hena asked her, had it been a good decision to move in here, to the old age home? She and Hena both agreed that the daily work of managing household tasks, cooking, paying bills, supervising servants and finding people to repair things were all much easier in the elder abode. She had decided to move into the home after their only (adopted) son had died from cancer, thinking, "If I have to cook another meal for just him [my husband] and me, I just can't bear it." Their only son hadn't married anyway; he had turned toward a spiritual life. He was a warm and great person and son, and then he had come down with cancer and died. They kept a large framed picture of him on the wall, garlanded by bright orange marigolds. She repeated that everything was convenient in the home—food, household upkeep, and not having to hire and manage servants.

However, she complained about the attitudes of both the serving staff and the manager, and said that she had not developed close relationships with anyone after about two years of residing there. About the manager, she described: "He doesn't really bother to get any news from us—*why* did we come here, leaving *saṃsār* (our households, families)? We don't have anyone at all. *How* will he understand all that? and *why* we came? He doesn't know anything at all about us or our background." Hena nodded sympathetically, and explained to me and for Gauri-boudi's benefit how Gauri-boudi and her husband had been *such* honored and dignified people in their society. He had been a well-respected doctor, and such a kind and wise man, and so good to and concerned for the welfare of others. They respected others and received respect. Gauri-boudi nodded and said that *this* was what she couldn't get them to understand here.

"Further, regarding the *jhis* (maids, staff)," Gauri went on, "they don't treat the residents with respect at all, and in fact they control the residents, keep them under their fists." She described her conversations with them (perhaps mainly those she has in her own mind?), using the "*tui*" form of address, the second-person pronoun reserved for one's juniors or inferiors or intimate childhood friends: "If this were your own grandfather, would you act like this? I'm thinking of you like my own grandchild; so, why can't you treat us like your own grandparents? It's because of *us*, after all, that you are here. If not for us, you would not have this job. We are not here because of you; you are here because of *us*."

She went on to describe her relations with the other residents: "At first, I used to try to mix with everyone, to get to know them, and offer them sympathy. After all," she commented, "*everyone* has come here out of pain (*sabāi to dukha-te eseche*)." But she found that they couldn't connect well. Some were less educated than she was. Others talked and complained repeatedly about the same things. Now she mostly sticks to herself, caring for her husband, reading, and choosing to receive her meals in their private room. The elder abode, to Gauri-boudi, is a convenient, even welcome, source of material sustenance, but not of close family-like bonds.

Yet the relatively alienating nature of elder-home relationships offers a protective benefit. Everyone I spoke with about this topic concurred that harsh words spoken between non-kin in an elder abode hurt far less than quarrels with kin. Where the ties of *māyā*—love, attachment, bodily-emotional bonds—are fewer, people may be more separate and lonely, but they are also more protected from pain. Suresh Chakravarti, a widower with one married daughter, explained: "Little arguments happen among people here, over food and things. That's just human nature. But if a non-related person (*parer lok*) says something, then it doesn't hurt nearly as much as it hurts when an "of one's own people" person (*nijer lok*) does . . . Where there is much *māyā*, there is pain (*kaṣṭa*)," he added. "That's why I like it here." He had mentioned earlier that he had tried to live with extended family for several years after his wife died, but that he "didn't receive right treatment there." Several ladies from the Loknath elder ashram commented similarly, while congregating on the three beds in the home's window-lined front room: "When you live with those your own age, your mind/heart stays much lighter (*man besī hālkā thāke*). We might argue a little, have a little disagreement of opinion, and quickly say one word; but then we quickly make up. That's it." Loosening one's ties of *māyā* by removing oneself from ordinary family-worldly life can also have spiritual benefits, a long-standing Hindu perspective that I will turn to next.

These stories illustrate that people understand the old age home in India, in vital, complex, and contradictory ways, to be both an instantiation of and failure of *sevā* (respectful service to elders), and both like and unlike a traditional joint family. The cultural categories of *sevā* and the joint family are central to people's understandings of what constitutes a normal Indian old age—and, in fact, it is difficult for many even to imagine aging outside of such a framework, of *sevā* and a multigenerational family. And thus these are two of the key cultural categories by which people construct and evaluate old age homes in India. Such ambivalent constructions and evaluations form an important part of the cultural process of making the old age homes Indian.

Spiritual Retreat in a Modern Forest

Elder residences in India are compared not only to the family but also to a traditional place of spiritual retreat in the forest, or *van* (pronounced *bon* in Bengali). According to the Hindu ethical-legal *Dharmaśāstra* texts, as a person enters old age, he[40] will move to the forest as a hermit, either with or without his wife, in a process of relinquishing material desires. The life phase of a forest-dweller, or *vānaprastha,* is the third of four life stages—of studenthood (*brahmacarya*), householder (*gṛhastha*), forest-dweller (*vānaprastha*), and finally renouncer (*sannyāsa*). In this third life phase, which works as a transition between material and spiritual life, the person is in a retreat from worldly life or *saṃsār,* living with as few material possessions and family ties as possible, as he prepares for the fourth and final life stage of *sannyāsa*—complete renunciation of the world, with a focus solely on God, spiritual realization, and release. The forest-dwelling life is described in *The Laws of Manu:*

> After he has lived in the householder's stage of life . . . , [an upper-caste man] should live in the forest, properly restrained and with his sensory powers conquered. . . . When a householder sees that he is wrinkled and grey, and [when he sees] the children of his children, then he should take himself to the wilderness. Renouncing all food cultivated in the village and all possessions, he should hand his wife over to his sons and go to the forest—or take her along.[41] . . . He should go out from the village to the wilderness and live [there] with his sensory powers restrained. . . . Constantly devoting himself to the

private recitation of the [Hindu scriptures], he should be controlled, friendly, and mentally composed; he should always be a giver and a non-taker, compassionate to all living beings. (Manu 1991:117; *The Laws of Manu* VI.1–8)

The model of the late-life forest-dweller is one with which all Hindus are familiar. Although most do not believe that they will actually physically move away from their households as they grow old, many even while living at home derive meaning and inspiration from the forest-dweller image, finding spirituality and detachment to be an appropriate focus of one's later years. So, even while remaining at home, many older Indians engage in activities such as prayer, spending time at temples or with a guru, attending spiritual lectures, reading scriptures and spiritual literature, bequeathing material possessions to descendants, abstaining from sexual relations, adopting a vegetarian diet, and passing time alone on the outskirts of the family.[42]

Interestingly and perhaps not surprisingly, the forest-dweller model has become a salient part of the mission of quite a few of the new senior residences in India, as well as of their members. As I noted above, the most common category of name of the old age homes springing up in and around Kolkata pertains to the concepts of forest-dwelling and spirituality. Such names include Forest-Dweller (*Vānaprastha*) Ashram (this is a fairly common name for the new elder residences across India),[43] Tapovan (a hermitage or site for meditation and religious practices, usually off in the countryside or high mountains), Bairag (renunciate), Gurujan Kunja (a spiritual garden retreat for respected seniors), and Milan Tirtha (a place of pilgrimage or "crossing" [*tīrtha*], from worldly to spiritual planes). Numerous elder residences are also named for well-known spiritual leaders, saints, and deities, such as Ramakrishna, Loknath, Mahadevananda Giri, Bholananda Giri, Mahaprabhu, Anandamayi Ma, Mahamaya, and Ma Kali. Several homes' names further highlight peace or *śānti* (e.g., Nest of Peace, Abode of Peace, Absolute Peace),[44] bearing connotations not only of spiritual serenity, but also of a related peaceful retreat from family strife. Many of the elder abodes refer to themselves as "ashrams," a term literally meaning both "shelter" and "stage of life," and implying a specifically spiritual haven.

Directors of such elder ashrams often explicitly emphasize their "traditional" spiritual missions. In the opening of chapter 3, I briefly introduced Sri Ashok Bose, a deeply spiritual-minded bachelor who had gone blind after retirement and who resided in the all-male Ramakrishna Math Home for Aged People run by the Ramakrishna Order. This home's director, himself a member of the Order and devotee of Ramakrishna, described the home's mission: to provide "a life away from the din of family, spent in solitary religious practices," "a site to pursue the *vānaprastha āśrama*," or the third and forest-dwelling phase of a Hindu man's life. An English-language brochure for this elder home describes the home's grounds as an ideal site for pursuing the ancient Hindu practice of *vānaprastha*: "The vast expanse of green covering three acres of land, the age old trees, the lily pool, the chirping of the birds, the serene ambience at dawn and dusk elevating the place to a *Vanaprasthashrama*, virtually reminds us of the ancient *Tapavana* [hermitage or site for religious practices] of the Sages away from the material world." One of this home's assistant managers reflected that the level of religious focus in their ashram "varies from person to person, boarder to boarder." He went on: "But most of us like at least the serenity, calmness, and environment of the place. There is always a spiritual rhythm."

An elder residence in Kerala, South India, similarly embraces *vānaprastha* or forest-dwelling in its revealing online mission statement.[45] The institution sees itself as drawing upon the spirituality of "ancient culture" to counter the degenerations of an excessively materialist "modern society" of "broken families," "mental turmoil," and a "strange sense of insecurity" impacting especially the aged. (Note that although in the United States a "broken family" connotes primarily marital divorce, in India, a joint family that divides into smaller nuclear units is what is most frequently described as "broken.") This home is called the Vrindavan Vanaprastha Ashram, after the holy north Indian temple city of Vrindavan where, according to tradition, Krishna frolicked in his childhood. Vrindavan is also well known for its ashrams for Hindu widows, which began to emerge as early as the early 1900s, and could be viewed as one forerunner of the contemporary ashrams for middle-class elders across India.[46] The Vrindavan Vanaprastha Ashram is situated along the banks of the Karmana River amid lush green coconut groves. Its website reads (in English):

> This is one Home where you can wake up to the chants of the mantras and bells from the nearby Sakti and Vishnu temples. Our ancient culture calls for four phases or Ashramas of one's life: Brahmacharya [student], Garhasthya [householder], Vanaprastha [forest-dweller], and Sannyasa [renouncer]. Vrindavan—the Home for the Aged—is inspired by this concept of the Vanaprastha [Forest-Dwelling]

Ashrama. Vrindavan offers a spiritual haven for us, away from the strife and toil of daily life and routines.

The modern society on one side has achieved progress in many realms. But on the other side it is encountering a few crises, too. An obsession with material gains, mental turmoil, broken families, and intellectual corruption are some of these crises, all of which have resulted in a strange sense of insecurity, with the aged being the worst affected.

Vrindavan Vanaprastha Ashram Project is a step to counter this insecurity, to offer a unique opportunity for those who are above fifty to live independent lives, to bring out their latent talents and above all to lead a life of spiritual solace and security.

The daily routines of the Vrindavan Vanaprastha Ashram's "inmates" include meditation, hymn-singing, yoga, Vedanta classes, and visits to nearby temples and woods.[47] At the same time, the Ashram offers "modern amenities," such as "self-contained spacious rooms," medical facilities and a library. It and others like it become a modern version of the ancient forest, where leaving one's (modern, broken) family and becoming "independent" acquire traditional meaning and value, where one can enjoy some of the comforts of modern living while still concentrating on traditional spiritual realization, and where the elder institution becomes not simply a Western invasion, but rather an ancient Hindu way of ordering the life course.

Elder-abode residents I grew to know also made frequent comparisons to *vānaprastha* or forest-dwelling to explain their circumstances, and then sometimes added the comment that old-age-home-living is not such a new and radically alien lifestyle after all. In the spring of 2003, early on in my research on India's old age homes, I visited a small, modest residence for six elders in the village outskirts of Kolkata and chatted with three of the residents, two men and a woman, in their common room. One question I had was, What is "new" about Indian society now so that old age homes are needed? Suresh Chakravarti insisted, however, that their arrangement is not, in fact, so new—for it fits with the long-standing Indian tradition of *vānaprastha:* "Old people used to go the forest or to Vrindavan [the holy city of Krishna known for its temples and ashrams]. I could go just as easily to Vrindavan, or to an 'old age home.' Now there's no need to go to Vrindavan, when I can have this. I can lead just as spiritual a life here." Amit Burman, a retired bachelor and ten-year resident of the Milan Tirtha elder home, called me into his private room one evening while I was spending the night there with my two daughters in the home's guest quarters. With his television still on in the background, he wished to share his reflections on the nature of India's old age homes. At first he presented old age homes as a product of modern, Western values and lifeways, but he quickly went on to interpret them as in keeping with "ancient" or "traditional" (*purano*) Indian spiritual practices:

> The whole world is undergoing a major transformation. Within just two decades, human relations have changed profoundly. . . . 'American civilization' is spreading throughout the world. For this reason, everyone has become 'self-centered.' No one wants to or has time to look after others. So, in old age, if one's children are very busy, and if a good [old age] 'home' can be found, then the old people will be very well situated if they go to the 'home.' . . .
>
> Now, you must know that the 'Indian conception' of earlier times was that of *vānaprastha* (forest-dwelling). When they grew old, people would leave their families and go to the forest, to focus on a spiritual life. This [old age home] is a 'modern' version of that ancient practice.

Sri Amit enjoys all the home's modern amenities, he commented, such as the square meals and air conditioning, but he stressed that a spiritual life is a strong motivating factor for him. He keeps a shrine in his room where he worships daily, and every few months he travels to spend about ten days at the ashram of his guru.

Several of the lady residents of Loknath also compared their elder ashram to the practice of *vānaprastha*. One afternoon they were asking me about the time I had spent living in the Bengali village of Mangaldihi, and I told them about one of the key themes in the narratives of the older people I had grown to know there. This is that *māyā*—a person's worldly ties of love and affection for other persons, places, and things—tends to increase rather than decrease as life goes on, and so that it is just when one is supposed to be ready to die in late old age that one's ties to the world feel the strongest and most painfully difficult to cut (Lamb 2000). The ladies nodded understandingly and commented together, "That's why we used to have a practice called *vānaprastha*—moving to the forest—so not as much suffering would happen. Because people would cut their *māyā* there [in the forest] before having to die." Ragini-di smiled and added in a rather enthusiastic tone, "That's like what we're doing in this elder ashram!"

At the beginning of chapter 4 I introduced Monisha Mashi ("Aunt" Monisha), who spoke with animated conviction of her and her husband's choice to sell their home, car, and belongings, to relinquish their servants and the trappings of upper-middle-class domestic and society life, after they had retired and their two daughters had moved abroad. They moved into the comfortable Milan Tirtha old age home on the banks of the holy Ganges River, explicitly to pursue the *vānaprastha* or forest-dwelling life of non-attachment. Within a few years her husband passed away, but Monisha Mashi continued to find fulfillment in her life there. I repeat some of Monisha Mashi's illuminating reflections from chapter 4, which she had shared with me over beer and lunch at the Saturday Club, one of Kolkata's finest old British-era institutions: "I came there [to the home] in the midst of full health. I don't own anything any more. But I received everything: everything out of nothing. The idea of *vānaprastha* is to forsake everything, and *then* to enjoy—to enjoy your life *through* abandonment (*tyāg*). I have everything I need living there!" Although maintaining an active life of volunteer community work and membership in several Calcutta social clubs, Monisha Mashi said that even while remaining busy and involved in the world, she aimed to do so with detachment. "Vedanta[48] says that one should try to reside in the world keeping *māyā* [attachments, ties] at bay. . . ." She acknowledged the difficulty of this detachment, but appreciated that cutting these ties to the world could bring true liberation and spiritual realization, at the end of life.

Shilpa Roychowdhury, a vibrant, dignified, thoughtful resident and co-founder of the Sraddhanjali old age home of Uttarpara, north Kolkata, had long planned to leave family life after she retired as an engineer. Widowed when she was only forty, she finished raising her son, brought a daughter-in-law into the family apartment, and slept in the same room with her beloved granddaughter for the first ten years of the girl's life. Shortly after her husband's death Shilpa-di first began to plan that she would enter a religious ashram upon retirement. "First one lives with family (*paribār*) and society (*samāj*)," she reflected, "and then it is time to turn to God." She often spoke compellingly of the value of detachment: "Everything of mine I left in [our home]. I didn't take anything from there. Aside from God, we don't have anyone or anything. I came alone and will have to leave alone. . . . I don't want to re-enter *saṃsār* (family-worldly life). If I enter it, with my son and wife, then they will become my own (*nije*). I would become accustomed to that closeness. Instead, I am living very independently (*svādhīnbhābe*). . . . No one is anyone's (*keu kārur nae*). Without abandoning, one can receive nothing. Only upon God am I dependent."

It becomes strikingly clear from such narratives that the traditional Hindu model of the value of renouncing ties to worldly life in one's later years is one that many elder-abode residents find highly compelling, and that they draw on to give meaning and purpose to life away from the family in elder housing. Even those who do not present the pursuit of *vānaprastha* as their motivating reason for entering an old age home very often spend much of their time, as do many older Hindus throughout India, focused on spiritual pursuits. Virtually all of the larger elder residences I found, those sizable enough to have one or more common rooms beyond simply the sleeping areas, contained a temple or worship space that residents visited, either alone or during morning and evening congregational gatherings, to worship, pray, and sing hymns. The majority of elder-abode residents (male and female, but especially female) also maintained in their rooms their own personal shrines of the kind that are found in most Hindu households. In these small bedroom shrines, residents place images of beloved deities, garlanded photographs of gurus and deceased senior kin (especially spouses and parents), incense, and daily flower and fruit offerings.

It is important to note, further, that quite a few residents expressed disappointment to me that their elder ashrams were not *more* spiritually focused. They had joined the ashram believing it to be a place focused on spirituality in keeping with the *vānaprastha* tradition, sometimes simply because of the use of "ashram" in many of the old age homes' names. (*Bṛiddhāśram*—ashram for elders—is the most common Bengali term employed to refer to these new senior residences.) But most of the old age homes I encountered in fact did not organize elaborate, extensive spiritual activities (beyond things like one or two temple gatherings per day), nor did most offer only vegetarian diets, as would be typical in a true Hindu religious ashram (although in many elder residences, a person can request a strict vegetarian diet, either for spiritual reasons or to maintain specific caste or family dietary mores).[49] Those who most successfully pursued a forest-dwelling life did so largely through their own efforts and state of mind.

Further, some choosing elder abodes are actually very secular and do not seem motivated by the *vānaprastha* image and aims at all. Among the most elite Bengali groups today, secularity is increasingly common, and so the few most elite (expensive, modern, posh) old age homes in Kolkata espouse a distinctly secular image, promoting modern, middle-

FIGURE 5.1. Lady residents gathered at the Swami Mahadevananda Giri Briddhashram temple.

class activities such as cocktail parties, card games, and trips to movie theaters and malls in lieu of temple worship and hymn-singing.

It is striking, too, that the dominant public discourse surrounding old age homes, introduced in earlier chapters, so negatively portrays the homes as a product of Westernization and the degeneration of Indian tradition, rather than as an innovative modern instantiation of the ancient Hindu tradition of aging in the "forest." Why? I suggest three reasons: First, *vānaprastha* is actually not central to the mission of many of the Indian old age homes and residents. Second, to become a forest-dweller is understood traditionally to be a voluntary act, whereas many elder-abode residents, as seen in chapter 4, are pushed into the homes by their kin or circumstances. Third, in some ways, there is a tension between spiritual (*vānaprastha*) and family (*sevā*) models of aging in Hinduism: to fully pursue one thwarts the other.[50] For most Indians, the pull of the family is even stronger than the pull of spiritual renunciation, and many who do find late-life renunciation to be a highly compelling life aim nonetheless strive to pursue spirituality within the folds of a loving, supportive family.

The Meanings of Activity and Inactivity

I will close this chapter on making a Western institution Indian by considering the significance of the striking absence of organized activities present in the majority of the old age homes I visited in India. Of course, residents did spend their time engaged in ordinary daily household-type activities, such as mealtimes and tea, bathing and dressing, chatting, taking morning walks, reading, and watching television. However, in all the homes I encountered—even those that offered some regular daily hymn-singing or card-playing opportunities, cultural programs, *pūjās* (religious celebrations or worship), and picnics to mark major holidays—almost no other organized activities were planned by proprietors, staff, or residents to order and fill up the day. This lack of organized activities may not strike most Indians as odd, but for one familiar with elder residences in the United States— replete with activity directors, printed calendars with a plethora of daily activity choices, and brochures advertising athletics, social events, arts and crafts, memoir writing, trips to museums and theaters, and adult education courses—the relative inactivity in the Indian institutions is striking.

How should one best interpret this conspicuous dearth of activities in Indian old age homes? One response could be that this lack resonates with the *vānaprastha* model of spiritual disengagement in late life and with broader Indian cultural understandings of personhood and aging. Old age is not, for most Indians, naturally a time when one should strive to prolong and make permanent an active adult life, pursuing the kind of "anti-aging" or "permanent adulthood" U.S. cultural model of aging described in opening this chapter. Instead, as the traditional Hindu model of the four life stages or ashramas suggests, many Indians find it highly appropriate for persons to become less active and vitally involved in the world as they grow older, partly as a technique to make the passage to new forms of existence after death smoother and easier, and partly as an opportunity to cultivate a spiritual awareness that can be lacking during earlier, busier life years (see Lamb 2000). Many Indians have a very processual understanding of personhood. Changes in old age and in dying are a normal, even meaningful and valued part of the human life course.

Further, the U.S. elder-home model of offering a broad menu of self-cultivating activities is quite an individualist and perhaps uniquely

American or Western model for any life stage. It was a U.S.-settled Bengali gentleman, whom I met in the Delhi airport as we were both making our way back to the United States in May 2006, who first made this point very clear to me. As we stood in the long luggage line and I reported to him some of my findings regarding Kolkata old age homes, he perceptively pointed out that the sort of active life—of making sure that each moment is filled with self-cultivating activities, if not with work, then with productive leisure practices such as exercise and hobbies—is a very American and individualist paradigm, not an Indian one, for persons of any age. "Do you even see younger Indians making sure that each moment of the weekend is filled with [self-developing] activities, hobbies, and exercise the way people do in the U.S.?" he asked. "True, I have not!" I concurred. As an enculturated American, I suppose, I had spent so many (to me) extremely boring, slow days simply sitting around middle-class flats in Kolkata over my two decades of visiting families there, relieved that I could often head out on my own busy research. My South Asianist colleague and friend Diane Mines also observed to me that when living in India she would be frustrated at the difficulty of finding calendars with empty daily spaces that one can fill in with all the activities one plans to do (that is, the numbers on Indian calendars are most often not encompassed within blank boxes). From this perspective, it makes sense that Indian old age homes are not designed around an elaborate set of organized, self-cultivating, active-life-prolonging activities, which for many elder-abode members would be a highly culturally unfamiliar way of ordering time and making personhoods. Marshall Sahlins reflects on what he characterizes as a particular Western cultural logic based on a certain kind of individualism, in which "each person takes the betterment of himself as his life project" (2005:23).

However, many residents spoke disapprovingly of what they perceived to be a real void of meaningful activity in the homes. For these, the elder residence had stripped away the most familiar framework for living a meaningful and fulfilling old age—the family and home—and yet offered very little else to take its stead. Kalyani-di of Aram (Comfort) described disparagingly, for instance, the emptiness, monotony, purposelessness, and utter inactivity of her old-age-home life: "We do nothing at all, nothing at all. Eat and sleep, eat and sleep. That's it. It's just a business." When I was invited to give talks comparing Indian and U.S. old age homes at places like the Dignity Foundation in Kolkata, an NGO and club for senior citizens, audience members would often comment that if their society is going to develop non-family-based, institutional modes of living like old age homes, then perhaps it would be best if these institutions also put forward Western-style, individual-focused activities. If we are no longer to focus on the family, then we had better develop the individual, the sentiment often seemed to be.

We see in this chapter the elaborate process by which those involved with old age homes in India construct the homes as complex local cultural instantiations of a globally emerging institution. Those designing and moving into India's old age homes are adopting some elements of Western ways of aging, such as living apart from families; but these elements take on unique meanings and forms. Further, other features of Western senior residences, such as a wealth of self-focused activities and intensive anti-aging medical technologies, are to date not being adopted at all. Instead, Indians are making use of the joint family, *sevā,* and forest as tropes to make meaning and sense of elder residences, reflecting powerful Indian cultural views of late life as a time both of receiving respectful care from juniors and of preparing for the new transitions of dying.

Just as the Western institution is not fixed, then, so neither is Indian tradition. In making the old age homes Indian, people creatively select certain features (and not others) of what they regard as a traditional past, bringing these features into new contexts of the present, where they take on new significances and forms. In some senses, in fact, old age homes can be regarded as a new way of maintaining the integrity of the nation in the absence of a "traditional Indian" family and spirituality. Elders are protected from the scourges of modernity by choosing, or being placed, in retirement homes that in some ways mimic tradition; and so commodifying elder care can ironically become an act not of destroying tradition but of (re)creating it.

6 LIVING ALONE AS A WAY OF LIFE

Consider four brief examples:

"Death from Loneliness at Eighty" reads one newspaper headline. A man's only son—an Indian Institute of Technology graduate—has settled in the United States. The story reports that the old father "jumped off the landing between the 8th and 9th floors, ending a solitary existence. . . . Neighbors said the loneliness was probably too much for the octogenarian to bear, a condition not uncommon in a city from which the young who will take care of the old are increasingly being driven away for lack of opportunities" (*The Telegraph* 2003a).

Narayan Sarkar, at age seventy, is a retired engineer who lives alone with his wife in their spacious south Kolkata home, their two married children settled in the United States. Although proud of their children's professional success abroad, he mourns their absence: "In our families, we raised our children—why? Our idea, our dream was that when we grew old, our sons and daughters-in-law would serve us (*sevā karbe*). And it is our dream, and a natural thing, to hope for this, to want this. We did this for our parents, and they for theirs."

Yet Viraj Ghosh, seventy-two—whose only son, an economist, has also settled in the United States—proclaims: "At this age, it's better to live separate. . . . If an old man says that he needs to have his son live with him, then the son won't advance, and the country won't advance." He resides with his wife in a flat their son has purchased for them in one of the new modern high rises springing up in south Kolkata, and Viraj-da spends hours each day socializing with friends, exercising at the apartment complex's gym, taking vigorous walks outdoors, meditating, reading, and playing music. "I am the happiest man in the world, living in heaven! I won't live anywhere other than here, surrounded by my circle of friends."

Responding to the growing number of middle-class elders living far from junior kin, the Agewell Foundation is a Delhi-based NGO that has sprung up to offer elder-care counselors for hire. Agewell offers services such as visits to chat over tea, escorts to the doctor or late-night wedding receptions, and the promise of presence at the time of death. NRI (non-resident Indian) junior kin who are able to supply money but not time or proximity can fund such services. Director and founder Himanshu Rath explains: "Imagine the counselor to be like a son . . . who takes the place of the natural child and performs the same duties for his elderly charge as a son would do." He adds: "A sad situation indeed where children cannot gift their parents' time. But this is a contemporary reality that has to be faced."[1]

In addition to moving into old age homes, increasing numbers of seniors among India's urban middle classes are also now living alone, in an arrangement that many describe as "unnatural," even "impossible" or "unthinkable" (*asambhab*), very "Western," and distinctly "modern." Abundant middle-class flats and large ancestral homes in Kolkata now house merely one to two persons—elders living singly, with a spouse, or with a live-in servant. Among the cosmopolitan Kolkata middle classes that this project focuses on, the common assessment is that the majority of families now have children living and working abroad—in cities such as Chicago, Boston, Houston, London, Hong Kong, Singapore, Sydney, and Dubai—or elsewhere in India's major cosmopolitan business centers, like Bangalore, Mumbai, and Delhi.

As with the rise of old age homes, much ambivalence surrounds this trend of independent, non–joint-family-based living. For some, living apart from children is part of a deplorable, poignant process of the waning of Indian traditions and values. From this perspective, living in a multi-generational, reciprocal family is a fading yet precious part of a more Indian, spiritual, slow-paced, materially humble, intimate, and emotionally sustaining lifestyle. Yet other interpretations of the trend are more positive. Like Viraj Ghosh, some deem that living separately can help both children and the nation "advance"—professionally and materially—bringing prestige to a family as well as to the nation of India. Living independently can also foster aged and gendered egalitarianism, and "freedom" from constraining traditional mores and tensions. It can even be enjoyable and fun, some find, as both age groups find the opportunity to pursue their own interests and engagements with peers. Nonetheless, the project of crafting an independent way of life in old age is not one that most Indians I have grown to know find unambiguously easy, or natural. As elders and their communities fashion new ways of living independently, they are also thus struggling to work out: What makes a good, viable life? a valuable, livable present and future? Is it material success and/or family intimacy? individualism and/or interdependence? consumerism and/or spirituality? modern, global cosmopolitanism and/or a more locally Indian tradition and culture?

Living Alone in India

According to the National Family Health Survey of India, more people in India are now living in single-person households than at any time previously. Those living singly still form a very small proportion of the population; in 2005–2006, just 5.2 percent of households were single-person, a number gradually increasing from 3.1 percent in 1989–1999 and 2.8 percent in 1992–1993.[2] Yet in public and media perceptions, living alone in India is a growing and uniquely *modern* phenomenon.

Significantly, many in India consider that elderly persons are effectively living "alone" if they do not reside with adult children, even if they are living as a married couple, or with a live-in servant. For instance, a *Times of India* article titled "Nation Leaves 11% of Its Elderly Alone" moves on to explain that "about 11% of India's 76.4 million people aged 60 years and above *do not have a person below 60 living with them*" (Bagga 2005, italics added). Under a column, "No Help at Hand," the author delineates: "8.5 million elderly Indians have nobody below 60 living with them," and "3.1 million of them are solitary" (that is, in single-person households).[3] A Kolkata seniors' organization, the Dignity Foundation, offers loneliness mitigation services to older "people *who live alone either single or as a couple*" (italics added).[4]

Elders I knew in Kolkata also frequently referred to themselves as "alone," "lonely," and "independent" when they were living without adult children, again even if they resided with a spouse or servant. For instance, one parent of two NRI children contacted me after a Dignity Foundation newsletter published a brief account of my research interests. "Perhaps I and my wife can be good material for your research," Dipesh Roy offered via email, "as we are NRI parents leading a lonely life and trying to anchor ourselves with NGOs like Dignity, etc." Another Dignity Foundation member, Uday Banerjee, described himself as "living alone with my wife." Recall that, as noted in chapter 5, in India a "broken" or "separated" (in Bengali, *pṛthak*) family refers most commonly to a joint or multi-generational household that has divided into smaller nuclear units, rather than, as is common in the United States, a family separated by marital divorce.

To describe in Bengali those living separately from children, Bengalis employ terms such as *ekā* (alone, single) and *eklā* (lonely, alone)—both derived from the root *ek,* "one," and having to do with being in a state of singularity or just one, like the English "alone"—all one. Both ordinarily have largely negative connotations, especially *eklā,* which often conveys the sense of feeling lonely or helpless in addition to simply being alone. There are contexts, however, when *ekā* or *eklā* can have positive connotations, especially when used as an adverb, as in "I did it all by myself (or all alone)" (*āmi ekā-i karechi*). A related term with distinctly more positive connotations is *svādhīn*—"independent," derived from the roots *svā* (self) and *adhīn* (dependent on or controlled by). *Svādhīn,* which is used also to refer to the nation of India after being freed from British rule, conveys a sense of that which is purposefully self-reliant, self-supporting and free, not under the authority of another.

Elders who speak of living "independently" or *svādhīn-bhābe* tend to phrase the matter as an act of deliberate choice and a purposefully cultivated attitude, as did Shilpa Banerjee, a widowed woman whose two married sons are both settled in the United States and who maintains a large Salt Lake[5] home on her own: "I *want* to live independently (*svādhīnbhābe*) now, and I would consider an 'old age home' in the future if I can no longer manage all on my own (*ekā-i*)." In contrast, those who describe themselves as living *ekā* (singly, alone) often present the situation as something not only uncomfortable, difficult, or lonely, but also as quite unthinkable or impossible (*asambhab*) and even not fully human. One woman living in an old age home explained her decision to move in, after she became a widow and had no sons (but only a daughter) she might live with: "*Ekā to thākā jāe nā*"—"Living doesn't happen alone" (or "One cannot live alone"). Another woman, a widowed math professor whose only children, both daughters, reside in the United States, described herself as living "completely alone" (*ekebāre ekā*), and yet reflected (in English) that "human beings have always lived together; it is not part of human nature to live alone." She went on, in Bengali: "We couldn't have even dreamed earlier that people would be living like this! . . . We had no 'concept' at all even that a person could live alone!" (*āmāder kono 'concept'-o chilo nā je ekjan ekā thākte pāre*).

Contrast such perceptions about living alone to those prevalent in the United States, where now 26 percent of households are single-person.[6]

Among those sixty-five and over in the United States, about 30 percent live in single-person households (a figure that has remained stable for the past twenty years), and about 50 percent live with only their spouse.[7] Such trends are not represented in ordinary public discourse as a problem. Rather, in the United States it is widely considered normal and even desirable for older people to live alone or especially with a spouse. What many people consider to be less than ideal is to be institutionalized. Generally, both in media coverage on older Americans and in everyday talk, the possibility of living with children does not even come up, let alone become represented—when co-residence does not occur—as a modern social crisis. (Daily talk and media stories *do,* however, consider topics such as how difficult it can be for adult children to help care for their elderly parents— emotionally, practically, and financially—especially if they live far away or are very busy with their careers and offspring.[8] The presumption in most such discourse is that the elder parents and adult children would not live together.) To the extent aging is presented as a problem in the contemporary U.S. news media, stories focus primarily on the economic burden that the booming aging population places upon the state, and on illnesses and health problems associated with aging.[9]

In contrast, the Indian media presents the occurrence of elders living alone as a serious modern social problem. Headlines read: "Alone and Insecure in the Winter of Life," "Loneliness, the Other Name for Old Age," "Loneliness, the Killer," "The Nest is Empty," and "Death from Loneliness at Eighty."[10] "Ageing Parents Home Alone" was the cover story of the 16 July 2007 issue of *India Today.* Blame is laid squarely upon the ways of modern society, and above all the contemporary younger generation. One journalist opens his story: "Used to joint family structures, the elderly these days do not have even their children to talk to, leading lonely lives fraught with anguish." He goes on:

> In our hurry to scale individual heights, is young India using the elderly as a stepladder before leaving them to fend for themselves? . . . While people are trying to better their lives while focusing on their careers, they are forgetting that they are leaving behind parents at home . . . While the present elderly population grew up in an environment that supported a joint family where there was no lack of people to communicate with, they now suddenly find themselves in a situation where even their own children are unavailable. . . . Often, the elderly have to keep themselves connected with their offspring

[only] through e-mails. . . . The problems remain constant for those
who toiled yesterday for our today. (Bag 2003:3)

Another story reports: "Bikas Chatterjee remains as lonely in death as he
was during the last few years of his life." His body lies alone in the morgue,
awaiting the arrival of his son from the United States (*The Telegraph* Staff
Reporter 2003b).

Fieldwork with Independent Elders in Kolkata

In my field research in Kolkata, I located elders living apart from
children through what could be considered "convenience" and "snowball"
sampling, rather than through a random sample of the general population.[11] Such non-random research methods can yield plentiful, valuable
research subjects, but it is important to keep in mind that my research
subjects are not necessarily representative of the population (of a city such
as Kolkata) as a whole.

I interviewed and spent time with friends, colleagues, and acquaintances I have known through years of doing research in Kolkata (quite a
few of whom now fit the profile of elders living apart from adult children);
with friends, neighbors, and relatives of this first group; with persons I met
in the apartment complex, Udita, where I lived for some months in 2006
and 2007; and with persons I met through participating in activities at
seniors' organizations, especially the Dignity Foundation of Kolkata and
the Laughing Club of Udita. For the purposes of this research, I considered persons to be living "independently" or "alone," in keeping with local
conceptualizations, if they were residing separately from their children—
with a spouse, or with a live-in servant, or completely singly. In all, I
casually associated with and had brief, often illuminating, conversations
with well over one hundred such persons, and I consider those I carefully
"studied" as research subjects to number thirty-four.[12] These thirty-four
are persons whom I interviewed at some length, usually in their homes,
sometimes at other sites, and often on more than one occasion. With some
(about thirteen) I also engaged in quite a bit of what anthropologists term
participant observation—hanging out together, sharing meals and outings, and exchanging emails, letters, gifts, and phone calls over a period of
several years. In some cases I also had contact with the children who lived
separately.

Of these thirty-four persons in my study, twelve were men and
twenty-two women. Eighteen were residing with a spouse only, nine lived

completely alone, and seven resided with one or more live-in servants; the children of nineteen were all living abroad (table 6.1). The parents of children abroad were often referred to as "NRI parents" or "parents of NRIs." Nine had at least one child living within India, though in a different city (and in most such cases, at least one other child was living abroad). Only three in my study had a child living in a separate household within Kolkata. One of these children was a daughter, and thus one with whom parents would not ordinarily expect to co-reside. The only persons in my study, a married couple, who had a son also living in the city were not originally from Kolkata. They had moved from the Punjab region of North India to Kolkata to be near their married son, a doctor. After his father retired, the son had purchased a flat for his parents to live in, a few miles from his home; but the two generations did not reside together. (This elder couple felt exceptionally lonely, especially initially.)

It is notable that, both within my study group of thirty-four and among the larger group of older persons living separately from children with whom I more casually interacted, few had sons and daughters-in-law residing right nearby in Kolkata, although such cases, of course, do sometimes occur. Neighbors of one such family described the family's story to me. The elder parents and daughter-in-law could not get along and were continuously fighting. The son blamed the situation mostly on his wife; but to make things easier and more peaceful for them all, he set his parents up in a separate flat. The son spent much of his time with his parents. More sensationally, newspapers and films periodically depict stories of modern kids who kick their parents even out into the streets, often motivated by greed for their elders' property. More commonly, one or more married sons will move out of a crowded joint family home, while at least one son will stay behind with his parents or bring his parents with him to his new home. That is, brothers in a joint family more easily separate from each other than do parents from *all* of their children, unless of course their children move far away for work or their children are all daughters. In Kolkata, to my knowledge, it is still rather uncommon for elder parents who have at least one son in the city to be living separately from all of their children.

In contrast, readers may recall that a good proportion—one-third—of old age home residents in my study had sons and daughters-in-law living right nearby (table 3.2). Why the difference? One reason is that it is in general much more expensive to set up a whole separate household than to reside in an old age home. Another reason is that many, although not

TABLE 6.1.
Locations of Children of Older Persons Living Alone

Parents have:	
All NRI (Non-Resident Indian) children living abroad	19
At least 1 child within India, though in a different city	9
At least 1 child in the same city, Kolkata	3
No children	3

Note: Based on 34 subjects

all, residents placed in old age homes are placed there at a point when they have become physically and/or emotionally frail, and in need of a lot of attention and *sevā,* respectful care and service. An old age home, but not independent living, can bestow such *sevā.* Nonetheless, in general there is much more stigma attached to old age home living than to residing alone. Those living alone are *not* generally considered to have been "thrown away" by their kin—especially if they have no sons or if their sons work far away and continue to offer financial support to their parents (which is common). Notably, however, those elders who are referred to in daily conversations with effusive enthusiasm as the "*most* fortunate" and "*happiest*" persons are almost always those living in multigenerational households with a married son or sons and grandchildren.

As my older informants make their lives apart from their children, practicing aging in new ways, I found that they are grappling with a core set of persistent and knotty questions, probing: What makes a good life? Can one bring together, or must one only choose between, sets of values that each seem at once compelling and yet, perhaps, radically opposed to the other? I frame these questions through exploring, first, the narratives of my informants whose children live abroad.

On Being the Parents of NRI Children

What makes a good life?—Independence and/or interdependence? Material success and/or family intimacy? Cosmopolitanism and/or Indianness? While doing fieldwork in Kolkata in the spring of 2006, I received the following email message, with the subject heading "Living Without Children."

Dear Sarah,

I am taking the indulgence of addressing you by first name as we have already met at Mrs. Dalmia's house at a Dignity Foundation meeting. I have just noted from our Dignity Foundation Kolkata Chapter Newsletter that you will be giving a talk on above subject on 6th May at Mrs. Dalmia's place to us. . . . Perhaps I and my wife can be good "material" for your research as we are NRI parents leading a lonely life and trying to anchor ourselves with NGOs like Dignity Foundation, etc. To have a proper perspective I briefly provide you with our background relevant to your focused area:

We have two children, daughter and son, both settled in USA. My daughter is married to her classmate, an American, while studying at University of Florida. They have a daughter. My son and daughter-in-law did their PhD from University of Texas, Austin. They were classmates in school in Kolkata. . . .

We visit them from time to time. Since we have to be with both the children, every trip lasts 4–6 months. It was exciting at the beginning but becomes a little boring gradually, as all of them go out and we remain confined at home, especially as they do not live in any mega city.

But once we are back in India, we feel lonely and try to keep ourselves occupied with some activities. Perhaps what I am saying is nothing new to you but it will help you to realize the mental state of NRI parents. We really do not know what to do after one of us is gone!! Socially in our country, it is a matter of pride to be NRI-parents but the euphoria is lost with the passage of time when both age and loneliness catch up.

Now on the lighter side: our granddaughter was here recently; she is 5 years old and could hardly follow Bengali. During her 10 weeks stay, however, she became fluent in Bengali (like you!) and enjoyed a CD on Hanuman and other mythological stories. Incidentally, have you read Swami Vivekananda and visited Belur Math and Ramakrishna Mission Institute of Culture at Gol Park, Ballyganj? You should also read Tagore and Saratchandra Chattopadhyay to know the roots of Indian/Bengalee Culture.

If you need any help/dialogue, please do not hesitate to get in touch with me, it will be a pleasure for us.

I look forward to hearing you on 6th May.

With best wishes from me and my wife Sarita,

—Dipesh Ranjan Roy

Dipesh-da's message echoes sentiments and dilemmas voiced by many: pride at their children's success abroad, yet misgivings and loneliness facing the break-up and dispersal of the family; the pleasure of making and receiving visits to and from children, yet the realization that these moments are ultimately short-lived and cannot constitute a whole way of living; regret and discomfort watching the newest generation gradually become distant from Indian and Bengali language and culture, even though a granddaughter enjoys absorbing Bengali words and stories.

I first met Dipesh-da, as he noted in his email message, at a Dignity Foundation gathering. A warm, silver-haired, and distinguished-looking man in his sixties, dressed in neatly-pressed, Western-style button-down shirt and pants, he approached me gregariously, telling me and others that I was like kin of his, as I was a countryman of his American son-in-law. He offered, then, too, that he would fit my research project. So I asked him, what should I know? How did he feel about his kids living abroad in the United States? Was he proud of them? Had he encouraged them to go? (These were probably too many questions at once, but we were milling around animatedly over tea and samosas, and the surrounding conversations were also very vivacious.)

Dipesh-da responded that, at first, he and his wife had been *so* proud of their children and delighted at their opportunities—"the chance to go to the U.S.! It's like El Dorado!"—an ultimate prize that one might spend one's life seeking. "We all think this at first," he went on. "But then, as the years go by—Now we are starting to feel lonely. There is some regret. It would be so nice if we could live closer together, so we could share our joys and sorrows. So we are beginning to feel very lonely (*eklā*)." Dipesh-da added that of course he and his wife had visited the United States several times, but that it is also lonely and boring there. The children, both husband and wife, go out to work all day long. "*Everyone* there is so busy with work," he observed, adding with an affectionate smile, "Even my *jāmāi* (son-in-law) is *really* a 'workaholic'!" And everything is so empty and spread out in the United States.

This theme—of being immensely proud of one's kids who receive the opportunity to go abroad, of training them and even pushing them to go, and yet later being hit with powerful qualms—was recurrent in my informants' narratives. For years, parents purposefully cultivate their children for professional careers abroad, then gradually come to regard such a path through an intensely ambivalent lens, though still never wishing quite to declare the path an outright mistake.

By the late spring of 2006 I had listened intently to many such narratives, and I wanted to probe further the long-term fluctuating process of parental aspiration and regret. I decided to seek out a retired couple whom I had come to know over twenty years earlier, when I had been in Kolkata (then Calcutta) as a graduate student on a language training program. At that time I had befriended the couple's two college-aged daughters, Manjari and Charu, and I recalled well how their parents, whom I addressed as Mashima and Meshomoshai (maternal Aunt and Uncle), had purposefully sought out my advice and direction, to assist in their daughters' aspirations for graduate study and marriage in the United States. Their elder daughter, Manjari, had been engaged to a Bengali graduate student at Northwestern University, near my own University of Chicago, but he had seemed to be developing "cold feet." The parents implored me to use any connections I might have to gain contact with the boy to find out what was wrong. Did he have an American girlfriend? Was he uncomfortable with an arranged marriage? Then when that engagement ended up falling apart, Manjari's parents arranged another match, again with a Bengali boy studying in the United States. The younger daughter, Charu, planned herself to pursue graduate studies in the United States, and she and her parents called on me to help her with the application process and essays. I had been very happy to be involved in these ways. That was back in the mid-1980s. Since then I had come to know that both girls had ended up settling in the United States. Every once in a while I was in contact with their parents. Recently, Meshomoshai had been telling me pensively by phone how many misgivings he had about his daughters' lives in America. I asked if I could more formally interview him about the whole process of pursuing and then living with the fact of children abroad.

I dropped in on Meshomoshai and Mashima one April morning. Theirs is a large, beautifully furnished flat on the twelfth floor of a sought-after apartment complex, with expansive views of the city. Mashima, as always, was dressed impeccably in a lovely silk sari and tasteful gold jewelry. Meshomoshai, a retired engineer, greeted me warmly and then settled into a handsome hand-carved antique chair in the front living room.

I opened by asking them to talk about how their daughters came to be in the United States, and how they felt about this move, then and now. Mashima interjected only occasionally, while Meshomoshai poured forth a long and contemplative narrative in a mixture of English and Bengali:

My first impressions of America were from two cousins. One went to MIT. He got top grades in electrical engineering and joined DEC [a leading company in the computing industry]. He talked of how America is such a good place. It always got stuck in my mind as a land of opportunities and facilities, and also of flexibility. . . . Then another cousin went to Caltech and traveled a lot across America, to almost forty-eight states. Again he gave the impression of America as a land of opportunities and facilities, and also, he felt, a land full of warm people. You see, we see the *English* as a very formal people, who look down upon us. But—and many others also have this impression—we think of the *American* people as very warm.

Before, though, the concept among Indians was that the very qualified children would go abroad for higher studies, to England mostly, but then they would return home! People would go abroad—their careers would advance, their knowledge would increase, they would receive training—and then they would come back! You saw this particularly with those in the Indian Civil Service. But in around the 1970s, two things happened. First, attention diverted from England to America. Second, the young people started not to come back. People are now going abroad and staying. . . .

When our daughters were in college, there was so much talk about who was going where, who was applying to which universities, who was taking the GRE. "Oh, she went there." "Oh, he went there." "Oh, he did this and now he is working at so and so." Listening to all this, I would sometimes get a little irritated. What is so lacking about life in India? But, as parents, we didn't get in the way at all. And we thought that when and if we *want,* our daughters would come back.

Meshomoshai portrays the parental role here as a fairly passive one; however, he and his wife had themselves been very agentive in cultivating their daughters for life in America—by sending them to elite English-medium schools when they were young, enrolling them in GRE prep courses, and seeking for their daughters only suitors among Bengali boys who were studying or working in the United States. Meshomoshai went on:

So, on the *same day* of Manjari's wedding, the *very next day* Charu left for the U.S., for graduate school. So, we lost two girls on the same day. [He paused as tears came to his eyes.] Of course, Manjari stayed in India with her in-laws for the first four months, but then she left for America.

During the marriage negotiations with Manjari's husband—he was doing his PhD there—we would ask if he was planning to return to India? And he said yes. We were comforted by that reply. . . .

Charu went to Syracuse University and completed her MA. Then she did come back for a few months, but she didn't find a good job here. So, she returned to the U.S. She thought she could work there or do a PhD. She became very independent. Meanwhile, we started marriage negotiations for her. . . .

He [referring to his younger son-in-law, now with a bitter tone, for the two are getting divorced] is absolutely *gaga* about America. "Why should I bother about India? What has India to offer that America doesn't?" That's his attitude. "America has blue sky, mountains, grocery stores. . . ." He comes here listing all the things that America has that India doesn't. . . . And, he's become very attracted by the consumerism and material-ism there. Manjari and Charu, to begin with, were also very impressed with America, but still in them, there is a little bal-ance—a sense of the value of Indian culture. But, their material desires and wants have multiplied. *That* is the basis of American society. . . .

And there's another important thing that I must mention. When they come back here, even our daughters somewhat find things here slow-moving, backward, and inefficient. And they question: "Why do you have servants? We don't have all that." We have to argue with them: "We are happy with the way things are here; and if we are not happy, then we are accus-tomed to it." And, we tell them, "There are problems in *each* country." About having domestic help, we say that this is the system that operates here. We try to treat our domestic help very well; and if we were to release them, how would they live and eat? And, we also see that *they* [people in America, as our daughters] *are always in a hurry.* There is *so much pressure* in the United States, and this is partly because people must do all the work themselves. . . .

And now I come to the next generation. There's that phrase—'A.B.C.D.—American-Born Confused Desi,'[13] which I think is very true. When our grandchildren were very young, they enjoyed it here. They got so much attention. Before, Manjari's daughter used to cry when she was leaving—she didn't want to leave her grandma. Manjari always planned a longer vacation here. But now they are always anxious to go back. Now it seems to us—it seems to us that they themselves—our daughters—are confused *deśis*. There [in the United States], they only remember small parts of their heritage. And even if Charu and Manjari are a little interested in their heritage, their children are not. For that reason, quite frankly, it seems that a distance has developed between us.

Mashima then spoke up. "So, actually, we never *wanted* that our children should go and stay there for good." She and Meshomoshai both paused, and then she went on: "But they see the glamour there, and also the education for their kids. There is less pressure there, and yet an *excellent* education, and so many opportunities for children."

Meshomoshai interjected, with a tone of bitterness, "Yes, it *is* the 'land of opportunities,' of course. As if all that adds up to your future."

Meshomoshai challenged what he has come to see as the prevailing and harmful assumption that material success is the most important measure of a meaningful life. Recently, since retirement, he has been reading spiritual works such as *Bhagavad Gita for Modern Times* and *Eternal Values for a Changing Society*, seeking ways to employ India's ancient spiritual wisdom to understand and curtail the excessive materialism and individualism of the modern and Western world. He feels that the general environment of impulsiveness, the desire for material gratification, and the milieu of individualism in America is not healthy, and that all this has contributed to their younger daughter's tragic divorce. "American culture—forgive me for saying this—is so easy," Meshomoshai reflected. "There are no rules. Materialism is so ready. People just act impulsively, pursuing immediate material gratification. All this has affected the life of our younger daughter. . . . It's a terrible situation there for her, from *our* point of view. Maybe people there say that divorce is not so terrible, but *we* think it is really terrible—that marriage is not something to be ended like that."

He and Mashima noted critically as well that many Americans, though they don't like to admit it, are quite "color conscious," and not much aware of or accepting of the wider world.

So, it is only with deep ambivalence that they continue to accept their children's lives abroad.

Narayan Sarkar, whose two children, a son and daughter, have likewise settled in the United States, also highlighted the tremendous tension between the pull for material prosperity—not only for oneself and one's family but also for one's nation—and the pull for family intimacy and tradition. A retired engineer living in a spacious south Kolkata home with his wife and a live-in child servant-assistant of about twelve, Narayan-da had begun several years earlier to edit a modest periodical for seniors called *Phire Dekhā,* "Looking Back." Subscribers, mostly other retired professionals, contribute writings and meet monthly for discussions. They speak often of the radical changes taking place in their families, nation, and world.

"As young men," he told, "we dreamed of our country's success, that it would be independent and prosperous. But now the young men have everything, and so they have no dream." The brilliant Indian boys of his own generation would work very hard to study at the best institutions, sometimes going abroad to England, in order to secure senior government positions or to become doctors *within India,* to help build the nation. These adults watched their country begin to prosper, and they themselves rose to a comfortable middle or upper-middle class. When they had children of their own, they gave these children everything they could. "People began to have smaller families—just one or two kids," Narayan-da recounted, "so they could give proper attention to each. They gave these children the *best* education; they did *everything* they could for these brighter girls and boys. Whatever they themselves had wanted to be but couldn't be—they tried to fulfill through their children. And they felt that their children *had* to go abroad to get the best chances, and the children were very easily getting chances abroad."

He was speaking, of course, not only of his peers' lives but his own. His one son had graduated from India's most elite institution, the acclaimed Indian Institute of Technology (IIT), and his daughter had achieved an MBA; both were prospering in the United States. He mentioned not only his children, but so many nieces, nephews, and friends' and colleagues' children who were all living and working in the United States, listing the professions and locations of each, one by one.

"Is this—so many children going abroad—a good or bad thing?" I inquired.

"My idea is that it is a *problem,* so it is bad," Narayan-da replied decisively. "My children who have such qualifications, why are they in *that* country (*odeśe*)? Why not in *our* country (*āmāder deśe*)?"

Narayan-da's wife, Manisha, interjected quietly: "They wouldn't get a good 'placement' here."

Yet Narayan-da insisted: "No, they *would* find a good job here. They should 'develop' their *own* country. 'All the well-educated kids should come back to India, to develop their country, and be near their parents.'"

Manisha-boudi, in an attempt to defend her children: "It's no one's fault (*doṣ*)."

Narayan-da replied, "I'm not accusing anyone. The answer is just this: you see, in our families, we raised our children—why? Our idea, our dream (*svapna*) was that when we grew old, our sons and daughters-in-law would serve us (*sevā karbe*). And it is our dream, and a natural thing, to hope for this, to want this. We did this for our parents, and they for theirs."

Narayan-da confronts a failed reciprocity, a radically new way of organizing families, generations, old age. He paused, then continued with an air of bitter irony, acknowledging that it was to a large extent his own agency that had brought him and his children to the current situation that he disparages: "A bonus of my career was that we gave them a good education. And then this—with that great education, they leave. I want *two* things, you see: I want maximum studying for my son. I want my son to do maximum studying, at the *best* schools, with the *best opportunities.* AND: I want that he will stay here, and that I will live with him."

Narayan-da yearns for two things at once that perhaps cannot both be had. He confronts prosperity displaced onto an alien nation, meaningless materialism, and loneliness. Some children abroad, he mentioned, do keep their parents happy and in an affluent condition by sending them money, but such material gifts bring little fulfillment.

Like Meshomoshai, Narayan-da ultimately condemns above all the excessive materialism of the current lifeway, a materialism that multiplies uncontrollably in a pointless fashion: "Now people are thinking only according to the clock. Whatever you earn, you have to spend. And whatever you desire, you have to earn. They have to run after that wild goose. You earn as much as you can to get those things—car, house, microwave." And in the process, families fall apart, elders are left alone, and India becomes a very different place.

These men's and others' sentiments are depicted unabashedly in an article titled "Is It Desirable If One's Children Settle Permanently Abroad?" appearing in a Bengali-language newspaper in June of 2003 (Choudhuri 2003). The article relates a range of parental opinions, under six separate headings:[14]

1) I'm at Peace If They Are Well.

   (It's the mother's first duty to consider the welfare of her children, isn't it? If we know that he is happy and well, then we will also be happy and well.)

2) I Would *Never* Want That.

   (My hope is that my son will go abroad for several years, acquire an education, and then return. I would never want him to stay there for good.)

3) It Brings Material Prosperity.

   (Spending just a few years working abroad can bring material prosperity. But I haven't yet heard that they plan to settle permanently. I do have the hope that one day they will return.)

4) I Would Like It If He Returned Home [to *Deś*].

   (We are facing difficult times now. We spend so much money and effort raising and educating our children, but there are no job opportunities here. Still, I will be *very* happy if my son returns home to settle permanently. But that all depends on him.)

5) Where Are the Jobs in This Country?

   (If after making much effort to find a good job here, one still can't find a job, then what else is there to do but go abroad?)

6) It's Our Disorderly Education System That Is Responsible.

   (These days our whole educational system is in a precarious state, and there are no good jobs here. However, how many more people do we have the capacity to send abroad?)

Despite the range in degrees of sanguinity and despondency in these narratives, a common theme stands at the forefront of each: the weighing of material prosperity versus family intimacy. On the one hand, children, their parents, and the nation seek out the affluence and prestige that comes from securing good jobs abroad; and yet on the other, it is only if children remain at home that people can sustain what they perceive to be a valued and *Indian* system of intergenerational reciprocity, co-residence, and family intimacy. In the article's accompanying cartoon, the (all male) children on one side leap wildly after foreign dollars and pounds, dressed in Western-style suits and doctors' coats, while their elder parents line up, somber and perplexed, outside a *bṛiddhābās* or old age home. I should note that there is some public discourse now that, as India's economy develops, more and more overseas children will begin to return, but so far such a trend is not widely apparent in Kolkata.[15]

Cultivating Independence

Even as NRI parents wonder whether material prosperity is really the ultimate meaningful "goose" to chase in life and worth this much sacrifice, a regular point of discussion among NRI parents is the pride and sense of accomplishment they feel in having fostered their and their children's mutual independence. They had promoted such independence by raising their children in cosmopolitan households, sending them to elite English-medium schools, funding higher education abroad, encouraging the pursuit of prestigious professional careers, and espousing bourgeois principles such as independence, freedom, self actualization, and personal fulfillment.[16]

Along these lines, some NRI parents present the older system of intergenerational living as flawed in certain respects—perhaps impractical, or restrictive, or fostering thwarted expectations. Basanti Chowdhury, a retired psychologist who lives alone with her husband, their one daughter settled in the United States and their son in Mumbai, reflected: "The old concept was that people stayed together—one must have a son to take care of one in old age. That concept *is* still there, but it's not practical. Why have those expectations in the first place? If one has no expectations and a child does do something for one, one can be *doubly* grateful." Nalini Mukherjee—who at eighty-three lived entirely alone save for a few live-in servants, her husband deceased and her two children in the United States—did not speak of a past system of generational co-residence with sentimentality. She commented that children enjoy joint family living, and that her own mother-in-law had been OK, but that for most adults, joint families are both good and bad. Her own two children abroad are very pleased with their lives there, and about herself, she described matter-of-factly: "I'm doing fine. I've adjusted. It's a very routine life, but I'm at peace. I've learned to accept all things. . . . I've become very independent (*svādhīn*)." Bharati Bose, a widowed math professor who lived absolutely alone, described her two daughters as "feminists," who cannot abide by the dress and other restrictions for women in India. Both feel very fulfilled working as professors in the United States, where they can easily insist on their right to wear pants rather than saris to campus every day. Some remark as well that many old people feel lonely even living with families. S. Swaminathan, a widower for the past twelve years who lives entirely alone, observed, "Generally we are a very family-oriented people. My whole life revolved around my children. Naturally, if I could stay with them, I would. But I can't, because they are abroad. My children would allow me to live there, but I wouldn't want to—I prefer to stay alone." Later he added, "Although I am alone, I don't feel lonely. . . . Some senior citizens stay *with* their families and feel lonely."

In fact, rather than settle permanently with their children abroad, many NRI parents very deliberately choose to remain in India, even when their children are urging the parents to join them. So, family togetherness does not always trump as a life aim, either for elders or for their children. The key reason elders provide for refusing to settle abroad is that such a move ends up entailing a relationship of utter dependence of the parent on the child. Although Indians widely find it normal and appropriate for an elder parent to depend on an adult child, most feel that the parent would, ideally, retain some significant degree of self-reliance. For instance, the whole family may be living in the *parent's* home, rather than the parent in the child's; the parent may maintain his or her own savings account and/or pension; the parent may have many relatives, colleagues, friends, and neighbors nearby with whom he or she can freely associate; and the parent may be able to get around independently to nearby markets, social contacts, and temples, by foot, bus, or taxi. However, in places like the United States, the elders find that they become utterly and completely dependent on their children, not only for material support but also for transportation, entertainment, and almost all social contact. They feel easily bored, isolated, and demeaned. Visits of up to several months can be very enjoyable, but not permanent residence.[17]

So some parents have quite purposefully cultivated independence in their children and themselves for years, preparing for separations. Basanti Chowdhury and her husband, for instance, sent their children to boarding schools from a young age, so that both they and their children could learn to live independently. They spoke disparagingly of one other son they knew who was so doted on by his parents that he had to return to India from the United States after just one year; but in contrast their children are able to get along very easily abroad. When Basanti's voice broke briefly as she offered, "But we do feel that we miss out, too. One misses out, too, when they are far away," her husband quickly chided her for her moment of sentimentality: "Life is like that! One can't have everything in life. That's why they've grown up so well." Basanti promptly re-donned a stalwart, optimistic stance, "Yes, our duty is to teach them, to *help* them, stand on their own two feet."

Those living alone purposefully develop new routines of filling up the time and managing independently—through practices such as delaying retirement (when possible),[18] exercising, devoting themselves to volunteer work, joining the flurry of new clubs for senior citizens, attending spiritual lectures, and going to cyber cafes in the evening even if one has a computer at home. NRI parents also exchange phone calls, emails, gifts, and visits with children and grandchildren; install webcams in their homes; and socialize with other kin and friends in the city. More frail, home-bound elders generally require the services of live-in servants, some of whom have worked for the elder and his or her family for years.

A common theme in elders' daily narratives is also that one must establish and maintain one's own financial autonomy. Narayan Sarkar, the editor of *Phire Dekhā* (*Looking Back*), reflected: "In my day, parents had to depend on their children. There was no other option and we imagined no other way. Now we—those of us who are growing old now, of my generation—have become very conscious of making our *own* provisions. So we won't have to stay with our children. It's a matter of personal prestige." He went on to explain how the young generation wants to go by their own style, which is often now a Western style, and this is not always acceptable to the old. A "clash of cultures" occurs when both generations try to live together. A Dignity Foundation member, a widowed gentleman who lived alone, commented:

> With the passage of time, we have witnessed so much change, and so parents have become cleverer now. For example, they

are not *so* generous to their children now. Modern parents will give some things to their children but will also keep property in their own name. Because they know that they cannot *count on* their children to provide for them. So, you see, I am more or less self-sufficient. At the same time, I love my children, and they love me. I pay visits to my children, and they pay visits to me. But, I do not *expect* them to support me.

A key theme of the blockbuster Bollywood film *Baghban,* along with the despicability of modern, selfish kids, is the self-sufficiency of the dyadic married couple: it is today wiser and better, more fulfilling and dependable, for elderly persons to plan to rely on each other and themselves, rather than to hope to depend on children. As narrated in chapter 2, the storyline unfolds first as a father and his wife, Raj and Pooja Malhotra, raise their four sons with great devotion and generosity, fully expecting the grown sons and daughters-in-law to care for them in return in their old age. But once the father retires and invests his remaining assets in his children, the children no longer have any use for the parents, treating them with contempt and neglect. In the end, the hero has published a best-selling novel based on his mistreatment at the hands of his sons; he becomes an overnight million-aire, the sons and daughters-in-law come groveling back, but the father has become wiser. He has come to realize that he needs no one other than him-self and his wife: "If I can raise children who can walk, talk, and understand anything, then I can also raise myself. I don't need to have any expectations of anyone because I am very fortunate. I am fortunate because life has given me such a partner that when I walk with her all the paths become easy, all the problems get resolved. And that partner is my wife."[19]

Love in the Time of Distance

Independence, however, does not entail a lack of love; many NRI parents emphasized this point to me. Although some have a hard time conceptualizing the persistence of real love—*bhālobāsā* (love), or *māyā* (ties, affection, conceived of as both bodily and emotional in nature)[20]—at a distance, absent daily material exchanges and co-residence, many others stressed that they basked in even long-distance love. "Out of sight is not out of mind!" Viraj Ghosh exclaimed regarding the sentiments of NRI parents. "Out of sight is *very* much in mind!"

Viraj Ghosh's sentiments were echoed by many, including Anjali and Sharad Das Gupta, who emphasized effusively, "Our daughter is *always* on our minds!" Sharing a very cheerful disposition, Anjali and Sharad resided only with each other in a lovely flat on the eighth floor with front-to-back windows offering pleasing cross-ventilation and panoramic views of the city. Anjali this day was dressed in a deep green silk sari and red shawl, her hair dyed black and pulled into an attractive knot; Sharad was just back from the market carrying bags of fresh vegetables and fruits. Their only daughter, son-in-law, and two young grandchildren reside in the United States, where the son-in-law is a professor and their daughter at present is staying at home to care for the children. They asked me if I knew of a poem by Rabindranath Tagore, which they found beautifully expressed their sentiments regarding living with their beloved daughter abroad. A young girl plays in the waves on the beach, so secure of her mother's devotion that she forgets even that her mother is there: "*Tomār pūjār chole, tomāe bhule thāki.*" "This is the attitude that we live by," Anjali went on, with an air of generous enthusiasm. "Our daughter is *always* on our minds! But *we* are happy because *she* is happy there! . . . We gave *everything* to our daughter, whatever maximum possible! And even when they call now, we come—we come *immediately!* We take the *best* presents from India, the *best* care, the *best* love! And this way, basking in our love, she can live there feeling very happy and secure."

Basanti Chowdhury emphasized as well that just as a parent does not forget a child, a child's love for his or her parents will be never-ending, no matter what the circumstances or distance of miles. Just after she stressed that parents should not *expect* their children to care for them, she remarked that, nonetheless, no matter how far away they live, children will always feel a pull or *ṭān* for their parents: "You know how they say in India . . . that when the body is burnt after death, and there are only ashes left, still the umbilical cord or *nāṛī* will not be burnt. . . . No matter how much we deny it, that pull, that *ṭān,* towards one's parents, one's mother especially, will *always* remain." Bengalis also frequently commented to me that Bengalis, and Indians in general, are very *āntarik* (deeply feeling, internal, heartfelt), "sentimental," and "emotional." They distinguished themselves from Americans in this regard, and explained that that's why independent living doesn't come naturally or effortlessly to them.

The Commodification of Care?
Elder-Focused NGOs and the Outsourcing of *Sevā*

To offer social, emotional, and practical support for elders living apart from junior kin, a new industry of extra-family aging is emerging in India. We have already examined the rise of old age homes in the nation, a largely market-based institutional form of non-family aging. Yet an increasing number of both charitable and for-profit elder-care organizations are also materializing to offer support to financially well-off elders living in their own homes—another form of outsourcing of care from the family to the market and NGO. Nonprofit nongovernmental organizations (NGOs) as well as private businesses provide services such as around-the-clock telephone help lines, escorts to doctors' appointments and late-night wedding receptions, meal delivery, and visits to chat over tea. It is often NRI children who fund the services for their parents in India, able to supply money but not time or proximity.

A couple in the Delhi suburbs, Mr. and Mrs. Saksena, has started one such business to look in on the elderly parents of NRI children. It is the children who are the paying "clients" (at $5.00/hour), and the Saksenas visit the senior parents as "friends of their son/daughter overseas." Their motto is, as Mr. Saksena reported to me by email, "to do whatever we are asked to do, provided it is not illegal," including routine visits to chat over tea; escorting to doctors' appointments, railway stations, airports, and social events; taking out on special occasions—to dinner, the movies, concerts, religious festivals; arranging cakes, flowers, and the like for birthdays or anniversaries; and, finally, being present at the time of death. Mr. Saksena continued to comment by email: "Typically, it takes anywhere between 24–48 hours for our non-resident clients to arrive in India. As such we have to be present with the [dying] elderly to provide emotional support and make arrangements for the funeral. Not a very pleasant task, but it has to be done."[21]

The Agewell Foundation, an NGO launched in 1999 in New Delhi, offers similar services: home visits, escorting, assistance filling out tax forms, platforms to socialize with fellow seniors, and a telephone helpline to aid in solving loneliness, legal, medical, financial, and other problems. NRI children can sponsor their parents, paying Rs. 5,000 (a little over $100) for a lifetime membership. As noted in the chapter's opening, Himanshu Rath, director and founder of Agewell, compares the hired counselors to "surrogate sons," explaining: "Imagine the counselor to be like a son . . . who takes the place of the natural child and performs the same duties for his elderly charge as a son would do. The presence of a younger person in the house gives these old people something to look forward to." Rath adds that the response from children who can't spend time with their parents has been overwhelming. "Agewell allows children to gift the membership to their parents. A sad situation indeed where children cannot gift their parents time. But this is a contemporary reality that has to be faced."[22]

The Dignity Foundation, founded in 1995 in Mumbai, offers "Senior Citizens Life Enrichment Services," with branches now in Kolkata, Pune, Navi Numbai, and Chennai.[23] This thriving organization provides a range of programs for senior members, many of whom are active volunteers in the program and who thereby assist themselves as they assist others, through forging meaningful post-retirement work and companionship. The organization offers monthly gatherings and lectures, subscription to the *Dignity Dialogue* periodical, computer training, day care for those with Alzheimer's, "loneliness mitigation" fieldtrips, second-career advice, companionship visits, and a telephone helpline staffed by both Dignity volunteers and a few paid social workers. The organization is not geared exclusively toward those who are living separately from children, for as a social worker from the Kolkata branch explained, some elders in the city are living *with* children and yet are lonely, abused, or neglected. Reportedly 50 to 90 percent of calls the Kolkata branch receives are related to loneliness, and the senior volunteers who pay visits to home-bound members go primarily to chat, have tea together, read aloud, inquire after the elders' health, and perhaps run a few small errands. Members are eligible to receive most services simply through paying the annual Rs. 1,000 ($20 to $25) dues.

Other similar organizations include Astha in Kolkata, founded in 1997 by a medical doctor, which offers for an annual fee an around-the-clock medical help line for seniors living alone, and is marketed not only to Kolkata seniors but also to their children living abroad. YourManInIndia (YMI) began as an enterprise offering healthcare for the aged parents of busy and distant NRIs and has now expanded to offer a full range of concierge services. The *Times of India* reports: "Busy yuppies outsource errands to new chore bazaar: From Looking after Old Parents to Walking the Dog, These Corporate Jeeveses Do It All" (Kamdar 2004).

As with old age homes, both positive and negative assessments abound regarding the outsourcing of care tasks from junior kin to private organizations. Indian gerontologists, in fact, frequently advocate developing alternatives to the family, at times presenting "traditional" family-centered modes of aging as "backward." Shovana Narayana is quoted as proclaiming, for instance, in a 2001 *Asian Age* article: "The self-sufficiency of the elderly is a very healthy trend. . . . The *problem* lies in the *rural mind set* where people consider their children as a support system for their old age" (Gupta 2001, emphasis added). The article comments approvingly that organizations such as Agewell help promote a "segment of old people who are financially independent, choose to stay on their own . . . [and] who can look after themselves without being burdens on their children" (Gupta 2001). Such attitudes are in keeping with ones commonly found in Western academic and policy literature on care work, where a frequent assumption is that it is better, more advanced, and more egalitarian for nations to develop both market- and state-based modes of care (for elders, the sick and disabled, and—more ambivalently—children),[24] so that the "burden of dependence" does not fall on unpaid family caregivers, especially women.

Much of the public and media discourse in India on the outsourcing of in-home care from the family to the market, however, is quite negative (although generally not nearly so scathing as public reactions to old age homes). Hearing of the emergence of hired elder care, a colleague's mother and grandmother used to implore her and other kin to please never let the private crevices of their bodies be touched or cared for by the hired hands of strangers/non-kin (*parer lok*). Critical newspaper coverage disparages not so much the organizations themselves as the wider society and especially the current generation of "impatient," "un-caring," "selfish" and "materialistic" younger people who have impelled such organizations to develop.

As is the case with the negative feelings toward old age homes, much of the discomfort surrounding elder-care organizations pertains not only to tensions regarding non-kin performing what kin would traditionally do, but also to the added anxiety of introducing *money* into a relationship where it ordinarily does not belong—that is, the commodification of care or *sevā*. Many Indians are profoundly uncomfortable transforming *sevā* from a fundamentally domestic social practice, embedded within relations of lifelong intergenerational reciprocity, to a public market-based commodity.[25] Keith Hart (2005) reflects in his "Notes towards an Anthropology of Money" that "money in capitalist societies stands for alienation, detachment, impersonal society, the outside," fundamentally antithetical to "a protected sphere of domestic life, where intimate personal relations hold sway, *home.*" Anthropologists (such as Carrier 1995, Gregory 1982, Mauss 1967)—as well as frequently their informants—have often distinguished in similar ways between "impersonal" commodity exchange (presupposing the independence of the transactors) and "personal" gift exchange (presupposing the reciprocal interdependence of the parties), although scholars such as Elizabeth Ferry (2005) and Jonathan Parry (1989) complicate the distinction as constructed across diverse cultural contexts.

In India, market exchange (for better and worse, in people's minds) *is* indeed very often specifically regarded as an impersonal medium of exchange. Using money as a medium, buyers and sellers may interact with mutual independence; no intimate bodily substances are transferred. This impersonality can be very useful in certain contexts; for instance, those concerned with matters of, say, caste purity may, using money, buy and sell items freely with people of diverse caste ranks without concern over undue intimate interaction or the transfer of polluting bodily substances. In contrast, *sevā* is ordinarily one part of a long-term intimate kinship relationship of reciprocal interdependence. *Sevā* ordinarily provides, then, not only the performance of certain tasks (serving tea, combing hair, paying bills) but also the forging and sustaining of intimate bodily and emotional intergenerational ties (chapter 2). Can it still be *sevā* if bought and sold on the market?

Finding herself facing just such a question, Papri Chowdhury, founder of a neighborhood-based organization for elders living alone called Jana Hitaya (For the Welfare of People), remarked fervently: "*Sevā* (service to and respect for the aged) is *not* something that can be bought or sold." Elder members themselves, or their junior kin (often from abroad), can request services from Jana Hitaya such as visits over tea, reading aloud, or escorting to the doctor or a spiritual program. But Papri is firm that she cannot *charge* for these services, this *sevā:* Instead, people who *wish to* make donations to the organization may do so at any time—but not at the same time that services are being rendered: "*Sevā* is not something that one can sell or buy. I am totally against the idea that only those who give money will receive *sevā.*"

In fact, Papri Chowdhury prefers to call her organization a "joint family," rather than an NGO, a term that connotes, she says, just as does money, the "distant" and "impersonal." Papri describes Jana Hitaya's work as "*sevār kāj*," the work of *sevā* or service to elders. She founded the organization with her husband and one other couple—all four in middle age (not yet retired, but with children grown and living abroad), and they offer, with the help of volunteers, home visits to elders; monthly gatherings (for spiritual lectures, music, and discussion); a periodical that publishes elder members' writings; escort services; an annual picnic; and occasional medical clinics at which local physicians donate their services. Jana Hitaya aims to "view senior citizens with *respect,* not *pity,*" and Papri states that she and the other volunteers espouse the Indian philosophy that "*I* am the one who is grateful, for I get the *opportunity* to do something for you."

Other elder-care organizations similarly tend to purposefully steer away from a straightforward commoditized "elder care for hire" framework, for instance by comparing hired counselors to "sons" (as does Agewell) or "friends of a son or daughter overseas" (the Saksenas), or by setting up the organization as a social "club," where "members" pay a fee to join but not to directly exchange money for services. Importantly, further, both the volunteers and the paid counselors or "sons" working for such organizations generally share with the elder care recipients a similar (middle- or upper-middle-) class background, making it easier for all parties involved to imagine the relationship as personal and kin-like.

Interestingly, and in contrast to prevalent Indian conceptions, it is precisely because paying for care work is impersonal that many North Americans prefer to hire a caregiver than to rely on a family member or friend, in order to maintain a cherished sense of independence (see Rivas 2002). So, with a degree of uncertainty mixed with relief and sometimes pleasure, some elders and their junior kin are turning to new public yet personal providers of care—to find "son-like" relationships among volunteers and paid visitors working for *sevā*-offering NGOs.

Relations with Servants

In thinking about the emerging trend in India of outsourcing elder care from the family, one must consider the long-term practice of hiring servants. The majority of middle- and upper-class families in both rural and especially urban India hire servants or "work persons" (in Bengali, *kājer lok*) to help with many features of household work, including cooking, dish and clothes washing, housecleaning, marketing, and various acts of serving, such as providing tea, water, snacks, and errands for persons of any age, and baby-sitting and elder-sitting for those needing special care.[26] This kind of arrangement has long existed in India and is not interpreted within daily and media discourse as a particular feature of modernity (pertaining to the intrusion of a capitalist economy into the domestic realm, or the global dispersion of India's young professionals, or the growing prevalence of women in the workforce). Indians widely regard it as perfectly acceptable, in fact, for servants to provide child and elder care, *if* the serving takes place in the context of a household where the adult householders (the parents of young children, or the children of old parents) also live. Since young children do not generally live separately from their parents, child care has not become in India the same kind of hot button issue that elder care has. When elder care by servants takes place in the absence of co-resident kin, *this* is, to many, a contemporary social problem.

To be sure, however, not all elders who live alone with the assistance of domestic workers find the situation to be problematic. Aparna Das Gupta, a widowed woman and retired professional whose only son and daughter-in-law reside abroad, lives with only her servant, a younger woman who has been with the family for more than twenty years. Several of my informants, in fact, had similar living arrangements. From the perspectives of the elders (I did not interview any domestic workers in meaningful depth), many of these long-term relationships work very well. Aparna Das Gupta stated warmly: "I don't feel like I am living alone; I have Shalini with me." Some companionship is provided, another person is there in case of emergency, tea and food are served, errands are run. Many employer-domestic worker relationships are, in fact, very affectionate and take on some kin-like qualities. Most employers and domestic workers refer to each other using kin terms, such as "sister," "elder brother's wife," or "aunt." And employers who have established long-term relationships with domestic workers give much more than simply a salary, customarily providing meals, gifts of clothing at major holidays, money to help pay for a child's schooling or wedding, small items of jewelry, doctor's fees, and emergency loans. Domestic workers in turn can be the source of forbidden pleasures for elders with restricted mobility, affectionately going against a family's or doctor's instructions, by surreptitiously supplying cigarettes, sweets for the diabetic, or extra spice in curries that are supposed to be bland.

However, many Kolkatans argue that it can be extremely trying and thorny attempting to set up domestic help for older people living alone, citing a number of prevailing causes for concern. First, servants do not generally provide *sevā* (respectful service toward elders), but rather *kāj* ("work," as reflected in the common Bengali term for servant noted above, *kājer lok*, "work person"). So, if only servants but no kin perform care work, is the elder receiving *sevā*? Second, solitary elders can be tediously stuck at home having to listen to the same monotonous stories of their servants, without a household full of other members to dilute and enliven the conversations. Third, it is very difficult these days to find capable and trustworthy servants. Finally, and relatedly, widespread public discourse has it that solitary elders are easy and vulnerable targets of theft and violence at the hands of their servants. Many sources relayed stories of servants pocketing gold chains as they massaged elders' shoulders, slowly making away with a lifetime of jewelry. The media also predictably presents the fact of an older person living alone—despite the existence of absent relatives—as the key cause behind the robbery and murder of elders at the hands of their servants. "City's Elderly, Tense and Tormented," reads one representative newspaper headline: "71-year-old Lalita Devi Goenka . . . was brutally murdered by her servants. . . . Though she has three daughters and two sons, she stayed alone in the city. . . . Her lonely existence was the prime reason for her being chosen as a target" (Times News Network 2004:6).

Hence, a relationship that many of the employer class feel has long worked very well in the context of large households—the hiring of workers to perform numerous domestic reproductive tasks, including elder care—becomes increasingly fraught in times of solitary living.

Peer Friendships and Clubs for Senior Citizens

Living alone requires not only negotiating care arrangements; for many, it also demands finding new modes of meaning beyond the family. The elder-focused NGOs surfacing in India frequently provide just such sources of meaning—offering not only novel forms of *sevā* but also new peer-oriented sites of sociality, activity, and identity. The NGOs emphasize the cultivation of peer friendships, "active/productive" aging, volunteer work, lifelong hobbies, fit bodies, age-specific magazines, and political awareness of having distinct "rights" and an "identity" as an international group of "senior citizens"[27]—pursuits especially appropriate for an individualistic, rather than centrally family-oriented, sense of self.

Senior citizens' clubs include the Dignity Foundation, Agewell, and Jana Hitaya, already introduced above. Others in Kolkata are the Indian Association of Retired Persons (part of the international ARP), Old Wine (a name chosen to highlight that some things, including people, get better as they age), the Non-Resident Indian Parents Association, and the Laughing Club of Udita. The Dignity Foundation is a particularly vibrant site of intimate peer friendships and volunteer work. In Kolkata, its more active members gather several times a week at the headquarters, to socialize and conduct various forms of business—accounting, planning programs, overseeing the Alzheimer's day care center, running computer training classes, and the like. Members carry a business card with the Dignity

Foundation logo and their names. Some become close friends, visiting each others' homes, calling each other almost daily on the phone, and going out together to movies and restaurants.

Relationships forged through Dignity can also explicitly substitute for the family. Priya Chatterjee, an active member, lived entirely alone and had no close kin of any kind in the city, not even nephews or nieces or cousins. A retired English professor, she had never married and still lived in her cherished childhood family home, but even now she felt keenly lonely and bereft after her last brother, who had shared the house with her, passed away twenty-five years earlier. Worried acutely about what might befall if she were to become seriously ill or bedridden, Priya-di began to investigate the possibility of moving into an old age home. She and I visited a few together, once accompanied by three other Dignity Foundation lady members on what seemed a very pleasant, lighthearted evening jaunt, followed by tea and snacks out. But when the manager of the home she liked best explained their admissions procedures, which included appearing before the board with two guarantors (ordinarily next of kin), who would agree to make decisions for her and manage her finances if she were to become incompetent, Priya-di became very distraught. "If we who have no one—If we *had* that kind of person who could look after us in such a way, then why would we be coming to an old age home?" But, she ended up deciding that fellow Dignity Foundation members could serve in the capacity of family guarantors. She chose two prominent male members (rather than some of her closest female friends), and these two members agreed to serve in this way, should she decide to move into the old age home.

The Laughing Club of Udita is another active senior citizens' group that I came to know well, formed in the Udita apartment complex in Kolkata where I resided for parts of 2006 and 2007.[28] Its members ranged in age from their fifties to eighties; their children were grown, largely married and, more often than not in this group, living separately, frequently abroad. The mixed-gender group met daily at 6:00 AM for laughter yoga— throwing heads back and arms out for exuberant, hearty laughing—as well as exercises, chatting, and (for those who wished to attend) Bhagavad Gita reading. In the early evenings, groups of men and women gathered separately for tea, snacks, and conversations, rotating among each others' flats and various outdoor congregating spaces. Several described the group as a lifeline—a reason to get up in the morning, engage with others, and replace family engagements that some experienced as sorely missing.

One of the group's early members, Mr. Gandhi, was featured in a *Telegraph* newspaper article on the club. "An old retired man finds a new family, setting an example to others of his age who follow suit," begins the story. Then:

> It's the fear that he remembers most. The year was 2002. And it was a cold, December evening. The night before, 77-year-old M. R. Gandhi, retired electrical engineer . . . , had moved with his wife into a plush high-rise complex. . . . He had gone for a late afternoon walk. . . . And as the sun went down and evening descended, Gandhi felt his spirits sink.
>
> Slowly, everyone else went indoors. But Gandhi didn't want to go inside. "I felt afraid," he recollects.
>
> In this new neighborhood, he knew no one. His children—a son and three daughters—their spouses and their children all lived separately, and at this age, alone and ailing, he found that life itself seemed like a long, cold, lonely winter. . . . "The only consolation was that my wife was there, but she too suffered from loneliness and it didn't help to talk to each other."

The story then jumps two years to 2004, with Gandhi in the midst of a Laughing Club gathering: "It's six in the early morning, at the center of the compound. The sun is up and the sky is blue. Gandhi, along with his wife and dozens of others—mostly elderly people over the age of sixty—are gathered on the sprawling, green lawn.[29] Some are jogging, others stretching, more walking and all of them, without exception, laughing. . . . Soon, [Gandhi] realized that he had a circle of friends in the compound. 'And they had become like family to me.'" Carrying on with the family metaphor, the accompanying photograph is captioned: "JUST LIKE KIN: Gandhi (third from left) enjoys a cup of tea with his friends" (Mitra 2004:15).

One morning following a Laughing Club gathering, a few lady members and I lingered to chat. They mentioned that women of their generation were so accustomed to living closely with family in large, crowded households that it was hard to get used to living alone now. "We felt so bad when we first moved here." They had each moved into the new high rise late in life, some into flats purchased by their children, leaving behind larger, now-empty family homes that were difficult to maintain and inappropriate for a solitary older person. But one of the women, Chameli, changed courses to proclaim animatedly: "Yet some are living separately from their children and are growing *accustomed* to that. Some are even feeling happy! Like some of our Laughing Club members!" She became

FIGURE 6.1. The Laughing Club of Udita. Members throw their arms open to the sky and laugh out loud.

very enthusiastic: "In your book, you can make *this* the last scene—those living without their children and who are *happy—laughing* even—in our Laughing Club!"

And, in fact, like other similar gated apartment complexes springing up around India's cosmopolitan centers, Udita functions not unlike a peer club for many of its well-off older residents—who join groups like the Laughing Club, look in on each other, visit, and gather outside in the evenings to chat. Each evening at Udita, a group of older women congregates on a low semi-circular wall and some lawn chairs just inside the complex's front entrance, while senior men gather outside the gates at the edge of the adjoining market and row of convenience stores. Udita resident and Laughing Club member Viraj-da and his wife lived in a flat that their U.S.-based son had purchased for them, and Viraj-da spent each day socializing with friends, exercising, meditating, reading, and playing music. He is the one who told me, as I quoted above: "At this age, it's better to live separate. . . . If an old man says that he needs to have his son live with him, then the son won't advance, and the country won't advance." He then went on, emphasizing the importance of peer ties: "I am the happiest man in the world, living in heaven! I won't live anywhere other than here, surrounded by my circle of friends."

Critically Reflecting upon Individualism as a Modern Lifestyle

This chapter has scrutinized the complex and varied lives and perspectives of older persons living "alone," in a situation that most had until recently considered extraordinarily novel. We have seen how older, middle-class elders living apart from junior kin, often very purposefully and strategically, work to fashion for themselves and their children independent lives—moving away from centrally family-focused to much more individual market-based and peer-focused forms of self and aging. However, by means of closing, I wish to present a narrative that highlights how the project of crafting an independent way of life in old age is not one that most Indians I have grown to know find unambiguously easy, or natural. Rather, it is a project they engage in with critical reflection, self-consciousness, effort, and generally some real ambivalence.

After I was invited to give a talk comparing ways of aging in India and the United States at one of the monthly Saturday evening gatherings of the Dignity Foundation, a lively and provocative discussion ensued on competing cultural models surrounding aging and intergenerational relationships. The gathering consisted almost entirely of older middle- and upper-middle-class persons who were living separately from their children. Conversations were in English, signifying the elite and diverse regional backgrounds of the participants. Referring to the joint family system in which children and parents in turn reciprocally provide care for each other, one gentleman commented, "That was a very sweet relationship, but it is dying now." Another member objected, "We can't get rid of that expectation level, though. The problem is that we have grown up *expecting* our children to care for us. If you"—he addressed this next comment to me, presumably as an American, or perhaps as a social scientist—"can show us how to *get rid* of this—our expectations—then there would be no problem." People smiled and nodded. A graceful dark-haired woman in about her seventies spoke up with an air of gentle, self-assured wisdom, "The main issue is: we should not demand money and love at the same time. We have to settle for one or the other. If we mistake one for the other, we will be disappointed." She went on:

> We invest in our children for years. But, we should *not* do
> so for the interest in the bank. We should not do so expect-
> ing anything in return. From the [Bhagavad] Gita, you should

know—that *disinterested* action is best.[30] If your child gives back to you, that is a blessing. But you should not give to the child *thinking* of the interest. *That* is the problem. It will *liberate* us to think of acting with *dis*interest!

The secretary of the group, Mr. Swaminathan, then stood up to offer a tale of an Indian doctor's experiences in Canada, illustrating how the "independent aging" and "individualism" of the West can be *too* extreme for an Indian's taste. An Indian doctor, settled in Canada, was practicing medicine there. He had an ailing, elderly Canadian patient who resided in a nursing home. One night, shortly after midnight, the man died. The doctor phoned the man's son. After the phone rang many times, the son picked up. The doctor told him, "I'm calling from the nursing home." The son asked, "Is there a problem?" The doctor: "Yes, I'm very sorry to say: Your father has passed away." The son replied (Mr. Swaminathan mimicked an irritated, angry voice), "Why did you have to wake me up and call me in the dead of night to tell me this? I have given the name of the undertaker. They will take the dead body away, and then you could reach me in the morning—I will go over then." The doctor was so disturbed by this interchange that he decided to leave Canada and return to India.

Murmurs came from around the audience, "Could this be true? Is this really a true story?" "Yes!" Mr. Swaminathan insisted, "I met the doctor myself, who told me this story." "Surely this must be an extreme case, though." "Indeed, this would *never* happen in India." But, an elegant middle-aged woman dressed in an ash-grey *salwar kameez* suit, offered softly, "In fact, it was a very practical reaction. True, the doctor could have simply called the undertaker, and then notified the son in the morning." This led to a conversation about the merits and demerits of individualism versus collectivism, as Western and Eastern or Indian ways of being.

As we departed into the darkening summer evening, the elegant, thoughtful woman in the ash-colored *salwar* came up to me and said, "See, if you weren't an individual, then you couldn't be going out like this, pursuing your work, giving talks, writing books. You would have to be home with your children and family." I said, "Yes, that's true. Though, still, I am *worried* about them." The meeting had gone on longer than I had expected and I had just turned on my mobile phone to see eight missed calls from where my two daughters were waiting for me in our rented Kolkata flat. The woman replied resolutely, "True, you can worry about them. But, still—you were able to come."

7 MOVING ABROAD

Toward the very beginning of this research project, when I was living in California, I met Matilal Majmundar, a retired minor railroad official from Gujarat who had come to be with his U.S.-settled children in his old age. He lived with his wife at his daughter's spacious Palo Alto home. "You are interested in Indian aging?" he inquired eagerly when I met him at an Indo-American seniors meeting. "Well, you must visit me." He had spent much of the past few years reflecting on "Indian" versus "American" modes of aging. When I arrived at his home, he apologized for having no tea (his wife was visiting their other daughter, and his daughter and son-in-law were of course at work).

I quoted at the beginning of chapter 1 from his anecdote about an acquaintance who complained of the difficulty of getting his morning cup of tea in his children's American home: "He gets up at six o'clock, he requires a cup of tea, he is moving here and there, waiting for a cup of tea. The children, they get up at 8:00, or 7:30, busy with all their activities. . . . At 9:00 or at 8:00–8:30 there will be a breakfast table, so many cups of tea and all these things." The acquaintance was put out that there was no one to prepare tea for him but was also disgruntled at the prospect of doing it himself. Matilal Majmundar teased the man: "You better go back to India. In India, if you take a second cup, or a third cup of tea, they will object, they will object. Here, you can take even *ten* cups of tea, prepare yourself, any material you use, your children will never object. But, if you want their *time,* they will object. They will object if you want their time. So, better go to India. Here is not the place for you."

This anecdote points to what I soon learned to be common images held by older Indians living in the United States: that even if maybe there is less material prosperity in India (i.e., people cannot always afford as many cups of tea as they might want), then at least families in India are closer, and old people are better served. America is the land of material prosperity; India is the land of intimacy, and time.

In this chapter I focus on older Indians who choose to move to the United States in late life to live with or near their U.S.-settled children. I found it interesting that many Indian Americans hold more idealized and conservative views of life in India than do those still living in India, and they see themselves as self-consciously grappling to create new, complex forms of family and aging across what can appear as gaping divides between nations and generations.

Since the passage of the 1965 U.S. Immigration and Naturalization Act, which allowed Asians with preferred occupational skills to enter the United States, Indians have been one of the fastest-growing immigrant groups.[1] Especially at first, the majority of Indians came as young professionals or students in graduate and professional schools. Thus, the Indian American population has been very "young" as a whole.[2] However, as earlier migrants have matured and put down roots, they have increasingly begun to express a deeply felt moral obligation and desire to bring their aging parents over from India. Many elders also speak of finding it natural to come to America in old age, to be with their children.

As I outlined in the book's introduction, most of my fieldwork with older Indian immigrants and their families took place in California, while I was living in the region as a postdoctoral fellow at the University of California at San Francisco. I joined as a volunteer and then as a board member the Indo-American Community Senior Center in the South Bay near Silicon Valley. Through the center, I spent time with many Indian American seniors and their families[3]—serving as a volunteer chauffeur; attending meetings, cultural programs, religious ceremonies, and late-morning tea breaks; and interviewing people about their life stories, hopes and dreams, losses and struggles. I also recruited research subjects through hanging out at a mixed-ethnic community senior center in Fremont, California, a city with a robust Indian immigrant population. After moving to Boston, I found research subjects through neighbors, colleagues, and friends of friends, and through the organization for Bengalis overseas, Prabasi. In both the San Francisco and Boston areas, Indian Americans live largely in mixed-ethnic (often primarily white) urban and suburban neighborhoods, in comfortable middle-class and upper-middle-class homes.[4] My Indian American informants have been mostly Hindu (though with some Sikhs and Jains), and largely Bengali and Gujarati (though with some Punjabis, other North Indians, and South Indians).

Why Come to the United States?

"Why did you decide to move to the United States?" was a question I often asked of Indian American elders. Nearly all replied that they came to be with their children. Some come first to visit, often to help with the births of grandchildren, not intending to stay permanently. They may travel back and forth between the two nations for several years, only later deciding to settle in the United States, and even then frequently maintaining a home and bank account in India for visits and an imagined eventual return. Others are called over by their children shortly after the elders' retirement, or when one parent is widowed, and make the move suddenly and for good.

When elaborating upon their decision to migrate, Indian American parents very frequently invoke a vision of an "Indian" system of lifelong intergenerational reciprocity: parents and children naturally live together throughout life, and juniors provide care for their senior parents, in return for all the effort, material cost, and love their parents expended to produce and raise them in infancy and childhood. One gentleman replied in a typical matter-of-fact fashion when I asked why he had come to the United States: "Because my only son is here. It is my son's duty to look after me." He described how he had educated his son, sending him to the United States with his own savings accrued from his modest salary as a high school principal. Now it is time for his son to provide for him. Another replied, "Naturally, to be with my son! I had taken care of him; now he will take care of me." Gopal Singh, a Punjabi Sikh man in his seventies, explained his immigration quite precisely in terms of his, and his children's, expectations to participate in a system of intergenerational reciprocity. He describes intergenerational exchanges not only of forms of material support, but also of bodies (via birth), affection, talk, and the "sharing [of] sorrows and happinesses":

> My wife and I were living in India. Our children [two daughters and one son, all of whom had become naturalized American citizens] thought that there is nobody to take care of us, as we had brought up our children. We . . . gave birth to them, provided a house for them, brought them up, gave them an education, and sent them to the United States for better life. . . . So, we came here to join our children, to spend the evening of our life

with our children. Because if we give to someone, we [in turn] need someone to care for us, to talk to us, to share our sorrows and happinesses. We shared the sorrows and happinesses of our children, and they share our sorrows and happinesses. . . . This is why we have come here, to live with our children and spend our old age.

Some speak very precisely also in terms of wanting to reap the rewards of the investment they have made in their children, claiming responsibility in large part for their children's successes. Seventy-five-year-old Matilal Majmundar, who provided the tea narrative opening this chapter, answered when I asked him why seniors come to America:

What they feel is that, they had brought up their children, spent so much money on them. And then, when [the children] become prosperous [in America], their wives or their husbands will get the benefit, [and] they [the parents] won't get it. You understand? That particular idea is there. Why should *we* not share the prosperity of our children, for which *we* were accountable?

Grown children also readily express their own desires to reciprocate toward their parents. "Culturally, I can't imagine it any other way," reflected Nita, musing about having her parents with her in her home. Some adult children further speak of wanting their parents to come live with them to help care for their own children while they may be out working, and to counteract what they see as the excessive "Americanization" that they and especially their U.S.-born children are experiencing. They hope that their parents will help preserve in their homes Indian cultural traditions surrounding not only family mores but also language, food, and religion.

Although the prevalent expectation in India, as we have seen, is that it is sons and daughters-in-law who provide parental care, in the U.S. context many senior parents do end up living with daughters, providing various explanations for such an unconventional arrangement. First, if a U.S.-settled daughter's parents-in-law do not wish to move to the United States, the daughter's marital home can become free for her own parents. Second, many Indian daughters in the United States are working and earning their own incomes, thus reducing the stigma that Indians attach to staying in a daughter's home—for parents would not be materially dependent on their son-in-law alone. Finally, it is entirely conventional for an Indian daughter to return to her natal home at the birth of her first child; but if it is not feasible to return to India for childbirth, it seems natural for her parents to come to the United States. They may then end up staying on. Other parents simply live with their American daughter for a good portion of each year, without making her home their only permanent one. Whether made up of daughters or sons, the multigenerational family becomes for many Indian Americans an enduring sign of a highly valued Indian identity, and of a "good" family and old age, forged across the disparate spaces of India and America.

Aging across India and America

Transnational living does not involve simply picking up people or cultural systems and importing them to another nation, however. After spending some time in the United States, most older immigrants, along with their families, end up self-consciously taking on practices, values, and modes of aging they regard as American, although often ambivalently with both eagerness and misgivings. In negotiating the intimate practices of their daily lives—making tea, cashing a government welfare check, taking a bus to a senior center, enduring a hospital stay—Indian Americans take some values, practices, and categories from one nation or culture ("Indian") and some from the other ("American"), living simultaneously across the two now overlapping worlds, transforming each cultural system, and themselves, in the process.

To examine more closely the making of such transnational lives through modes of aging, let us consider the transactions that take place between senior Indians and adult children after they have lived for some time in the United States. It may be useful for readers here to refer again to table 2.1, which sketches core features of what many both in India and abroad regard as the "traditional" Indian system of intergenerational reciprocity. Many of the exchanges that my informants imagine to constitute an "Indian" intergenerational system are, in America, halted, reversed, or displaced onto the state (see table 7.1).

1. Transactions of Material Support:
Families, the State, and the Production of Independent Selves

Most of the adult children in the Indian American families I know in the San Francisco and Boston areas do provide a substantial degree of material support for the elderly parents they help bring over from India.

TABLE 7.1.
Images of "Indian" and "(Indian) American"
Intergenerational Transactions

		"Indian"	In America
Media of transaction	Phase 1: Initial giving (parents → children)	Phase 2: Reciprocated giving, the repaying of debts (children→ parents)	Phase 2
Material Support	Food, clothing, money, shelter, education	Food, clothing, money, shelter	State takes over much (though children still provide some or much)
Services	E.g., serving food, daily care, cleaning bodily wastes—all requiring a great deal of effort	e.g., serving food and tea, daily care, cleaning bodily wastes (if parent becomes incontinent)	Halted (unreciprocated) and/or reversed (parents → children)
Emotional Support	Love, affection	Love, respect	Lost? due largely to a scarcity of time and American "independence"
Body	Given via birth	Children reconstruct for parents as ancestors via funeral rites	Halted (unreciprocated) or minimized

Of the thirty-two immigrant elders I work with most closely, for instance, twenty-one, or about two-thirds, live in the homes of their adult children, where they are provided shelter and food (or at least food supplies), and often a bit of spending money. Those who do not live with their children tend nonetheless to receive quite a lot of material support from them, such as money deposited regularly in a bank account, the gift of a car, payment of medical expenses, and air tickets to and from India. However, the state also ends up taking over some or much of the responsibility of providing for these senior immigrants—in the form of Supplemental Security Income welfare benefits,[5] Medicare, state-subsidized senior apartments (which some move into), senior bus passes, discounted lunches at senior centers, and the like—resulting in a whole new configuration of the social-moral relationship between old people, families, and the state.

At first, many are perplexed by such a system of state support of the elderly. Vitalbhai Gujar, for instance, described to me the confusion he experienced during his initial interview with welfare agents. Nearing seventy, he had come to the United States from Gujarat, India, several years earlier to live with his only son, a naturalized American citizen and an engineer who was married to a Gujarati-born woman. Gujar regularly attended a nearby multiethnic senior center, where once or twice a year social service agents would come to speak about the federal Supplemental Security Income (SSI) program for the elderly and how to apply. He thus went to inquire at the local social service office. He recalls the puzzlement he felt: "Why are they calling me indigent, when my son makes money?" Vitalbhai Gujar in fact had no resources of "his own" in the United States, having come to this country too late in life to begin new work, and having had (like most of his compatriots) to leave behind any assets in India due to Government of India regulations restricting the outflow of money from the nation.[6] But he had considered himself appropriately well provided for in the household of his son. In India, he stressed, he would not consider himself, nor be considered by others (the community *or* the state), to be "indigent."

Vitalbhai Gujar went on, though: "If the American government defines things this way, and if we are living in America, then why not accept?" In fact, many like Gujar who immigrate to the United States late in life do end up accepting SSI benefits. Among the senior members of the San Francisco South Bay Indo-American community center where I volunteered, directors estimated that anywhere from 50 to 75 percent were receiving SSI. Of the thirty-two people I work with most closely who are over age sixty-five, 75 percent receive SSI.[7] Further, not only do many senior immigrants receive SSI, but they also make use of senior bus passes, state-subsidized senior apartments, discounted lunches at senior centers, Medicare, and the like.

These older immigrants come to see SSI and other such state programs for the elderly as part of a quintessentially "American" way of doing things, and of aging. In America, many Indians explain, children do not provide for their parents—and this is not due (necessarily) to moral laxity on the part of children. Rather, older parents do not even expect or want their children to support them. They value independence and self-sufficiency, and are averse to being "burdens" on their children. The state also does not ordinarily expect adult children to care for their parents, a presumption Indian immigrants encounter in their own interactions with state agencies, such as when applying for SSI. Swapna Goswami, a Bengali woman now in her sixties who (unlike most of my informants) moved with her husband and children to the United States when her children were young, explained: "The American government doesn't think working men and women should care for their parents. People should support themselves by working and setting aside retirement funds, and by getting SSI." At an Indo-American seniors' meeting, a member told the group a story of an Indian son who took his father to see a surgeon in the United States. The doctor said to the son (encouraging the son to get his father on Medicare), "Why should *you* have to pay for the surgery?" He concluded, "What a different kind of society from ours this America is!"

Some find disturbing this novel mode of imagining the relationship between an old parent, an adult child, and the government. Vitalbhai Gujar, who nonetheless was using SSI, said to me:

> Have you heard of the *buṛo āśram?* old age home? . . . Seniors from India are using the U.S. government like an old age home. They come here, and the U.S. government takes care of all medical expenses, food. [I asked, "Do you think that's wrong?"] Yes! And it's bad for families, too. My son is not taking on his responsibility of caring for me! And then their children are not learning from them—they think just that the government should do it. . . . They're forgetting the Indian system.

Swapna Goswami spoke disapprovingly of a Gujarati friend who lived with her husband in state-subsidized senior housing: "She says she is here to see her kids. But I say, 'If you come to be with your kids, then why don't you live with them?' . . . It's an abuse of SSI, and an abuse to old people, to allow them to be supported by SSI and not their kids."

Many of the immigrants I know, however, have gradually come to value and even enjoy dimensions of what they see as an American mode of aging, in which elders support themselves or are supported by the state, rather than being dependent on their children. Many praise the generosity and prosperity of the U.S. government, which can support its aged. A good proportion of senior Indian immigrants, especially those who are still married, end up using their SSI money to seek out their own apartments, some in state-subsidized senior complexes. One morning I discussed such modes of aging with two older Punjabi Sikh men, Gopal Singh and Teja Singh—two good friends who had been in the United States for over ten years. At the time, I did not yet know either of them well. I had just recently begun research on the subject and still assumed that most Indian seniors would prefer to live with their children:

> GOPAL SINGH: So, the [Indian] seniors have decided that they would like to live close to their family, but prefer their independence and freedom. We prefer our independence and personal freedom.
>
> TEJA SINGH: As the American seniors.
>
> SL: So, some decide to live separately?
>
> TS: Yes, yes. Independent living means respectable living. But, [only those] who are getting this SSI, who are getting medical coverage—then only can one live independently here.
>
> GS: Yes, Indian elderly see the American elderly living in the senior homes [subsidized senior apartment complexes] in USA, and their lives are *excellent.*
>
> SL: Oh, you think their lives are excellent? [surprised]
>
> GS and TS: Yes!
>
> SL: Would you like to do that also?
>
> GS: Yeah, we would like!
>
> TS: I'm living that way! I'm living that way right now!

On another occasion, Gopal Singh spoke to me eagerly about how one doesn't even need to depend on children here, since the state provides for so much—SSI, Medicare, senior centers. "Why, we can even call 911 if something goes wrong. We tried it once," he said with delight. "Why would we have to live with our children?"

A senior Gujarati man, Manubhai Daiya, explained his transition to such an "American" mode of living. When he and his wife first came to this country in 1986, they came to be with their daughter (a naturalized citizen) and help care for her children while she and her husband worked. Then six years later, he explained: "After we became senior in American parlance—that is, age sixty-five—we received SSI. So we thought we may as well launch out on our own, and accustom ourselves to American life." So saying, he and his wife moved into a separate apartment, where they are supported almost entirely by SSI. He describes with enthusiasm the "independence" and "freedom," and the reduction in family conflict, they have enjoyed since moving into their own home. One active member of the Bay Area Indian American seniors community and a close informant, eighty-four-year-old Harikrishna Majmundar, went so far as to compile a book, *Mapping the Maze: A Guide to Welfare for Elderly Immigrants* (2003), in which he draws on years of giving informal advice to senior Indians about SSI, Medicare, and other programs of the U.S. welfare system. The cover of the book depicts an elderly couple on a complicated yet happy journey to an independent home.

Others underscore that even in India, where people ordinarily expect children to support their elderly parents, they would not want to be *entirely* dependent on their children. Especially among those in this group of middle- and upper-middle-class families (those well-off enough to fund passage to the United States), people would hope to retain at least some resources in their own name until they die—perhaps a retirement pension, or a separate savings account, or some family property—to help ensure that they maintain a degree of independence, respect, and leverage over their children throughout their old age. Elder Indian Americans thus express feelings of discomfort and humiliation in having to ask for *everything* from their children, even any little bit of pocket money to ride the bus, buy a small gift for a grandchild, purchase a new pair of sneakers, or make a temple offering. Many thus feel relieved and grateful if they are able to receive SSI or find a part-time job. Lata Parikh, who was able to earn a small salary working in a child care center and who also received SSI, told about life in the United States: "You have to earn your pocket money! You know, if you don't have any other and have to beg from your children [laughs a little, sheepishly]. Of course, they don't mind, but . . . you don't feel like asking them for *every penny* you spend." Vitalbhai Gujar described, "If I have to ask my daughter-in-law for bus fare, for five to ten dollars, and then if she asks, What happened to the last twenty? How that makes me feel. I am thinking, 'And I should be the head of the family?' The SSI money the government gives—it liberates me, and her."

Yet, some express some humiliation regarding their position of semi-dependence on the U.S. government. Two of my male informants likened their position to that of the Indian "house son-in-law" (*ghar jāmāi*), with the U.S. government in the role of their father-in-law. In India, the house son-in-law arrangement is one in which parents of only daughters bring an in-marrying son-in-law or *ghar jāmāi* into their own home. A *ghar jāmāi* is generally from a poor family and does not stand to inherit much from his own parents. He agrees to move into his wife's household in exchange for the property he will live on and inherit from his father-in-law, but this is a rather embarrassing position for him, less prestigious than the usual male pattern of continuous patrilocal residence. Older immigrant Indian men similarly leave behind rights to their own property in India to move to a new land, where they may be provided for by their "father-in-law" (the U.S. state), but in the process lose prestige.

SSI money and part-time jobs, then, cannot make seniors independently wealthy or even, in most cases, fully independent of their children. Nonetheless, their own income makes it possible for senior immigrants to function in important part as self-supporting, as well as to participate in the life of the nation as independent consumers. They begin to cultivate a kind of egalitarian autonomy, still fused with hierarchical interdependence, made possible in part by working with American policies that displace the material management of aging from the family onto individuals and the state.

2. Transactions of Services: Unreciprocated Flows in a Land of No Time

Another major transformation that transpires in the working out of intergenerational relations in Indian American families involves the transaction of services. Recall that in a more conventional Indian family system, adult children provide not only material support for their aging parents but also key services or *sevā* (respectful care), including cooking and serving food and tea, tending to household chores, providing companionship and entertainment, and nursing during periods of frailty. The common perception among Indian seniors in America is that juniors do not end up reciprocating such services to their parents (or at least not as much as the parents expect and would like), which is a key source of tension and perceived failure and disappointment on the part of seniors. The main problem (expressed by juniors and seniors) is that juniors are too busy working (they don't have any *time*) to serve their elders. In addition, both juniors and seniors gradually assume what they regard as a general U.S. culture of egalitarian self-sufficiency—where people do not rely on servants either, and the expectation is that each individual cares for him or herself. Finally, though, elder parents in the multigenerational Indian American family often end up taking on the household's domestic services (including childcare, cooking, and cleaning)—thus reversing the expected direction of transactional flows by extending *their* phase of serving into old age. Such practices involve major transformations in both generational and gendered relationships.

Many of the conversations at the Indo-American Community Senior Center where I hung out revolved around the problem of the children's inability or disinclination to provide services. One morning, while about ten members sat chatting over tea, chairs arranged in a circle around the common room, Ajit Parikh commented, "The children have gone the American way. They say, 'Help yourself.'" A few others chimed in, emphatically, "But we can't *blame* them. When we come to this country, we must accept certain things. Our attitudes must change." Parikh nodded in agreement, but went on:

> But in coming here, at first I felt a big shock. *Shock* that they could be this way. I came, there was snow everywhere. It was cold. I didn't know how to drive. And the children were so busy. They had their work, and took care of themselves, expecting me to do the same. . . . But slowly the snow melted, the flowers came out, I learned how to drive, I joined meetings, and in the Indian way, I looked after the grandchildren—one of the greatest joys. [After a brief pause, however, he added wistfully—] But then the grandkids grow up and go the American way.

On another occasion, the group discussed how children, both sons and daughters-in-law, are so busy during the week. Life is so busy here. They take up the American lifestyle of working so hard. "Therefore, we hardly see them at all." "They have no time for us." "And we don't want to interfere." Vitalbhai Gujar contributed: "In India people are very poor but they are more relaxed. Here, people are worrying about every minute—time. They have *so much*—big houses, everything—but still they don't know when or how to stop." I asked if their children would at least drive them to meetings and such on weekends. Those present at the center that day knew how to get there by bus, but there were many senior members who only attended on the weekends. Deepak Shankar replied with a smile, "No, the children don't drive us anywhere on weekends either, because they are too lazy!" Ajit Parikh jumped in, "No! No! Don't use that word. They are not lazy. It's just that on five or six days they are so busy, so on Sunday they want to work on the house, clean it, fix the garden, be at home, all that." "OK, OK," Shankar responded with a grin, "I accept—the euphemism." Then he added to me as an aside, "A spade is called a spade by some; others use euphemisms and flowery language."

Many offer very interesting contemplations on the nature of time as a scarce resource in the United States, a problem lying at the root of differences in elder and junior expectations. Matilal Majmundar reflected perceptively:

> You know if a wealthy man has got much money, he might have some complaints. If a poor man finds that this fellow is complaining, [then] even if that wealthy man has got a real complaint, this [poor] man will say, "Oh, it's an excuse. A man with money, what complaint has he got?" Similarly, what has happened [is] that, in the respect of time, the seniors have got *so much time* at their disposal, and the youngsters have got only *one* difficulty—of time! *All* other things they have got! But they have no *time*. So, whenever the old people complain, these [young] people say, "Oh, you've got sufficient time, you can do so many things. *How* can you complain?" So, their real complaints are not taken into account. They are considered an excuse.

The speakers' deeper complaint in this scenario is that their children are not paying any attention to them. Elder parents expect and crave from their children not merely material items, like food or tea or money, but more fundamentally acts of serving that require care and time—phenomena that are conspicuously scarce in the United States.

Another major concern among many seniors is, as one put it, the "fear of going to a nursing home, that our children will throw us into a nursing home." Ajit Parikh explained to me: "What happens is, with the people working, and there being no servants, it is a very difficult thing for the children to look after the ailing elderly. And so the nursing homes play a very important role in looking after the elderly." The Parikhs now live in a senior apartment complex (after residing with their Indian son, American daughter-in-law, and grandchildren for many years), and their friends, an Indian couple, had recently been admitted to a nursing home. "And in fact," Ajit Parikh went on, "you get used to that type of living." But most I spoke with did not at all like the idea of ending up in a nursing home, where the care may be professionally superior and adequately funded by their children or the state, but where the elder is radically cut off from kin. And so, many immigrant parents hope to be able to return to India—where they may have a remaining relative—a child, niece, nephew, or cousin—who may be able to care for them, and where they could afford to hire servants to help. Still, many worry about not being able to carry out such plans: "Just when you have the most need to go is when you aren't able to go!" Lata Parikh exclaimed at a seniors' meeting, as people envisioned their own future infirmities.

The absence of cooking can loom as a formidable problem, especially for senior men who may have never learned in India, as we have seen, even to prepare a cup of tea. Vitalbhai Gujar was proud to have learned to make tea for himself; but he still did not cook. Every morning he looked in the refrigerator to see if his daughter-in-law had left any prepared food there for his lunch. Rarely did he find any; so he would take the bus to an Indian restaurant, where he was able to buy lunch with his SSI money, sometimes meeting up with a friend or two. One day as we were chatting in the car on our way to the community center, Vitalbhai narrated:

> I am proud to say that *never,* not *once,* in all my five years here, have I ever asked my daughter-in-law for a cup of tea. . . . The problem with Indian seniors here is that they don't bend. I say, just as [we accept that] in India the cars drive on the left and then here they drive on the right, we have to change our ways about other things. *The daughter-in-law here is not the same as the daughter-in-law in India.* If you can't accept that, you should *not* stay here—you should go back to India. Just because a senior may only need five hours of sleep at night and wake up at five AM doesn't mean that he can ask his daughter-in-law for a cup of tea at that hour.

A little later he explained:

> I never invite people to my house, because I wouldn't be able to offer them Indian hospitality, and I don't want to ask my

daughter-in-law to do it. If I were to do it myself, I would have to go to the kitchen for ten to fifteen minutes, and then we couldn't chit chat, and I would have to worry, is there enough milk [in the tea]? enough or too much sugar? . . . But, if someone like *Nita's father* [a good friend] comes, then we might *help each other* and make some tea ourselves.

Older women tend not to complain too much about cooking, but they still note its absence. I asked Gauri Das Gupta, a Bengali woman in her eighties who spends about half of every year with her only son in San Francisco and half in a Kolkata old age home, if her American daughter-in-law, Jill, does the cooking. She replied, with resignation and acceptance, "*Bou?* [daughter-in-law?] Cooking? She doesn't pay much attention. How could she? She comes back from work at ten or eleven. My son, there's no exact time he returns. Therefore, I don't eat much. When I get hungry, I eat a bit."

Furthermore, as I have noted, it is often the seniors themselves who end up providing the household's domestic services, and senior women in particular are frequently the ones who end up taking on such responsibilities as cooking, child care, and housecleaning, to facilitate the external paid work of their daughter-in-laws or daughters. However, men also take on domestic work. Even those who might, in their previous lives in India, never have prepared one cup of tea may take up vacuuming or other duties. Manubhai Detha, now seventy-two, had arrived in the United States from Gujarat, and told me with some pride mixed with chagrin that he makes eighty chapatis a day for his working children in their extended household of eight, while he also supplies the after-school child care. Vitalbhai Gujar teased: "Here, all seniors get their BSC degrees—degrees in babysitting and cooking! We are all babysitters and cooks!" So, gendered as well as generational relations are transformed—as older men become newly domestic, and older women remain domestic beyond their normal years of domesticity. In so doing, they perform services that a servant might otherwise do, and reverse the mother-in-law/daughter-in-law relationship as it is more commonly played out and perceived in India.

Many say that they do not mind doing such work, which gives them a feeling of purpose and closeness to their grandchildren, and allows them to transmit to the young ones "Indian culture." Senior Indian parents frequently also describe their performance of household work as a beneficial means of contributing to what they see as a primary aim of life in America—material prosperity through work. Nirmala Shankar, in her late fifties, had moved with her husband from Mumbai to be with their married son and daughter-in-law after the younger couple had children. She recounted with apparent satisfaction how she and her husband did all of the cooking, shopping, and cleaning: "This way our children can concentrate on their employment." However, senior parents do not like being taken for granted by their children, or scolded by their children if they do not do things (such as taking phone messages in English) the right way. Matilal Majmundar proclaimed, in discussing the plight of Indian seniors here:

> It is one thing to be acquainted with the grandchildren, it's one thing to love them. And, it is a second thing to be responsible for them, to babysit them. *That* they don't like. . . . They [Indian seniors] complain severely. "What is this? Are we babysitters? They are saving money, they are saving babysitters' money [because of] us. Are we babysitters? Huh? And at this age we have to do all these things?" So, this is their complaint.

Ajit Parikh described his own ambivalence regarding his babysitting role. He told of how his son and son's wife had both been working, while their children were cared for by an American babysitter. One day the babysitter invited her boyfriend over and they had beer in the home. "After that, my son asked me to come to help raise the grandchildren," so they wouldn't need to rely on American babysitters or daycare. "So, I did that, and I received a bit of satisfaction, and sometimes not satisfaction. I consider it all a state of mind. When I'm happy, I think I have the best of both worlds here. And when I'm unhappy, I think it's a devil of a place and I want to go back to India. There is no panacea."

3. Transactions of Sentiments: Intimacy Lost?

Another crucial dimension of the working out of Indian American modes of family and aging concerns the exchange of sentiments. The problem is not a matter simply of who provides the material support, or who performs the labor of household services, but of a lack of closeness, a loneliness, the feeling of being trapped in a house all day surrounded by cold fog or snow, without even a phone call from a son. An important component of Indian perceptions of junior-to-senior intergenerational service or *sevā* is love and honor. This is what many Indian seniors feel to be the most seriously lacking in the United States—the gift of the sentiments of love and respect that make up close intergenerational relations.

Lata Parikh's story of her and her husband's arrival in America captures her sense of isolation and neglect by children who have no time:

> It was the month of December. And it was in Columbus, Ohio. Full of snow—all over. . . . Arrived, and absolutely a new country, new things. And in the morning, you look out, and all you see is white white white white white white everywhere, nothing else! [She took a deep breath, recalling her shock.] And I said, "Oh, my God! What are we going to *do*?" And the children were very busy! They didn't have any time!

Swapna Goswami was weeping one afternoon when I dropped by, because it was the final day of a three-day weekend and her son, who lived in a neighboring apartment, had not yet visited. Her husband told me gently, "Her problem is that she is living between East and West. Like an Indian mother, she still thinks that her son should call her every day, come over to see her every day. But he has lived in America most of his life. He won't do that." This particular family had immigrated when their children were still young, when Swapna's husband took a job as a professor at a U.S. university. Swapna explained to me:

> The children were raised here, so they are really more like Americans. They love us; they really do love their parents, but they don't like to come visit us. My son doesn't have any time for us. I tell him, "Look at all your commitments—you have your work, your friends, your tabla [her son played this traditional Indian drum as a hobby]. And *then* us. We come right after your tabla! You can't even put us, your father, before your tabla? The whole weekend will go by, and he won't even call once. And he lives there, right next to us!

A little later, she added: "Even if my son wanted me to live with him, I wouldn't go. I'm very sensitive. I don't want to hurt and be hurt. The solution is to live away, to be less involved."

Swapna-di agonizes over which country would have been a better place to raise her children, weighing the competing benefits of material prosperity and emotional intimacy:

Sometimes I wonder whether it would have been better if I had stayed in India, lived and raised the children there. When we first came here, we didn't know that we would stay. We thought about going back; but my husband didn't want the children to face all the hardships they would face in India. They wouldn't have the same opportunities there that they had here—for a really good education, good careers. We wanted to give them the best that we could. So we raised them here. And now my son is a computer engineer, and the youngest daughter a doctor. But sometimes I wonder whether it would have been better to stay in India. Sure, maybe my son will make billions and billions. But what is so important about the money? What is really important in life is some satisfaction, fulfillment. If we had stayed in India, would we have been *happier? closer?*

Ajit and Lata Parikh reported to me that in India, senior parents remain the virtual head of the household. If a wedding invitation comes, it will be addressed to the household's most senior member. If an important decision is to be made, the elder will be consulted. In reality, Ajit acknowledged, elderly parents even in India often do not have that much authority. "But that *virtual head feeling* should be there." In America, he professed, it's not. Dhirubhai Kumar, who traveled each year between his Bay Area son's family and his original Ahmedabad home, told of the blow he felt when his "Americanized" son would not take his seventy-year-old wife to the doctor: "So, my eldest son, I told him that it is better that she should go for X-ray, and that tomorrow will you take her to the doctor for X-ray. He said, 'I have to go play tennis.' [Pause. Deep sigh.] And in India, if anybody says like this, it's an insult."

Many, further, are unconvinced that their children really want them here. Matilal Majmundar reflected, "We give the general impression, all the seniors give the general impression that they are here because their children desire that they should be near to them. In fact, the children are not that much particular. They don't mind, but they are not that much particular. Because it's a botheration after all. Old people are a botheration."

Such waning ties of parent-child intimacy transpire in the context of a wider U.S. society where sociality in general is thin. Many are struck by what they perceive to be the widespread lack of intimate sociality in America. My informants report that everything in the United States is so quiet, spread out. Often there are no signs at all of people in their neighborhoods—only houses, lawns, and trees. One wonders: Where could all the people be? Priyanka Majmundar reflected on the striking contrasts between the daily experiences of sociality in the two nations:

> In India, there is so much involvement from the morning on! At six o'clock in the morning, the milkman would come. And he wouldn't simply give milk and go away, but we'd talk [about] something. "So, how are you today? Where are you going to go? Do you have any work? Can I help?" and so on. Then the newspaper man would come, and he would say a few words, "Oh, I'm sorry, I'm late today. Tomorrow I will be on time." Then [Priyanka laughed as she spoke], a neighbor would come, saying, "I'm going to the market, do you want me to bring anything for you? Some vegetables or something like that?" So, this way, there is always involvement with the people.
>
> Here, many ladies are confused. Because *from morning til night* they are alone. So, if somebody calls [on the phone] they are very happy, but in some homes the messages are to be recorded [by the answering machine], so [the elder ladies] are not to pick up the phone.

Priyanka-ben[8] and her husband currently reside in a separate guest cottage on the grounds of their married daughter's Palo Alto home. Priyanka says that they enjoy the living arrangements: "Our children feel that we are here, so they don't worry about us. But it's better to be separate, because we can invite our friends, or have tea whenever we want, or make snacks in the microwave." Still, she described the strikingly different living arrangements in India, with animated warmth:

> In India, [people live in a] much smaller place! Mostly just one house, not even independent rooms! Children and grandmothers and grandfathers, they sleep together. At night we were sleeping together—all! See the difference of culture! And here, sometimes, if all the bedrooms are occupied, and some guests come, people say, "No, there is no room." And we say, "Why? Why is there no room? We can all sleep together! The living room is there! This room is there! We shall spread the mattresses and sleep!"

Anil Bhusan, in reflecting on the marked contrasts between America and India at an Indo-American Community Senior Center gathering, offered:

> And then there is socializing: in India, you go next door, there is someone to talk to, socialize with. Here, you must telephone first. There is socialization only by appointment! They say, "Come over sometime." You say, "OK, how about tomorrow?" "Oh, tomorrow? Tomorrow I'm not free." And they say this, smiling all the time! [He and those gathered smiled, too, in recognition.] People here are so busy. Socialization by appointment only!

In a land of individual privacy, relationships with not only children but also the wider society are sparse and attenuated.

4. Transactions of Death: Technology, Individuality, and the Body

Finally, the structure and meaning of family relationships are reshaped as Indian seniors negotiate dying across Indian and U.S. contexts. Older Indian immigrants are struck by American attempts to control and preserve the body as long as possible, coupled with the construction of death as an *end* to the individual body/self, rather than a means for expressing, reshaping, and extending family relationships. American strivings for bodily immortality are apparent in the pervasive popular cultural techniques aimed at keeping even the very old body fit and young looking—via hair dyes, facelifts, anti-wrinkle creams, exercise routines, sporty youthful clothing, and the like. These strivings are also manifest, even more powerfully, in the United States' elaborate, advanced medical technology geared toward keeping the body alive seemingly indefinitely.[9]

Many of my informants contrast such practices to an "Indian" system, in which one thinks of the body as something that naturally fades and passes away at the end of life—like a tree loses its leaves, or a rice plant drops its seeds and withers to the earth—thereby opening pathways towards new forms of life following. An important part of the Hindu funeral ritual is cremation, the final dissolution of the body, which frees the soul or *ātmā* to take new paths—to ancestorhood, and to reincarnation in a new body or, perhaps, ultimate liberation (*moksha, mukti*). Sons or other close male descendants ritually reconstruct an ancestral body for the parent, through preparing *piṇḍas,* or rice balls, intended to nourish the departed spirit as well as to produce a new ancestral body, just as the parent once gave the child his own body at birth (Knipe 1977:114–115, Lamb 2000:171–176, Nicholas 1988:377–388, Parry 1982:84–86). Descendants then continue to remember, honor, and nurture the ancestor, ideally for generations, through ongoing ritual performances or *śrāddhas.* In such a system, death is an important means of expressing and extending intergenerational family ties (see Lamb 2000:144–180, Parry 1994) and a passage on to important new existences.

Indian Americans struggle with how to sort through these intermingling practices and attitudes, to construct an acceptable mode of aging and dying out of the interplay of India and their new home. Indians living in the United States often cease performing rituals of reconstructing ancestral bodies for and serving parents after death. Although Hindu funeral rites may be performed in the United States (most major metropolitan areas now house several Hindu temples), many juniors as well as seniors feel that such ritual attention to ancestors is no longer important in the U.S. context. Other parents state that even if they would like these rituals to be practiced, they cannot expect their children to do so here because of factors such as the lack of time and good priests, and the alien cultural milieu. Some doubt whether the elaborate Hindu funereal transactions between sons and parents really amount to anything anyway. Suresh Trivedi, a man from Gujarat in his eighties, queried in irritation one morning to a gathering of a few friends at the Indo-American senior center: "What is this boy [my son]? When I go, he will put flowers, he will put my photo, and flowers and all these things on the photo. He will pray and all these things. What is the use of all this when in normal life he is maltreating me?"

Some, who say they have always had quite secular views anyway, embrace what they see as not merely an "American," but a more broadly modern, rational, secular way of approaching dying. Matilal Majmundar, for instance, mused: "If you go to India, they will definitely talk to you, 'Oh, there is life after death,' and all these things. Nothing. In their heart they know that there is no life. Once you go, then you are completely forgotten out of history. There will be no trace." Their whole family has cultivated a "secular outlook on life that fits very well in America," and he does not expect his children to perform *śrāddhas* for him.

However, some remain very keen on finding ways to be ritually processed after death as a Hindu. They may hope to return to India to die or plan explicitly transnational funerals, instructing their children to send their ashes back to relatives remaining in India, so that proper funeral and ancestral rites can be at least minimally practiced there—ensuring insertion into a ritual economy that promises ancestral eternity, and practicing, in a very literal way, dying on a transnational scale.[10]

Confrontations with U.S. medicine provoke intensely ambivalent feelings. Many juniors as well as seniors see as one of the main benefits of living abroad the advanced, state-of-the-art medical care available for elders in the United States. However, at the same time, they are hesitant and fearful about becoming overly embroiled in life-prolonging technology. Matilal Majmundar exclaimed, as quoted in chapter 5: "I have visited the nursing home. I have visited, yes, and I have seen people suffering. I tell you, such a bad situation has come over here. That because of medical facilities, we are living too long." When I asked Arjun Varma if he had compared Indian and U.S. ways of thinking about aging, his reply focused on very different attitudes towards medicine and technological control: "Lots of things are different. . . . In India, we leave many things to God. 'So, let God take care of it.' That is our attitude. Or: 'Let it happen. What can you do?' That sort of thing. But, here, you have to have a life *plan*. You have to take care of things, control your own life." So, one thing American elders do, as he described it, is seek elaborate medical attention. But, "In India, the resources often aren't there. And even when they have resources, they may think, 'Let come what may.' . . . That's the main difference." He went on:

> For example, I know a particular man [in India] who had cancer. He could not take anything in, but what did he do? He did not go to the hospital. He went to his house and then called his sons. And then he died in that house, without any [medical] care. So, there is a lot of difference in attitude. Even those who can afford it, they will think—is it necessary to go to the hospital? Even if they can have all the best medical attention, they will not choose it.

One case of a medicalized death was discussed in detail at several Indo-American seniors' meetings. A senior Gujarati man (whom I had not known personally) had had a heart attack. His son called 911, so he was taken to the hospital. There he was put on life support technology and died over a period of weeks. The ordinary Hindu dying rituals such as lying on the floor—practiced to help purify the person and body, loosen worldly ties, and help the soul (ātmā) leave at the moment of death (Lamb 2000:158–160; Madan 1987:134–135)—could not be practiced in the hospital. At one point, the man's son and wife indicated that he should be put on the floor, but the nurses did not understand or could not accept the request. So he died in the hospital, in bed, hooked up to machines. In musing over the event, people reflected that in the "Hindu" way, the body would be discarded when old and used, like old clothing; but in the U.S. system, a call to 911 results in attempting to keep the body alive as long as possible.

Thus death and dying in the United States become less family events, moments for expressing and extending intergenerational family ties, and increasingly medicalized and bodily matters. Dying, in this view, is perceived to be located outside of the family and, instead, in hospitals (and in the state, through phenomena such as Medicare and 911), and managed through a highly advanced, admired, at times welcomed, and yet disturbingly binding and individualizing medicine.

In scrutinizing the transactions of goods, services, sentiments, and bodies practiced by older Indian immigrants and their children, we see four major dimensions of transformation from a perceived "Indian" to a creatively hybrid "Indian American" mode of aging and family. First, modes of exchange within families become modified toward a lifetime unidirectional flow from parents to child, thus radically altering cultural notions of life course and entitlement. Aging becomes redefined to make elders *lifetime* givers to their children, rather than principally reciprocal receivers. Incidentally, this is also the way that native-born Americans tend to think of intergenerational exchanges, commonly believing that there should be a one-way (and thus non-reciprocal) lifetime flow of resources from seniors to juniors, ending if possible with an inheritance left to juniors after death (as discussed further in chapter 8).

A second dimension of change in this reworking of Indian American aging is that the government, in the United States, takes over much of the support of elders that children would otherwise provide—supplying not only material support (such as SSI money or subsidized housing), but also the performance of services. Senior immigrants who wish to can seek out daily companionship, entertainment, cooked meals, and even trips to the hospital through state-funded programs such as community senior centers and 911 operations.

Third, Indian immigrants describe aging and family life in America as entailing increased "independence" and "personal freedom," coupled inevitably with a loss of intimacy. When people imagine the ways intergenerational relations work in India, they speak of love as being inextricably wrapped up with the giving of services and material support: All three dimensions of a parent-child relationship are tied together, as almost one and the same. So, if services and material support are provided by the state or by an "independent" self, and not by children, then love—no longer embodied in material things—becomes abstract, tenuous, uncertain. Parents and children become "independent" and "free," but in the process they lose love.

Finally, all this takes place in a perceived context of prosperity. Pursuit of material success is the main reason seniors provide to explain their juniors' passage to the United States; but it is pursued and embraced with ambivalence.

Particular Transnational Lives

Before closing this chapter, I wish to focus in a bit more detail on a few individuals' stories, as a means of pointing (more fully than can be done through generalizations) to the varied, complex, ambivalent, and deeply felt ways that Indian American aging is worked out through particular people's daily practices and reflections.

MATILAL MAJMUNDAR

After retiring as a minor railroad official, Matilal-bhai[11] came to the United States in 1985 to join his wife, Priyanka, and their eldest daughter. Priyanka had come two years earlier to see her second grandchild born, and finally Matilal-bhai decided to join them. "When I came over here," he told, "I was completely bored. I used to take a bus, I and my wife, to East Ridge, and then come back by the second bus, spending our time like that, talking together. And I was very much doubtful whether it was correct for me to come over here." A very outgoing person, he would try to strike up conversations with other people on the bus, but he recalls that "out of ten, seven people would snub me." He rationalized: "Americans don't communicate much, first of all, and secondly, they are not very free with people of other nations. . . . Unless you are willing to suffer some humiliation, you will never be able to come here."

Many years have since passed, and Matilal-bhai now describes with effusive pleasure how he has achieved the best of both the American and Indian worlds, living with his wife in the guesthouse of his daughter's Palo Alto home. His daughter and husband supply room and board for the senior couple, and they receive the rest of what they need (spending money and medical expenses) from the government. Priyanka does all the cooking and after-school child care for her daughter and son-in-law, and Matilal helps with homework, plays cards, and watches TV with the grandchildren. The whole extended family dines together. Several years ago, he decided to become a U.S. citizen so that he could vote (he is keen on defending the rights of African Americans and immigrants) and be assured of receiving the welfare benefits citizens are guaranteed. Because of the professional success and material prosperity of his daughter and son-in-law, and what Matilal sees as the real generosity of a wealthy state that can offer benefits to senior immigrants, Matilal feels that he—who was a relatively menial civil servant in India and had married his wife of a higher class through a love marriage sixty years earlier—has finally been able to bring his wife the comfortable and prestigious living that she deserves.

Now Matilal-bhai spends the bulk of his time organizing and providing advice for more newly arrived senior Indian immigrants. He writes a column on aging in a local newspaper, travels the country to give talks on aging at various Indo-American community centers, and is a central figure in the Indo-American Community Senior Center in the Bay Area. At the local library he serves as a math tutor to adults who are working to complete their GED.[12] He recounted:

> I have been telling people that when I came over here I suf-
> fered a lot of difficulties. So now that I have passed that stage,
> my work is that others should not suffer those difficulties that
> I have suffered. . . . This stage, when I have no trouble of my
> own—my financial, no trouble; health, no trouble; no trouble
> of spending my time! [He smiled grandly.] So, I am *perfectly*
> satisfied with my life! So my work now is to see that I may be
> useful to others.

As for his plans for dying, he says he does not care what his children do or do not do afterwards (he is the one who asserted that there is no life after death, and "once you go, then you are completely forgotten out of history"); but he has worried about how to manage a decrepit old age. He reflects, "My wife and I have spent a lot of time discussing what will happen if we cannot take care of ourselves. . . . We don't want to be dependent on the children, . . . and we don't want to go to a nursing home." Ideally, he and his wife would return to India in late, decrepit old age, but realistically, such a journey may then be impossible. "The only consolation is that if one of us goes first, the other will not have much time more to pass."

GOPAL SINGH

This older Punjabi Sikh man, also introduced above, frequently speaks of all the positive, wonderful, great things about life in the United States. He exclaims: "This is the heaven on earth! . . . Old age is a gift from God when spent in dignity, as in this country." He speaks of U.S. seniors: "Anyway, they are happy. They take pleasure in meeting together, meeting friends, they go to picnics, and everybody is happy. . . . We see smiling faces everywhere." He talks about living alone here (with his wife), apart from his children: "I prefer an independent life. I like to live on my own instead of living with relatives. I am happy now."

It was difficult, however, for him to arrive at such positive assessments. I was not able to witness directly the complex process of his working out a life in the United States, having met him twelve years after his arrival and being myself a native member of the nation/culture he is struggling to comprehend, and thus someone to whom he might not wish to reveal everything. But the arduous process of gradually reworking his own taken-for-granted assumptions about the world, family, the United States, and India seep through his writing and discussions.

Singh has been writing a book on his reflections on aging in America. The book, large portions of which he read to me, has been ten years in the making. Much of it is prescriptive, happy, and cheery in tone, and reads like a positive advice manual for living as a senior Indian in the United States. One gets the feeling that in writing and reading the book, Gopal Singh is trying to convince and edify not only others of the principles he lays out, but himself. His own painful stories, though not explicitly narrated, help shape the book—for instance, when he writes of what an Indian senior should *not* do here, such as be crushed at an Americanized child's divorce (it turns out that one of his children did divorce), or expect children to take their parents with them on their family vacations. I found one particularly poignant sequence of passages striking. After relating how senior Indians in the United States may do best to decide to live "independently" apart from their children, he goes on to narrate: "Never turn up uninvitedly, unexpectedly at your children's place. When you are living independently, that is. *Never* drop in at your children's house unexpectedly or uninvitedly. You have to *call* them first that you are coming." (I envisioned him dropping in on his kids and being painfully turned away, or being profoundly shocked by what he confronted there.) Yet he read the next passage with increasing eagerness, tears coming to his eyes:

> Keep your door open for your children: *They* need not call! Tell them
> [just to] press the door and come in—at *any* time! They are welcome.
> . . . When they want to come, they are *always* welcome, day and night,
> without any calling. We feel great pleasure in meeting our children!
> . . . Children visit parents off and on. . . . One can almost see the glow
> of happiness on the faces of old parents when children visit.

Singh resides now with his wife in a senior apartment complex where several other Indian couples live, in the same city as his children. He has lunch every day with his closest friend, another Punjabi, and they frequently stroll together to a nearby non-ethnic senior center, for discussion, events, and card playing. He sees his kids primarily on the weekends, and he takes his wife to the local Sikh temple each Sunday.

ADULT CHILDREN OF SENIOR IMMIGRANTS

Adult children of senior immigrants feel many of these same predicaments and pleasures—of being pulled and drawn in different directions, with their parents, in/at the conjuncture of disparate cultural systems. Pranab Das Gupta (son of Gauri Das Gupta, introduced above) has been in the United States for more than thirty years, since college, and views himself as "absolutely American." He describes cuttingly his widowed mother's expectations that she be cared for by her son in old age as "old-fashioned" and part of a "medieval view of life," but imperative nonetheless. "There's no question I have to do it," he said. He and his American wife, Jill, support his mother entirely, which is not always easy for them. (Pranab, however, is "totally opposed" to SSI for seniors whose children can afford to support them.) They have her spend half the year with them and half the year in a Kolkata old age home, in this way preserving some time and space for themselves as an American married couple, and also allowing her to maintain her ongoing emotional attachments to India.

The elder woman travels to and from India on the airplane by herself, with a credit card and calling card supplied by her son in case anything goes wrong. Pranab often appears quite short with her, "Ma, the tea is dripping!" "Don't you know where the biscuits are?" But he also tends to her needs affectionately, bringing Bengali books for her from the university library, cooking occasional meals, and sometimes taking his work home so that she will not have to be alone all day.

Nita (Matilal and Priyanka Majmundar's daughter), much less ambivalently, finds immense value and pleasure in living with and supporting her parents in their old age. She asked her parents to come from India to live with her, her husband, and their children, "because culturally I couldn't imagine it any other way." Her parents receive SSI money but in a reduced amount, because Nita and her husband provide them housing (the guest cottage) and food (they all eat their meals together in the front house). Nita and her husband are busy and successful professionals (both having immigrated from India to pursue higher education in the United States), and over the years Nita's mother has performed most of the family's child care and cooking to enable the younger couple to work. Nita's only regret, she says, is that there is not enough time to spend with her parents. She yearns to be even closer to them and speaks nostalgically of the life she remembers having in India, when family members could just sit together and talk endlessly. She once told me, a bit baffled, that she believes her parents have become even more "American" than she and her husband. She muses with some regret, "My parents have become *so* independent here that sometimes they don't give us the *chance* to help them."

So, seniors in Indian American transnational families strive, with an ambivalent mixture of nostalgia and creative resourcefulness, to construct a meaningful aging through the competing expectations and values traversing India and the United States, generations and eras—of family and individualism, time and material prosperity, intimacy and professional success, the spirit and technology, locality and cosmopolitanism, tradition and modernity. Indians living in the United States take some symbols, practices, and policies from what they see as India, some from the United States, and some from a more broadly dispersed global modernity, in the process reciprocally constructing while creatively intermingling these diverse overlapping worlds. Much changes in the passage from India. Familial economies become less multiplex, and key aspects of reproduction are displaced onto the state. An ethos of freedom and egalitarianism is fostered, in part, by state support of individuals, which works toward leveling status differences of age and gender, but in the process, eroding the moral density that dependency engenders. Here, semi-autonomy is partly symbolized by the ability to exercise the power to consume (even if under state subsidy), in a context in which material prosperity and consumption are eminent values. An immediate, present-time, and individualistic focus is cultivated, too, via powerful practices of preserving the body and self of *this* life as long as possible, in the face of uncertainty that life and its relationships will hold any value or continuance afterward. At the same time, most Indian American seniors, in diverse ways and degrees, also nurture various precious images and values of a dearly remembered India, such as that of intimate intergenerational reciprocity, a slowness of daily time, and an acceptance of worldly, bodily, transience. Thus, senior Indian Americans may brew their own cup of tea, acquiring the supplies from their juniors' coffers; they may enjoy SSI welfare payments, but reside intimately with their families; they may die in a U.S. hospital hooked up to medical technologies, but as a Hindu striving to be put on the floor where worldly attachments are fewer. In these ways, they forge their lives, reinterpreting "India" and "America" and the complex meanings of aging, via intricately multivalent global processes of cultural production.

8 CHANGING FAMILIES AND THE STATE

During my fieldwork period in Kolkata, a recently retired man in his sixties committed suicide by hanging. In the suicide note published in the local newspapers, he blamed his son and daughter-in-law, with whom he lived along with his wife, for causing his death by the mental and physical torture he received at their hands. The son and daughter-in-law were jailed. Newspapers reported: "Elderly Alipore Clerk Blames Son's Wife Before Suicide" and "Tortured Father Takes Life."[1]

Curious, I went to see the Officer in Charge (OC) at the local police station. I sat across from his large black desk in a comfortable airy room with both the ceiling fans and air conditioner switched on. The officer quickly ordered tea for me, and a generous cup with several biscuits promptly arrived. The officer himself seemed to be in his late forties or early fifties. He commented that he had a son studying engineering at SUNY-Albany, but I learned nothing more about his own family life. Hearing of my general research interests, he brought up spontaneously the particular case that had caught my attention:[2] "There was one incident of torture of a father-in-law by his son and daughter-in-law. . . . The father had to commit suicide by hanging himself. He left a suicide note, categorically stating that the suicide was due to mental torture inflicted by his son and daughter-in-law." He went on, situating the legal case in a broader context of contemporary social change: "The younger generation these days has become so materialistic and self-centered. Most sons nowadays don't want to live in a joint family (ekānnabartī paribār). The tendency is to live separately, away from the parents. . . . Even ladies studying subjects in the university like sociology and human rights—even they now have the tendency to want to live alone as just husband and wife." One might expect, his comments implied, that those concerned with human rights should instead be concerned with serving their elders.

The officer went on to estimate that about 25 percent of today's youth still do wish to stay with their parents. "But the other 75 percent no longer want to live jointly," while the parents still expect co-residence and *sevā* (filial service); this is what leads to conflict. "It is only the most serious cases of fighting (*mārāmāri*) and suicide that come to the police."

"What happens in such cases?" I asked.

"The parties are called to the police station, and negotiation occurs. We try to get the sons, daughters-in-law and parents to work it out, and we tell the sons and daughters-in-law that they should care for their parents. But, if they don't seem to be able to come to an agreement, then the suggestion is given that they should live separately." A bit later, the Officer in Charge added, "I think that in such cases, the parents should simply leave the house and live separately; that would be better."

While we spoke, he busied himself flipping through the pages of a large ledger to find the case of the father who had committed suicide. "Yes, here it is—case number 85, 28–4–2005." He read from the register: "Ranjit Chakraborty, aged approximately sixty-five years, committed suicide by hanging in the bathroom, due to being mentally and physically tortured by his son and daughter-in-law in their house on Pritambar Ghatak Lane."[3]

"Hmm," I mused. "What kind of torture was inflicted on the father?"

The OC's reply was offered in a matter-of-fact tone, "Oh, they didn't feed him. They didn't maintain him properly—giving him tea and water, serving and attending to him (*cā dāoyā, jal dāoyā, sevā-śuśrūṣā karā*). You know, all that is required for the proper caring of old men" (as if to imply, in a somewhat bored tone, "You know, the normal kind of torture of parents").

He added that the mother, the man's wife, also came forward to take a stand against her son and daughter-in-law, and the two younger ones were taken into custody. Charges were filed against them, and the young couple remained in jail for two months.

As an American, I found the exchange to be fascinating. There was no mention in either the police officer's comments or the newspaper coverage that the recently retired sixty-five-year-old man had been physically or mentally disabled. Presumably, if the senior man had been capable of engineering alone his own hanging in the bathroom, he was also physically capable of preparing his own tea. It was hard for me to imagine a U.S. court jailing a son and daughter-in-law for failing to serve an able-bodied father tea and water.[4] However, the Bengali officer's frank comments revealed how taken-for-granted is the assumption in Kolkata that it is normal and appropriate, even if not always assured, that adult children care for their elders.

Over recent years, the state in India has become increasingly involved in matters of aging—but not, for the most part, in order to shoulder responsibilities once held by the family, an effort that began in the United States around the turn of the twentieth century and has transpired in many other nations around the world as well. Rather, state efforts in India—through police-mediated dispute resolution, legislation, and the courts—have been aimed predominantly at enforcing family care. The central premise is that the family is the proper moral, cultural and legal site of care for the aged. What "used to" happen "naturally"—intimate support within the haven of the sustaining Indian joint family—may need now to be mandated by the state, but it is not to be discarded. Some Indian gerontologists, journalists, and policy makers, however, do advocate that the Indian government should assume a greater role in caring for the aged—arguing at times that state support of the elderly is a crucial sign of a "developed" nation, and that "traditional" family-centered modes of aging are "backward."

In this chapter, I examine recent developments regarding the role of the state in elder care in India. I also probe contrasts in Indian and U.S. policies, using the perspectives of my older Indian American informants to help illuminate and complicate assumptions underlying both systems. Focusing on the state, this chapter continues to probe a question running throughout the book: Where is the best site of elder care—the family, the individual, the market, or the state? And what kinds of social, cultural, moral, and economic principles and models of personhood are entailed by the competing answers to this enduring question?

Legislating Parental Care: The Maintenance and Welfare of Parents and Senior Citizens Bill of 2007 and the Courts

In December 2007 the Indian Parliament, seeking to enforce family care of the elderly as a legal obligation, passed a bill titled the Maintenance and Welfare of Parents and Senior Citizens Bill of 2007.[5] Under the law, children may be fined 5,000 rupees and jailed for up to three months if found guilty of neglecting parents. Relatives other than children are also obligated to support childless senior citizens (any citizen of India aged sixty or older) if they stand to inherit property from their aged kin. The Bill gives parents powers to disinherit errant children and other kin from their property. Furthermore, it calls upon (though it does not require) state governments to establish old age homes in every district, to take care of indigent older persons with no kin able to provide support. The Bill also proposes to provide better medical facilities for senior citizens, by calling upon government hospitals to set aside sufficient beds for the elderly, and it asks that state governments establish suitable mechanisms for protecting the life and property of older persons who are economically self-sufficient and living alone voluntarily or involuntarily.

At the heart of the Bill is the stipulation that adult children have not only the moral but also the legal obligation to care for their elderly kin. The premise is that children in Indian society have always been morally obligated to support their aged parents, but that due to the decline of the joint family system in contemporary times, children are now frequently failing to fulfill these obligations. Moral systems must now be backed by legal systems; thus the need for a parental maintenance law. Under "Need for the Legislation," the opening remarks for the Bill specify:

> The traditional norms and values of the Indian society laid stress on showing respect and providing care for the aged. The aged members of the family were normally cared for by the family itself. However, in recent times, society is witnessing a gradual but definite withering of the joint family system, as a result of which a large number of parents are not being maintained by their children, as was the normal social practice. . . . With their dwindling financial resources and weakening health, parents are often being perceived as a burden, even while living within the family. Many older persons are now living with spouse and without children, while many persons, especially widowed women, are forced to spend their twilight years alone. . . . Unfortunately, the time has come when the moral obligation of children to look after their parents in their old age has to be backed by a legal obligation.[6]

During evidence, the Secretary of the Ministry of Social Justice and Empowerment proclaimed, "It is an established fact that family is the most desired environment for senior citizens/parents to lead a life of security, care and dignity." Thus the core aim of the proposed legislation is to "ensure that the children perform their moral obligation towards their parents."[7]

This is not the first time that state or central governments in India have attempted to legislate parental care. The current Maintenance and Welfare of Parents and Senior Citizens Bill of 2007, passed by India's Central Government Parliament, draws heavily on similar legislation enacted by the State of Himachal Pradesh in 2001, the "Himachal Pradesh

Maintenance of Parents and Dependents Act, 2001." This Act makes persons legally obligated to provide adequate maintenance to parents, as well as to other dependents (minor sons, unmarried daughters, and widows), who are unable to support themselves.[8] Section 125 of the Criminal Procedure Code 1973 similarly requires persons with sufficient means to provide a monthly allowance for the maintenance of parents, wives, and minor children unable to provide for themselves.[9] The Hindu Adoption and Maintenance Act of 1956 likewise compels Hindu men and women to provide for elderly parents, minor sons, and unmarried daughters in need. In addition, under this Act a Hindu man must provide for his wife, widowed daughter-in-law, and widowed daughter unable to obtain maintenance from her father-in-law, her own son or daughter, or the estate of her deceased husband.[10]

Previously, such laws were applied largely in order to secure the rights of dependent younger women—wives, daughters-in-law, and widows. According to Ahana Chakraborty of the Human Rights Law Network of Kolkata, who has practiced as a human rights attorney for the past twenty years and whom I interviewed in May 2006, until recently parents rarely availed themselves of such maintenance laws. "They did not want to come forth and proclaim, 'My son is not feeding me, not looking after me.' They didn't know about the law, and they would be embarrassed to speak out," because of the stigma involved in confessing that one's children do not care for one. Furthermore, she explained, a lawsuit is complicated to initiate, requires spending money to hire a lawyer, and can take years to process.

Nonetheless, some parents have been coming forward over recent years to demand maintenance from their children under Section 125. Chakraborty described one of her recent cases, a not untypical scenario. One woman's husband, as he grew older, put his bank account in his wife's and sons' names. He had wanted the account to be in his sons' names in addition to his wife's in case the mother died (so the money would pass easily to his sons), and so the older woman would have her sons there to help her manage the account. But after the older man died, his sons wrote a letter to the bank and filed paperwork removing their mother's name from the account and forbidding her to withdraw any money. The mother contacted the Dignity Foundation[11] for help, and Dignity referred her to Mrs. Chakraborty and the Human Rights Law Network. Chakraborty wrote a letter to the bank explaining the situation, while in the meantime initiating a Section 125 case. The 125 case is still pending, but the mother has access to the bank account money. I asked, "She didn't feel uncomfortable going this route, taking legal action against her sons?" "Yes, perhaps," was the reply. "But how else will these parents eat? They are often left with *nothing*—no money, no home, no food."

The new Maintenance and Welfare of Parents and Senior Citizens Bill of 2007 is intended to make claiming maintenance from children much easier for aged parents. The Bill's prefatory remarks make plain: "Even though a provision already exists under the Criminal Procedure Code 1973 (Section 125) for maintenance of parents, the procedure of going through the Court is both time consuming and cumbersome in addition to being expensive."[12] Under the proposed new legislation, special tribunals will be established in all districts across the nation. Senior citizens unable to support themselves based on their own earnings or property, and wishing to claim maintenance from one or more children or relatives, will appear before the tribunal. In this process, no party may be represented by a legal practitioner. A conciliation officer will first attempt to resolve, within one month, the disputes and differences between parents and children amicably. If these efforts fail, the tribunal will take action, giving each party the opportunity to be heard. If the tribunal is satisfied that the senior citizen is unable to take care of him or herself and that there is neglect or refusal of maintenance on the part of children or obligated relatives, it may order the children or relatives to provide a monthly maintenance allowance, not to exceed 10,000 rupees (around $200). Children who fail to provide the specified maintenance may be fined and jailed for up to one month or until payment is made. All proceedings are to be carried out promptly, resolved in no more than ninety days. A parent or senior citizen who is unsatisfied with the decision of the original tribunal may make an appeal to an appeals tribunal; however, junior kin may not initiate an appeal. Finally, a child or relative who abandons a senior citizen—who "leaves such senior citizen in any place with the intention of wholly abandoning such senior citizen"—may be fined up to 5,000 rupees and jailed for up to three months.[13] The law is to apply to all Indian citizens, whether living in India or abroad. Lawmakers acknowledge that it will pertain especially to the propertied classes, as the indigent would not be able to provide a monthly maintenance allowance to an elder even if so ordered.

For the purposes of this Bill, "children" include biological and adoptive sons and stepsons, daughters, grandsons, and granddaughters, but not minors. "Relatives" include any legal heir of a childless senior citizen who is in possession of or stands to inherit his or her property after his death. A "senior citizen" is any citizen of India age sixty or older, while there is no minimum age requirement to be a "parent." "Maintenance" includes "provision of food, clothing, residence and medical attendance and treatment"—that is, meeting the aged person's needs "so that the senior citizen may lead a normal life."[14] It is noteworthy that the culturally long-recognized although uncomfortable relationship between elder care and inheritance (discussed in chapter 2) becomes legally formalized in this bill; relatives who stand to inherit from the elder are those specifically obligated to provide maintenance.

The language of gender is interesting in both the older and newer parental maintenance laws. It is striking that no differentiation is provided in these bills between the obligations of a son or a daughter, even though according to prevalent cultural and social structural principles in India it is sons who are generally responsible for their parents in late life, while daughters once married are freed from such obligations, assuming instead responsibilities for their parents-in-law. Further, nowhere in the lengthy text of the Maintenance and Welfare of Parents and Senior Citizens Bill of 2007 is the role of the daughter-in-law addressed. Social workers and legal counselors in Kolkata with whom I discussed the matter, however, reported that under existing laws, daughters-in-law can indeed be obligated to provide parental maintenance. In fact, reportedly, it is common for a daughter-in-law to be jointly involved in such a case with her husband, or to be pursued independently if her husband is deceased. Presumably under the new 2007 maintenance law, a widowed daughter-in-law who has inherited or stands to inherit property from her parents-in-law could also in that regard be classified as a relative of a childless elder obligated to provide support.

According to those I interviewed, however, Bengali elders almost never think to legally pursue a daughter for maintenance—except perhaps in the relatively uncommon circumstance when a daughter and her husband have taken on the formal obligation to care for an elder parent in exchange for inheriting the parent's property, when no sons exist.[15] In perusing the newspaper coverage on legal disputes between parents and children that my research assistant and I gathered from 2003 to 2008, I have not encountered any cases where the courts have explicitly blamed a daughter. Daughters, in fact, not infrequently figure as rescuers—freeing parents from locked rooms or dire situations of neglect received at the hands of sons and daughters-in-law, bringing the cases to the attention of the police. In contrast to the common image of the benign, loving, generous daughter (who is not culturally obligated to provide for her parents, so that anything she does offer is an act of liberal generosity and love, while anything she fails to provide is not her fault), the figure of the negligent and deliberately spiteful daughter-in-law is a familiar and old one in the Indian imagination. The courts and police seem to easily include the daughter-in-law in their assessments of blame, as we saw in the case opening this chapter; when a man committed suicide after undergoing "torture" at the hands of his juniors, both the son and daughter-in-law were jailed.

As my own informants for this project did not include any individuals or families whom I knew to be involved in legal disputes over elder maintenance, I cannot move on now to examine their personal stories. However, it is illuminating to probe further the underlying assumptions and models—about aging, personhood, gender, the nature of the family, and the relationship between the family and the state—evidenced in discourses surrounding such legal disputes published in local newspapers and judges' opinions.

"Court Orders Son and Daughter-in-Law to Grasp Parents' Feet and Beg Forgiveness":[16] *Gender, Generation, and Family Values in the Courts*

During the five-year period from 2003 through 2008 when I examined local coverage on the topic, newspapers reported that increasing numbers of cases regarding disputes between elderly parents and junior kin have come to the attention of the police and courts—reportedly about fifteen to twenty cases per month in and around Kolkata (e.g., B. Bandyopadhyay 2005).[17] In a featured Sunday piece titled "Old Age Angst," under the subheading, "Courts Whip Cruel Sons," it is reported that "in the last few years, elderly parents have filed numerous petitions before the Calcutta High Court against their children," described as "cruel, uncaring and selfish offsprings" (Gupta 2005).

The key players in the disputes are almost always a parent or parents and their son(s) and/or daughter(s)-in-law. Often the disputes involve property. For instance, in one reported case, this one transpiring in Delhi, a son allegedly compelled his father at knifepoint to execute a general power of attorney in the son's favor; but the case was brought to the High Court, where the chief justice issued a warning to the son to sort out his "differences" with his parents or else face a police probe into the parent's allegations (*Telegraph* 2004). In another case, when a widowed mother refused to transfer the family home to her son's name, the son and daughter-in-law began to threaten and mentally torment her. This was followed by physical beating. The son argued that he was going to retire soon and therefore needed to have the home in his name right now. The torture reached such a height that the widowed mother felt forced to leave the home, taking refuge with her daughter. When a complaint with the police brought no redress, she filed a suit in the High Court. The High Court decreed that whenever the mother wishes to return, the police should escort the elder woman back to her rightful home with her son and daughter-in-law. If the elder woman further complains of torture, harsh steps will be taken against the junior couple (*Anandabajar Patrika* 2007).

Other cases revolve around more mundane generational conflict. For instance, in one case a daughter-in-law allegedly began to lock up the household kitchen, hiding the key, so that her fifty-seven-year-old mother-in-law had no access to it; and she began ill-treating the older woman whenever the son was out (although the son reportedly tried to persuade his wife to be kind to his mother). In this case, the Calcutta High Court judge ordered the family—the widowed mother, daughter-in-law, son, and grandchildren—to eat their meals together daily for a fortnight, and then to report back to the court after two weeks. During this time, both the mother-in-law and daughter-in-law were to have equal access to the kitchen, and share in the cooking. Three weeks later, the newspapers reported that the judge's directive appeared to have worked:

> A family that eats together, stays together. The adage proved to be true on Monday when a family—on the verge of splitting up a month ago—appeared as a close-knit unit in court. . . . After eating together for three weeks, the family appeared in court and told the judge that they had ironed out their differences. A pleased judge wished them a happy Puja (*Times News Network* 2007a).[18]

Another older woman, following a spat with her two daughters-in-law, stormed out of the home telling her kin not to worry about her, and wandered the streets for two days until the police picked her up. She was reluctant to return home, but finally after the police offered her tea and promised to bring her back to the station during the upcoming Puja celebrations, she provided the names of her sons, who arrived to escort her home (*Telegraph* 2005b, *Times News Network* 2005a).

Many cases, as reported in the papers, are born from a mixture of economic concerns and the impact of a social-cultural milieu of changing values. "Aged Mother Dumped at Station" and "80-year-old United with Family, Nightmare Ends" (Debnath 2008a and 2008b) report on the Kolkata police's efforts to compel an errant son and daughter-in-law to provide for their octogenarian mother. The younger couple, Dulal and Padma Sardar, apparently had their reasons for attempting to rid their lives of the older woman, claiming that they could not afford to care for her and that they needed her bedroom. "They even offered a solution to the eighty-year-old woman," the reporter recounts. "She could either take her own life by throwing herself before the next train or go to any of her two daughters for shelter" (Debnath 2008a). The son and daughter-in-law proceeded to leave her by the railway tracks with a few belongings and small pillow stuffed in a bag. At least three local trains sped by. Finally, a subsequent train driver spotted the elderly woman, dressed in the plain white garb of an old Bengali widow, and a few Good Samaritan passengers alighted. They tried first to take the old woman to her daughter's house. But the daughter was not at home and the daughter's husband refused to take the elderly woman in; so the Good Samaritans escorted the woman to the police station, where she was provided with food and a bed. Past midnight, the police tracked down and summoned to the station the son and daughter-in-law. There the couple was warned about the law—that it is mandatory for all children to take care of their elderly parents or else be fined or imprisoned. But the police offered the son a second chance if he agreed to pledge in writing that he would take care of his mother and never drive her out again. The police escorted the reunited family back to their home and woke up the neighbors, requesting them to keep an eye out and inform the police if they noticed any future wrongdoings. The newspaper story ends: "Every day more and more elderly people are being abandoned by their children either when they shift to other places for work or simply because of the generation gap. Calcutta High Court has, in recent times, seen a flurry of cases when elderly people have sought legal resort after being tortured or driven away by their offspring" (Debnath 2008a).

In yet another intergenerational dispute, a widowed mother inherited her husband's home upon his death.[19] The trouble began when her youngest son began to threaten the older woman that he would expel her from the home if she refused to sign the property over to him. Apprehending being ousted, the mother filed a case in the Alipore, Kolkata court. Her son filed a counter-petition, claiming that the woman was in fact not his mother but merely his father's "kept woman" (*rakshitā*), and that she therefore had no right to the family property. Deeply offended by this statement, Calcutta High Court Judge Biswanath Samaddar summoned the son to appear before him in court, amid a crowd of curious onlookers. *Anandabajar Patrika* reports: "Right from the beginning, Justice Samaddar felt extremely anguished. He repeatedly reminded the audience that the High Court can never support such a horrifying erosion of values" (*Anandabajar Patrika* 2008b). The older woman had four children—two sons and two daughters. None of the other children disputed her identity as their true mother. Judge Samaddar proclaimed, "Only a mother can say who her offspring are. Hence, the Court cannot disregard a mother's account." The judge cautioned the son, "The High Court does not want to hear about this subject a second time. If the sacred (*pabitra*) relationship between the mother and son gets tainted, that does not augur at all well for society. The values which human beings have nurtured over centuries cannot be allowed to degenerate out of mere self-interest (*svārtha*)."

At this point, the son stood up in court and began to scream: "That I called my mother a kept woman is an offense! But my mother called my wife a prostitute! What about that?"

The judge replied, "We do not want to know what your mother told your wife. But she never used any obscene word [like *rakshitā* or kept woman] in court."

The story concludes: "The Judge ruled that both sides should sit with their lawyers and solve the issue through discussion. The relationship of affection, attachment, fondness and respect existing between mother and son should be revived. After fifteen days a report on this should be submitted to the High Court" (*Anandabajar Patrika* 2008b).

The son sought a directive to the media not to publish the report of the proceedings, but the judge rejected the plea, arguing that "if he was so concerned about his social image he should not have used such words against his mother in court" (Prahladka 2008).

In another case, a widowed mother, son, and daughter-in-law were called to court after the mother complained that the younger couple did not take care of her or provide her with food, but were renting out her portion of the family home and keeping the proceeds. The *Anandabajar Patrika* staff correspondent reports:

> Today, right at the beginning of the case, the judge asked [the son], "What is this? You don't take care of your mother, give her food? This old woman had to come to the court—aren't you ashamed?" With

folded hands, [the son] replied, "Sir, I have committed a wrong, my Lord. I apologize. From now onwards, I shall take care of my mother."

The judge decreed that the mother must be paid each month the full proceeds from the rental, proclaiming in an emotion-filled voice, "A mother cannot be compared with anyone. You wait and see, your mother will save from that amount and give to you at your hour of emergency." The judge then asked the aged woman whether 4,000 rupees a month would suffice for her maintenance. The woman replied meekly, "I have small expenses. Whatever I save I will give to him. I am advancing toward death." In closing, "the Judge spoke to [the son] affectionately, 'Take care of your mother. You see, you will be happy.'"[20]

In still further cases: A judge warns a neglectful son, a government employee, to mend his ways if he cares for his job (Gupta 2005). Another judge orders a son and daughter-in-law to grasp their parents' feet and beg for forgiveness, and then come back to report to the court after the quarrels are settled, warning: "Remember, your own children will be grown one day. I hope you will have no regrets" (Bhattacharyya 2003).

Some common themes emerge in these stories. First, elders are dependent (appropriately, as are young children). Second, the family is the proper site of elder care. Third, locating elder care within the family is not simply a matter of tackling the (limited) problem of how the elderly of a society should be sustained, but is rather a pivotal part of a much broader vision of the proper functioning of society as a whole. This broader vision is evident in Judge Samaddar's proclamations: "If the sacred (*pabitra*) relationship between the mother and son gets tainted, that does not augur at all well for society" (*Anandabajar Patrika* 2008b). Fourth, in parental maintenance disputes, the courts seem to be strongly biased in favor of the elders, at least as the stories are reported in the papers. That is, the foundational presumption seems to be that elder parents are, without question, trustworthy and deserving—simply by virtue of their being parents and old—and thus, sons (and daughters-in-law) can say little in their own defense.[21]

As noted above, the courts and the public previously used family maintenance laws to emphasize the protection not of elders but of vulnerable younger women, notably abandoned and abused daughters-in-law and wives. My readings of contemporary media stories, as well as my limited number of conversations with attorneys, social workers, and the police, suggest that the courts are increasingly working now to protect elderly parents. This is perhaps because elders seem to be gradually losing in relative social power and so are suddenly more in need of legal succor. To some extent, the abused and powerless elderly parent is taking the place of the abused and powerless daughter-in-law in the public imagination. An *Anandabajar Patrika* news story titled "Homeless mother-in-law, beaten by her daughter-in-law, wanders the streets" opens along these lines: "So long it was heard that the mother-in-law throws the daughter-in-law out of the home. Now the complaint is that the daughter-in-law has thrown her mother-in-law out of the old woman's own home, and thrown her father-in-law out as well" (7 April 2005). What was once the era of gerontocratic patriarchy, many today argue, is now becoming an era of aged and gendered egalitarianism, individualism, and independence.

Some (elders in particular) contend that the Indian courts should work to remedy what they see as the growing imbalance in favor of the young in the wider society, with even stricter elder-rights measures. In the suicide note left by the retired Alipore clerk whose story opened this chapter, the sixty-five-year-old writes in severe distress:

> If a woman is tortured, the first thing police do is arrest her in-laws, even though they are elderly. What if I am tortured by my daughter-in-law? All 498A [a section that deals with physical and mental torture of women] does is put people like us behind bars, it will never put my daughter-in-law behind bars. Police should look into this discrepancy and if need be change the law, for I am ending my life unable to bear the torture meted out to me by my daughter-in-law. (Times News Network 2005b)[22]

One 2003 Calcutta High Court ruling specified, in favor of the younger wife and generational independence, that if a wife desires to live separately (*pṛthak*) with her husband, away from her in-laws, then arrangements must be made. This ruling provoked a flurry of agitated letters to the editor from older *Anandabajar Patrika* readers, assembled in a 16 October 2003 collection titled "Let aged father and mother go to hell."[23] One letter, submitted by Krishnadas Chattopadhyay of Birbhum, a district a few hours northwest of Kolkata by train, reads:

> The above verdict of the Calcutta High Court, based on equal rights of man and woman, has no doubt supplied another weapon of waywardness to society's modern women (*ādhunikā*), who believe in the theory of equality of men and women and who are now happy. On the pretext that "I am unable to adjust," if the wife, soon after

marriage, refuses to stay with her husband's mother, father, or relatives, and in that case, if the husband decides . . . to live separately in order to fulfill the immediate pleasures of his wife, breaking a tradition of discipline, and in that case, if the parents remain dependent on the income of their son, then what will the parents do? In my ordinary thinking, I am not able to understand how this verdict of the Honorable Court is going to benefit society!

According to traditional social norms (*pracalita niyamānusāre*), a woman grows up nurturing the dream in her mind that she will enter into marriage, leave behind her familiar surroundings, hold the hand of a man, attempt to adjust to a totally new environment with the strength of her own education and culture, and take on the role of an ideal wife, daughter-in-law, and mother. This verdict of the Court will destroy all such good qualities of the feminine spirit and give rise to indiscipline. . . . This historic, 'great' verdict of the Honorable Court has no doubt snatched in a second the smiles from the faces of helpless, aged parents and widowed sisters and unemployed brothers. For, according to this world's current fashions, no modern woman (*ādhunikā*) would like the money earned by her husband or herself to be spent to maintain the entire [husband's] family. . . .

The fact is that as a result of this new edition of the equal rights of women and men, the human society is being transformed into an animal society (*paśusamāj*). Like animals and birds, in the present society, the role of parents will be simply to educate the son effortlessly until he can be on his own. Then it will be just "you and me."

"You and me," or in Bengali, "*tumi o āmi,*" is meant here to indicate the romantic, self-focused, dyadic couple of husband and wife, apart from parents and wider kin. In a society where children grow up to live separately from their parents, people become like animals—among whom neither generation, following a short-lived period of dependent infancy, depends on or maintains close ties with the other.

Murarimohan Manna of Howrah, on the outskirts of Kolkata, likens the moving out of the son and daughter-in-law to the shooting of one's parents, writing:

I felt a bit sad to read this news—"If the wife wants to stay with her husband separately, arrangements must be made." Today I am aged seventy-one years. Since my earliest consciousness, I have seen that sons live along with their aged parents and extend all kinds of care and service (*sevā*) to them. I too have taken similar care of my parents. At present they are no more.

Now, following this news, if all sons desert their parents and live with their wives, renting places elsewhere, then there should have been one law, as follows, in the Constitution of India: As soon as one reaches the age of retirement (sixty), sons can shoot their parents to death. Then daughters-in-law won't have to go anywhere else. They could live in peace in their own homes. I plead with the Government of India to please pass a similar law!

These letters are accompanied by a sketch meant to portray a modern, young, nuclear-style family: a husband, wife, and one young son are seated on a modern furniture set—a matching couch and armchair—with a television in the background, the remote control in the wife's hand and a mobile phone in the husband's.

It is amid such an environment of generational and gendered strife and uncertainty that the new Maintenance and Welfare of Parents and Senior Citizens Bill, and high-profile court cases in favor of parental support, are transpiring. According to the papers, however, it is only with heavy hearts that lawmakers are implementing such measures. In a story titled "House Tears for the Aged," published in the *Telegraph,* 7 December 2007, the reporter recounts: "The Upper House passed a bill to ensure the aged are well looked after, with tearful members regretting that the country should ever have needed such legislation."

The Ambivalent Role of the State in Elder Care

Not all policy makers in India agree, however, that the best site of elder care is inevitably the family, and some are calling for the state to take on a greater role. One *Telegraph* editorial, spurred by a report of a middle-class elderly woman abandoned on the streets by her sons, critiques the absence of a welfare system in India, which creates "inordinate dependence on the family. . . . To blame [the current situation of the elderly] on the demise of the joint family is to misrepresent the complex, systemic and political nature of the problem—an evasive moralism behind which governments often hide" (*The Telegraph* 2006).

To depend as a nation exclusively on the family for elder care is not, many argue, merely inadequate; it is also "backward." "Independent India is rapidly marching towards achieving the desirable goal of being a welfare state," gerontologists S. Irudaya Rajan, U.S. Mishra, and P. Sankara Sarma (1999:141) argue—and implementing effective social security programs is an essential part of that goal. In their *India's Elderly: Burden or Challenge?*

Rajan et al. recommend that the Indian government should support old age homes and pension plans, and that aging individuals should cultivate a dependence on the self—through savings, exercise, and an open-mindedness about living in old age homes—as one can no longer count on, and *should* no longer count on if one is modern and educated, depending on children in old age. Shovana Narayana comments: "The self-sufficiency of the elderly is a very healthy trend. . . . The *problem* lies in the *rural mind set* where people consider their children as a support system for their old age" (in Gupta 2001, emphasis added).

Such views are consistent with assumptions in international development discourse: state support for the elderly, in the form of pension schemes and elder-care institutions, is taken internationally to be one of the core signs of a "developed" nation. Economist Robert Palacios of the World Bank, for instance, remarks: "In the past fifty years, policymakers in India have made precious little progress towards providing a viable alternative to the family as the main source of income security for the elderly" (2002a). In "The Future of Global Ageing" Palacios examines the dramatic worldwide expansion of formal pension schemes for the elderly during the twentieth century, contrasting the achievements of "rich, developed" nations to those of the "poor, young countries of the developing world." Rich and developed countries, he asserts, have state pension schemas in place, while poor countries still rely inordinately on the family. India finds itself here among the "poor" countries: "In India, home to one-eighth of the world's population over 60, more than two-thirds of old women reported depending on transfers from children in the early 1990s." Although currently "practically every country in the world has some formal pension scheme," Palacios reveals, those in place in poor and middle-income countries are limited, targeted only at alleviating poverty, and thus cannot operate as a comprehensive alternative to the family in the way that pension schemes can in rich and developed nations (2002b: 786–789).

We see here a clear developmental teleology: as a nation progresses from being poor to being rich, developing to developed, its elders will progress from relying on the family to relying on the state and individual self.[24] Of course, many who espouse current neoliberal policies would argue that the free market and ethical self-responsibility are even more efficient, desirable, and advanced than a welfare state (see, e.g., Ong 2006).[25] These are very different cultural models than the one, as seen in earlier pages, held by some Indians—that to turn away from a system of lifelong intergenerational family transfers is not to progress, but to *regress* from a more natural, humane, and civilized to an unnatural and even animalistic state of being.

Social Security and Cultural Models of Personhood and Family

Modest state-based social security systems have gradually come into existence in India, beginning in the British colonial era, when retirement benefits for government employees were established, and continuing after Independence. The Indian Constitution embraces a concept of social security establishing that the state should make itself responsible for ensuring a minimum standard of material welfare to all its citizens (see Kumar 2003:49, Gokhale 2003:225). Some government programs to support the elderly are in place beyond the new legislation aimed at pressing families to support their own elders. These programs come in three major forms: retirement pension schemes for employees in the "organized sector" (primarily government employees), modest old-age pensions for the destitute, and limited government support for voluntary non-governmental organizations providing services to the aged, such as HelpAge India and Agewell Foundation.[26] In addition, the new Maintenance and Welfare of Parents and Senior Citizens Bill, although it emphasizes family care, includes some minimal recommendations to expand state social security programs by calling upon (though not requiring) state governments to establish old age homes for the destitute and encouraging government hospitals to set aside sufficient beds for the elderly.

About 10 percent of India's working population is employed in the organized sector and eligible to receive retirement pensions (after a mandatory retirement age of about sixty).[27] These include primarily employees of the government and other major enterprises, such as manufacturing, mining, and port and railway companies (Kumar 2003:45–55), as well as employees of large transnational corporations. The Government of India spends about 6 percent of its revenue on pensions for its employees (Kumar 2003:62). However, the vast majority, about 90 percent, of India's workforce comprises the "unorganized sector," and is thus not eligible for employee-based pensions. The majority of these are agricultural workers; there are also rickshaw pullers, taxi drivers, shopkeepers, carpenters, domestic servants, etc. Beginning in the 1950s, India's individual states began implementing old-age pension programs for destitute older persons, offering an average of about 150 rupees, or $3.00 to $4.00 USD, per month. In 1999, the Central Government instituted the first National Old-Age Pension Scheme (NOAPS)—offering 75 rupees (or around $1.50) per month to persons over sixty-five who are considered destitute, defined as "having little or no regular means of subsistence from their own income or through financial support from family members or other sources."[28] In April 2006, the government increased the pension amount to 200 rupees per month. Applicants must provide certification of being above sixty-five years of age along with proof of their destitute status.[29] Although modest, the funds enable recipients to purchase basic food supplies. The funds can also, I found in conducting supplemental research with recipients of such pensions, provide the recipients with enhanced status and clout within their families. (In the context of a very poor family, 200 rupees per month is a notable income, enabling an elder to purchase a grandchild a few biscuits, contribute modestly to a household's expenses, and in a sense buy some degree of attention and care.) Several studies have concluded, however, that there are problems in the disbursement of the old-age pensions for the destitute, including cumbersome application procedures, irregular payments, and lack of awareness on the part of potentially eligible recipients (Kumar 2003:59, Sreevastava 2004).

It is clear that state support for the aged is still quite limited in India, and this is due, I suggest, to a mixture of both economic exigency (India is poor) and cultural principles (family is best). Many Indians—policy makers, government officials, and the public—would like to see India develop more extensive and generous forms of social security for elders but acknowledge that India is still quite a poor nation with limited governmental capability. It is also significant that the existing modest social welfare programs for the elderly in India are only for those with no family to rely on. This is unlike, as we will see further shortly, the U.S. Supplemental Security Income (SSI) program for the low-income aged. A U.S. SSI recipient could have children with assets in the millions, and this information would not even be relevant. A U.S. elder's *spouse's* assets do count; the U.S. government considers husbands and wives to be appropriately financially interdependent. But the existence of children or their assets does not even come into consideration in calculating SSI eligibility—revealing very different Indian and U.S. cultural models of personhood, family, and in/dependence over the life course.

The significance of sons in determining eligibility for aged welfare programs in India became clear during my visit to the single government old age home in West Bengal, one of only a handful of government old age homes in the nation.[30] The Home for Old and Infirm Political Sufferers was first established in the mid-1960s when the Left Front Government came to power in West Bengal; its mission was to provide shelter to aged freedom fighters who had fought for India's independence from Britain in the first half of the twentieth century, and to other "political sufferers" who had been injured or imprisoned protesting various Congress Government policies since Independence. In the beginning the home housed sixty boarders, all male; but by the time of my visit in 2006, there were only fourteen political sufferers remaining. In 1989, the home opened its doors to destitute older women and men, with a capacity of near seventy.

My research assistant Hena and I made the journey on a bright, pleasant day in late April, with high clouds floating against a pastel blue sky, unseasonably dry and mild following the dramatic, cooling thunderstorms of the previous evening. We took the car about an hour and a half from Kolkata along crowded narrow roads into the South 24 Parganas District, past guava and lychee groves, rice and sugarcane fields, descending at the Champahati Railway Station. From there we walked ten or fifteen minutes to the home, asking for directions along the way. We frequently left the car and driver at a major thoroughfare, finding it less awkward to negotiate the final stretches of a journey to an old age home by foot or cycle rickshaw in a region where private cars remained relatively uncommon luxuries. This old age home was popularly known as the *Pānchtalā Bāṛi,* or Five-Story Building, the only such grand edifice amid the semi-rural backdrop of the district—an old, majestic zamindar's[31] mansion sold to the government years ago. Painted a pale yellow, it stood in the bend of a quiet cobblestone road.

Since it was the day immediately following an election—a major holiday in West Bengal, when all businesses are closed and many return to their home towns or neighborhoods to vote—the superintendent was not present. But we were able to speak with a welcoming caretaker, who took us inside the spacious front office on the ground floor. Since we had not obtained official permission to visit, we were not allowed upstairs to take a look around, but the caretaker was happy to chat with us about the history of the place and its current operations. Sixteen staff currently care for sixty-eight boarders, the majority now female, after the days of housing political sufferers were nearly over. To qualify for admission, the candidate or person bringing the candidate must fill out an application, and then there

FIGURE 8.1. Home for Old and Infirm Political Sufferers.

is an investigation to determine that the person is truly destitute (*dustha*). It is not enough, the caretaker explained, if the person has a son whose economic condition is fine but who simply doesn't want to look after his parent. The candidate must be in a terrible condition (*abasthā khubi khārāp*), with no one who could possibly care for him or her. The boarders are mostly brought by others, such as the police, who find them on the streets. They are in general highly grateful to have a place to stay, receiving a roof over their heads, a fan, food, and *sevā* (respectful care). They sleep dormitory style, three to six persons to a room. A doctor comes three days a week and is offered an honorarium. The home is almost fully funded by the West Bengal Government, with some additional assistance from the Central Government and various non-governmental organizations.

As we were chatting with the manager in the front office, an older gentleman entered. He was dressed in Western-style pants and shirt that seemed in quite decent condition, clean and relatively new. He himself also appeared physically and mentally fit, and had a pleasant, quiet, dignified presence. His face had not been shaven for a few days, and there was a subtle harried air to him, but he otherwise came off quite well. He inquired demurely and politely, "What are the procedures for admission to this place?"

The caretaker asked if he inquired for himself.

"Yes," responded the gentleman.

The caretaker began to explain the procedures, but then, after a pause, advised, "I wouldn't want you to waste your time going through the application process if you won't qualify. May I ask, is the matter quite urgent? Do you need a place right away?"

"Yes, it is a bit urgent," the gentleman humbly replied.

"OK," the caretaker offered respectfully. "Can you tell me if you have any sons?"

"Yes, two sons."

"Do you mind if I ask—what do they do?"

"One has a small electric business," the older man replied, "and the other works for the railway."

"Oh, then, no, sorry, you won't qualify," the caretaker responded, still gently but decisively. "If sons exist, it won't happen" (*chelerā thākle habe nā*).

"Even if they don't support me at all?" the gentleman persisted hopefully.

"That's right, even if they don't support you at all."

Eagerly curious about the gentleman and his situation for our research, and keen to help him if we could, Hena and I initiated conversation. We told him about other homes we knew of. He was worried that he couldn't afford much, but said that as a former factory worker, he had compiled some savings, and using the interest from the savings could afford to pay about 1,000 rupees per month, as long as he didn't also have to put down a deposit. He did not reveal why he could no longer live with his sons, with whom he used to stay before he had moved to his sister's daughter's home a few weeks earlier. He appreciatively had us write down a few addresses and phone numbers of those old age homes we had visited that we had both liked and that had low fees. Shortly after, the gentleman, Hena, and I departed, going our own ways.

This was a fascinating interaction to witness, and one point it plainly brought home is that although the state is increasingly involved in matters of old age care in India, a central premise underlying the state's involvement is that care of the aged by the family (notably sons) is best, most normal, most appropriate—culturally, morally, and economically. Such a premise does not go entirely unchallenged, as some assert that it is time for India to deemphasize the role of the family. Further, some argue that to attempt to legislate family care is futile; if a family does not out of its own volition wish to care for its elderly, will the existence of laws accomplish the task?[32] So it is with complex ambivalence that members of the Indian public approach recent developments regarding state involvement in elder care in India.

America as a Deluxe Retirement Home? Competing Views of Aging, Family, and the Person-State Relationship in the United States

> Have you heard of the buṛo āśram? old age home? . . .
> Seniors from India are using the U.S. government like an old age home. They come here, and the U.S. government takes care of all medical expenses, food. . . .
>
> —VITALBHAI GUJAR, Indian immigrant
> to the United States, age seventy

> The U.S. welfare system has . . . become a form of deluxe retirement home for many elderly from the Third World.
>
> —ROBERT RECTOR of the Heritage Foundation,
> testifying before the U.S. Congress, February 6, 1996

Two different possible answers to the question of the proper site of elder care are apparent in the Indian and U.S. contexts. Indian state policies emphasize the home and sons, and yet in the United States, the government itself has become a natural provider of elder care, as part and parcel of a developed welfare state and a cultural emphasis on individual self-reliance. (The state steps in, when necessary, to help aged individuals rely on themselves.) The comments of Vitalbhai Gujar above and those of other Indian Americans from chapter 7 reveal how many older immigrants come to view U.S. state support of the elderly, ambivalently, as a quintessential part of American culture and way of life. In the neoliberal climate of the mid-1990s, however, U.S. policy makers began to express concern that aged immigrants were using the welfare system too much, and it was in this context that Robert Rector of the conservative Heritage Foundation think tank was invited to testify to Congress, making his argument that the U.S. welfare system had inappropriately "become a form of deluxe retirement home" for elderly immigrants "from the Third World" (U.S. Congress,

Senate 1997:109). By exploring the clash of values between the U.S. and Indian state models of elder care, I aim to further illuminate assumptions underpinning both systems.

Interestingly, as with the origins of old age homes in the United States that we briefly examined in chapter 3 (finding there that the concept of the old age home did not really take hold in the United States until the early 1900s), the concept of state support for the elderly is also relatively new and not a "primordial" American tradition. Historian David Hackett Fischer notes, in his *Growing Old in America,* that "114 old age pension bills were introduced in Massachusetts between 1903 and 1929, and not one of them was passed. The legislature preferred to deal with the problem by passing a law which made it a criminal offense for a child with means to fail to support an aged parent" (1978:159). Michel Dahlin also notes that "the failure of the family was an important theme in the campaign for old age pensions" in early twentieth-century America (1993:125). "The family was supposed to be the primary source of aid for the dependent elderly," Dahlin relates, "but reformers argued that the family, especially the working-class family, was no longer able to perform this role as a result of industrialization, at least not without making sacrifices that middle-class reformers considered unacceptable, such as sending children to work at a young age or over-crowding homes" (p.125).

So, in such a climate of debate over the proper site of elder care—the family or the state—Congress implemented the Social Security Act of 1935, the first major U.S. program of federal old-age benefits. Its central function was to establish a pension system for aged persons, calculated as a percentage of former wages.[33] Interestingly, the providing of Social Security pensions to the elderly impacted the family in ways that had not been predicted. According to Dahlin, "it freed the old from financial dependence on children and led, not to happy and conflict-free co-residence, but to a sharp decrease in co-residence of the elderly with their children in the years following its adoption" (Dahlin 1993:126).

Since 1935, Congress has broadened the Social Security Act many times. The Medicare health insurance initiative, a major amendment to the Social Security Act, became law in 1965. Medicare is the nation's largest health insurance program, providing federal money to cover most of the health needs of individuals aged sixty-five or over and making medical care more fully accessible to the elderly than ever before in American history (Fischer 1978:192).[34] In 1974 the Supplemental Security Income (SSI) program was implemented to provide a nationally uniform guaranteed minimum income for the low-income aged (as well as the blind and disabled). Supplemental Security Income can be combined with Social Security (if so, the recipient receives a proportionally lesser amount), and it can also be drawn upon by those not eligible for Social Security, such as those who have not accrued Social Security credits through regular employment.

Federal, state, and local government funds also support a myriad of other programs for elders in most major cities and towns across the United States: senior transport services and senior centers that offer such activities as classes, social events, games, outings, discounted meals, and the like. According to some of my Indian American informants—such as Gopal Singh, the Punjabi Sikh immigrant in his seventies quoted in chapter 7—one doesn't even need to live with one's children in America, since the state provides so much: SSI, Medicare, senior centers. "Why, we can even call 911 if something goes wrong. . . . Why would we have to live with our children?" Indian immigrant perceptions are indeed that state care for the aged, as opposed to family care, is such a normal, central part of "American culture" that the U.S. government can be likened to an old age home. As explored in chapter 7, many senior Indian Americans enjoy, admire, praise, and partake in U.S. state services for the elderly, although not for most without some ambivalence, uncertainty, and discomfort, as Vitalbhai Gujar expressed when I asked him if he thinks it's wrong that older Indian Americans are using the U.S. government like an old age home. "Yes!" he replied. "And it's bad for families, too. My son is not taking on his responsibility of caring for me! And then their children are not learning from them—they think just that the government should do it. . . . They're forgetting the Indian system."

The 1996 Congressional Hearing: The Use of SSI by Immigrants

I turn to focus now more specifically on the Supplemental Security Income (SSI) program and the debates over its use by immigrants that ensued in the U.S. Congress and among my older Indian American informants in the late 1990s—as these debates reveal very interesting competing models of aging, family, and the person-state relationship. In February 1996, Congress held a hearing before the Subcommittee on Immigration of the Committee on the Judiciary, to debate the merits of the use of Supplemental Security Income and other welfare programs by immigrants

(U.S. Congress, Senate 1997). From the beginning of the SSI program, initiated in 1974, legal aliens (non-citizen immigrants) were eligible to receive benefits under the program, provided they met other eligibility requirements pertaining to age, blindness or disability, and financial resources.[35] In fact, until about the mid-1990s the subject of immigration barely entered into any of the congressional dialogue surrounding SSI. For instance, Congress's ten-year assessment of the program considers participation by "race"—"white," "black," "other" and "not reported"—but nowhere provides data pertaining to the immigrant status, whether alien or citizen, of participants (U.S. Congress, Senate 1984). By 1988 there was concern that "minorities" of longer standing in the country, including Blacks, Hispanics, American Indians, and Asian/Pacific Islanders, were underrepresented in the SSI-aged program, and outreach efforts were established to increase minority participation, through foreign-language radio announcements and the outplacement of bilingual staff in diverse community centers (U.S. Congress, House 1989a; Sexton 1997; Young and Kawabori 1995).

But by the 1990s, some began to be concerned that immigrants were *over*-utilizing SSI, including Robert Rector and William Lauber of the Washington-based conservative public policy research institute the Heritage Foundation, who wrote a report titled, "America Is Becoming a Deluxe Retirement Home" (Rector and Lauber 1995). This report caught the attention of the U.S. government. Robert Rector was invited to testify at the congressional hearing on the use of SSI by immigrants, where he made the assertion that "the U.S. welfare system has already become a form of deluxe retirement home for many elderly from the Third World" (U.S. Congress, Senate 1997:109).

Two factors are likely significant here, spurring the new concerns. First, there was in fact a real increase in the number of alien residents receiving aid from the Supplemental Security Income program over the years leading up to the hearing. From 1982 to 1994, the number of aged immigrants receiving SSI had risen by 379 percent (U.S. Congress, Senate 1997:2). This increase was probably due in part to enhanced efforts on the part of the government to recruit non-whites for the program. In addition, the rate of immigration increased over this same period, undercutting the conclusion that immigrants are now simply demonstrating an increased propensity to go on welfare (pp. 5–6, 43, 74–75). Second, recent decades had also witnessed a changing racial makeup of the immigrant body. Until 1965, immigrants to the United States came primarily from Europe, but by the mid 1990s, Asian and Latino immigrants had come to make up 75 percent of the entering immigrant population (Hing 1997:2). It is probably not a coincidence that when immigrants from regions other than Europe became predominant in the United States, the discourses of opportunistic immigrant elderly grabbing at benefits they do not deserve acquired salience.

Ultimately, a welfare reform bill was passed in August 1996 decreeing that immigrants would no longer be entitled to receive SSI benefits, unless or until they became naturalized citizens.[36] A year later a grandfather clause was amended to the bill allowing those receiving SSI benefits at the time of the new law to remain in the program.[37] These rulings impacted many of my informants and were widely discussed, especially among older members of the Indo-American Community (formerly Senior) Center in the San Francisco South Bay where I volunteered. For, as I related in chapter 7, many members of the community had been receiving SSI benefits, and in fact social welfare officials had been coming to the center once or twice a year to recruit members for the program and instruct them on how to apply. Thus many I knew were confused and somewhat hurt by the changes in policy.

These debates over SSI use by immigrants highlight some very interesting differences in cultural understandings of parent-child and senior-state relationships, forms of reciprocity and in/dependence, and calculating productivity over the life course. Interestingly, although testifiers in the Congressional hearing frequently invoked a notion of culture when discussing immigrant "others" (in statements such as "Asian reverence for aged parents" and "the Chinese tradition of close family ties"),[38] there seemed to be little or no recognition that U.S. government policies and documents are themselves replete with particular cultural assumptions and models not universally shared, obvious, or natural.

The Proper Site of Elder Care: Children or the State?

Probably the most salient cultural principle that the SSI program and debates over its use throw into relief is the matter of who should properly care for a society's aged: children or the state? In America, many Indians explain, children do not provide for their parents—and this is not due to moral laxity on the part of children, but rather to the existence of a very different cultural system. Programs like SSI and Medicare exemplify the American cultural principle of state versus family care for the aged.

At first, as we saw in chapter 7, many Indian Americans are puzzled by this alternative way of conceptualizing intergenerational relations, by the shift from an "Indian" perspective in which it is the responsibility of adult children to care for aged parents, to an "American" one in which parents are either self-supporting or supported by the state. Many older immigrants from India are, in fact, eligible for the SSI program (before 1996, after having spent at least three years in the country, and after 1996, only if they become naturalized citizens). This is because most have immigrated post-retirement and so are not employed in the United States and have not accrued U.S. social security credits. In addition, most senior immigrants from India have little or no resources of their "own," due to Government of India regulations restricting the outflow of currency from the nation and the unfavorable rupee to dollar exchange rate. So, even though many older immigrants may have a home or a retirement pension in India, they have almost no independent resources in the United States. Although most do receive support from their U.S.-settled children, they find that from a U.S. government perspective, being dependent on children is not an ordinary, expected, or required arrangement. If an elder (immigrant or not) happens to be living in a household for which the child is financially responsible, this is considered by the SSI program "living in another person's household." The elder parent could still be eligible for SSI but would simply receive a reduced amount (one taking into account that housing expenses are being covered). Thus, Indian immigrant elders are in an ambiguous class position—if considered as senior members of their (for the most part) middle-class families, they are in one position; but if regarded (as by the U.S. government) as separate "individuals," they are quite poor, even below the poverty line.[39]

Vitalbhai Gujar told of the confusion he felt when he first went to inquire at a local social security office about SSI benefits. Nearing seventy, Gujar had come to the United States several years earlier to live with his only son, a naturalized American citizen, and his daughter-in-law and granddaughter, in the younger couple's comfortable middle-class home in Fremont, California. The SSI program is especially for the "indigent" aged, Gujar learned, but he was told that he qualified, although his son makes a fine living. The SSI application form similarly perplexed him, when he was instructed to check the box, "I am living in another person's household." He explained: "Indian seniors are so confused by the USA's SSI. US officers say that their son and daughter-in-law's house is 'another person's house.' They say, 'You're living in another person's household.' But Indians don't understand this." I asked, "In India, would you call it 'your' house?" "No, the family house," he answered decisively, without pause, "the *family* house."

In general, my Indian American informants are right in their reading of the SSI program's underlying assumption, that it is not appropriate or expected for aged parents to depend on their children. I perused several congressional hearings as well as government documents on SSI, searching for some dialogue on the appropriateness (or not) of expecting adult children to support their parents in old age, or on whether the resources of children should be taken into account when assessing a senior person's eligibility for SSI.[40] I could find virtually no explicit discussion of the matter (so taken-for-granted or doxic is the assumption), except more recently when the discussion centered on immigrant practices. For instance, Norman Matloff, professor of computer science at the University of California at Davis and member (through his wife) of the Bay Area Chinese American community, testified to Congress: "Many of the recipients' children are upscale professionals. . . . Moreover, a senior will typically have several sons and daughters in the U.S., whose *total* income—and thus their collective ability to support the senior—is of course much higher even" (U.S. Congress, Senate 1997:91). He went on to deplore that such welfare use "was helping to erode Chinese family tradition" and runs "directly counter to the popular image of Asian reverence for aged parents" (p. 92, 94). Robert Rector of the Heritage Foundation added: "Most noncitizens on SSI . . . have relatives capable of supporting them" (p. 111), and Susan Martin of the U.S. Commission on Immigration Reform declared: "Historically, many ethnic groups have established mutual aid societies that help support new immigrants" (p. 34).

U.S. policy makers, however, do not pay heed to the financial resources of the multiple children, extended families, and/or ethnic support groups of non-immigrant older Americans when seeking to ascertain whether they are in need of public assistance. A 1980 informational pamphlet on the SSI program simply states cursorily: "Nor does the Federal law require support by relatives" (U.S. Department of Health and Human Services 1980:2). The 2008 Supplemental Security Income pamphlet on the www.socialsecurity.gov website does not mention children or relatives at all. As far as calculating eligibility for SSI is concerned, the federal government assumes only that a child (until the age of eighteen, if unmarried) shares in the income and resources of his or her parents, and that a husband and wife who live together share their income and resources. An immigrant, if sponsored, also shares in the resources of the sponsor until he or she becomes a naturalized citizen. Otherwise, each person is assessed as a separate individual.

Senator Edward Kennedy (Democrat, Massachusetts) was one of the participants in the 1996 hearing more outspoken in favor of immigrant rights, and he asserted: "In no case, however, should [senior] immigrants remain the wards of their sponsors once the immigrants become American citizens" (U.S. Congress, Senate 1997:57). His statement was meant to speak against the double standard being proposed—that only immigrant children care for their parents while "Americans" need not—but it also reveals the depth of his cultural views that it is unsuitable to expect adult children to support their parents, as wards, in their old age.

The basic model of parent-child relationships evident in government discourses surrounding the Supplemental Security Income program is consistent with that found in the wider U.S. society. Anthropological research has found that Americans, especially among the white middle classes, expect financial resources to flow in a unidirectional manner from parents to child throughout a lifetime. Parents support their children as minors, and even strive later to continue to provide some material assistance to children as adults, ending ideally with leaving an inheritance at death. However, most middle-class, white Americans find it an anathema to think of reversing the direction of intergenerational transfers to become financially dependent on their children in old age (Clark 1972, Hashimoto 1996, Hunt 2002, Kalish 1967, Simic 1990, Vesperi 1985),[41] although they do welcome non-monetary transfers, such as affection, love, visits, phone calls, and assistance with errands and trips to the doctor. I quickly sketch these contrasting models in figure 8.2. It is significant that there are several common English terms to indicate child and spousal support (child support, allowance, alimony) but none that connote parental support.

Calculating Reciprocity and Ideologies of Age

Also highlighted in the 1996 debates on SSI use by immigrants were competing cultural models of reciprocity and productivity over the life course. In both the Indian and U.S. models, for an elder to receive care, whether from children or the state, ideally he or she has to have earned it through participating in a relationship of long-term reciprocity—with

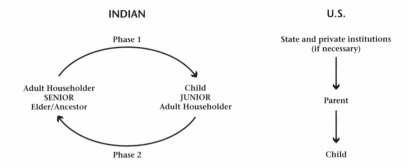

FIGURE 8.2. Models of intergenerational relations and elder support.

children, in the Indian model, or with the state, in the U.S. model. (This adds another dimension to the illustration in figure 8.2; I have added it in figure 8.3.) Many older Indians in the United States believe that state care of the elderly is "the American way," and I would say that Americans to a large extent agree with such a premise; but—as the 1996 congressional hearing on immigrant use of SSI made clear—really only to the extent that the elderly have formerly contributed to the state, through working and paying taxes. As Senator Alan Simpson (Republican, Wyoming) put it in his opening remarks: "Immigrants should be able to earn their way into our generous network of social support, but we should no longer permit unfettered access to welfare by newcomers who have not worked in our country and who have not contributed to these taxpayer-supported assistance programs, such as SSI" (U.S. Congress, Senate 1997:2). In response to a comment offered by Jane Ross of the U.S. General Accounting Office, who spoke of the problems inherent in bringing a set of people to the country "who are too old to work," Senator Simpson replied: "Isn't that it right there? . . . If you come to the United States . . . and you are a parent of 60 or 65 and you have put nothing into Social Security or SSI and suddenly you begin to draw and you draw the same benefit that a citizen draws?" (p. 47). Throughout the hearing, elderly immigrants in fact were presented as dangerously thwarting the quintessential "American" values of productivity, self-reliance, and the work ethic; they were described as those "who are too old to work" (pp. 41, 47), who are unemployable "because of their age and other infirmities" (p. 54), and who, problematically, "clearly have no other means of support but their children" (p. 47).

Because of this association of the elderly with economic dependence, there was an underlying current of ambivalence about the idea of accepting aging immigrants to the United States at all. The Heritage Foundation's Robert Rector expressed this sentiment directly: "Nations with very large and generous welfare systems have to be very careful . . . about [the] immigration of two groups that are very likely to end up on . . . welfare: . . . persons with low skills and . . . elderly and near-elderly people" (U.S. Congress, Senate 1997:109). UC-Davis Professor Norman Matloff recommended "reduced yearly quotas and/or restrictions on the eligibility of elderly parents for immigration" (p. 101), and stated, "the fact that working-age immigrants are productive does not mean that we should then admit for immigration their elderly parents who will go on welfare" (p. 89). Daniel Stein, director of the Federation for American Immigration Reform, commenting in 1997 on these congressional debates on National Public Radio, took it perhaps furthest: "And the system should not allow immigrants to bring elderly parents here over the age of fifty-five as a general rule."[42] (Not all recommended such a harsh policy, however, as Senator Kennedy declared that the opportunity for parents to join their children "in their golden years and be near their grandchildren . . . should be a joy available to all Americans, not just the wealthiest Americans" [p. 57].)

Significantly, the Indian Americans I spoke with about this matter were not unconcerned about partaking in a relationship of reciprocity with the state. Rather, they tended to envision the units involved in the reciprocal exchanges quite differently (see Figure 8.3). Congressional testifiers stressed that *only those individuals* who had previously paid taxes to the American government should rightly be eligible for welfare. A common argument in the Indian American community was that—when looked at on a *family* level—aged immigrants are indeed deserving of welfare benefits, because in general their professional children pay much more in taxes than the elders receive in welfare payments. One woman, Premalata Bhusan, explained, "My son said to me [about SSI], 'You take.' I said, 'No, I won't. What have I done for this country?' He said, 'You have donated three children to this country, and we pay so much tax.'"

Further, in many of the multigenerational Indian American households, it is the very domestic labor of the senior parents—who provide babysitting, cooking, and cleaning—that enables the junior tax-paying children to work (chapter 7). Many of the seniors who perform this work do not feel that it is "natural" that they do so. Most come from social classes in India where they were accustomed to having servants perform much

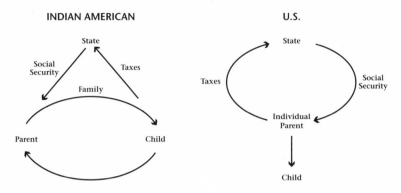

A. Parent-child and family-state reciprocity   **B. Individual-state reciprocity**

FIGURE 8.3. Indian American and U.S. models of reciprocity and parent-child-family-state financial transactions.

of the household cooking and cleaning. Moreover, in a more "Indian" system, seniors would be the *recipients,* rather than the providers, of *sevā* or service, as their sons and daughters-in-law would gradually take over the household's domestic and financial responsibilities, including the care of their elders. Nonetheless, most I know seem to find that their domestic work makes sense in the context of North America, and becomes a valuable contribution to what they perceive to be the main reason for their families being in the United States—the careers of their children.

The U.S. government, however, does not officially recognize this kind of unpaid domestic labor as a form of productive work. "Productivity" in much governmental parlance is measured in terms of paid labor and tax-paying, not in terms of the unpaid domestic (re)production and support of laborers for the work force—a fact that has, of course, been noted by feminist critics of capitalist societies as well (e.g., Rubin 1975). Certain U.S. government policies do in fact recognize a *husband and wife* as mutual parts of a productive joint family unit. For instance, a homemaker wife can earn Social Security credits through her working husband. But the state has no such system of recognizing the domestic contributions of an older parent to an adult child's household.

And so, a system that stresses radical individualism and paid productivity does not take into account the broader kinds of potential productive contributions to the state, society, and family that many Indians recognize older people as offering—such as having earlier produced and raised children (who, among other things, can now work and pay taxes), or being able to perform domestic work (which facilitates the external employment of children), and contributing in more diffuse ways to the maintenance of family ties, love, and "Indian" traditions. Ambivalent attitudes about aging in the United States and Western Europe are not limited, of course, to aged immigrants. In a society where individual productivity is so highly valued, anything less—as Foucault exposes (1965, 1979)—is frequently disciplined or despised (see also Cole 1992, Graebner 1980, Vesperi 1985:71).

Answers to the question of where is the best and proper site of elder care vary vastly from society to society, and contain within them their own moral codes, developmental logics, and models of personhood.

AFTERWORD

One spring evening, toward the end of my fieldwork for this book, I was sitting on the narrow front veranda of the modest old age home Aram with two of my closest resident friends, Kalyani-di and Uma-di. A luminous moon was rising, a few pedestrians and cyclists were making their way down the adjoining lane in the thickening dusk, we brushed away mosquitoes. Inside the home the background drone of the television could be heard, along with the sounds of the evening dinner preparations. I mentioned that I should be getting home to where my daughters would be waiting. Kalyani-di and Uma-di commented to me then, wistfully and affectionately, that even my own days of living closely with a family—with my girls and me at home—are short-lived. "Soon when you give their marriages, you will wonder: When will I see them again? For us," Uma-di added softly, "those days have already arrived."

I realized poignantly that they were absolutely correct. Further, I became conscious that the processes my informants—my guides and interlocutors[1] —had been dealing with are in certain respects processes of the human condition that we all share: the experience of change and loss as one moves through the life course.

Yet my research was also about difference. In some respects, this book has been a reflection on increasing independence and individualism; on ways of living that many Americans (I among them) take for granted, accept as natural and normal, but that many of my Indian informants find bizarre.

A month or so later, I returned to the United States. As we parted, I gave my daughter's mobile phone as a gift to Kalyani-di and Uma-di, hoping it would help them stay in touch with their families, perhaps me, and the wider world.

As I close the pages of this book, there are a few quick points I would like to bring home. One aim of my project has been to argue that it is illuminating and productive to do close ethnographic research on social change with older persons as key informants. Popular and academic studies of aging tend to assume, explicitly or implicitly, that the old are not innovative agents in processes of social-cultural change. Scholarly and media discourses in the West tend to present the key "problem" of aging as merely that of how to care for increasing numbers of dependent elderly—assumed to be passive subjects requiring tending. In contrast to these assumptions, I have investigated the unique and complex ways that older persons themselves are actively involved in the making and remaking of a society.

Many of my older informants saw themselves as grappling with the most profound social-cultural change—even more than the young people in their society. Both older and newer (to put it simply) models of living were very real, live and present for them. Those of the senior generation grew up with the older model and in many ways were upholding it, bringing it into the present, reconstructing and interpreting it. At the same time, these seniors were very often actively taking on new worlds—by purposefully sending their children abroad, or moving out of extended family homes to nuclear units and elder residences, or joining senior citizens' organizations that emphasize peer-oriented individualism and independence. True, other elders were passively "thrown away" by children to places like old age homes. Yet one must recall, as Marx points out, that people make their own lives even though not always under conditions of their own choosing. Even those who were "thrown away" were conspicuously involved in complex processes of cultural production, as the very act of moving from an extended family household to an elder residence compelled them to rethink received ideas and practices, in creative and interesting ways.

We have seen an extensive diversity of perspectives at play in this study of aging in India and abroad today. Amartya Sen (2005) writes of how argument has pervaded Indian history, literature, politics, and everyday life, producing "the simultaneous flourishing of many different convictions and viewpoints" (p. ix). This argumentative tradition is certainly vibrantly apparent in contemporary debates over aging and modernity. No one dominant "Indian" model emerges as to how best to craft meaningful lives and forms of aging in a present characterized, for so many, by a profound sense of both unsettling and promising social-cultural change. What is clear is that the Indian public is actively and critically debating and reflecting on change. In his essay "On Modernity," first delivered in Bengali in Calcutta as a public lecture, Partha Chatterjee asserts that "there cannot be just one modernity irrespective of geography, time, environment and social conditions" (1997:198), and that "to fashion the forms of our own modernity, we need to have the courage at times to reject the modernities established by others" (p. 210). Amartya Sen espouses, in a slightly different vein, a "critical openness," which includes "the valuing of a dynamic, adaptable world, rather than one that is constantly 'policing' external influences and fearing 'invasion' of ideas from elsewhere" (2005:124). Given the intense cultural and intellectual interconnections between the "East" and the "West," Sen goes on to argue, "the question of what is 'Western' and what is 'Eastern' (or 'Indian') is often hard to decide, and the issue can be discussed only in more dialectical terms" (p. 132).

I use Chatterjee's and Sen's words as a launching point for a brief closing relativistic note. A central thesis of this book is that there is no one compelling way of answering the question of how best to age, what shape(s) the family should take, and the proper social-moral relationship among individuals, genders, families, the market, and the state. Neither a model of lifelong intergenerational reciprocity (which has prevailed in India) nor one of individual independence (more dominant in the United States) can be considered essentially natural or unnatural, humane or inhumane, advanced or backward, advantageous or detrimental. Rather, both models serve as different cultural interpretations of the proper workings of aging and society, of finding meaning in the human life course, of being in the world.

Of course, many Indian and American readers, in fact myself included, may accept as a given that it *is* simply better to have some provision for the poor beyond the family. Not every elder will be able to rely on an adult child or amassed independent savings. For those with no one or nothing, is it not absolutely more ethical to have a state safety net to offer relief? By chalking up all difference to "alternative modernities" or "contrasting cultural systems," one risks masking real problems of global inequality (cf. Ferguson 2006:192), such as the fact that only some states have the economic resources for a robust social welfare system. But beyond the basic assertion that alleviating poverty is desirable, it becomes difficult to make a viable pan-cultural argument. Is it necessarily better or worse, more or less "advanced" or "backward," to pay no heed to an adult child's capacity to support an elder parent when determining whether or not the elder is needy?[2] or to reside in separate nuclear households rather than in multigenerational families? or to foster generational independence rather than lifelong mutual interdependence? Many readers in India and the United States may harbor, consciously or unconsciously, a conventional teleological model of the developmental march of modernity. With such a model in mind, some may have a hard time relinquishing the notion that it *is* simply "better" (more modern or up-to-date or enlightened or egalitarian or enjoyable) to have a system that fosters generational independence—self-sufficient, free, unencumbered adults—rather than lifelong mutual interdependence and multi-generational co-residence. Even I, influenced by my own upbringing in the United States and my feminist inclinations, have the tendency to feel that the individualistic, nuclear-family-style system is more desirable. (It's the one I suppose I have chosen to live in.) But, *is* it?

Renato Rosaldo, in his eloquent, simple and provocative essay, "Of Headhunters and Soldiers: Separating Cultural and Ethical Relativism" (2000), puts forward a definition of cultural relativism as follows:

> Relativism argues for engagement, for dialogue between cultures. This is not the kind of easy cosmopolitanism that implies enormous privilege—the capacity, for example, to spend three days in the Bali Hilton. It's a deeper form of knowing that entails some recognition that I am one among others. I'm not the center of the universe.
>
> This argues against ethnocentrism, against what could be called cultural imperialism (imposing a set of norms on people who might not want to inhabit those norms), against projection (laying something you see inside yourself on somebody else). The effort in relativism is to determine what that other person is actually thinking.

Taking up such principles, we are able realize that the things we believe and do, take for granted and think of as superior, often inspire other people's revulsion—and vice versa. Our own systems are just one of many possible ways of organizing lives in the world. By engaging in the anthropological project of making the familiar strange and the strange familiar, we widen our sense of the horizons of the possible, helping to promote self- and cross-cultural understanding—a vitally important project in our remarkably diverse and increasingly interconnected world.

NOTES

Acknowledgments

1. For those familiar with my earlier book, *White Saris and Sweet Mangoes,* I should note that this Hena (Hena Basu of Basu Research and Documentation Service in Kolkata) is not the same Hena (Hena Mukherjee) who devoted her energies to working with me as a research assistant in the village of Mangaldihi in 1989–1990. Both Henas have been invaluable research assistants and close friends.

1. Introduction

1. I use 'single quotation marks' to signify words spoken in English in an otherwise Bengali conversation. As I discuss further below, residences for elders are most frequently referred to by Indians in English as "old age homes," signifying the perceived Western-originating nature of these institutions.

2. As I examine further in chapters 7 and 8, immigrants who become citizens can be eligible to receive the kinds of welfare benefits the United States government offers to any citizen over 65 with limited means, including Supplemental Security Income (SSI) and Medicare.

3. As the book's following pages reveal, both tea and time—in relation to family, intimacy, and modernity—are in fact recurring tropes in my informants' narratives. Tea takes time to prepare. Time is essential for true intimacy, among family or friends. *Āḍḍā*—a quintessential Bengali way of forming and enjoying friendships—entails endless, lengthy, time-expending talk, often over tea. Tea is something that Indians commonly drink several times a day—generally at least first thing in the morning, then again with breakfast, and then in the afternoon. Tea is what guests are offered when dropping in to visit. And seniors and superiors (in what many hold up as traditional or proper Indian contexts) rarely prepare their own tea, but rather are offered it by servants, daughters-in-law, or other juniors. The new old age homes in India always specify how often tea is offered, and residents who like their homes readily cite being served tea. Older immigrants to the United States, particularly men, often describe their adjustment to American (busy and individualist) lifestyles by narrating how they have finally learned to make their own tea.

4. Rajan and Kumar (2003:78–79), based on 1992–1993 National Family Household Survey data, report that 88 percent of the elderly in India co-reside with their adult children. Although co-residence is declining, gerontologists concur that the strong majority of Indian elderly still do live with their children. See Jamuna 2003:127–128, Basu 2006.

5. For instance, those who can speak English well comprise only about 5 percent of India's population; and just about 9 percent of households in India have a refrigerator (Derné 2005:108; see also Fernandes 2006:81, Table 3). I discuss below and in chapter 2 the varying criteria used to define the Indian middle classes, a fast-growing group that includes, scholars estimate, between 100 and 250 million persons, or about 9 to 22 percent of the population.

6. See especially Lamb 2000:90–99. For other important anthropological works on aging in India, see Van Willigen and Chadha 1999, and Vatuk 1975, 1980, 1987, 1990, 1992, 1995.

7. HelpAge India's (soon-to-be-updated) 2002 guide to old age homes lists eight hundred across India (HelpAge India 2002; see also Sawhney 2003), and since its publication new elder residences have been springing up at a fast pace. From 2004–2006, I was able to locate seventy-one old age homes in Kolkata and its suburbs.

8. As Eric Gable nicely writes, reflecting on his and James Ferguson's different accounts of their subjects' experiences of modernity in Africa: "Nowadays in anthropology, when we compare two fieldwork encounters and find them to be divergent, we can account for such divergence in a variety of ways. One way would be to scrutinize the motives, both conscious and unconscious, of the authors of the ethnographic accounts in question. Ethnographers are authors; they write, as Geertz, Clifford, Marcus, and others made us all see in the 1980s, 'fictions,' . . . stories that each of us constructs, reflecting our biographies, our preoccupations, our libraries. . . . Ethnography can be a window into the lives of others and it can also be a mirror" (2006:411 n.14).

9. Most residents of old age homes feel compelled to state publicly that their families did not want them to move in (whether or not the assertion is fully true). This saves the family's prestige and represents the elder as loved and served.

10. I use double quotes here and elsewhere to highlight the constructed or representational nature of a phrase or concept. So, here, I draw attention to "American culture" as represented by my informants, rather than as a fixed, independently existing entity.

11. For more on population aging, see Barbagli and Kertzer (2003:xiv–xviii), Kinsella 1997, Peterson 2002, United Nations 2001. Chakraborti 2004 and Rajan, Sarma and Mishra 2003 focus on the demography of Indian aging.

12. "World Population Ageing: 1950–2050," Department of Economic and Social Affairs, Population Division—http://www.un.org/esa/population/publications/worldageing19502050 (United Nations 2001; accessed 9 November 2008).

13. Watson Wyatt Worldwide and Center for Strategic and International Studies (CSIS) report, "Global Aging—The Challenge of the New Millennium." http://www.watsonwyatt.com/research/printable.asp?id=W-315 (accessed August 2008).

14. See Beijing Review 2007, Eckholm 1998, Jianhua 2006, and Shea 2005.

15. See Kotlikoff and Burns 2004, Peterson 2000, Wilmoth and Longino 2006.

16. Some analysts do, however, integrate demographic and social-cultural concerns when thinking about India's future. To cite just one example: in an article titled "Pension Issues and Challenges Facing India," H. T. Parekh presents figures on population aging in the nation and predicts that "due to a variety of sociological and demographic reasons, the role of the family in providing retirement financing is likely to be less prominent in the future" (2006:4638).

17. Grand Western social science theorists of modernity include August Comte, Karl Marx, Max Weber, and Emile Durkheim. More recent influential works that emphasize and examine the universality of core modern transformations include Berman 1988; Foucault 1979, 1980; Giddens 1990; Habermas 1987; Harvey 1989; Jameson 1991, 2002; and Latour 1993.

18. For works that take this argument and/or explore particular or alternative modernities, see Appadurai 1996; Appadurai and Breckenridge 1995; Chakrabarty 2001; Chatterjee 1997; Comaroff and Comaroff 1997; Dube and Banerjee-Dube 2006; Errington and Gewertz 1996; Ferguson 1999; Foster 2002; Gable 2006; Gaonkar 2001; Gewertz and Errington 1996; Goodale 2006; Hodgson 2001; Knauft 2002; Liechty 2003; LiPuma 2000; Lynch 2007; Mills 1999; Nonini and Ong 1997; Ong 1996, 1997; Pigg 1996; Rofel 1999; Taylor 2001; and Van Hollen 2003.

19. Anna Lowenhaupt Tsing writes relatedly of how anthropologists are still, somewhat unsatisfactorily, grappling with just how to get beyond the unhelpful dichotomizing of the "global blob and local detail"—"an imagery in which the global is homogenous precisely because we oppose it to the heterogeneity we identify as local" (2004:58).

20. I am indebted to Eric Gable (2006:409), who inspired me to pull out my copies of Geertz and find this still relevant and important passage. Gable observes that, in much of his work, Geertz "tried to show how societies might experience the same or equivalent histories, yet interpret them in dramatically different ways, revealing in the process the contours of culture" (2006:409).

21. These questions are inspired by Dilip Gaonkar's (2001) and Dipesh Chakrabarty's (2001) contributions to *Alternative Modernities* and Marshall Berman's (1988) *All That Is Solid Melts into Air.*

22. M. N. Srinivas, most notably in *Social Change in Modern India* (1968), and Milton Singer (*When a Great Tradition Modernizes,* 1972) are two anthropologists who several decades ago produced highly influential theories of social and cultural change and the modern in India, expressing many insights that are still compelling today. Other more recent works on South Asian modernity in various regions and historical periods include Breckenridge 1995, Chakrabarty 2002, Gold and Gujar 2002, Liechty 2002, Mankekar 1998, Pigg 1996, van der Veer 2001; and see the next note below.

23. For significant works on gender, sexuality and modernity in South Asia, see P. Chatterjee 1989, 1990, 1993; N. Chatterjee and Riley 2001; Derné 2000; Lynch 2007; Mankekar 1999; Srivastava 2004a, 2004b; and Van Hollen 2003.

24. As mentioned earlier, Cohen (1988) and more briefly I (Lamb 2000, especially pp. 88–98) do examine how visions of aging are tied to various Indian conceptualizations of modernity. However, there is more work to be done. First, a lot has transpired in the relatively short time since Cohen and I did our earlier research, including a surge of old age homes. Second, both Cohen and I concentrated rather narrowly only on *negative* stories of modernity. Third, this current project focuses on the ways older people themselves as agents reflect upon, experience, and fashion modernity, rather than simply (as Cohen's work concentrates on) the ways old people and old age are *represented by others* (such as their families, their communities, gerontologists, the state, and the media).

25. See, for instance, Wardlow 2006:8–9, 20; Comaroff and Comaroff 1997:365–404; Keane 2002:68; LiPuma 1998, 2000:128–152; and Taylor 1992.

26. McKim Marriott first coined the term "dividual" to refer to a notion of more or less "open" persons whose capacities for exchanging properties with other people, places, and things make them composite and hence divisible or dividual in nature—embedded in multiple external relations—rather than relatively closed, contained, solid, and distinct as *in*dividuals (Marriott 1976:111). This is a suggestion that has spread in Melanesian (e.g., M. Strathern 1988:13, 348n.7) and South Asian studies. For further discussions of dividual, sociocentric, relational and/or familial notions of personhood in South Asia, see Daniel 1984; Lamb 1997, 2000; Roland 1988; and Shweder and Bourne 1984. As I have argued elsewhere, for most people, different forms of (dividual or individual) personhood cross-cut their lives—highlighted in varying contexts and life phases—and so are not neatly dichotomous (Lamb 1997).

27. Habitus, very briefly, refers to a person's beliefs and dispositions, the social-cultural structures or principles that exist in people's bodies and minds (Bourdieu 1977, Mauss 1979[1935]).

28. "A Profile of Older Americans: 2006—Living Arrangements." Administration

on Aging 2006. Available at http://www.aoa.gov/PROF/Statistics/profile/2006/6.aspx. Among those 65 and over in the United States in 2005, about 30.1 percent of all non-institutionalized persons lived alone, and over half (54.8 percent) lived with only their spouse. The proportion living alone increases with advanced age: among women aged 75 and over, for example, nearly half (47.7 percent) lived alone. About 9.5 percent of persons 65 and over in the United States in 2005 lived in nursing homes and other senior housing.

29. Comte's discussion comes from chapter VI, "Social Dynamics; or, Theory of the Natural Progress of Human Society." Bennett Berger comments that what Comte failed to foresee is that, in Western Europe and the United States at least, increased life expectancy seems to have brought with it an extension of the definition of youth (1960:13–14), a trend I discuss at the beginning of chapter 5—our efforts to stave off (forever, if possible) the period of old age.

30. See, for notable studies of youth cultures and youth agency, many of which highlight in particular the making of the modern and global: Amit-Talai and Wulff 1995; Berliner 2005; Bucholtz 2002; Cole 2004; Dolby and Rizvi 2008; Durham 2000, 2007; Fong 2004; Gable 2000; Gillespie 1995; Hall 2002; Honwana and de Boeck 2005; Liechty 2002; Lukose 2008; Maira 2002, 2004; Maira and Soep 2005; Sharp 2002. Rachana Agarwal usefully alerted me to several items on this list.

31. Madhulika Khandelwal's chapter 6, "Elders and Youth," presents a more complex account of the varied perspectives and strategies of elder Indian immigrants in New York City.

32. Of course, as I explain in further detail below, I was deliberately concentrating in this research on those who were *not* living in conventional arrangements with their grown children. Nonetheless, it is significant that the vast majority (near 100 percent) of my research subjects for this project had grown up in multi-generational and often joint family households.

33. The retirement age in the West Bengal government sector is fifty-eight and in the Government of India sector sixty. The private sector has no fixed rule.

34. Laura Ahearn (2000) and Sherry Ortner (2006) provide particularly lucid discussions of the concept of agency.

35. Susan Rasmussen makes a similar argument in analyzing several different types of musical performances popular among Tuareg youth and elders: "These data challenge some anthropological tendencies to associate rigid structural oppositions such as 'traditional/modern' with static age categories. . . . They suggest that 'traditional' and 'modern' beliefs and practices do not line up so neatly . . . according to one or another age or generation" (2000:142).

36. In 1946, only 18.2 percent of U.S. mothers with children under eighteen were employed, but maternal employment rates have steadily risen, to 48.8 percent in 1976 and 70.0 percent in 1996 (Hoffman 1998:2). Lois Hoffman remarks: "There are few social changes that are so easy to document as the increased employment of mothers in the United States" (p. 2). See also Vlasblom and Schippers (2004), "Increases in Female Labour Force Participation in Europe: Similarities and Differences."

37. The popular and scholarly literature on anxieties surrounding maternal employment is too vast to cite. For just a few further examples, see "Study Links Working Mothers to Slower Learning" (Lewin 2002), "Angst and the Working Mother" (*New York Times* Editorial Desk 2002), and Suzanne Venker's *7 Myths of Working Mothers: Why Children and (Most) Careers Just Don't Mix* (2004).

38. Of course, the putting of women without resources or freedom to work caring for the children of more privileged women is not at all new in the United States; it is

just increasingly transnationally arranged. There is a long history in the United States of domestic nannies and slaves (in the U.S. South) caring for other women's children.

39. Ehrenreich and Hochschild here are recounting the narrative of Josephine Perera, the nanny and transnational mother featured in Nilita Vachani's documentary film, "When Mother Comes Home for Christmas."

40. Except if that extra-family care takes place in a nursing home. As I explore in the chapters below, many Americans are concerned about the quality of elder care in nursing homes, although most are comfortable with the concepts of up-scale retirement communities, hired in-home help, and living singly or as a married couple.

41. For discussions of cultural values surrounding aging and intergenerational relationships in the United States, see chapters 3–8 below, and Clark 1972; Hunt 2002:109–110; Kalish 1967; Lamb 2000:52–53, 2005; Margolies 2004; Simic 1990; and Vesperi 1985.

42. Among middle-class families in India, it is rare for a mother to migrate abroad without taking her children with her (although recently many sons and daughters-in-law are migrating transnationally without their parents). In Sri Lanka, however, many young mothers have been migrating to work as domestics in wealthier oil-producing countries of the Middle East, leaving behind young children (Gamburd 2000). To quell this trend, the Sri Lankan government announced in March 2007 its plans to ban mothers with children under five from working overseas, although after being swamped by protests from local and international human rights groups, the cabinet is reconsidering.

43. I discuss this case further in chapter 8.

44. Black 2006; *New York Times* 1989; *St. Louis Post-Dispatch* 2000; Seff 2003; Arthur 2004; Abaya 2006.

45. Bengal is a region in the northeast of South Asia, shared primarily now by the state of West Bengal, India and the nation of Bangladesh (formerly East Pakistan). Bengalis are the main ethnic community of this region and speak the language of Bengali or *Bangla*. The majority of Bengalis in West Bengal are Hindu, though with a sizable minority of Muslims, and the majority of Bengalis in Bangladesh are Muslim; although before the partition of India and Pakistan in 1947, Hindus and Muslims lived freely across both regions. Many of the Hindu Bengalis now living in Kolkata, and many of this study's informants, are originally from the region that has become Bangladesh.

46. Although residents paid to stay in these as in other homes, the Peerless and Birla Group corporations subsidized their costs and viewed the homes in part as merit-producing, charitable enterprises, as I discuss further in chapter 3.

47. There is no uniformly accepted term to refer to people from the Indian subcontinent living in the United States. "South Asian," the phrase most widely used in academic circles, refers to persons from the contemporary nations of India, Pakistan, Bangladesh, Sri Lanka, Nepal, and Bhutan (although masking what many perceive to be deep differences of language, religion, ethnicity, etc.). People of Indian descent in the United States refer to themselves by a variety of labels, including "Indian American," "Indo-American," Deshi or *Deśi* (of the *deś* or homeland; primarily used by youth), and simply "Indian." "Asian Indian" has been the official U.S. Census category since 1980. See Anand 1994; Das Gupta 2006; George 1997:52 (n.3); Kibria 1996; Leonard 1997, 2000; Natarajan 1993; Nelson 1992; Prashad 1999; Radhakrishnan 1996; Shankar 1998; and Shukla 2003 for further discussions of these labels and their social-political ramifications.

48. Immigrants from India in the United States have, on the whole, had a high socio-economic status, following the 1965 U.S. Immigration and Naturalization Act, which allowed Asian immigrants to enter the United States on the basis of preferred

occupational skills. The 2000 U.S. Census lists Asian Indians as having the second highest annual median household income among all U.S. ethnic groups, $70,708, just below the Japanese median family income of $70,849 (available at http://www.census.gov/prod/2004pubs/censr-17.pdf, p.18 of the report; accessed 15 September 2008).

2. The Production of Tradition, Modernity, and a New Middle Class

1. The Bengali term for children (*chelerā*) can mean either children in general or sons in particular. Sons, with daughters-in-law, are widely regarded as those most responsible for caring for their parents.

2. Messages from Subbulakshmi Jagadeesan, Government of India Ministry of Social Justice and Empowerment, and Prime Minister Manmohan Singh. Heading: "The Nation felicitates its senior citizens on the International Day of Older Persons." *Anandabajar Patrika,* 1 October 2004.

3. For notable works that examine processes of constructing tradition as part of the very project of fashioning modernity or working out the present, see Chatterjee 1997, Gable 2006, LiPuma 2000 (p. 77 passim), Hobsbawm and Ranger 1983, Jackson 1995, and Lynch 2007 (p. 249 n. 4). Partha Chatterjee writes that "it is superfluous to call this an imagined past, because pasts are always imagined" (1997:210). Liisa Malkki writes, in *Purity and Exile:* "that the 'worlds made' through narrations of the past are always historically situated and culturally constructed, and it is these that people act upon and riddle with meaning" (1995:104).

4. For more on *sevā* and elders, see Cohen 1998, Lamb 2000:59–66, and chapter 5 below.

5. McKim Marriott (1976) first coined the term "dividual," which was later taken up by Marilyn Strathern (1988:13, 348–349 n. 7) and other Melanesianists, to convey such a notion of persons, common in South Asia, as composite and hence "dividual" or divisible in nature, existing in a social and cultural world of particulate "flowing substances" (see also Marriott and Inden 1977 and Marriott 1990). Inden and Nicholas 1977; Daniel 1984; Lamb 1997, 2000; and Zimmermann 1979 also examine conceptualizations of fluid and open persons in various South Asian contexts.

6. According to Clifford Geertz, for instance, Westerners see the person as a "bounded, unique, more or less integrated motivational and cognitive universe, a dynamic center of awareness, emotion, judgment and action organized into a distinctive whole and set contrastively against other such wholes and against its social and natural background." Geertz characterizes this Western conception of the individual as "a rather peculiar idea within the context of world cultures" (1983:59).

7. I have been told variations of this tale numerous times in India and also found it printed in a newsletter for the Dignity Foundation "Senior Citizens Life Enrichment Organization" based in Mumbai. It appears as well in Knowles 1893, under the title "How the Wicked Sons Were Duped" (pp. 241–242). The blockbuster Bollywood film *Baghban,* described shortly below, features a very similar theme.

8. I take this example from Lamb 2000 (p. 47), which focused on village life. I found that in visits to this and neighboring villages over 2003–2007, anxieties over the impact of modernity were present but not as salient as they were among the urban middle classes.

9. These initial passages are taken from newspaper stories: Young 2007, Gentleman 2007, Das 1999, Baruah 2004. Lawrence Cohen's (1998) *No Aging in India* also cites prevalent media narratives of the modern "fall" of the joint family.

10. For instance, see Wadley (1994, 2002) for discussions of family types in

Karimpur, North India, from 1925 through 1998. Over this period, nuclear families were consistently the largest group (2002:19). Cohen (1998) explores narratives of modern "bad families" from the colonial era to contemporary times. Vatuk (1990) examines the anxiety New Delhi elders express regarding becoming "burdens" on their children. See also the perspectives of Bengali villagers on the multiple kinds of enduring forces that interfere with successful joint family living in "Conflicting Generations: Unreciprocated Houseflows in a Modern Society" (Lamb 2000:70–111).

11. See Dube 1988, Lamb 2000:207–212, Raheja 1995, Raheja and Gold 1994:73–120, and Sax 1991:77–126 for analyses of the shifting positions of women in Indian families.

12. In Bengali, the suffixes "di" for *didi* or older sister, and "da" for *dādā* or older brother, are often used as a sign of both respect and closeness. Other kin terms, such as aunt (mashi, pishi, mami, kakima, jethima), uncle (mesho, pisho, mama, kaka, jethu), and elder brother's wife (boudi), are also used as suffixes. Bengalis, like other Indians, generally find it disrespectful to refer to a person senior to oneself by first name only.

13. "*Bāpre bāp!*" is a common Bengali exclamation indicating amazement, fear, surprise or incredulity.

14. See chapter 5 for an analysis of the meanings *ekānnabartī paribār,* frequently glossed as joint family, which literally means a family whose members all eat together or share a hearth.

15. For accounts of the *āśrama dharma* schema in the *dharmaśāstra* texts, see Kane (1968–1975:vol. 2) and Manu (1885, 1991).

16. See especially chapter 6, "Our Culture, Their Culture" in *The Argumentative Indian* (Sen 2005:121–138).

17. *Bartaman,* Letters to the Editor, 11 August 2005, p. 4; translated from the Bengali by my research assistant Hena Basu.

18. Aparna Sen, introductory editorial message in the unnumbered front matter pages of *Sananda,* 1 February 2003. Translated from the Bengali by my research assistant Hena Basu.

19. Translations from Hindi have been provided by my research assistant Rachana Agarwal.

20. Letter to the editor, *Telegraph,* 30 June 2005.

21. Subham Dutta, *Sunday Newsline,* Kolkata, 3 June 2007—Section "P.S.," p. 6.

22. For works on the growth of the Indian middle classes since the economic liberalization policies of the 1990s, see Beteille 2001; G. Das 2002:279–290 passim; Derné 2005; Fernandes 2006; Mazzarella 2003, 2005; T. Ray 2006; Radhakrishnan 2006; and Sridharan 2004. Liechty 2002 examines the making of middle-class culture in Nepal.

23. To Sridharan, the "elite" middle class consists of those in the "high" income group with salaries in 1999 above Rs. 140,000 (or $3,200) annually; the "expanded" middle class includes those of both "high" and "upper middle" income groups, with annual incomes above Rs. 105,000; and the "broadest" middle class corresponds to the high, upper middle, and middle income groups, those with annual salaries of Rs. 70,000 and up (2004:411–413). See also Fernandes 2006:82, Table 4.

24. Although Kolkata is the third largest city in India, with an extended metropolitan population of over 14 million, since the independence of India in 1947 it has not been a major economic hub (though from 2000, the city has been experiencing some economic rejuvenation).

25. "NRIs remitted over $24 billion back home in 2006," report dated June 8, 2007. NRI-worldwide.com—"The website for the great Indian diaspora." http://nri-worldwide.com/cgi-local/ts.pl?action=fetch&area=nrifacts (accessed 9 November 2008).

26. See the Indian Embassy site: http://www.indianembassy.org/policy/PIO/

Introduction_PIO.html (accessed 9 November 2008), and Dhooleka Raj's chapter 7 of *Where Are You From? Middle-Class Migrants in the Modern World,* "Being British, Becoming a Person of Indian Origin" (2003:165–183).

27. For newspaper coverage of this new complex, see Mookherjea 2007.

28. The first McDonalds and Pizza Hut franchises appeared in India in 1996; the first mall opened in 1999.

29. Bist 2004, "The Great Indian Mall Boom."

30. The old person, however, was not absent from earlier anti-colonial Indian nationalist discourses. Consider, for instance, Lawrence Cohen's analysis of the figure of the Westernized Indian middle-class "babu" carrying his wife on his shoulder but with a chain around his old mendicant mother's neck. This is the image of "Ghar Kali" that adorns the cover of Cohen's *No Aging in India: Alzheimer's, the Bad Family and Other Modern Things.* Cohen writes of the "apocalyptic vision of modernity" depicted in the popularly circulated nineteenth-century lithograph, in which "the old mother's abjection suggests the fallen present of the babu's Calcutta" (1988:171), "babu" referring to the Bengali middle-class Westernized gentleman.

31. See also Anannya Bhattacharjee, who observes that in the United States, "women's bodies become the site for the preservation of India" (1992:31), and Sunita Mukhi, who examines how Manhattan India Day celebrations pronouncedly link girl/womanhood and Indian nationalism (1998).

32. Rupal Oza (2006), however, examines what she finds to be widespread "moral panic" centering on the woman in the post-1990s India of economic liberalization, surrounding particularly the new public (sexually "open" and indiscriminate) nature of women's bodies in contemporary visual media, such as advertisements, television, magazines, and billboards.

3. The Rise of Old Age Homes in India

1. A lungi is one of the most popular men's garments for everyday wear in West Bengal, a long cotton cloth that can be wrapped around the waist and extends below the knees, generally worn within the household only by those in the middle classes but worn much more widely by those in the laboring classes.

2. As introduced in chapter 2, *vānaprastha* literally means forest dweller, and is presented in Hindu texts (such as the *Laws of Manu*) as the third stage of life (*āśrama*), during which a man (with or without his wife) leaves behind his married children and material possessions to dwell in relative solitude in the forest, focusing on spiritual cultivation. A brochure for the Ramakrishna Mission Home for Aged People describes the home's grounds as an ideal site for pursuing *vānaprastha:* "The vast expanse of green covering three acres of land, the age old trees, the lily pool, the chirping of the birds, the serene ambience at dawn and dusk elevating the place to a *Vanaprasthashrama,* virtually reminds us of the ancient *Tapavana* [place suitable for religious practices] of the Sages away from the material world."

3. In Lamb 2000 (pp. 62–66) I examine Bengali conceptions of elders as those who generally possess the potent capacity to give blessings (*āśīrbād*), largely because of their seniority.

4. See Pigg 2001:512–524 for an interesting discussion of the use of English terms to discuss taboo topics and mark as modern.

5. For further discussions of *sevā* and elders, see chapters 2 and 5, Cohen 1998 and Lamb 2000:59–66.

6. After India's independence in 1947, many Anglo Indians, who identified strongly with British culture, emigrated from the nation to settle in the United Kingdom or elsewhere in the Commonwealth of Nations, such as Australia and Canada.

7. See the introduction for a more detailed account of the nature of my fieldwork in old age homes from 2003 to 2006. In 2007 I again made fieldwork visits to the old age homes I knew best but did not concentrate then on uncovering new homes, although I could tell from a quick perusal of newspaper advertisements and articles that several new elder residences had sprung up over the past year.

8. The population of India is about 80 percent Hindu and 13 percent Muslim. In addition, 2.3 percent of the Indian population is Christian and 1.9 percent is Sikh, with "other" and "unspecified" at 1.9 percent (2001 Census, https://www.cia.gov/cia/publications/factbook/geos/in.html; accessed 9 November 2008).

9. Samia Huq and Nehraz Mahmood, personal communication.

10. See also Liebig 2003 for a quite detailed account of her survey of the physical amenities of and services offered by forty-eight old age homes that she visited across India in 1997–1998. My observations here are very similar to hers.

11. The older, free homes for the aged around India tend to be even larger. For instance, Kolkata's Little Sisters of the Poor Old Age Home currently houses 150 elders, and the West Bengal government home for "old and infirm political sufferers" and destitute women houses sixty-eight. See also Liebig 2003:170–171.

12. In chapter 5, I analyze the ways relationships in the elder homes are constructed as both like and unlike those in a family or joint family.

13. For an examination of Bengali attitudes regarding the inappropriateness of living with married daughters, see Lamb 2000:83–88.

14. Cultural and personal attitudes regarding sleeping and living alone are explored further in chapter 5.

15. Outside of West Bengal, many old age homes (Liebig 2003:166 found 52 percent of the forty-eight homes she surveyed) offer strictly vegetarian diets, in keeping with the traditions of many (non-Bengali) Hindus. HelpAge India's *Old Age Homes: A Guide Book* for some reason advises that all Indian old age homes should serve only vegetarian foods (2000:48). Bengali Hindus of all castes tend to consider especially fish (and often also eggs and mutton) an essential and precious part of the diet.

16. Chapter 5 analyzes Bengali categories of "family," "joint family," "home" and "homey," and compares these to the qualities of old age homes.

17. Mukund Gangopadhyay himself has one married son and two married daughters.

18. As throughout this book, I use 'single quotation marks' to indicate English terms inserted into an otherwise Bengali conversation.

19. Hochschild (2001) and Menzies (2005) are two works from a growing popular literature on the time bind in contemporary North American life.

20. I have termed "society ladies" the active group of upper-middle-class and upper-class women volunteers in Kolkata. These are largely well-to-do housewives who devote a lot of their time to social causes, often through various women's and community clubs such as the Rotary Club and the Inner Wheel Society. A few of these groups have been actively involved in founding certain old age homes. Others plan organized visits to old age homes several times per year, to chat with the residents and offer things like cultural programs and gifts of sweets, fruit, and shawls.

21. See chapter 2 for a discussion of the historical context of debates surrounding

women and social change in colonial and postcolonial India, as well as Chatterjee 1989, 1990, 1993; and Lamb 2000:92–99.

22. The sacred thread, a long white string worn over one shoulder, is one sign of an upper-caste Hindu man's status.

23. Zamindars are major landowners.

24. At http://www.satyajitray.org/films/pather.htm (accessed 15 September 2008).

25. At http://film-i.blogspot.co/203_12_01_archive.html (accessed 22 October 2008).

26. The Calcutta Metropolitan Institute of Gerontology (CMIG), introduced in chapter 2, is an innovative institute focusing primarily on helping the city's elderly poor.

27. Contemporary marriages in India are commonly classified into two categories: "arranged" and "love" marriages. (These English terms are often the ones used, although Indian language equivalents exist.) People hope and expect that love will also develop in an arranged marriage, of course; but an arranged marriage is one that is facilitated and approved primarily by parents or other senior kin, while a love marriage is one in which the members of the couple have met and make the decision to marry (largely or entirely) on their own. The arranged marriage is the more traditional and widely accepted and respected form of marriage, although love marriages are becoming increasingly common, especially among urban cosmopolitan classes.

28. E.g., Hareven 2000:15, Kertzer 1995, Laslett 1972.

29. Before 1800, less than 6 percent of the U.S. population lived in cities (U.S. Census 1990, United States Summary, Table 4: "Population: 1790 to 1990"). Available at www.census.gov/population/censusdata/table-4.pdf (accessed September 2008).

30. See Greven 1970, Hareven 2000:3–30.

31. See Costa 1999; Hareven and Uhlenberg 1995; Kertzer 1995:373; Ruggles 1995; D. S. Smith 1979, 1981. Kertzer makes the important remark, "The fact that people establish their own households at marriage need not exclude a phase of complex family coresidence as a part of the normal life course" (1995:376), aiming to complexify our notions of a simple, dominant, and static Western nuclear family system. Significantly, many more older, widowed *women* moved in with extended family members than men (Costa 1999, Hareven and Uhlenberg 1995). Although some American widowed women continue to live as dependents with other family members, the proportion has decreased significantly from 1890 (57 percent) to 1990 (14 percent) (Costa 1999:42). The U.S. census data provided by Hareven and Uhlenberg show that more than three-fourths of all older widows were living with children in 1910 (1995:285).

32. Tamara Hareven's (2000) research on French-Canadian immigrant workers in an American industrial community from 1880 to 1930 importantly complicates, however, the more popular, simple view that urban migration and industrialization meant that extended kin networks were no longer important, while the "isolated nuclear family" took over, for under the harsh economic conditions of early industrial capitalism, family members needed each others' support. Nonetheless, the proportion of elderly persons living with kin (other than a spouse) in the United States has dropped significantly: in 1890 it was usual for the aged (particularly the widowed) to live with kin; now, the majority live alone (Ruggles 1995:259, 264, 271; Costa 1999).

33. See ElderWeb 2006, Haber 1982 and Haber 1993 for discussions of the history of elder housing in the United States.

34. See, for example, ElderWeb (www.elderweb.com) for descriptions of these various senior housing options.

35. See http://agingstats.gov/Agingstatsdotnet/Main_Site/Data/2008_Documents/Health_Care.pdf; search Indicator 36 (accessed 9 November 2008).

36. However, Americans tend to feel much more comfortable and sanguine about senior residences other than nursing homes, such as retirement housing, as I will continue to explore in the following chapters.

37. I have borrowed the phrase "horror stories" from Michele Gamburd (2000:209–231), who uses it similarly to refer to the sensationally negative media narratives surrounding the lives of migrant housemaids from Sri Lanka working in the Middle East. See also Caitrin Lynch's discussion of the "moral panic" (2007:114 ff.) surrounding women's factory work in contemporary Sri Lanka.

38. This vision—that no one is allowed to go in or out—is not at all true for most old age homes in India, where people come and go regularly.

39. Subho Das Gupta's "Janmadin" appeared in 2001 in Das Gupta's collection, *Śudhu Tomār Janya* ("Just for You"), pp. 32–35, and was translated for me by my research assistant Hena Basu.

4. Becoming an Elder-Abode Member

1. In India, alcohol consumption is largely limited to sophisticated, urban elite circles and, in some communities, to working class and lower caste men. Among the urban elite, it can be a sign of modernity, cosmopolitanism, and sophistication. In Kolkata's sophisticated social clubs, like the one Monisha Mashi and I were attending, male and female guests do commonly enjoy drinks of beer and whiskey, although it is still relatively unusual to find women of Monisha Mashi's generation partaking of alcohol.

2. See chapters 2 and 5, where the notion of *vānaprastha* is scrutinized in further depth.

3. See chapters 2 and 5, as well as Lamb 2000, Savishinsky 2004, Tilak 1989, and Vatuk 1980, for a further examination of the notion and value of worldly detachment in late life for Hindus.

4. Vedanta is a branch of Hindu philosophy, meaning the "end" or culmination of the Vedas (the ancient texts regarded as the scriptural foundation of Hinduism, written down from about 1500 to 500 BCE). Vedanta is constituted by the Aranyakas, or "forest scriptures," of which the Upanishads form the chief part. As a young woman, Monisha Mashi had received an MA in Vedanta Studies, although women of her era in India rarely studied that far.

5. As throughout this book, English terms used in an otherwise Bengali conversation are in 'single quotation marks.'

6. *Sannyās* is the final life stage presented in the Hindu Dharmasastra texts, during which a person leaves behind all ties to family, belongings and place, focusing solely on God and spiritual release.

7. The scant existing literature on India's old age homes includes informative survey-type works such as Liebig 2003 and Sawhney 2003, and editorial-style commentaries such as Narasimhan 2004.

8. A key theme in many older Bengali women's life stories is how loved and happy they were in their father's households in their childhoods (see also Lamb 2001a:24).

9. Kalyani-di does not mention how her children were cared for during the periods when she was away from home working. Presumably, as is common among working class families in the region, the older children helped to cook and look after the younger children. She never mentioned having or being able to afford servants.

10. "*Bāh!*" is an expression of pleasure, enthusiasm, delight.

11. Cohen's Varanasi, Lamb's Mangaldihi, and Vatuk's New Delhi informants also

tie property to good treatment in old age (Cohen 1998:241; Lamb 2000:79, 86–87; Vatuk 1990:78–80), as does the immensely popular Hindi film *Baghban* (Chopra 2003), discussed in chapter 2. See also the discussion in chapter 2 (pp. 36–37) of the ambiguous role property has long played in the Indian intergenerational system.

12. This son's explanation of his motive seemed to be more of an excuse than a reason, however, since placing his mother in an old age home required more money than having her stay at home. (This was not Kalyani-di's observation, but rather my own.)

13. Kalyani-di had also referred above vaguely to not having received peace (*śānti*) at home after she had quit work. It seems perhaps that she as well as her son and daughter-in-law were uncomfortable with her being a non-earning dependent. She also stressed to me on numerous occasions how much she had enjoyed being active and out of the house, amid the world, as a working woman.

14. I discuss such a notion of Bengali women as passive recipients of action as well in Lamb 2000:186.

15. Several of the old age homes I encountered were kept locked and guarded in such a fashion, although the majority were much more open.

16. A *boumā* is a daughter-in-law. The term literally means "wife-mother," as the daughter-in-law is viewed as a wife and mother of/for the family line.

17. *The Laws of Manu* (in Sanskrit, *Manusmriti* or *Manavadharmasastra,* and informally known as Manu) is widely known as a foundational work of Hindu law and society, compiled and written about 200 CE in India.

18. The full passage from *The Laws of Manu* goes thus: "A girl, a young woman, or even an old woman should not do anything independently, even in (her own) house. In childhood a woman should be under her father's control, in youth under her husband's, and when her husband is dead, under her sons.' She should not have independence" (1991:V.147–148, p. 115).

19. Failed reciprocity was also a key theme in Lamb 2000 focusing on aging, gender, and families in a village region of West Bengal, India.

20. For further discussion of the relationship between parents and married daughters, see Lamb 2000:83–88. In the relatively rare matrilineal communities of India, such as the Malayalam-speaking populations of Kerala, there is a much greater incidence of parents living with married daughters.

21. I discuss the two components of this second premise in some detail in Lamb 2000:71–83.

22. Mukund Gangopadhyay is the one whose narrative I cited in chapter 3, about how old age homes represent the ruination of modern society during the contemporary degenerate Kali Yuga.

23. See Figure 3, "Households by Size: 1970 to 2003," in "America's Families and Living Arrangements: 2003" (U.S. Census Bureau 2004). In 2003, single-person households were the second most common type (at 26.4 percent of all households), after two-person households (at 33.3 percent). Available at http://www.census.gov/prod/2004pubs/p20–553.pdf (accessed 7 November 2008).

24. Note, however, that the notion that one may not wish to be a "burden" on children does also have roots in Indian traditions, as Vatuk (1990) explores.

25. See Lamb 2000 (especially chapters 1 and 4) for a detailed exploration of what kinds of acts, to Bengalis, entail the sharing of bodily substances and emotional states, and the meanings and impacts of such acts.

26. As explained above, *boumā* is generally translated as "daughter-in-law" but literally means "wife-mother," as she is a wife and mother of the family line. *Boumā* and *bou*

are often used interchangeably, and any member of a family (including a daughter or sister, as Bulbul demonstrates shortly) can refer to a *boumā* as "our *boumā*." A *husband,* however, would only refer to his wife as his *bou* (wife), not *boumā*. Note also that Bulbul does not broach the notion that a daughter could "throw her parents out," since daughters are not socially or morally expected to care for their parents.

27. This description surprised me, because her father had always struck me as a quite gentle person. I had, however, seen him become animated in a strongly disparaging, even angry way when speaking of certain current political events and the rise of old age homes in the country.

28. See note 27 in chapter 3 for an explanation of "love" versus "arranged" marriages.

29. Bulbul herself had lived with her in-laws for many years after marriage, although eventually she did persuade her husband to leave the small-town joint family home to move to Kolkata, where she felt that they and their sons would have better economic and educational opportunities.

30. Here Bulbul is alluding to the lines from the *Laws of Manu* that I introduced earlier: a woman should never be independent, but should be given support and guidance by her father in childhood, her husband in youth, and her sons in old age (Laws of Manu V.148, Manu 1886:195, 1991:115).

31. The move to a *śvaśur bāṛi* or marital home is generally one of the most dramatic and wrenching moves in an Indian woman's life (see Dube 1988, Jeffery and Jeffery 1996, Lamb 2000:207–211, Raheja 1995, Sax 1991:77–126).

32. In Lamb 2000 (pp. 213–238) I provide a much fuller discussion of the rigorous set of practices prescribed for Bengali Brahman widows.

33. "Hostel" is the term ordinarily used to refer to what Americans more readily call a dormitory—a residence, commonly for students, where groups of similar-aged (usually young), and generally same-gendered, peers live together.

5. Tea and the Forest

1. Marshall Sahlins (1994, 1999) and Ulf Hannerz (1996) were two of the first to employ the phrase "indigenization of modernity." Jonathan Inda and Renato Rosaldo prefer the term "customization" to "indigenization" because it seems less ideologically loaded and does not carry the same connotations of connection to the soil (2002:30, n. 22). Appadurai 1996, Liebes and Katz 1990, Lynch 2007, Michaels 2002, Srinivas 2006, and Van Hollen 2003 provide some rich ethnographic examples and analyses of these sorts of processes. Inda and Rosaldo (2002:12–25) provide a perceptive summary of some of this literature. See also the discussion of "alternative modernities" in chapter 1.

2. See chapter 3 for further discussions of the history of old age homes in the West.

3. As throughout the book, I use 'single quotation marks' to indicate English terms employed in an otherwise Bengali conversation.

4. Homi Bhabha elaborates on the notion of cultural hybridity, pushing beyond dichotomies of Self and Other, East and West, in his 1994 *The Location of Culture* (1994). Amartya Sen writes: "Given the cultural and intellectual interconnections, the question of what is 'Western' and what is 'Eastern' (or 'Indian') is often hard to decide, and the issue can be discussed only in more dialectical terms" (2005:132).

5. See, for example, ElderWeb (www.elderweb.com) for descriptions of these various senior housing options.

6. As I discuss in chapters 7 and 8, state-supported "Senior Centers" in most larger

U.S. towns and cities likewise facilitate similar aims, particularly those of maintaining independence and an active life.

7. See, for examples, Weeks and Cuellar 1981, which compares the elderly in nine different ethnic groups in San Diego to an "Anglo-white" sample; Sokolovsky 1990; Stack 1996:107–121; and Tate 1983.

8. One example: ads for Crest's Rejuvenating Effects Gel invite: "Restore your smile and help it look younger, longer."

9. For instance, the American Academy of Anti-Aging Medicine, in a piece titled "Meditate on This: Buddhist Tradition Thickens Part of the Brain," reports on a study indicating that "regular meditation may slow age-related thinning of the frontal cortex"—posted on the "Anti-Aging Library" portion of its website: http://www.worldhealth.net/p/meditate-on-this-buddhist-tradition-thickens-parts-of-the-brain-2005–12–02.html (accessed 15 September 2008).

10. The Xtend-Life company, for instance, produces a Total Balance vitamin complex intended to "slow down the aging process and promote vitality and well-being," available at http://www.antiaginginfo.net/anti-aging-vitamins.htm (accessed 15 September 2008).

11. See, for instance, Belluck 2006. Nintendo's Brain Age is one new big-selling product of the anti-aging industry, which is branching into brain games "offering the possibility of a cognitive fountain of youth."

12. Viagra, for instance, a drug used to treat erectile dysfunction, is targeted primarily toward older men, and has been one of the most lucrative drugs in the pharmaceutical industry, with the United States its largest market (Berenson 2005). Books such as the revised classic *The New Love and Sex after 60* (Butler and Lewis 2002) are also top-selling.

13. See, for examples, Luisa Margolies's (2004) "Lesson 5: Enough is Enough: Prolonging Living or Prolonging Dying?" (pp. 225–236), and Muriel Gillick's (2006) *Denial of Aging: Perpetual Youth, Eternal Life, and Other Dangerous Fantasies.*

14. Administration on Aging 2006; see also Johnson and Weiner 2006:vii, 3; Margolies 2004:179.

15. For instance, in 2002 in the United States, only 21.6 percent of deaths among people age sixty-five and older occurred at home, and just 5.5 percent of deaths occurred among outpatients in emergency rooms, while 39 percent and 28.4 percent of deaths occurred in in-patient hospital units and in nursing homes, respectively. The figures are similar for people of younger ages, demonstrating a more general phenomenon of medicalizing death in the United States (Centers for Disease Control and Prevention, Worktable 309, "Deaths by Place, of Death, Age, Race and Sex: United States, 2002, available at http://www.cdc.gov/, search Worktable 309; accessed September 2008).

16. For instance, homosexuality was classified as a "disease" in the Diagnostic and Statistical Manual of Mental Disorders (DSM) until 1973. "Drapetomania" was a psychiatric diagnosis proposed in 1851 by physician Samuel A. Cartwright of the Louisiana Medical Association to explain the "disease of mind" inducing slaves to flee captivity. See also Conrad and Schneider's 1992 *Deviance and Medicalization: From Badness to Sickness.*

17. Anthropologist Nancy Scheper-Hughes writes about the medicalization of hunger in Brazil, where government physicians as well as patients often label hunger as "nerves" (*nervios*), prescribing a variety of quick-fix pills (for insomnia, anxiety, even appetite stimulation) without daring to voice politically charged, morally blaming, and overwhelmingly difficult-to-solve problems such as hunger, poverty, and inequality (1993:167–215).

18. The concept of medicalization was named by medical sociologist Irvin Zola in his seminal 1972 article, "Medicine as an Institution of Social Control." See also Conrad 2007. To say that something is "medicalized" does not necessarily imply that the phenomenon cannot be viewed as having any valid biomedical dimensions, but rather that one could and even perhaps should well view the phenomenon as *also* or even *more primarily* a social, political-economic, or natural life-course one.

19. http://www.worldhealth.net/event/about_1.php (accessed August 2006; no longer available). Anthropologist Courtney Mykytyn has done very interesting research on the recent emergence of "anti-aging medicine" in the United States (2006a, 2006b). See also American Academy of Anti-Aging Medicine (2000–2006) and Klatz 2000.

20. Ibid.

21. For an in-depth exploration of Hindu Bengali attitudes toward death and dying, see Lamb 2000:115–180.

22. Joel Savishinsky's retired American informants, however, often found the taboo on speaking about death bothersome, frustrated with children and others unwilling to broach the topic (Savishinsky 2000).

23. Several of these passages can occur concurrently. For instance, rituals transforming one into an ancestor do not preclude the soul or *ātmā* also being able to move on to other new forms of existence. See Gold 1988:59–132, Inden and Nicholas 1977:62–66, Lamb 2000:144–180, Madan 1987:118–141, Parry 1994, and Stone 1988 for further discussions of Hindu perceptions of death.

24. The names of the seventy-one old age homes I located in the Kolkata region fall into a relatively limited number of interesting categories:

> 1) something related to *vānaprastha* or spirituality (this was the most numerous category, which I will explore shortly),
>
> 2) something related to *sevā* or serving and respecting elders,
>
> 3) something related to household-like hospitality and warmth (such as Hospitality, Nest of Affection),
>
> 4) something related to compassion or providing shelter for the otherwise adrift or abandoned (such as Site Full of Mercy, Auspicious Shelter, Source of Support),
>
> 5) something related to positive feelings (such as Happy Home, Ashram of Joy),
>
> 6) something related to being near the end of life (such as Sunset Glow, Lamp at Sunset, Retirement),
>
> 7) something related to beginning a new life (such as New Nest, New Horizon), and finally
>
> 8) a few named for specific locations, saints, or people (such as the founder or founder's parents).

25. The implication here is that Sri Ashok had earlier served the Mission (for he had long been a disciple) or society (by working). Now in late life it was his turn to stop working and receive *sevā* in return.

26. See also Cohen 1998 and Lamb 2000 for detailed discussions of *sevā* and aging.

27. Why were not more male elder-abode residents (comfortable being) supported by their sons? One factor is that it is common among this class of individuals choosing old age homes to be practicing and upholding "modern" and "Western" values of independence, values facilitated by the modern pension system. Also, even in more conventional

contexts, for instance as Vatuk (1990) and Lamb (2000) found working with those living in multigenerational households in New Delhi and Mangaldihi, men generally prefer to maintain some financial autonomy when moving to a retired phase of life of increasing dependence on sons. Further, older men normally would be living with their sons in a family home that they themselves had worked to establish and support over many years, so that even if the older man is no longer bringing in new cash earnings, his earlier contributions to the household as well as the junior members' indebtedness to him are both readily apparent in the material form of the house. As I discussed in chapter 4, Indian women in general have conventionally held much less financial autonomy than men, and dependence on sons in old age is often viewed as a natural and fitting extension of dependence on fathers in childhood and husbands in adulthood.

28. *Ekānna* is a term derived from Sanskrit from the roots *ek* (one) and *anna* (rice, meal, food). *Bartī* is a suffix indicating location or place. So, *ekānnabartī* indicates a place where meals are shared, and an *ekānnabartī paribār* is a family (*paribār*) whose members all eat together. Interestingly, *ekānna* is also the Bengali term for the number fifty-one (an auspicious number), and so some Bengalis believe that the phrase *ekānnabartī paribār* (or joint family) literally implies "fifty-one members of a household"— that is, a family of many members living together. Experts in the history of the Bengali language, however, state that the "fifty-one" and "one-meal" meanings of *ekānna* are simply homonyms, and that *ekānnabartī paribār*, glossed as joint family, derives from the "one-rice" or "shared-meal" meaning of *ekānna* and not the word's unrelated numerical sense (Clinton Seely, personal communication). Nonetheless, both popularly understood meanings can fit, as the two main characteristics of a joint family or *ekānnabartī paribār* in most Bengalis' minds are that its members all eat together, and it is large in size.

29. *Chele* can mean boy, young man, son, and/or child, depending on the context.

30. This is the old age home where Monisha Mashi, with whom I shared a beer at the Saturday Club (chapter 4), resided and where my daughters and I spent the night in the guest quarters.

31. See the brief discussion in chapter 2 above, and Daniel 1984, Inden and Nicholas 1977, Lamb 2000 (especially pp. 27–36), Marriott 1976, and Marriott and Inden 1977 for analyses of Indian conceptions regarding the fluid and open nature of persons, whose bodily and emotional relationships with other persons, places, and things are formed through the intimate sharing of bodily substances.

32. Cohen 1998 (pp. 116–120) and Lamb 2000 (pp. 78, 91, 95, 136–137) also introduce Aloka Mitra and the Navanir homes.

33. Close friends—peers of similar age and rank—tend not to use kin terms with each other, simply calling each other by name. One may also call a junior by name, even if that person stands in a junior kin-like relationship to one (such as younger sister or son or niece). However, it is disrespectful to call a senior person by name only. One may address a senior person by simply using a senior kin term, or by employing the kin term following the personal name, as in Monisha Mashi (Monisha Aunt), or Kalyani-di (Kalyani–older sister).

34. Lawrence Cohen (1988:116, 118–119) provides an interesting and revealing discussion of how the female residents of Navanir are called *māsimās* (aunties) rather than mothers, as the aunt figure is close yet peripheral. Compared to the mother, the aunt maintains only a tenuous connection to a household and kin, with weak claims upon family support.

35. Regrettably, for this research project I did not interview any staff members pri-

vately, out of the context of their work environment, so I do not know well their own perspectives on their work and the elder institutions.

36. The Ashram Mata lamented, crying after her daughter's untimely death at forty-two, "Why did *she* go? There are so many people here [in this elder ashram] for whom if they died their relatives (*bāṛir lok,* "home's people") would be happy and relieved and even find peace, for whom there aren't even any people to cry, who even would just lie rotting with no one even to take them to the cremation ground, if not for us. Why couldn't one of *them* die instead of my daughter? At such a young age!" Hena found her plea selfish, saying that she should have wished for her *own* death rather than an ashram member's. I felt I could relate to the Ashram Mata's pain and was interested in the way she characterized the ashram residents as those who had no one.

37. I have never encountered the term *bāṛi* (house, home) in the name of an old age home either, instead finding terms such as ashram (spiritual shelter, refuge), abode (*ābās, niketan,* and *nivās*), nest (*nīṛ, bāsā*), and the English 'home.' A "nest" (*nīṛ* or *bāsā*) is understood by Bengalis as a resting place or temporary residence, distinct from a real ancestral or family home (*bāṛi*) (also see Inden and Nicholas 1977:7). The terms I have translated as "abode" here (which could also be glossed as residence or dwelling) are terms that carry both more temporary and more formal (as in poetic or literary) connotations than *bāṛi.*

38. In Lamb 1997 and 2000 (pp. 207–221), I examine Bengali notions about women's relative transformability or flexibility over the life course. Bengalis do in general also speak of women as, perhaps even more than men, valuing crowded togetherness in daily life, as Margaret Trawick also found among the women she knew in Tamil Nadu (1990:73; also see Lamb 2000:207).

39. As I have noted elsewhere, Bengalis and other Indians use kin terms in many social settings, especially when addressing and referring to those senior to oneself, to signify both respect and closeness.

40. In the *Dharmaśāstra* texts, the life stage schema applies specifically to an upper-caste man's life. Little explicit attention is given to defining the appropriate stages of a woman's life, which are determined by her relationships to the men on whom she depends for support and guidance—her father, her husband, and finally her sons (*The Laws of Manu* V.148, Manu 1886:195, 1991:115).

41. Wendy Doniger finds one commentator who interprets Manu to intend that if a wife is young, she should be left with her sons, and if she is old, then her husband should take her along to the forest; another suggests that if the wife wishes to go, her husband should take her (1991:117 n. 3).

42. Many scholars have written about how spirituality and "forest-dwelling" inform conceptions of old age and daily life practices of Hindus, including Hiebert (1981:215–221, 225–226), Lamb (2000:115–143), Roy (1992:138–145), Savishinsky 2004, Tilak (1989) and Vatuk (1980, 1990:73–75).

43. See, for instance, Lawrence Cohen's analysis of a Vanaprastha Ashram in Hardwar, northern India (1998:113–115).

44. The Bengali forms of these names are Santi Neer, Santiniketan and Prasanti.

45. Available at http://www.sambodh.org/NEW/2002/vana/vana.htm (accessed 15 September 2008).

46. Vrindavan's ashrams for Hindu widows are populated primarily by Bengali women, many of whom were widowed in their childhoods and sent forcibly to Vrindavan by families who did not wish to keep an inauspicious widow. Other women

choose the path, hoping to find a meaningful way to live as a widow, focused on spirituality. The widows spend their days singing hymns and receive just barely enough rice, clothing, and shelter from the ashrams and passing pilgrims to scrape by. Widows' ashrams have received considerable negative press recently (e.g., Tripathi 2006) and have been hauntingly depicted in films such as *Moksha* (Butalia 1993) and *Water* (Mehta 2005).

47. Vedanta is a branch of Hindu philosophy, meaning the end, or culmination, of the Vedas, the ancient texts regarded as the scriptural foundation of Hinduism.

48. As noted above, Vedanta is a branch of Hindu philosophy; it comprises the Aranyakas or "forest scriptures," of which the Upanishads form the chief part. As a young woman, Monisha Mashi had received an MA degree in Vedanta Studies.

49. For instance, upper caste Bengali widows, in particular, are traditionally expected to eat only vegetarian foods, which means avoiding not only all meats, fish, and eggs, but also onions, garlic, and certain kinds of dal.

50. For discussions of the tension between the values of attachment and renunciation in Hindu Indian society and the life course, see Dumont 1980 [1960], Gold 1989, 1992; Lamb 2000 (especially chapter 4 and pp. 140–142); and Madan 1987.

6. Living Alone as a Way of Life

1. The quoted passages are from Sokhal 2000, one of about twenty clippings Himanshu Rath, director and founder of Agewell Foundation, offered me when I met with him for several hours in March 2003 to discuss Agewell and his general views on aging.

2. For the 2005–2006 figures, see Table 2.2 "Household Composition" of the National Family Health Survey India-3 (http://www.nfhsindia.org/nfhs3_national_report.html, Volume I>Chapters>Chapter 02, Household Population and Housing Characteristics. Table 2.2 is on p. 23); for the 1998–1999 figures, see Table 2.5, "Household Characteristics" of the NFHS-2 (available at http://www.nfhsindia.org/india2.html); for the 1992–1993 figures, see Table 3.6, "Household Composition" of the NFHS-1 (available at http://www.nfhsindia.org/india1.html. These sites were accessed in 15 September 2008). According to the Census of India 2001, less than 1 percent of the total Indian population of 1.03 billion live in single-person households ("Household Size"—available at http://www.censusindia.gov.in/Census_Data_2001/Census_data_finder/H_Series/Household_Size.htm; accessed 15 September 2008).

3. My search of the Census of India 2001 data produces just slightly different figures: of persons aged sixty or older, 4 percent lived in single-person households and 7 percent as an elderly couple. Of those who did live alone, a larger number are females: 2.1 out of 38.3 million (5.5 percent) of older women aged sixty years and above. See Census of India 2001: "Data Highlights: HH-5: Households with number of aged persons sixty years and above by sex and household size," pp. 2–4, available at http://www.censusindia.gov.in/ (accessed 15 September 2008).

4. Available at http://www.dignityfoundation.com/lmp.htm (accessed 15 September 2008). The Dignity Foundation is a "Senior Citizens Life Enrichment Organization," founded in 1995, with chapters now in Chennai, Kolkata, Hyderabad, Jamshedpur, and Visakhapatnam.

5. Salt Lake City is a relatively new, well-to-do, planned community on the northeastern outskirts of Kolkata, of largely spacious single-family homes. Built in the mid-1970s, and then populated by many families raising sophisticated children, it is now

well known for having a preponderance of large homes housing merely one to two older adults, whose professional adult children have moved abroad.

6. Figure 3, "Households by Size: 1970 to 2003," in "America's Families and Living Arrangements: 2003" (U.S. Census Bureau 2004). In 2003, single-person households were the second most common type of household, with two-person households being the most common. In India in 2005, single-person households were the second *least* common type (just ahead of 8-person households), following 4, 5, 3, 6, 2, 7, and 9+-person households, in that order. In 1992–1993, single-person households were the very least common type, following 5, 4, 6, 9+, 7, 3, 2, and 8-person households, in that order. (See note 3 above for the sources of this National Family Health Survey India information.) In terms of percentages of the population, in India (in 2001) less than 1 percent of persons (.735 percent) lived in single-person households (note 3 above), while in the United States in 2000, 9.7 percent of the population lived singly.

7. U.S. Census Bureau, accessed at www.census.gov, September 2007: Single Person Households Age 65 and Older in 1999: 2000 Census, Tables No. 60 and 61; and "A Profile of Older Americans: 2003"—http://www.aoa.gov/PROF/Statistics/profile/2006/6.aspx.

8. For example, see the discussion of the "sandwich generation" in chapter 1.

9. My research assistant Naomi Schiesel analyzed U.S. media stories on aging appearing between 2002 and 2007 in major U.S. newspapers and magazines.

10. Bandhopadhyay 2005, Bag 2003, *Telegraph* Staff Reporter 2005a, *Telegraph* Staff Reporter 2005b, Santhanam 1998, and *Telegraph* Staff Reporter 2003a.

11. Convenience sampling involves studying those known to or accessible to the researcher (as when a professor uses college students, or a researcher uses volunteers who have responded to signs or ads). In snowball sampling, one begins by identifying a few persons who meet the criteria for inclusion in the study, and then asks these initial subjects to recommend others they know who also fit the criteria.

12. In cases of married couples, only if I interacted closely with and interviewed both partners have I considered both as research subjects.

13. A.B.C.D. refers to a modern South Asian American youth unsure about his or her cultural identity. *Deśi* is derived from the term *deś*, meaning (in many north Indian languages) "land" or "country of origin/belonging." *Deśi* means "local" or "indigenous," in contrast to *bideśi*, "foreign," and is used to refer to people or things of South Asian origin.

14. I have translated the six headings verbatim and summarized their contents in parentheses.

15. Guruchuran Das, an acclaimed columnist and former CEO of Procter & Gamble India, also comments relevantly: "Our children are leaving or have left to go abroad, and this is another source of discontent. We did not create enough jobs at home because of mistaken economic policies. Our children are forced to look abroad for opportunities—many of them never to return. When friends and children leave, life begins to feel insipid" (2002:282).

16. T. E. Woronov (2007) relatedly analyzes how many middle-class Chinese parents are cultivating in their children a perceived American-style independence and self-actualization that will bring them and their nation success in the era of capitalist globalization.

17. These are the kinds of reflections I heard, at least, from NRI parents who have chosen to remain in India; the next chapter explores the perspectives of parents who have decided to move.

18. However, mandatory retirement at age fifty-eight, sixty, or sixty-two is widespread in India, for those holding professional jobs.

19. Chopra 2003. Translations from the Hindi were made by my research assistant Rachana Agarwal.

20. For more on the Bengali concept of *māyā* as bodily and emotional ties of affection and attachment, see Lamb 2000 and chapter 2 of this volume.

21. See also Sundaram 2001 for a discussion of the Saksenas's business.

22. This discussion was published in Sokhal 2000 (see note 1 above). The Agewell Foundation website can be found at: http://www.agewellindia.org/about_us.htm (accessed 9 November 2008).

23. The Dignity Foundation website can be found at: http://www.dignityfoundation.com/lmp.htm (accessed September 2008).

24. Interestingly, in Western academic and policy literature, there is much more ambivalence about locating child care outside the family than care for the elderly, sick, or disabled. This is consistent with deep, not always recognized and scrutinized, cultural assumptions in Western Europe and North America that it is normative for children to be dependent on and cared for by their parents, especially the mother, but not for elderly parents to be dependent on their adult children. See, for instance, Meyer (2000).

25. Around the world, however, care work is becoming increasingly commodified. Pierrette Hondagneu-Sotelo writes, for instance, of global trends in the organization of care work: "In the current postindustrial context, many reproductive services are commodified, removed entirely from the household (e.g., fast food, dry cleaners, car washes), or they are now performed for pay in the household." Of course, this is a complex transition, but Hondagneu-Sotelo writes that, "I believe it is suggestive of an historical trajectory. . . . The work of caregiving and cleaning, once relegated to wives, mothers, and grandmothers, is increasingly commodified and purchased on a global market" (2000:161). Pei-Chia Lan (2002) examines the commodification of elder care and the "subcontracting" of filial piety among Chinese immigrant families in California.

26. A worker who is hired especially to provide care for a young child or frail elder—helping to dress, bathe, toilet, feed, and supervise—is generally considered an ayah (nanny or nurse) rather than simply a more general "work person," although ayahs frequently also perform broader household cooking, cleaning, and serving tasks.

27. The use of the now internationally current English phrase "senior citizens" is similar in some respects to the modern creation of a partly consumer culture-driven, partly political "global gay" identity around the world as examined, for instance, in Altman 2001.

28. The first Laughing Clubs were launched in Bombay by Dr. Madan Kataria in the 1990s and have since spread throughout India and to Europe and the United States, promoting laughter yoga as a means to improve health, reduce stress, and increase happiness. Although not specifically founded for older persons, India's laughing clubs tend to have more older than younger members, and Udita's club was made up entirely of those who considered themselves to be "senior."

29. Generally not "dozens" but about eight to twenty of the approximately thirty-five members gather daily.

30. The Bhagavad Gita is an ancient Sanskrit text which many view as a classic summary of the core beliefs of Hinduism.

7. Moving Abroad

1. For discussions of the history of South Asian immigration to the United States, see Agrawal 1991, Bacon 1996, Das Gupta 2006, Hing 1993:69–73, Jensen 1988, Leonard 1997, Lessinger 1995, Shukla 2003, and Visweswaran 1997.

2. The 1990 U.S. Census counted Asian Indians age sixty-five and over at only 1.6 percent of the population (Winokur 1994:12). The 2000 U.S. Census counted them at 4.0 percent (Census 2000 SF2 Tables DP-1). Many older Indians, however, move back and forth between India and the United States, often retaining Indian nationality and legal residency, and thus are not included in the U.S. census.

3. For a discussion of the term Indian American, see chapter 1, note 47.

4. Because of the terms of the 1965 U.S. Immigration and Naturalization Act, as noted in the text, immigrants from India in the United States have, on the whole, had a high socio-economic status. The class backgrounds of Indian Americans are becoming somewhat more varied, however, as newcomers immigrate under the Family Reunification Act. Still, the 2000 U.S. Census lists Asian Indians with the second-highest annual median household income among all U.S. ethnic groups. See chapter 1, note 48.

5. The federal Supplemental Security Income program was established in 1974 to provide a nationally uniform guaranteed minimum income for the aged, blind, and disabled. Until 1996, both citizens and legal immigrants could receive benefits under this program. Following 1996, only immigrants who become citizens can be eligible. I discuss the SSI program and its underlying assumptions in much more detail in chapter 8.

6. The Government of India began to lift some restrictions on its currency after 1991, in a series of ongoing reforms. Now non-resident Indians can withdraw some assets from India, although the unfavorable rupee to dollar exchange rate still leaves many older, retired expatriates with few independent resources abroad.

7. It is important to note that of all the Indian immigrant seniors I knew who were receiving SSI, each was a recent immigrant, having come to the United States late in life to be with their children. Of the fewer senior Indian Americans I know who migrated to the United States sufficiently early in their lives to work, and thus earn Social Security credits and amass retirement funds, none are receiving SSI.

8. In Gujarati, the suffix "ben," meaning sister, is often added to a woman's name as a sign of respect and closeness, similar to "di" or "didi" (older sister) in Bengali.

9. The section on medicalizing and prolonging the end of life in chapter 5 examines such trends in more detail.

10. Writer Tahira Naqvi's short story "Dying in a Strange Country" poignantly portrays an older Pakistani woman's gripping fears of dying in the United States when she visits her Connecticut-settled son. See also Firth 1997 for a rich look at beliefs and practices surrounding death and dying in a British Hindu community.

11. Like "ben" meaning sister, "bhai" meaning brother is often added as a suffix to Gujarati men's names as a sign of respect.

12. GED refers to the "General Equivalency Diploma" to indicate a high school level of education.

8. Changing Families and the State

1. "Elderly Alipore Clerk Blames Son's Wife Before Suicide" (Times News Network, *Times of India,* Kolkata, April 29, 2005). "Tortured Father Takes Life" (Staff Reporter, *Telegraph,* Kolkata April 29, 2005).

2. I took notes but did not record our conversation while the officer spoke in a mixture of Bengali and English.

3. The gentleman's name and address were part of the public record, reported in the newspapers, so I have chosen not to use a pseudonym in this case.

4. Elder abuse is a crime in all fifty U.S. states. Legal definitions of elder abuse vary considerably from state to state, but in almost all states, protective interventions or prosecution are authorized or required only if the elders are mentally or physically impaired (Bonnie and Wallace 2003:35). "Neglect" usually is associated exclusively with persons who have a legal duty to provide care—who have formally assumed a custodial or caregiving role; while in most states anyone can be found to have committed "abuse" (such as a physical act causing pain or injury, or financial exploitation). In legal definitions of, and academic texts examining, elder abuse in the United States, adult children are not singled out as the paradigmatic caregivers. Nowhere in any of the materials my research assistant Naomi Schiesel and I examined is it stated that an adult child has an inherent responsibility to care for an elderly parent. However, an adult child could be prosecuted for elder abuse if the other conditions applied (such as that the elder parent is physically or mentally impaired, and the child has assumed the responsibility for care or custody of the parent). In fact, in the almost 90 percent of elder abuse and neglect incidents with a known perpetrator, two-thirds of the perpetrators are the adult children of the elderly parent (Tatara et al. 1998:12). See also American Bar Association Commission on Law and Aging 2005; Jogerst et al. 2003; Tatara 1995; and "Elder Rights and Resources," Administration on Aging, Department of Health and Human Services—http://www.aoa.gov/eldfam/Elder_Rights/Elder_Abuse/Elder_Abuse.aspx.

5. Earlier versions of the bill were introduced in the Indian Parliament in 2005 and 2006 under slightly different names: "The Older Persons (Maintenance, Care and Protection) Bill, 2005" and "The Parents and Senior Citizens (Welfare and Maintenance) Bill, 2006." The text of the 2007 bill is available at http://www.prsindia.org/docs/bills/1182337322/scr1193026940_Senior_Citizen.pdf (accessed 15 September 2008). For a bill to be enacted into law as an Act, it must pass both houses of Parliament and be signed by the president. As of this writing (May 2008), the Maintenance and Welfare of Parents and Senior Citizens Bill, 2007, has been approved by the Parliament but not yet finalized as an act. National and international newspaper coverage of the bill includes: Chauhan 2007, Desai 2007, Dholabhai 2007, Gentleman 2007, Ghildiyal 2005, Ghoshal 2007, Salvadore and Mukherjee 2007, Sarkar 2008, *Telegraph* 2007, Tikku 2007, and *Times News Network* 2007b.

6. Standing Committee on Social Justice and Empowerment (2007–2008), Twenty-Eighth Report: "The Maintenance and Welfare of Parents and Senior Citizens Bill, 2007": p. 9 (see note 5 above for link).

7. Ibid., p. 10.

8. The law was first introduced to the Himachal Pradesh state government in 1997, taking four years to be fully implemented as an act. The 1997 version of the bill's preface reads: "Aged and infirm parents are now left beggared and destitute on the scrap heap of society. It has become necessary to provide compassionate and speedy remedy to alleviate their sufferings" (quoted in Ravindranath 1997). Retired chief justice and chairman of the state Human Rights Commission Chittatosh Mukherjee commented on the legislation: "As long as there were strong family bonds, there was no need for written law to dictate that you have to care for your parents" (ibid.).

9. Code of Criminal Procedure 1973, Section 125: "Order for maintenance of wives,

children and parents," available at http://www.vakilno1.com/bareacts/CrPc/s125.htm (accessed 15 September 2008).

10. "Laws: The Hindu Adoptions and Maintenance Act of 1956" (Act No. 78, 1956), available at http://www.vakilno1.com/bareacts/hinduadoptionsact/hinduadoptionsact. htm (accessed 15 September 2008).

11. The Dignity Foundation, a "Senior Citizens Life Enrichment Services Organization," is a non-governmental organization based in Mumbai and with branches in Chennai, Kolkata, Hyderabad, Jamshedpur, and Visakhapatnam—introduced in chapters 2 and 6. See http://www.dignityfoundation.com/.

12. Standing Committee on Social Justice and Empowerment, "The Maintenance and Welfare of Parents and Senior Citizens Bill, 2007": p. 10.

13. Ibid, p. 53 (Chapter VI, clause 24).

14. Ibid, pp. 44–45 (Chapter I.2.a–h, and Chapter II.4.2).

15. In such an arrangement, the son-in-law is referred to as a "house son-in-law" or, in Bengali, *ghar jāmāi* (see Lamb 2000:87 and chapter 7).

16. This is an abbreviated headline from an *Anandabajar Patrika* news story reported by Arunodoy Bhattacharyya, "Court Reprimands Son and Daughter-in-Law for Torture and Orders Them to Embrace Parents' Feet and Ask for Forgiveness" (*Atyācār karāy bhartsanā, mā-bābār pā dhare kshamā cāite nirdeś korter*), 27 June 2003, p. 1. As described in chapter 2, the gesture of a junior family member bowing to touch the feet of a senior expresses deep respect.

17. From 2003 through 2008, my research assistant Hena Basu scoured the English and Bengali papers daily for relevant stories pertaining to court and police cases concerning disputes between elders and their junior kin. The newspapers popular in Kolkata that she searched included primarily the *Telegraph;* the *Times of India, Kolkata;* the *Hindustan Times; Anandabajar Patrika;* and *Bartaman.*

18. Puja here refers to Durga Puja, the major festival of the year for Bengali Hindus, during which time families gather together, exchange gifts, share meals, and pay homage to the Goddess Durga, and when schools and offices frequently close for an extended holiday. Other newspaper stories on this case include: "Simply Cook and Co-Exist Together" (*Telegraph,* 22 September 2007, p. 22), and "Justice Refuses to Take Sides in *Saas-Bahu* War" (Prahladka, *Hindustan Times,* 22 September 2007).

19. "Only a Mother Can Say Who Her Child Is, High Court Cautions Son (*Santān kār balben śudhu mā, cheleke hūśiyāri hāikorter*)" (*Anandabajar Patrika* 2008b, April 24, p. 16), and Prahladka 2008—"Court Rebuke for Insult to Mother" (*Hindustan Times,* 24 April, Kolkata Live section, p. 3).

20. *Anandabajar Patrika* 2008a, "*Māke dekhen nā, lajjā kare nā! Mucalekā nila court*" [You Don't Take Care of Your Mother—Don't You Feel Ashamed?! Court Requires Son to Post Bond]. March 19, p. 1.

21. Such elder bias, to the extent it exists, could be bolstered by the fact that the majority of judges are themselves of a relatively senior generation, and of course elder bias resonates as well with the widespread (though not unequivocally sustained) principle in Indian society—that elders are deserving of respect.

22. Section 498A ("Husband or relative of husband of a woman subjecting her to cruelty") was added to the Indian Penal Code in 1983. Widely known popularly as "the Dowry Law," it reads: "Whoever, being the husband or the relative of the husband of a woman, subjects such woman to cruelty shall be punished with imprisonment for a term which may extend to three years and shall also be liable to fine." The section elaborates

the meanings of cruelty, one of which includes driving the woman to suicide: "any willful conduct which is of a nature as is likely to drive the woman to commit suicide or to cause grave injury or danger to life, limb, or health (whether physical or mental) of the woman." Text available at http://www.vakilno1.com/bareacts/IndianPenalCode/S498A. htm (accessed 15 September 2008).

23. The original Bengali is "*Buṛo bāp-mā culoe jāk,*" which literally means, "Let old parents go to the funeral pyre" or to the "oven" (*culo*). *Culoe jāk* carries a meaning similar to the English idioms "go to hell," "go to the dogs," or "go to ruins."

24. James Ferguson (2006) incisively scrutinizes the ways such familiar teleological developmental narratives present an "evolutionist temporalization of difference" (p. 182).

25. As seen in earlier chapters, cultivating both the market and the individual are indeed also strategies Indians are utilizing to tackle aging, in the form of market-based old age homes and NGOs (such as the Dignity Foundation) promoting individual self-reliance.

26. For accounts of Indian government social security programs for the elderly, see Kumar 2003; Parekh 2006; Rajan 2001; Rajan, Mishra, and Sarma 1999; and Shankardass 2000.

27. West Bengal government employees retire at age fifty-eight and Government of India employees at sixty. Fixed retirement ages in private companies vary, but generally fall near age sixty.

28. "National Social Assistance Program," available at http://arunachalpradesh.nic. in/nsa.htm (accessed 15 September 2008); Kumar 2003:60; and Sreevastava 2004.

29. As of April 2008, a proposal is under consideration to lower the age of eligibility to sixty years or higher.

30. The caretaker of the Home for Old and Infirm Political Sufferers thought that his was the only government old age home in India; however Rajan, Mishra, and Sarma report in 1999 the existence of three government old age homes, in the states of Haryana, Rajasthan, and West Bengal (1999:240–241). Central and state governments do also provide some financial assistance to various non-governmental old age homes, especially those that serve the poor (see, e.g., Gokhale 2003:225, Table 2).

31. Zamindars are major landowners. During the periods of Mughal and British rule in India, zamindars operated as feudal landlords collecting land revenue of a district for the government.

32. Such skeptical views about the efficacy of the new Maintenance and Welfare of Parents and Senior Citizens Bill are offered in two editorials, "Present Tense, Future Imperfect" (Salvadore and Mukherjee 2007) and "Sowing Seeds of Bitterness" (Desai 2007). Sarah Salvadore and Roshni Mukherjee ask, "But will this Bill be able to better the lives of the elderly? If the intent is missing, will any law, rule, regulation bring any change in the way children mistreat their elderly parents?" Ashok Desai envisages that with the new legislation, "the children who are taken to court will almost certainly fight. They will say that the parent is not their parent and cannot prove he is, that they are too poor to support him, that they are ready to take care of him but he pisses in the washbasin, that he blew up the millions he had inherited and is now coming to them for a dole, . . . , etc., etc.," concluding: "This legislation is going to create an enormous new industry—the dirty linen washing industry" (2007:18).

33. The full text of the Social Security Act of 1935 is available at http://www.ssa. gov/history/35actpre.html (accessed 15 September 2008). See also Fischer 1978: 183–184. Fischer notes that the Social Security program, as enacted in 1935, "was extraordinarily

weak and ineffectual by the standards of welfare legislation in other western nations" at the time (pp. 183–184).

34. In general, individuals are eligible for Medicare if they hold U.S. citizenship or have been a permanent legal resident for five continuous years, and are sixty-five years or older. Some disabled people under sixty-five are also eligible.

35. The aged are defined as persons sixty-five years or older. Individuals and couples are eligible for SSI if their resources or assets total no more than $2,000 for an individual or $3,000 for a couple, and if their incomes fall below the Federal maximum monthly SSI benefit. In 1996 this was $470 for an individual or $705 for a couple, and in 2008, $637 for an individual or $856 for a couple; a table with this information is available at http://www.ssa.gov/OACT/COLA/SSIamts.html (accessed 15 September 2008). Certain assets are not counted, however, such as the home one lives in, one's car (usually), burial plots, and up to $1,500 in burial funds (available at www.socialsecurity.gov— "Supplemental Security Income (SSI)," accessed 15 September 2008). For a five-year period following the alien's entry to the United States, the assets of the alien's sponsor would also be taken into account in calculating eligibility (initially this period was set at three years, but it was revised upward in 1994).

36. #H.R. 3507, 104th Congress, second session, now Public Law 104–193.

37. Immigration-Related Welfare Provisions in the Balanced Budget Act, Public Law 105–133.

38. U.S. Congress, Senate 1997:92–94.

39. On the whole, immigrants from India in the United States have had a high socioeconomic status. See chapter 1, note 48.

40. U.S. Congress, House 1989a, 1989b, 1996; U.S. Congress, Senate 1984, 1997; U.S. Department of Health and Human Services 1980.

41. In many African American families, however, adults do feel compelled to financially support the older parents and especially grandparents who raised them (see Stack 1996). The more dominant U.S. model is that, while adult children may provide many forms of emotional and practical care to their elderly parents, they ideally will not offer full financial support or intimate bodily care (such as bathing and toileting), or co-reside.

42. The Federation for American Immigration Reform, according to its web page, is a nonpartisan "organization of concerned citizens who share a common belief that our nation's immigration policies must be reformed to serve the national interest. FAIR seeks to improve border security, to stop illegal immigration, and to promote immigration levels consistent with the national interest—more traditional rates of about 300,000 a year" (http://www.fairus.org; accessed 15 October 2008). See also Daniel Stein interview, March 19, 1997, on NPR's *Talk of the Nation,* available at http://www.npr.org/templates/story/story.php?storyId=1011313 (accessed 15 September 2008).

Afterword

1. Diane Mines writes about culture as a "'co-production' of the ethnographer and her informants or, perhaps better stated, her guides and interlocutors" (2005:209).

2. For those who are not reading this book's chapters in sequence, I will mention that the two sides of this question, regarding the proper configuration of state support for the aged, are examined closely in chapter 8.

BIBLIOGRAPHY

Abaya, Carol. 2006. "The Sandwich Generation: Don't Quit Work to Care for Mom." *Herald News* (Passaic County, New Jersey), 15 October, sec. Life: B07.

Administration on Aging. 2006. "Elder Rights and Resources." Department of Health and Human Services. http://www.aoa.gov/eldfam/Elder_Rights/Elder_Abuse/ Elder_Abuse.aspx (accessed 15 October 2007).

Administration on Aging. 2006. "A Profile of Older Americans 2006: Living Arrangements." Department of Health and Human Services. http://www.aoa.gov/ prof/Statistics/profile/2006/6.aspx.

Agrawal, Priya. 1991. *Passage from India: Post 1965 Immigrants and Their Children.* Palos Verdes, Calif.: Yuvati.

Ahearn, Laura. 2000. "Agency." *Journal of Linguistic Anthropology* 9(1–2): 12–15.

Altman, Dennis. 2001. "Rupture or Continuity? The Internationalization of Gay Identities." In John C. Hawley, ed., *Post-Colonial, Queer: Theoretical Intersections,* 19–41. Albany: State University of New York Press.

American Academy of Anti-Aging Medicine. 2000–2006. *Anti-Aging Medical News.* http://www.worldhealth.net/p/4243.html

American Bar Association Commission on Law and Aging. 2005. *Information about Laws Related to Elder Abuse.* Washington, D.C.: National Center on Elder Abuse.

Amit-Talai, Vered, and Helena Wulff, eds. 1995. *Youth Cultures: A Cross-Cultural Perspective.* London: Routledge.

Anand, Rajen S. 1994. "What Should We Call Ourselves? Let's Debate." *India-West,* 18 February.

Anandabajar Patrika (Kolkata). 2003. "*Buṛo bāp-mā culoy jāk*" [Let Aged Father and Mother Go to Hell], 16 October, sec. CE: 4.

———. 2005. "*Boumār prahāre bāṛichāṛā śāśuṛi ghurchen pathe pathe*" [Homeless Mother-in-Law, Beaten by Her Daughter-in-Law, Wanders the Streets], 7 April.

———. 2007. "*Mā-bābār upare atyācāre kaṛā byabasthā*" [Harsh Measures to Tackle Torture of Parents], 18 September.

———. 2008a. "*Māke dekhen nā, lajjā kare nā! Mucalekā nila korṭ*" [You Don't Take Care of Your Mother—Don't You Feel Ashamed?! Court Requires [Son to] Post Bond], March 19: 1.

———. 2008b. "*Santān kār balben śudhu mā, cheleke hūśiyāri hāikorṭer*" [Only a Mother Can Say Who Her Child Is, High Court Cautions Son], April 24: 16.

Appadurai, Arjun. 1996. *Modernity at Large: Cultural Dimensions of Globalization.* Minneapolis: University of Minnesota Press.

———. 1997. "Discussion: Fieldwork in the Era of Globalization." *Anthropology and Humanism* 22: 115–118.

Appadurai, Arjun, and Carol Breckenridge. 1995. "Public Modernity in India." In Carol A. Breckenridge, ed., *Consuming Modernity: Public Culture in a South Asian World,* 1–20. Minneapolis: University of Minnesota Press.

Arthur, Kate. 2004. "Surviving the Push and Pull of the Sandwich Generation."
  Pantagraph (Bloomington, Ill.), 2 March, sec. Focus: p. D1.

Bacon, Jean. 1996. *Life Lines: Community, Family, and Assimilation among Asian Indian
  Immigrants.* New York: Oxford University Press.

Bag, Shamik. 2003. "Loneliness, the Other Name for Old Age." *Hindustan Times,*
  13 August, sec. HT City: 3.

Bagga, Chirdeep. 2005. "Nation Leaves 11% of Its Elderly Alone." *Times of India,*
  Kolkata, 26 May.

Bandhopadhyay, Atin. 2005. "Alone and Insecure in the Winter of Life." *Sunday Times of
  India,* 24 April: 2.

Bandyopadhyay, Bimal. 2005. "*Jelāe bayaskader nirāpattāy najar dite puliśke nirdeś rājyer*"
  [The Government Directs Police to Monitor the Safety of District's Elderly].
  Bartaman (Kolkata), 7 August.

Barbagli, Marzio, and David I. Kertzer. 2003."Introduction." In David I. Kertzer and
  Marzio Barbagli, eds., *The History of the European Family, Volume Three: Family
  Life in the Twentieth Century,* xi–xliv. New Haven, Conn.: Yale University Press.

Baruah, Bonita. 2004. "Family Matters: The New Joint Venture." *Sunday Times of India,*
  Kolkata, 26 September: 11.

Basu, Saumitra. 2006. Some Social, Economic and Behavioral Problems of the Aged
  Inhabiting Calcutta City: An Anthropological Approach. PhD diss., University of
  Calcutta.

Beijing Review. 2007. "The Development of China's Undertakings for the Aged (II),"
  11 January. http://www.bjreview.com/document/txt/2007–01/08/content_52416_2.
  htm (accessed 15 September 2008).

Belluck, Pam. 2006. "As Minds Age, What's Next? Brain Calisthenics." *New York Times,*
  27 December. http://www.nytimes.com/2006/12/27/health/27brain.html (accessed
  15 September 2008).

Berenson, Alex. 2005. "Sales of Impotence Drug Falling, Defying Expectations."
  New York Times, 4 December. http://www.nytimes.com/2005/12/04/business/
  yourmoney/04impotence.html (accessed 15 September 2008).

Berger, Bennett M. 1960. "How Long Is a Generation?" *British Journal of Sociology* 11(1)
  (March): 10–23.

Berliner, David. 2005. "An 'Impossible' Transmission: Youth Religious Memories in
  Guinea-Conakry." *American Ethnologist* 32(4): 576–592.

Berman, Marshall. 1988. *All That Is Solid Melts into Air: The Experience of Modernity.*
  New York: Viking Penguin.

Beteille, Andre. 2001. "The Indian Middle Class." *Hindu,* 5 February.

Bhabha, Homi. 1994. *The Location of Culture.* New York: Routledge.

Bhattacharjee, Anannya. 1992. "The Habit of Ex-Nomination: Nation, Woman, and the
  Indian Immigrant Bourgeoisie." *Public Culture* 5(1): 19–43.

Bhattacharyya, Arunodoy. 2003. "*Atyācār karāy bhartsanā, mā-bābār pā dhare kshamā
  cāite nirdeś korṭer*" [Court Reprimands Son and Daughter-in-Law for Torture and
  Orders Them to Embrace Parents' Feet and Ask for Forgiveness]. *Anandabajar
  Patrika.* 27 June: 1.

Bist, Raju. 2004. "The Great Indian Mall Boom." *Asia Times Online,* 24 July. http://www.atimes.com/atimes/South_Asia/FG24Df01.html

Black, Rosemary. 2006. "Curse of the Sandwich Generation." *Daily News: New York's Hometown Newspaper,* 29 July, sec. Now: 27.

Bloch, Maurice, and Jonathan Parry. 1989. "Introduction: Money and the Morality of Exchange." In Jonathan Parry and Maurice Bloch, eds., *Money and the Morality of Exchange,* 1–32. Cambridge: Cambridge University Press.

Bonnie, Richard J., and Robert B. Wallace, eds. 2003. *Elder Mistreatment: Abuse, Neglect, and Exploitation in an Aging America.* Panel to Review Risk and Prevalence of Elder Abuse and Neglect, National Research Council. Washington, D.C.: National Academies Press.

Bourdieu, Pierre. 1977. *Outline of a Theory of Practice.* Translated by Richard Nice. Cambridge : Cambridge University Press.

Breckenridge, Carol A., ed. 1995. *Consuming Modernity: Public Culture in a South Asian World.* Minneapolis: University of Minnesota Press.

Brody, Jane E. 1998. "Personal Health: A Valuable Guide to Successful Aging." *New York Times,* 14 April, sec. F: 7.

Bucholtz, Mary. 2002. "Youth and Cultural Practice." *Annual Review of Anthropology* 31: 525–552.

Butalia, Pankaj, director. 1993. *Moksha* (Salvation). London: Jane Balfour Films.

Butler, Robert N., and Myrna I. Lewis. 2002. *The New Love and Sex after 60,* revised ed. New York: Ballantine.

Carrier, James G. 1995. *Gifts and Commodities: Exchange and Western Capitalism since 1700.* New York: Routledge.

Centers for Disease Control and Prevention. 2006. "Deaths by Place of Death, Age, Race and Sex: United States 2002," Worktable 309, http://www.cdc.gov/nchs/data/dvs/mortfinal2002_work309.pdf

Chadsey, John N. 1879. "Out from the Poor-house." Music for the Nation: American Sheet Music, 1870–1885. The Library of Congress: American Memory. http://memory.loc.gov/ammem/smhtml/smhome.html (accessed 15 September 2008).

Chakrabarty, Dipesh. 2001. "*Adda,* Calcutta: Dwelling in Modernity." In Dilip Parameshwar Gaonkar, ed., *Alternative Modernities,* 123–164. Durham, N.C.: Duke University Press.

———. 2002. *Habitations of Modernity: Essays in the Wake of Subaltern Studies.* Chicago: University of Chicago Press.

Chakraborti, Rajagopal Dhar. 2004. *The Greying of India: Population Ageing in the Context of Asia.* New Delhi: Sage Publications India.

Chatterjee, Nilanjana, and Nancy E. Riley. 2001. "Planning an Indian Modernity: The Gendered Politics of Fertility Control." *Signs* 26(3): 812–845.

Chatterjee, Partha. 1989. "Colonialism, Nationalism, and Colonialized Women: The Contest in India." *American Ethnologist* 16:622–633.

———. 1990. "The Nationalist Resolution of the Women's Question." In Kumkum Sagari and Sudesh Vaid, eds., *Recasting Women: Essays in Indian Colonial History,* 233–253. New Brunswick, N.J.: Rutgers University Press.

———. 1993. *The Nation and Its Fragments: Colonial and Postcolonial Histories.* Princeton, N.J.: Princeton University Press.

———. 1997. "Our Modernity." In *The Present History of West Bengal: Essays in Political Criticism,* 193–210. Delhi: Oxford University Press.

Chatterji, Shoma A. 2004. "Perceptions of Age in Contemporary Films." Files of the author.

Chauhan, Chetan. 2007. "Law to Protect Elders from Wicked Kin." *Hindustan Times* (Kolkata), 24 July: 2.

Chopra, Ravi, director. 2003. *Baghban.* India/UK: B.R. Films.

Choudhuri, Ajanta. 2003. "*Santāner Bideśe Sthāyibhābe Thākā Ki Kāmya?*" [Is It Desirable If One's Children Settle Permanently Abroad?] *Sangbād Pratidin,* 14 June: 10.

Clark, Margaret. 1972. "Cultural Values and Dependency in Later Life." In Donald O. Cowgill and Lowell D. Holmes, eds., *Aging and Modernization,* 263–274. New York: Appleton Century Crofts.

Cohen, Lawrence. 1998. *No Aging in India: Alzheimer's, the Bad Family, and Other Modern Things.* Berkeley: University of California Press.

Cole, Jennifer. 2004. "Fresh Contact in Tamatave, Madagascar: Sex, Money, and Intergenerational Transformation." *American Ethnologist* 31(4): 573–588.

Cole, Jennifer, and Deborah Durham. 2007. "Introduction: Age, Regeneration, and the Intimate Politics of Globalization." In Jennifer Cole and Deborah Durham, eds., *Generations and Globalization: Youth, Age, and Family in the New World Economy,* 1–28. Bloomington: Indiana University Press.

Cole, Thomas R. 1992. *The Journey of Life: A Cultural History of Aging in America.* Cambridge: Cambridge University Press.

Comaroff, John L., and Jean Comaroff. 1997. *Of Revelation and Revolution, Volume 2: The Dialectics of Modernity on a South African Frontier.* Chicago: University of Chicago Press

Comaroff, Jean, and John L. Comaroff. 1999. "Occult Economies and the Violence of Abstraction: Notes from the South African Postcolony." *American Ethnologist* 26: 279–303.

Comte, Auguste. 1974[1855]. *The Positive Philosophy of Auguste Comte.* Freely translated and condensed by Harriet Martineau, with an introduction by Abraham S. Blumberg. New York: AMS Press.

Conrad, Peter. 2007. *Medicalization and Society: On the Transformation of Human Conditions into Treatable Disorders.* Baltimore, Md.: Johns Hopkins University Press.

Conrad, Peter, and Joseph W. Schneider. 1992. *Deviance and Medicalization: From Badness to Sickness.* Philadelphia: Temple University Press.

Coontz, Stephanie. 1992. *The Way We Never Were: American Families and the Nostalgia Trap.* New York: Basic Books.

Costa, Dora L. 1999. "A House of Her Own: Old Age Assistance and the Living Arrangement of Older Nonmarried Women." *Journal of Public Economics* 72(1): 39–59.

Dahlin, Michel R. 1993. "Commentary: Symbols of the Old Age Pension Movement: The Poorhouse, the Family, and the 'Childlike Elderly.'" In K. Warner Schaie and W. Andrew Achenbaum, eds., *Societal Impact on Aging: Historical Perspectives,* 123–129. New York: Springer.

Daniel, E. Valentine. 1984. *Fluid Signs: Being a Person the Tamil Way.* Berkeley: University of California Press.

Das, Gurcharan. 2002. *India Unbound: The Social and Economic Revolution from Independence to the Global Information Age.* New York: Anchor Books.

Das, Tina. 1999. "Old Age Home to Make Life a Pleasant Experience for Elderly." *Asian Age,* 5 September.

Das Gupta, Monisha. 2006. *Unruly Immigrants: Rights, Activism, and Transnational South Asian Politics in the United States.* Durham, N.C.: Duke University Press.

Das Gupta, Subho. 2001. *Śudhu Tomār Janya.* Kolkata: Modern Kalam.

Debnath, Sukumar. 2008a. "Aged Mother Dumped at Station." *Hindustam Times.* Kolkata Live, Saturday, 26 April: 1.

———. 2008b. "80-year-old United with Family, Nightmare Ends." *Hindustan Times,* Kolkata Live, 27 April: 1.

Derné, Steve. 2000. *Movies, Masculinity and Modernity: An Ethnography of Men's Filmgoing in India.* Westport, Conn.: Greenwood Press.

———. 2005. "Globalization and the Making of a Transnational Middle Class: Implications for Class Analysis." In Richard P. Appelbaum and William I. Robinson, eds., *Critical Globalization Studies,* 177–186. New York: Routledge.

Desai, Ashok. 2007. "Sowing Seeds of Bitterness." *Businessworld* 27(19) (1 October 2007): 18.

Dholabhai, Nishit. 2007. "Right to Home for Parents." *Telegraph,* Calcutta Sunday, 9 September: 1.

Dolby, Nadine, and Fazal Rizvi, eds. 2008. *Youth Moves: Identities and Education in Global Perspective.* New York: Routledge.

Dolby, Nadine, and Fazal Rizvi. 2008. "Introduction: Youth, Mobility, and Identity." In Nadine Dolby and Fazal Rizvi, eds., *Youth Moves: Identities and Education in Global Perspective.* 1–14. New York: Routledge.

Dube, Leela. 1988. "On the Construction of Gender: Hindu Girls in Patrilineal India." *Economic and Political Weekly,* 30 April: 11–19.

Dube, Saurabh, and Ishita Banerjee-Dube. 2006. "Introduction: Critical Questions of Colonial Modernities." In Saurabh Dube and Ishita Banerjee-Dube, eds., *Unbecoming Modern: Colonialism, Modernity, Colonial Modernities,* 1–31. New Delhi: Social Science Press.

Dumont, Louis. 1980[1960]. "World Renunciation in Indian Religions." Appendix B of *Homo Hierarchicus,* 267–286. Chicago: University of Chicago Press.

Dupont, Joan. 2000. "An Indian Director's Stirring Vision of Old Age." *International Herald Tribune,* 28 January. http://www.iht.com/articles/2000/01/28/fest.t.php (accessed 15 September 2008).

Durham, Deborah. 2000. "Introduction: Youth and the Social Imagination in Africa." *Anthropological Quarterly* 73(3): 113–120.

———. 2007. "Empowering Youth: Making Youth Citizens in Botswana." In Jennifer Cole and Deborah Durham, eds., *Generations and Globalization: Youth, Age, and Family in the New World Economy,* 102–131. Bloomington: Indiana University Press.

Dutta, Subham. 2007. "Hello! Old Age." *Sunday Newsline* (Kolkata), 3 June, sec. P.S.: 6.

Eberstadt, Mary. 2004. *Home-Alone America: The Hidden Toll of Day Care, Behavioral Drugs, and Other Parent Substitutes.* New York: Sentinel.

Eckholm, Erik. 1998. "Homes for Elderly Replacing Family Care as China Grays." *New York Times,* May 20. http://query.nytimes.com/gst/fullpage.html?res=9502E5DF1 539F933A15756C0A96E958260&sec=health&pagewanted (accessed 15 September 2008).

Economist. 2004. "Feral and Furious: Teenagers Alone." Sec. Books and Art, 13 November.

Ehrenreich, Barbara, and Arlie Russell Hochschild, eds. 2002. *Global Woman: Nannies, Maids, and Sex Workers in the New Economy.* New York: Henry Holt.

ElderWeb. "Illustrated History of Long Term Care." http://www.elderweb.com/home/ node/2806 (accessed 15 September 2008).

Errington, Frederick, and Deborah Gewertz. 1996. "The Individuation of Tradition in a Papua New Guinean Modernity." *American Anthropologist* 98(1): 114–126.

Ferguson, James. 1999. *Expectations of Modernity: Myths and Meanings of Urban Life on the Zambian Copperbelt.* Berkeley: University of California Press.

———. 2007. *Global Shadows: Africa in the Neoliberal World Order.* Durham, N.C.: Duke University Press.

Fernandes, Leela. 2006. *India's New Middle Class: Democratic Politics in an Era of Economic Reform.* Minneapolis: University of Minnesota Press.

Ferry, Elizabeth Emma. 2005. *Not Ours Alone: Patrimony, Value, and Collectivity in Contemporary Mexico.* New York: Columbia University Press.

Firth, Shirley. 1997. *Dying, Death and Bereavement in a British Hindu Community.* Leuven, Belgium: Peeters.

Fischer, David Hackett. 1978. *Growing Old in America,* expanded edition. New York: Oxford University Press.

Fong, Vanessa. 2004. "Filial Nationalism among Chinese Teenagers with Global Identities." *American Ethnologist* 31(4): 631–648.

Fortes, Meyer. 1984. "Age, Generation, and Social Structure." In David I. Kertzer and Jennie Keith, eds., *Age and Anthropological Theory,* 99–122. Ithaca, N.Y.: Cornell University Press.

Foster, Robert J. 2002. "Bargains with Modernity in Papua New Guinea and Elsewhere." In Bruce M. Knauft, ed., *Critically Modern: Alternatives, Alterities, Anthropologies,* 57–81. Bloomington: Indiana University Press.

Foucault, Michel. 1965. *Madness and Civilization: A History of Insanity in the Age of Reason.* Translated by Richard Howard. New York: Times Mirror.

———. 1979. *Discipline and Punish: The Birth of the Prison.* Translated by Alan Sheridan. New York: Vintage.

————. 1980. *The History of Sexuality.* Vol. 1, *An Introduction.* Translated by Robert Hurley. New York: Vintage.

Francese, Peter. 2003. "Well Enough Alone." *American Demographics,* 1 November 2003: 9.

Gable, Eric. 2000. "The Culture Development Club: Youth, Neo-Tradition, and the Construction of Society in Guinea-Bissau." *Anthropological Quarterly* 73(4): 195–203.

————. 2006. "The Funeral and Modernity in Manjaco." *Cultural Anthropology* 21(3): 385–415.

Gamburd, Michele. 2000. *The Kitchen Spoon's Handle: Transnationalism and Sri Lanka's Migrant Housemaids.* Ithaca, N.Y.: Cornell University Press.

Gaonkar, Dilip Parameshwar. 2001. "On Alternative Modernities." In Dilip Parameshwar Gaonkar, ed., *Alternative Modernities,* 1–23. Durham, N.C.: Duke University Press.

Geertz, Clifford. 1968. *Islam Observed: Religious Development in Morocco and Indonesia.* New Haven, Conn.: Yale University Press.

————. 1983. "'From the Native's Point of View': On the Nature of Anthropological Understanding." In *Local Knowledge: Further Essays in Interpretive Anthropology,* 55–70. New York: Basic Books.

Gentleman, Amelia. 2007. "India Moving to Punish Neglect of Elderly Parents." *Boston Sunday Globe,* The World, 4 March: A11.

George, Rosemary Marangoly. 1997. "From Expatriate Aristocrat to Immigrant Nobody: South Asian Racial Strategies in the Southern Californian Context." *Diaspora* 6(1):31–60.

George, Sheba Mariam. 2005. *When Women Come First: Gender and Class in Transnational Migration.* Berkeley: University of California Press.

Gewertz, Deborah, and Frederick Errington. 1996. "On PepsiCo and Piety in a Papua New Guinea 'Modernity.'" *American Ethnologist* 23(3): 476–493.

Ghildiyal, Subodh. 2005. "Care for Your Parents, or Else . . ." *Times of India, Kolkata,* 3 July.

Ghosh, Goutam. 1998. "Homes of the Future?" Special issue on "Ageing" with the Sunday Magazine, *Hindu,* 18 October. Online edition: http://www.hinduonnet. com/folio/fo9810/98100260.htm (accessed 15 September 2008).

Ghoshal, Somak. 2007. "Loving Wisely and Well." *Telegraph* (Calcutta), 4 October: 11.

Giddens, Anthony. 1990. *The Consequences of Modernity.* Stanford, Calif.: Stanford University Press.

Gillespie, Marie. 1995. *Television, Ethnicity and Cultural Change.* New York: Routledge.

Gillick, Muriel R. 2006. *The Denial of Aging: Perpetual Youth, Eternal Life, and Other Dangerous Fantasies.* Cambridge, Mass.: Harvard University Press.

Goffman, Erving. 1961. *Asylums: Essays on the Social Situation of Mental Patients and Other Inmates.* Garden City, N.Y.: Doubleday.

Gokhale, S. D. 2003. "Towards a Policy for Aging in India." In Phoebe S. Liebig and S. Irudaya Rajan, eds., *An Aging India: Perspectives, Prospects, and Policies,* 213–234. New York: Haworth Press.

Gold, Ann Grodzins. 1988. *Fruitful Journeys: The Ways of Rajasthani Pilgrims.* Berkeley: University of California Press.

———. 1989. "The Once and Future Yogi: Sentiments and Signs in the Tale of a Renouncer-Kin." *Journal of Asian Studies* 48:770–786.

———. 1992. *A Carnival of Parting: The Tales of King Bharthari and King Gopi Chand as Sung and Told by Madhu Natisar Nath of Ghatiyali, Rajasthan.* Berkeley: University of California Press.

Gold, Ann Grodzins, and Bhoju Ram Gujar. 2002. *In the Time of Trees and Sorrows: Nature, Power, and Memory in Rajasthan.* Durham, N.C.: Duke University Press.

Good, Byron. 1994. *Medicine, Rationality, and Experience: An Anthropological Perspective.* Cambridge: Cambridge University Press.

Goodale, Mark. 2006. "Reclaiming Modernity: Indigenous Cosmopolitanism and the Coming of the Second Revolution in Bolivia." *American Ethnologist* 33(4): 634–649.

Graebner, William. 1980. *A History of Retirement: The Meaning and Function of an American Institution, 1885–1978.* New Haven, Conn.: Yale University Press.

Gregory, C. A. 1982. *Gifts and Commodities.* New York: Academic.Greven, Philip J. 1970. *Four Generations: Population, Land, and Family in Colonial Andover, Massachusetts.* Ithaca, N.Y.: Cornell University Press.

Gullette, Margaret Morganroth. 1997. *Declining to Decline: Cultural Combat and the Politics of the Midlife.* Charlottesville: University of Virginia Press.

———. 2004. *Aged by Culture.* Chicago: University of Chicago Press.

Gupta, Aparna. 2001. "To Light Up That Wrinkled Face." *Asian Age,* 2 October.

Gupta, Jayanta. 2005. "Old Age Angst." *Sunday Times of India, Kolkata,* 2 October: 2.

Haber, Carole. 1982. *Beyond Sixty-Five: The Dilemma of Old Age in America's Past.* Cambridge: Cambridge University Press.

———. 1993. "Over the Hill to the Poorhouse: Rhetoric and Reality in the Institutional History of the Aged." In K. Warner Schaie and W. Andrew Achenbaum, eds., *Societal Impact on Aging: Historical Perspectives,* 90–113. New York: Springer Publishing Co.

Habermas, Jurgen. 1987. *The Philosophical Discourse of Modernity: Twelve Lectures.* Translated by Frederick G. Lawrence. Oxford: Oxford University Press.

Hall, Kathleen D. 2002. *Lives in Translation: Sikh Youth as British Citizens.* Philadelphia: University of Pennsylvania Press.

Hall, Stephen S. 2000. "The Recycled Generation." *New York Times Magazine* (30 January, 2000): 30–35, 46, 74, 78–79.

Hannerz, Ulf. 1996. *Transnational Connections: Culture, People, Places,* 44–55. London: Routledge.

Hansen, Karen. 2005. *Not So Nuclear Families: Class, Gender, and Networks of Care.* New Brunswick, N.J.: Rutgers University Press.

Hareven, Tamara K. 2000. *Families, History, and Social Change: Life-Course and Cross-Cultural Perspectives.* Boulder, Colo.: Westview.

Hareven, Tamara K., and Peter Uhlenberg. 1995. "Transition to Widowhood and Family

Support Systems in the Twentieth Century, Northeastern United States." In David I. Kertzer and Peter Laslett, eds., *Aging in the Past,* 273–299. Berkeley: University of California Press.

Hart, Keith. 2005. "Notes towards an Anthropology of Money." *Kritikos* 2 (June 2005). http://garnet.acns.fsu.edu/~nr03/notes%20towards%20an%20anthropology%20 of%20money.htm (accessed 15 September 2008).

Harvey, David. 1989. *The Condition of Postmodernity: An Enquiry into the Origins of Cultural Change.* Oxford: Basil Blackwell.

Hashimoto, Akiko. 1996. *The Gift of Generations: Japanese and American Perspectives on Aging and the Social Contract.* Cambridge: Cambridge University Press.

Havighurst, R. J. 1961. Successful Aging. *The Gerontologist.* 1(1): 8–13.

HelpAge India. 2000. *Old Age Homes: A Guide Book.* New Delhi: HelpAge India.

———. 2002 [1995]. *Directory of Old Age Homes in India 2002.* New Delhi: HelpAge India.

Hiebert, Paul G. 1981. "Old Age in a South Indian Village." In Pamela T. Amoss and Stevan Harrell, eds., *Other Ways of Growing Old: Anthropological Perspectives,* 211–226. Stanford: Stanford University Press.

Hindu Staff Reporter. 2004. "Old Age Homes Against Our Culture: Vaiko." *Hindu* September 14. http://www.thehindu.com/2004/09/14/stories/2004091405490300. htm (accessed 15 September 2008).

Hindu Special Correspondent. 2004. "More Control Over Old Age Homes Sought." *Hindu* (Sunday, December 05). http://www.hinduonnet.com/2004/12/05/stories/2004120505330500.htm htm (accessed 15 September 2008).

Hing, Bill Ong. 1993. *Making and Remaking Asian America Through Immigration Policy 1850–1990.* Stanford, Calif.: Stanford University Press.

———. 1997. *To Be an American: Cultural Pluralism and the Rhetoric of Assimilation.* New York: New York University Press.

Hobsbawm, Eric, and Terence Ranger, eds. 1983. *The Invention of Tradition.* New York: Cambridge University Press.

Hochschild, Arlie Russell. 2001. *The Time Bind: When Work Becomes Home and Home Becomes Work.* New York: Owl Books.

———. 2003. *The Commercialization of Intimate Life: Notes from Home and Work.* Berkeley: University of California Press.

Hodgson, Dorothy L., ed. 2001. *Gendered Modernities: Ethnographic Perspectives.* New York: Palgrave.

Hoffman, Lois Wladis. 1998. "The Effects of the Mother's Employment on the Family and the Child." http://parenthood.library.wisc.edu/Hoffman/Hoffman.html (accessed 15 September 2008).

Hondagneu-Sotelo, Pierrette. 2000. "The International Division of Caring and Cleaning Work." In Madonna Harrington Meyer, ed., *Care Work: Gender, Labor and the Welfare State,* 149–162. New York: Routledge.

———. 2001. *Domestica: Immigrant Workers Cleaning and Caring in the Shadows of Affluence.* Berkeley: University of California Press.

Honwana, Alcinda, and Filip De Boeck, eds. 2005. *Makers and Breakers: Children and Youth in Postcolonial Africa.* Oxford: James Currey.

Hunt, Robert C. 2002. "Economic Transfers and Exchanges: Concepts for Describing Allocations." In Jean Ensminger, ed., *Theory in Economic Anthropology,* 105–118. Walnut Creek, Calif.: AltaMira.

Inda, Jonathan Xavier, and Renato Rosaldo. 2002. "Introduction: A World in Motion." In Jonathan Inda and Renato Rosaldo, eds., *The Anthropology of Globalization: A Reader,* 1–34. Malden, Mass.: Blackwell.

Inden, Ronald B., and Ralph Nicholas. 1977. *Kinship in Bengali Culture.* Chicago: University of Chicago Press.

Jackson, Jean. 1995. "Culture, Genuine and Spurious: The Politics of Indianness in the Vaupes, Colombia." *American Ethnologist* 22(1): 3–27.

Jameson, Fredric. 1991. *Postmodernism; or, the Cultural Logic of Late Capitalism.* Durham, N.C.: Duke University Press.

———. 2002. *A Singular Modernity: Essay on the Ontology of the Present.* New York: Verso.

Jamuna, D. 2003. "Issues of Elder Care and Elder Abuse in the Indian Context." In Phoebe S. Liebig and S. Irudaya Rajan, eds., *An Aging India: Perspectives, Prospects, and Policies,* 125–142. New York: Haworth Press.

Jayaraaj, Rajasekharan Nair, director. 2000. *Karunam* (Pathos). India: Harvest Films.

Jayaswal, Rajeev. 2006. "India to Become Hub for Elderly Care." *Times News Network,* 17 March.

Jeffery, Patricia, and Roger Jeffery. 1996. *Don't Marry Me to a Plowman! Women's Everyday Lives in Rural North India.* Boulder, Colo.: Westview Press.

Jensen, Joan M. 1988. *Passage from India: Asian Indian Immigrants in North America.* New Haven, Conn.: Yale University Press.

Jianhua, Feng. 2006. "Gender Pressure: With the country's sex-ratio imbalance growing ever wider, China is promoting a program to improve the situation for girls and elderly people with no sons." *The Beijing Review,* 28 September. http://www.bjreview.com/nation/txt/2006–12/10/content_50371_2.htm (accessed 15 September 2008).

Jogerst, Gerald J., MD, Jeanette M. Daly, RN, PhD, Margaret F. Brinig, JD, MA, PhD, Jeffrey D. Dawson, ScD, Gretchen A. Schmuch, MSW, and Jerry G. Ingram, MSW. 2003. "Domestic Elder Abuse and the Law." *American Journal of Public Health* 93(12): 2131–2136.

Johnson, Richard W., and Joshua M. Wiener. 2006. "A Profile of Frail Older Americans and Their Caregivers." The Retirement Project, Occasional Paper No. 8, February 2006. Urban Institute. http://www.urban.org/url.cfm?ID=311284 (accessed September 2008).

Kaiser Family Foundation. 2005. "The Public's Views on Long-Term Care." Kaiser Health Poll Report. May/June. http://www.kff.org/healthpollreport/june_2005/upload/KHPR-June-July-Long-Term-Care-Printable-Version.pdf (accessed 15 September 2008).

Kalish, Robert. 1967. "Of Children and Grandfathers: A Speculative Essay on Dependency." *Gerontologist* 7: 65–69.

Kamdar, Seema I. 2004. "Busy Yuppies Outsource Errands to New Chore Bazaar: From Looking After Old Parents to Walking the Dog, These Corporate Jeeveses Do It All." *Times of India, Kolkata.* Wednesday, 1 September:12.

Kane, Pandurang Vaman. 1968–1975. *History of Dharmasastra.* 2nd ed. 5 vols. Poona Bhandarkar Oriental Research Institute.

Keane, Webb. 2002. "Sincerity, 'Modernity,' and the Protestants." *Cultural Anthropology* 17(1): 65–92.

Keith, Jennie. 1977. *Old People, New Lives: Community Creation in a Retirement Residence.* Chicago: University of Chicago Press.

Kertzer, David I. 1995. "Toward a Historical Demography of Aging." In David I. Kertzer and Peter Laslett, eds., *Aging in the Past,* 363–383. Berkeley: University of California Press.

Khandelwal, Madhulika S. 2002. *Becoming American, Being Indian: An Immigrant Community in New York City.* Ithaca, N.Y.: Cornell University Press.

Kibria, Nazli. 1996. "Not Asian, Black or White? Reflections on South Asian American Racial Identity." *Amerasia Journal* 22(2): 77–86.

Kinsella, Kevin. 1997. "The Demography of an Aging World." In Jay Sokolovsky, ed., *The Cultural Context of Aging: Worldwide Perspectives,* 2nd ed., 17–32. Westport, Conn.: Bergin and Garvey.

Klatz, Ronald. 2000. "Making the Quantum Leap to Human Immortality in the Year 2029." *Anti-Aging Medical News* 1 (October): 1–12.

Knauft, Bruce, ed. 2002. *Critically Modern: Alternatives, Alterities, Anthropologies.* Bloomington: Indiana University Press.

Knipe, David. 1977. "*Sapindikarana:* The Hindu Rite of Entry into Heaven." In Frank E. Reynolds and Earle H. Waugh, eds., *Religious Encounters with Death: Insights from the History and Anthropology of Religions,* 111–130. University Park: Pennsylvania State University Press.

Knowles, J. Hinton. 1893. *Folk-Tales of Kashmir.* London: Kegan Paul.

Kotlikoff, Laurence J., and Scott Burns. 2004. *The Coming Generational Storm: What You Need to Know about America's Economic Future.* Cambridge, Mass.: MIT Press.

Krucoff, Carol. 1985. "Mothers or Others: The Effects of Substitute Care on Children." *Washington Post,* 18 December, sec. Health: 12.

Kumar, S. Vijaya. 2003. "Economic Security for the Elderly in India: An Overview." In Phoebe S. Liebig and S. Irudaya Rajan, eds., *An Aging India: Perspectives, Prospects, and Policies.* Pp. 45–65. New York: Haworth Press.

Lamb, Sarah. 1993. Growing in the Net of Maya: Persons, Gender, and Life Processes in a Bengali Society. PhD diss., University of Chicago.

———. 1997. "The Making and Unmaking of Persons: Notes on Aging and Gender in North India." *Ethos* 25(3):279–302.

———. 2000. *White Saris and Sweet Mangoes: Aging, Gender and Body in North India.* Berkeley: University of California Press.

———. 2001a. "Being a Widow and Other Life Stories: The Interplay between Lives and Words." *Anthropology and Humanism* 26(1): 16–34.

———. 2001b. "Review of *Social Aging in a Delhi Neighborhood*, by John van Willigen and Narender K. Chadha; and *India's Elderly: Burden or Challenge?*, by S. Irudaya Rajan, U. S. Mishra, and P. Sankara Sarma." *Journal of Asian Studies* 60(2): 589–91.

———. 2002a. "Intimacy in a Transnational Era: The Remaking of Aging among Indian Americans." *Diaspora* 11(3): 299–330.

———. 2002b. "Love and Aging in Bengali Families." In Diane P. Mines and Sarah Lamb, eds., *Everyday Life in South Asia*, 56–68. Bloomington: Indiana University Press.

———. 2005. "Cultural and Moral Values Surrounding Care and (In)Dependence in Late Life: Reflections from India in an Era of Global Modernity." *Journal of Long Term Home Health Care* 6(2):80–89.

———. 2007. "Aging Across Worlds: Modern Seniors in an Indian Diaspora." In Jennifer Cole and Deborah Durham, eds., *Generations and Globalization: Family, Youth, and Age in the New World Economy*, 132–163. Bloomington: Indiana University Press.

Lan, Pei-Chia. 2002. "Subcontracting Filial Piety: Elder Care in Ethnic Chinese Immigrant Families in California." *Journal of Family Issues* 23(7): 812–835.

Laslett, Peter. 1972. "Introduction: The History of the Family." In Peter Laslett and Richard Wall, eds., *Household and Family in Past Time*, 1–89. Cambridge: Cambridge University Press.

Latour, Bruno. 1993. *We Have Never Been Modern*. Translated by Catherine Porter. Cambridge, Mass.: Harvard University Press.

Leonard, Karen Isaksen. 1997. *The South Asian Americans*. Westport, Conn.: Greenwood Press.

———. 2000. "State, Culture, and Religion: Political Action and Representation among South Asians in North America." *Diaspora* 9: 21–38.

Lessinger, Johanna. 1995. *From the Ganges to the Hudson: Indian Immigrants in New York City*. Boston: Allyn and Bacon.

Lewin, Tamar. 2002. "Study Links Working Mothers to Slower Learning." *New York Times*, July 17, A:14

Liebes, Tamar, and Elihu Katz. 1990. *The Export of Meaning: Cross-cultural Readings of Dallas*. New York: Oxford University Press.

Liebig, Phoebe S. 2003. "Old-Age Homes and Services: Old and New Approaches to Aged Care." In P. S. Liebig and S. I. Rajan, eds., *An Aging India: Perspectives, Prospects and Policies*, 159–178. New York: Haworth. (Also published in *Journal of Aging and Social Policy* 15(2/3):159–178, 2003.)

Liechty, Mark. 2002. *Suitably Modern: Making Middle-Class Culture in a New Consumer Society*. Princeton, N.J.: Princeton University Press.

LiPuma, Edward. 1998. "Modernity and Forms of Personhood in Melanesia." In M. Lambek and A. Strathern, eds., *Bodies and Persons: Comparative Perspectives from Africa and Melanesia*, 53–79. Cambridge: Cambridge University Press.

———. 2000. *Encompassing Others: The Magic of Modernity in Melanesia.* Ann Arbor: University of Michigan Press.

Lukose, Ritty. 2008. "The Children of Liberalization: Youth Agency and Globalization in India." In Nadine Dolby and Fazal Rizvi, eds., *Youth Moves: Identities and Education in Global Perspective*, 133–149. New York: Routledge.

Lynch, Caitrin. 2007. *Juki Girls, Good Girls: Gender and Cultural Politics in Sri Lanka's Global Garment Industry.* Ithaca, N.Y.: Cornell University Press.

Madan, T. N. 1987. *Non-Renunciation: Themes and Interpretations of Hindu Culture.* New Delhi: Oxford University Press.

Maira, Sunaina Marr. 2002. *Desis In The House: Indian American Youth Culture in NYC.* Philadelphia: Temple University Press.

———. 2004. "Imperial Feelings: Youth Culture, Citizenship, and Globalization." In Marcelo Suarez-Orozco and Desiree B. Oin-Hilliard, eds., *Globalization: Culture and Education in the New Millennium*, 203–234. Berkeley: University of California Press.

———. 2005. "The Intimate and the Imperial: South Asian Muslim Immigrants and Youth After 9/11." In Sunaina Maira and Elisabeth Soep, eds., *Youthscapes: The Popular, the National, the Global*, 64–81. Philadelphia: University of Pennsylvania Press.

Maira, Sunaina, and Elisabeth Soep, eds. 2005. *Youthscapes: The Popular, the National, the Global.* Philadelphia: University of Pennsylvania Press.

Majmundar, Harikrishna. 2003. *Mapping the Maze: A Guide to Welfare for Elderly Immigrants.* Palo Alto, Calif.: H. J. Majmundar. http://www.geocities.com/mappingthemaze/Mapping-the-Maze.htm (accessed 15 September 2008).

Malkki, Liisa. 1995. *Purity and Exile: Violence, Memory, and National Cosmology among Hutu Refugees in Tanzania.* Chicago: University of Chicago Press.

Mankekar, Purnima. 1998. "Entangled Spaces of Modernity: The Viewing Family, The Consuming Nation, and Television in India." *Visual Anthropology Review* 14(2): 32–45.

———. 1999. *Screening Culture, Viewing Politics: An Ethnography of Television, Womanhood, and Nation in Postcolonial India.* Durham, N.C.: Duke University Press.

Mannheim, Karl. 1952[1927]. "The Problem of Generations." In Paul Kecskemeti, ed., *Essays on the Sociology of Knowledge, by Karl Mannheim.* Pp. 276–320. London: Routledge.

Manu. 1886. *The Laws of Manu.* Translated by G. Buhler. Vol. 25, *Sacred Books of the East.* Oxford: Clarendon Press.

———. 1991. *The Laws of Manu.* Translated by Wendy Doniger, with Brian K. Smith. New York: Penguin.

Margolies, Luisa. 2004. *My Mother's Hip: Lessons from the World of Eldercare.* Philadelphia: Temple University Press.

Marriott, McKim. 1976. "Hindu Transactions: Diversity without Dualism." In Bruce Kapferer, ed., *Transaction and Meaning: Directions in the Anthropology of Exchange and Symbolic Behavior*, 109–142. Philadelphia: Institute for the Study of Human Issues.

———. 1990. "Constructing an Indian Ethnosociology." In McKim Marriott, ed., *India through Hindu Categories,* 1–39. New Delhi: Sage Publications.

Marriott, McKim, and Ronald Inden. 1977. "Toward an Ethnosociology of South Asian Caste Systems." In Kenneth David, ed., *The New Wind: Changing Identities in South Asia,* 227–238. The Hague: Mouton Publishers.

Mauss, Marcel. 1967 [1925]. *The Gift: Forms and Functions of Exchange in Archaic Societies.* Translated by Ian Cunnison. New York: W.W. Norton.

———. 1979 [1935]. "Body Techniques." In *Sociology and Psychology: Essays.* Translated by Ben Brewster, 97–123. London: Routledge and Kegan Paul.

Mazzarella, William. 2003. *Shoveling Smoke: Advertising and Globalization in Contemporary India.* Durham, N.C.: Duke University Press.

———. 2005. "Middle Class." In Rachel Dwyer, ed., *South Asia Keywords.* http://www.soas.ac.uk/southasianstudies/keywords/keywords-in-south-asian-studies.html (accessed 12 November 2008).

Mehta, Deepa, director and writer. 2005. "Water." Canada: Deepa Mehta Films.

Menzies, Heather. 2005. *No Time: Stress and the Crisis of Modern Life.* Vancouver: Douglas and McIntyre.

Meyer, Madonna Harrington, ed. 2000. *Care Work: Gender, Labor and the Welfare State.* New York: Routledge.

Michaels, Eric. 2002. "Hollywood Iconography: A Walpiri Reading." In Jonathan Inda and Renato Rosaldo, eds., *The Anthropology of Globalization: A Reader,* 311–324. Malden, Mass.: Blackwell.

Mills, Mary Beth. 1999. *Thai Women in the Global Labor Force: Consuming Desires, Contested Selves.* New Brunswick, N.J.: Rutgers University Press.

Mines, Diane P. 2005. *Fierce Gods: Inequality, Ritual, and the Politics of Dignity in a South Indian Village.* Bloomington: Indiana University Press.

Mitra, Dola. 2004. "All In It Together." *Telegraph.* 20 January: 15.

Moggach, Deborah. 2004. *These Foolish Things.* London: Chatto and Windus.

Mookherjea, Sohini. 2007. "Life Begins at 60: Specially designed apartments are being built just for senior citizens to take care of their needs and bring the spring back into their lives." *Telegraph* June 15: 12.

Mukhi, Sunita Sunder. 1998. "'Underneath My Blouse Beats My Indian Heart': Sexuality, Nationalism, and Indian Womanhood in the United States." In Shamita Das Gupta, ed., *A Patchwork Shawl: Chronicles of South Asian Women in America,* 186–205. New Brunswick, N.J.: Rutgers University Press.

Mykytyn, Courtney Everts. 2006a. "Anti-Aging Medicine: A Patient/Practitioner Movement to Redefine Aging." *Social Science and Medicine* 62(3): 643–653.

———. 2006b. "Anti-Aging Medicine: Predictions, Moral Obligations, and Biomedical Intervention." *Anthropological Quarterly* 79(1): 5–31.

Naqvi, Tahira. "Dying in a Strange Country." *Dying in a Strange Country: Stories.* Tahira Naqvi. Toronto: TSAR Publications, 2001. 1–16.

Narasimhan, Sakuntala. 2004. "Old Age Home Horrors: We Need Some Kind of Monitoring Mechanism for Old Age Homes." *Deccan Herald, Consumer Bytes,*

24 August 2004. http://www.deccanherald.com/archives/aug242004/cbytes2.asp (accessed 15 September 2008).

Narayan, Kirin. 2002. "Placing Lives through Stories: Second-Generation South Asian Americans." In Diane P. Mines and Sarah Lamb, eds., *Everyday Life in South Asia*, 425–439. Bloomington: Indiana University Press.

Natarajan, Nalini. 1993. "Introduction: Reading Diaspora." In Emmanuel Nelson, ed., *Writers of the Indian Diaspora: A Bio-Bibliographical Sourcebook*, xii–xix. New York: Greenwood Press.

Nelson, Emmanuel S. 1992. "Introduction." In Emmanuel Nelson, ed., *Reworlding: The Literature of the Indian Diaspora*, ix–xvi. New York: Greenwood Press.

New York Times. 1989. "Juggling Family, Job and Aged Dependent." 26 January, B: 8.

New York Times Editorial Desk. 2002. "Angst and the Working Mother." *New York Times*, 20 July, A:12.

Nicholas, Ralph. 1988. "*Śrāddha*, Impurity, and Relations between the Living and the Dead." In T. N. Madan, ed., *Way of Life: King, Householder, Renouncer*, 369–379. New ed. Delhi: Motilal Banarsidass.

Nonini, Donald M., and Aihwa Ong. 1997. "Chinese Transnationalism as an Alternative Modernity." In Aihwa Ong and Donald M. Nonini, eds., *Ungrounded Empires: The Cultural Politics of Modern Chinese Transnationalism*, 3–33. New York: Routledge.

Ong, Aihwa. 1996. "Anthropology, China and Modernities: The Geopolitics of Cultural Knowledge." In Henriette Moore, ed., *The Future of Anthropological Knowledge*, 60–92. London: Routledge.

———. 1997. "Chinese Modernities: Narratives of Nation and Capitalism." In Aihwa Ong and Donald M. Nonini, eds., *Ungrounded Empires: The Cultural Politics of Modern Chinese Transnationalism*, 171–202. New York: Routledge.

———. 2006. *Neoliberalism as Exception: Mutations in Citizenship and Sovereignty.* Durham, N.C.: Duke University Press.

Ortner, Sherry. 2006. *Anthropology and Social Theory: Culture, Power, and the Acting Subject.* Durham, N.C.: Duke University Press.

Oza, Rupal. 2006. *The Making of Neoliberal India: Nationalism, Gender, and the Paradoxes of Globalization.* New York: Routledge.

Palacios, Robert. 2002a. "The Challenge for India: Do New Initiatives Go Far Enough?" *Insights* 42 (June). Global Action on Aging. http://www.globalaging.org/pension/world/india.htm (accessed 15 September 2008).

———. 2002b. "The Future of Global Ageing." *International Journal of Epidemiology* 31: 786–791. http://ije.oxfordjournals.org/cgi/content/full/31/4/786 (accessed 15 September 2008).

Parekh, H. T. 2006. "Pension Issues and Challenges Facing India," *Economic and Political Weekly* 11 November: 4638–4641.

Parreñas, Rhacel Salazar. 2002. "The Care Crisis in the Philippines: Children and Transnational Families in the New Global Economy." In Barbara Ehrenreich and Arlie Russell Hochschild, eds., *Global Woman: Nannies, Maids, and Sex Workers in the New Economy*, 39–54. New York: Metropolitan Books.

————. 2005. *Children of Global Migration: Transnational Families and Gendered Woes.* Stanford, Calif.: Stanford University Press.

Parry, Jonathan. 1982. "Sacrificial Death and the Necrophagous Ascetic." In Maurice Bloch and Jonathan Parry, eds., *Death and the Regeneration of Life,* 74–110. Cambridge: Cambridge University Press.

————. 1989. "On the Moral Perils of Exchange." In Jonathan Parry and Maurice Bloch, eds., *Money and the Morality of Exchange,* 64–93. New York: Cambridge University Press.

————. 1994. *Death in Banaras.* Cambridge: Cambridge University Press.

Peterson, Peter G. 2000. *Gray Dawn: How the Coming Age Wave Will Transform America—and Most of the World.* New York: Three Rivers Press.

————. 2002. "The Shape of Things to Come: Global Aging in the Twenty-First Century." *Journal of International Affairs* 56: 189–210.

Pigg, Stacy Leigh. 1996. "The Credible and the Credulous: The Question of 'Villagers' Beliefs' in Nepal." *Cultural Anthropology* 11(2): 160–201.

————. 2001. "Languages of Sex and AIDS in Nepal: Notes on the Social Production of Commensurability." *Cultural Anthropology* 16(4): 481–541.

Prahladka, Deepak. 2007. "Justice Refuses to Take Sides in *Saas-Bahu* War." *Hindustan Times,* 22 September.

————. 2008. "Court Rebuke for Insult to Mother." *Hindustan Times,* Kolkata Live, 24 April: 3.

Prashad, Vijay. 1999. "From Multiculture to Polyculture in South Asian American Studies." *Diaspora* 8:185–204.

Radhakrishnan, R. 1996. "Is the Ethnic 'Authentic' in the Diaspora?" In R. Radhakrishnan, ed., *Diasporic Mediations: Between Home and Location,* 203–214. Minneapolis: University of Minnesota Press.

Radhakrishnan, Smitha. 2006. "Global Indians" and the Knowledge Economy: Gender and the Making of a Middle-Class Nation. PhD diss., University of California, Berkeley.

————. 2008. "Examining the 'Global' Indian Middle Class: Gender and Culture in the Silicon Valley/Bangalore Circuit." *Journal of Intercultural Studies* 29(1): 7–20.

Raheja, Gloria Goodwin. 1995. "'Crying When She's Born, and Crying When She Goes Away': Marriage and the Idiom of the Gift in Pahansu Song Performance." In Lindsey Harlan and Paul R. Courtright, eds., *From the Margins of Hindu Marriage: Essays on Gender, Religion, and Culture,* 19–59. New York: Oxford University Press.

Raheja, Gloria Goodwin, and Ann Grodzins Gold. 1994. *Listen to the Heron's Words: Reimagining Gender and Kinship in North India.* Berkeley: University of California Press.

Raj, Dhooleka. 2003. *Where Are You From? Middle-Class Migrants in the Modern World.* Berkeley: University of California Press.

Rajan, S. Irudaya. 2001. "Social Assistance for Poor Elderly: How Effective?" *Economic and Political Weekly,* 24 February: 613–617.

Rajan, S. Irudaya, and Sanjay Kumar. 2003. "Living Arrangements among Indian

Elderly: New Evidence from National Family Health Survey." *Economic and Political Weekly* 38:75–80.

Rajan, S. Irudaya, U.S. Mishra, and P. Sankara Sarma. 1999. *India's Elderly: Burden or Challenge?* New Delhi: Sage Publications.

———. 2003. "Demography of Indian Aging, 2001–2051." In Phoebe S. Liebig and S. Irudaya Rajan, eds., *An Aging India: Perspectives, Prospects, and Policies,* 11–30. New York: Haworth Press.

Rangaswamy, Padma. 2000. *Namaste America: Indian Immigrants in an American Metropolis.* University Park: Pennsylvania State University Press.

Rasmussen, Susan J. 2000. "Between Several Worlds: Images of Youth and Age in Tuareg Popular Performances." *Anthropological Quarterly* 73(3): 133–144.

Ravindranath, Sarita. 1997. "*Sans* Everything . . . but not *Sans* Rights." *Statesman,* 1 February.

Ray, Satyajit, director. 1958. *Pather Panchali (Song of the Road).* India: Government of West Bengal.

Ray, Tirna. 2006. "The BMC's Changing." *Telegraph,* March 19. http://www.telegraphindia.com/1060319/asp/opinion/story_5982551.asp# (accessed 15 September 2008).

Rector, Robert, and William Lauber. 1995. "America Is Becoming a Deluxe Retirement Home." *Social Contract* (Fall 1995): 58.

Reeves, Terrance J., and Claudette E. Bennett. 2004. "We the People: Asians in the United States, Census 2000 Special Reports," CENSR-17. Washington, D.C.: U.S. Census Bureau. Archived at: http://www.census.gov/prod/2004pubs/censr-17.pdf (accessed 15 September 2008).

Rivas, Lynn May. 2002. "Invisible Labors: Caring for the Independent Person." In Barbara Ehrenreich and Arlie Russell Hochschild, eds., *Global Woman: Nannies, Maids, and Sex Workers in the New Economy,* 70–84. New York: Henry Holt.

Rofel, Lisa. 1999. *Other Modernities: Gendered Yearnings in China After Socialism.* Berkeley: University of California Press.

Roland, Alan. 1988. *In Search of Self in India and Japan: Toward a Cross-Cultural Psychology.* Princeton, N.J.: Princeton University Press.

Rosaldo, Renato. 2000. "Of Headhunters and Soldiers: Separating Cultural and Ethical Relativism." *Issues in Ethics* 11(1) (winter 2000). http://www.scu.edu/ethics/publications/iie/v11n1/relativism.html (accessed 15 September 2008).

Rowe, John W., and Kahn, Robert L. 1999. *Successful Aging.* New York: Random House.

Roy, Manisha. 1992 [1972]. *Bengali Women.* Chicago: University of Chicago Press.

Rubin, Gayle. 1975. "The Traffic in Women: Notes on the 'Political Economy' of Sex." In Rayna R. Reiter, ed., *Toward an Anthropology of Women,* 157–210. New York: Monthly Review Press.

Ruggles, Steven. 1995. "Living Arrangements of the Elderly in America: 1880–1980." In Tamara K. Hareven, ed., *Aging and Generational Relations Over the Life Course: A Historical and Cross-Cultural Perspective,* 254–271. New York: Walter de Gruyter.

Sahlins, Marshall. 1994. "Goodbye to Tristes Tropes: Ethnography in the Context of Modern World History." In Robert Borofsky, ed., *Assessing Cultural Anthropology,* 377–294. New York: McGraw Hill.

———. 1999. "What Is Anthropological Enlightenment? Some Lessons of the Twentieth Century." *Annual Review of Anthropology* 28:i–xxiii.

———. 2005. "The Economics of Develop-man in the Pacific." In Joel Robbins and Holly Wardlow, eds., *The Making of Global and Local Modernities in Melanesia: Humiliation, Transformation and the Nature of Cultural Change,* 23–42. (Originally published in 1992 in the journal *Res* [21] 13–25).

Salvadore, Sarah, and Roshni Mukherjee. 2007. "Present Tense, Future Imperfect." *Times of India,* 28 February, sec. Calcutta Times Leisure section: 1.

Santhanam, Kausalya. 1998. "The Nest Is Empty." *Hindu Folio* Sunday Magazine, 18 October. http://hinduonnet.com/folio/f09810/98100320.htm (accessed 15 September 2008).

Sarkar, Svapan. 2008. "*Āsche āin, mā bābāke nā dekhle hate pāre jel-o*" [In a New Law, Not Looking After Parents Could Even Send One to *Jail*]. *Anandabajar Patrika,* 22 April, sec. CE.

Savishinsky, Joel S. 2000. *Breaking the Watch: The Meanings of Retirement in America.* Ithaca, N.Y.: Cornell University Press.

———. 2004. "The Volunteer and the Sannyasin: Archetypes of Retirement in America and India." *The International Journal of Aging and Human Development* 59(1): 25–41.

Sawhney, Maneeta. 2003. "The Role of Non-Governmental Organizations for the Welfare of the Elderly: The Case of HelpAge India." In P. S. Liebig and S. I. Rajan, eds., *An Aging India: Perspectives, Prospects and Policies,* 179–191. New York: Haworth.

Sax, William S. 1991. *Mountain Goddess: Gender and Politics in a Himalayan Pilgrimage.* Oxford: Oxford University Press.

Scheper-Hughes, Nancy. 1993. *Death Without Weeping: The Violence of Everyday Life in Brazil.* Berkeley: University of California Press.

Seager, Henry Rogers. 1910. *Social Insurance: A Program of Social Reform.* New York: Macmillan.

Seff, Marsha Kay. 2003. "Parent Care: Caregiver Between a Rock and a Hard Case." *Copley News Service,* December 22.

Sen, Amartya. 2005. *The Argumentative Indian: Writings on Indian Culture, History and Identity.* New York: Penguin.

Sengupta, Uttam. 2005. "New Deal for the Old: Isn't It Time the Government Tried to Find Out What Actually Happens in Old-Age Homes?" *Telegraph,* 20 April: 19.

Sexton, Joe. 1997. "Immigrants Don't Know What to Believe About S.S.I." *New York Times,* 10 May: A21.

Shankar, Lavina Dhingra. 1998. "The Limits of (South Asian) Names and Labels: Postcolonial or Asian American?" In Lavina Dhingra Shankar and Rajini Srikanth, eds., *A Part, Yet Apart: South Asians in Asian America,* 49–66. Philadelphia: Temple University Press.

Shankardass, Mala Kapur. 2000. "Societal Responses." *Ageing: A Symposium on the Greying of Our Society,* special issue of *India Seminar* (488) (April 2000). http://www.india-seminar.com/2000/488.htm (accessed 15 September 2008).

Sharma, Aruna, and Vinay Menon. 2000. "Senior Citizens' Homes: Life in a Cocoon." *Hindustan Times,* 14 November.

Sharp, Lesley Alexandra. 2002. *The Sacrificed Generation: Youth, History, and the Colonized Mind in Madagascar.* Berkeley: University of California Press.

Shea, Jeanne L. 2005. "Sexual 'Liberation' and the Older Woman in Contemporary Mainland China." *Modern China* 31(1): 1–33.

Shukla, Sandhya. 2003. *India Abroad: Diasporic Cultures of Postwar America and England.* Princeton, N.J.: Princeton University Press.

Shweder, Richard A., and Edmund J. Bourne. 1984. "Does the Concept of the Person Vary Cross-Culturally?" In Richard A. Shweder and Robert A. LeVine, eds., *Culture Theory: Essays on Mind, Self, and Emotion,* 158–99. Cambridge: Cambridge University Press.

Simic, Andrei. 1990. "Aging, World View, and Intergenerational Relations in America and Yugoslavia." In Jay Sokolovsky, ed., *The Cultural Context of Aging: Worldwide Perspectives.* Pp. 89–108. New York: Bergin and Garvey.

Singer, Milton. 1972. *When a Great Tradition Modernizes: An Anthropological Approach to Indian Civilization.* Chicago: University of Chicago Press.

Smith, D. S. 1979. "Life Course, Norms, and the Family System of Older Americans in 1900." *Journal of Family History* 4: 285–299.

———. 1981. "Historical Change in the Household Structure of the Elderly in Economically Developed Societies." In J. G. March et al., eds., *Aging: Stability, and Change in the Family,* 91–114. New York: Academic Press.

Sokhal, Sonali. 2000. "Bright Twilight." *Cardmembers' EXPRESSION India.* June: 54–55.

Sokolovsky, Jay. 1990. "Bringing Culture Back Home: Aging, Ethnicity, and Family Support." In Jay Sokolovsky, ed., *The Cultural Context of Aging: Worldwide Perspectives,* 201–221. New York: Bergin and Garvey.

Sreevastava, Pradeep. 2004. "Poverty Targeting in Asia: Country Experience of India." ABD (Asian Development Bank) Institute Discussion Paper No. 5, February 2004. http://adbi.adb.org/files/2004.02.05.dp005.poverty.india.pdf (accessed 15 September 2008).

Sridharan, E. 2004. "The Growth and Sectoral Composition of India's Middle Class: Its Impact on the Politics of Economic Liberalization." *India Review* 3(4): 405–428.

Srinivas, Mysore N. 1968. *Social Change in Modern India.* Berkeley: University of California Press.

Srinivas, Tulasi. 2006. "'As Mother Made It': The Cosmopolitan Indian Family, 'Authentic' Food and the Construction of Cultural Utopia." *International Journal of Sociology of the Family* 32(2): 191–220.

Srivastava, Sanjay. 2004a. "Introduction: Semen, History, Desire and Theory." In Sanjay Srivastava, ed., *Sexual Sites, Seminal Attitudes: Sexualities, Masculinities and Culture in South Asia,* 11–48. New Delhi, India, and Thousand Oaks, Calif.: Sage.

———. 2004b. "Non-Gandhian Sexuality, Commodity Cultures and 'a Happy Married Life:' Masculine and Sexual Cultures in the Metropolis." In Sanjay Srivastava, ed., *Sexual Sites, Seminal Attitudes: Sexualities, Masculinities and Culture in South Asia,* 342–390. New Delhi, India, and Thousand Oaks, Calif.: Sage.

Stack, Carol. 1996. *Call to Home: African Americans Reclaim the Rural South.* New York: Basic Books.

Stone, Linda. 1988. *Illness Beliefs and Feeding the Dead in Hindu Nepal.* Lewiston, N.Y.: Edwin Mellen Press.

Strathern, Marilyn. 1988. *The Gender of the Gift: Problems with Women and Problems with Society in Melanesia.* Berkeley: University of California Press.

Sundaram, Viji. 2001. "Delhi Couple Fill On for Absent NRI Children." *India-West* 26(30) (1 June): A36.

Tagore, Rabindranath. 1913. *Gitanjali* (Song Offerings). A collection of prose translations made by the author from the original Bengali, with an introduction by W. B. Yeats. London: Macmillan.

Talk of the Nation. 1997. "Welfare Reform," transcripts, 19 March. Washington, D.C.: National Public Radio.

Tatara, Toshio. 1995. *An Analysis of State Laws Addressing Elder Abuse, Neglect, and Exploitation.* Washington, D.C.: National Center on Elder Abuse.

Tatara, Toshio, Lisa Blumerman Kuszmeskus, and Edward Duckhorn. 1998. *The National Elder Abuse Incidence Study: Final Report.* Washington, D.C.: The National Center on Elder Abuse in Collaboration with Westat.

Tate, N. 1983. "The Black Aging Experience." In R. McNeely and U. Colen, eds*., Aging in Minority Groups,* 95–107. Beverly Hills, Calif.: Sage.

Taylor, Charles. 1992. *Sources of the Self: The Making of the Modern Identity.* Cambridge, Mass.: Harvard University Press.

———. 2001. "Two Theories of Modernity." In Dilip Parameshwar Gaonkar, ed., *Alternative Modernities,* 172–196. Durham, N.C.: Duke University Press.

Telegraph. 2003a. "Death from Loneliness at Eighty." 22 July, sec. Nation: 1.

———. 2003b. "Last Wish Denied, Last Rites Await Son's Arrival." 23 July: 1.

———. 2004. "HC Glare on Son for Abusing Parents," 31 March, sec. Nation: 6.

———. 2005a. "Loneliness, the Killer." 9 August: 7.

———. 2005b. "Sita, 72, with Two Sons, Leaves Home, Roams Streets," 29 September, sec. Calcutta: 13.

———. 2005c. "Tortured Father Takes Life," 29 April, sec. Calcutta.

———. 2006. "Unaccommodated." 11 March: 18.

———. 2007. "House Tears for the Aged," 7 December, sec. Nation: 5.

Tikku, Aloke. 2007. "Look After Your Parents, or Else . . ." *Hindustan Times,* 7 December, sec. Nation: 4.

Tilak, Shrinivas. 1989. *Religion and Aging in the Indian Tradition.* Albany: State University of New York Press.

Times News Network. 2004. "City's Elderly, Tense and Tormented." *Times of India,* 1 October, sec. City: 6.

———. 2005a. "Deserted Widow Rescued by Cops." *Times of India, Kolkata,* 29 September.

———. 2005b. "Elderly Alipore Clerk Blames Son's Wife before Suicide." *Times of India, Kolkata,* 29 April.

———. 2007a. "'Eat Together' Recipe Reunites Feuding Family." *Times of India, Kolkata,* 16 October: 5.

———. 2007b. "Elders Get Legal Shield against Neglect." *Times of India, Kolkata,* 23 Feb, sec. Nation: p. 10.

Trawick, Margaret. 1990. *Notes on Love in a Tamil Family.* Berkeley: University of California Press.

Tripathi, Purnima S. 2006. "The Living Dead." *Frontline* 23(16) (August) 12–25.

Tsing, Anna Lowenhaupt. 2004. *Friction: An Ethnography of Global Connection.* Princeton, N.J.: Princeton University Press.

United Nations. 2001. "World Population Ageing: 1950–2050." Department of Economic and Social Affairs, Population Division. New York. http://www.un.org/esa/population/publications/worldageing19502050 (accessed 15 September 2008).

United States Congress, House. 1989a. "The Elimination of Poverty among the Elderly: Supplemental Security Income Reform." Hearing before the Subcommittee on Retirement Income and Employment of the Select Committee on Aging. 100th Congress, second session, 16 September 1988. Washington, D.C: U.S. Government Printing Office.

———. 1989b. "Supplemental Security Income Program." Joint Hearing before the Subcommittee on Human Resources of the Committee on Ways and Means and the Select Committee on Aging. 101st Congress, first session, March 2, 1989. Washington, D.C. U.S. Government Printing Office.

———. 1996. "Supplemental Security Income (SSI)." In *1996 Green Book: Background Material and Data on Programs within the Jurisdiction of the Committee on Ways and Means,* 257–326. Washington, D.C.: U.S. Government Printing Office.

United States Congress, Senate. 1984. The Supplemental Security Income Program: A 10–Year Overview. U.S. Senate Special Committee on Aging. 98th Congress, second session. Washington, D.C.: U.S. Government Printing Office.

———. 1997. "The Use of Supplemental Security Income and Other Welfare Programs by Immigrants." Hearing before the Subcommittee on Immigration of the Committee on the Judiciary. 104th Congress, second session, 6 February 1996. Washington, D.C.: U.S. Government Printing Office.

U.S. Census Bureau 2004. "America's Families and Living Arrangements: 2003." http://www.census.gov/prod/2004pubs/p20–553.pdf (accessed 7 November 2008).

U.S. Department of Health and Human Services. 1980. *A Guide to Supplemental Security Income.* Washington, D.C.: U.S. Government Printing Office.

Vachani, Nilita, director and producer. 1995. "When Mother Comes Home for Christmas" (documentary film). Greek Film Centre.

Van der Veer, Peter. 2001. *Imperial Encounters: Religion and Modernity in India and Britain.* Princeton, N.J.: Princeton University Press.

Van Hollen, Cecilia. 2003. *Birth on the Threshold: Childbirth and Modernity in South India.* Berkeley: University of California Press.

van Willigen, John, and Narender K. Chadha. 1999. *Social Aging in a Delhi Neighborhood.* Westport, Conn.: Bergin and Harvey.

Vasudeva, Pakshi. 2006. "Old, But Free." *Telegraph,* 14 February, CE: 16.

Vatuk, Sylvia. 1975. "The Aging Woman in India: Self-Perceptions and Changing Roles." In Alfred de Souza, ed., *Women in Contemporary India and South Asia,* 142–163. New Delhi: Manohar Publications.

———. 1980. "Withdrawal and Disengagement as a Cultural Response to Aging in India." In Christine Fry, ed., *Aging in Culture and Society,* 126–148. New York: Praeger.

———. 1987. "Authority, Power, and Autonomy in the Life Cycle of North Indian Women." In Paul Hockings, ed., *Dimensions of Social Life: Essays in Honor of David G. Mandelbaum,* 23–44. Berlin: Mouton de Gruyter.

———. 1990. "'To Be a Burden on Others': Dependency Anxiety among the Elderly in India." In Owen Lynch, ed., *Divine Passions: The Social Construction of Emotion in India.* Pp. 64–88. Berkeley: University of California Press.

———. 1992. "Sexuality and the Middle-Aged Woman in South Asia." In Virginia Kerns and Judith K. Brown, eds., *In Her Prime: New Views of Middle-Aged Women,* 155–172. Urbana: University of Illinois Press.

———. 1995. "The Indian Woman in Later Life: Some Social and Cultural Considerations." In Monica Das Gupta, Lincoln C. Chen, and T. N. Krishnan, eds., *Women's Health in India: Risk and Vulnerability,* 289–306. Bombay: Oxford University Press.

Venker, Suzanne. 2004. *7 Myths of Working Mothers: Why Children and (Most) Careers Just Don't Mix.* Dallas, Tex.: Spence Publishing Co.

Vesperi, Maria E. 1985. *City of Green Benches: Growing Old in a New Downtown.* Ithaca, N.Y.: Cornell University Press.

Visweswaran, Kamala. 1997. "Diaspora by Design: Flexible Citizenship and South Asians in U.S. Racial Formations." *Diaspora* 6(1): 5–29.

Vlasblom, Jan Dirk, and Joop J. Schippers. 2004. "Increases in Female Labour Force Participation in Europe: Similarities and Differences." *Utrecht School of Economics Discussion Paper Series* 04–12: 28 pages.

Wadley, Susan S. 1994. *Struggling with Destiny in Karimpur, 1925–1984.* Berkeley: University of California Press.

———. 2002. "One Straw from a Broom Cannot Sweep: The Ideology and Practice of the Joint Family in Rural North India." In Diane P. Mines and Sarah Lamb, eds., *Everyday Life in South Asia,* 11–22. Bloomington: Indiana University Press.

Wardlow, Holly. 2006. *Wayward Women: Sexuality and Agency in a New Guinea Society.* Berkeley: University of California Press.

Watson Wyatt Worldwide and Center for Strategic and International Studies (CSIS) report, "Global Aging—The Challenge of the New Millennium" http://www.watsonwyatt.com/research/printable.asp?id=W-315 (accessed 15 September 2008).

Weeks, J., and Jose Cuellar. 1981. "The Role of Family Members in the Helping Networks of Older People." *Gerontologist* 21: 338–394.

White, Merry Isaacs. 2002. *Perfectly Japanese: Making Families in an Era of Upheaval.* Berkeley: University of California Press.

Williams, Joan. 2000. *Unbending Gender: Why Family and Work Conflict and What to Do About It.* New York: Oxford University Press.

Wilmoth, Janet M., and Charles Longino Jr. 2006. "Demographic Trends That Will Shape U.S. Policy in the Twenty-First Century." *Research on Aging* 28(3): 269–288.

Winokur, Julie. 1994. "Cowboys and Indians: Indo-Americans Have Made Great Strides in the West, but Now They Are Returning to Traditional Values." *San Jose Mercury News,* 15 May.

Woronov, T. E. 2007. "Chinese Children, American Education: Globalizing Child Rearing in Contemporary China." In Jennifer Cole and Deborah Durham, eds., *Generations and Globalization: Youth, Age and Family in the New World Economy,* 29–51. Bloomington: Indiana University Press.

Wulff, Helena. 1995. "Introduction: Introducing Youth Culture in its Own Right: The State of the Art and New Possibilities." In Vered Amit-Talai and Helena Wulff, eds., *Youth Cultures: A Cross-Cultural Perspective,* 1–18. New York: Routledge.

Wyatt, Watson. 2008. "Global Aging—The Challenge of the New Millennium." Center for Strategic and International Studies (CSIS) report. http://www.watsonwyatt.com/research/resrender.asp?id=W-315 (accessed 12 November 2008).

Young, Jeffry J., and Justin Kawabori. 1995. "Strangers No More: SSI and the Asian Pacific Senior: Final Report [microform]." Washington, D.C.: U.S. Administration on Aging.

Young, Linda. 2007. "India: Proposed Law Would Fine or Imprison Adult Children Who Abandon Parents." *AHN (All Headline News),* 1 March.

Zimmermann, Francis. 1979. "Remarks on the Body in Ayurvedic Medicine." *South Asian Digest of Regional Writing* 18:10–26.

Zola, Irvin K. 1972. "Medicine as an Institution of Social Control." *Sociology Review* 20(4): 487–504.

INDEX

"Parents of Indian Americans" refers to Indian seniors who immigrate to the United States to be with their children.

"Parents of NRI (non-resident Indian) in the United States" refers to Indian seniors who reside in India, and whose children are permanent residents of the United States.

Pseudonyms of interviewees are alphabetized in direct order (e.g. Vitalbhai Gujar).

46–49, 72–73; changes in Bengali Middle Class (BMC), 48–49; definitions of, 27, 279n23; elder abandonment, 249; English language knowledge of, 27; as living alone, 173–74; retirement pensions, 58; rise of old age homes, 72–73; women's agency in, 49–50; women's transnational migration, 277n42

Milan Tirtha (old age home), xiii, 62, 90–91, 143, 149, 156, 166

Mines, Diane, 170, 297n1

Mitra, Aloka, 150, 288n32

modernity, 4, 5, 6, 11, 29, 41, 88–89; in accounts of "throwing away" (*phele dāoyā*), 85–89; aging and, 4, 5, 11, 40–46, 275n24, 278n10; alternative forms of, 9–11, 13, 269–70; *artha* (material wealth), 1, 70, 157; Bengali terms for, 8, 41, 69; commodification of elder care, 196–98, 292n25; consumerism, 16–17, 46, 48–49, 72–73, 196–98, 292n25; decline of the joint family, 4, 41–46, 68, 69; economic liberalization in India, 46–47; elder agency, 45–46; emergence of old age homes, 41, 68–69, 70–73, 78, 132; English as language of, 38, 75; failed reciprocity, 42–44, 86–88, 98–100, 103–104; generational differences and, 14–19, 269; independent living, 173; individualism, 9, 12; individualistic modes of personhood, 12; the middle class and, 46–47, 48–49; money, 16–17, 80–81, 196, 197; nuclear families, 37–38, 72, 109–10, 111, 112, 148, 271, 282nn31,32; outsourcing of elder care, 172–73, 194–95, 198–200; rapid social change and, 44–45; seniors as agents of, 18; social science theories of, 8–10, 274n17; and spiritual awareness, 40; transnational migration, 46–47; welfare system in India, 249–50; Westernization of culture, 9, 10, 11–12; women as face of, 50; women's agency in, 49–50, 96–99, 100–101. *See also* globalization; independence; individualism; individual-

ity; materialism; NRI (non-resident Indian) children in the United States; single living/single-person households; tradition

Moggach, Deborah, 36

moksha (release), 39, 141, 225

Monisha Mashi, 90–92, 166, 283n1

Mukherjee, Roshni, 296n32

Mukund Gangopadhyay, 69–70, 281n17, 284n22

Muslims, xiii–xiv, 24–25, 59, 96–97

mutual aid societies, 83–84, 262

Mykytyn, Courtney, 287n19

Nalini Mukherjee, 189–90

Narayan Sarkar, 186–87

Narayana, Shovana, 195–96, 250

National Family Health Survey of India, 174

National Old-Age Pension Scheme (NOAPS), 252

Nava Nir (old age home), 79, 150

neoliberal policies, 250

NGOs. *See* Agewell Foundation; Dignity Foundation

Nicholas, Ralph, 153

911 emergency line, 227, 228, 258

Nirmala Shankar, 221

NOAPS (National Old-Age Pension Scheme), 252

NRI (non-resident Indian) children in the United States, 179t6.1; A.B.C.D. (American-Born Confused Desi), 185, 291n13; attitudes toward traditional Indian values, 184, 190; elder-care services, 172–73, 194–95, 232–33, 256–57, 258; growth of communities, 47; immigration of elderly parents, 233, 264–65; independence of, 190–91; outsourcing of elder care, 172–73, 194–95, 198–200; parents' pride in, 87, 180, 181, 182, 186–88; remittances, 47, 279n25; *sevā* offered by, 215–18. *See also parents headings*

nuclear families, 11, 37–38, 41, 68, 72, 109–10, 111, 112, 148–49, 271, 282nn31,32

nursing homes: American attitudes

TRACKING GLOBALIZATION

Illicit Flows and Criminal Things:
States, Borders, and the Other Side of Globalization
EDITED BY WILLEM VAN SCHENDEL AND ITTY ABRAHAM

Globalizing Tobacco Control:
Anti-Smoking Campaigns in California, France, and Japan
RODDEY REID

Generations and Globalization:
Youth, Age, and Family in the New World Economy
EDITED BY JENNIFER COLE AND DEBORAH DURHAM

Youth and the City in the Global South
KAREN HANSEN IN COLLABORATION WITH ANNE LINE DALSGAARD,
KATHERINE GOUGH, ULLA AMBROSIUS MADSEN, KAREN VALENTIN,
AND NORBERT WILDERMUTH

Made in Mexico:
Zapotec Weavers and the Global Ethnic Art Market
W. WARNER WOOD

The American War in Contemporary Vietnam:
Visual Culture and Commemoration
CHRISTINA SCHWENKEL

Street Dreams and Hip Hop Barbershops:
Global Fantasy in Urban Tanzania
BRAD WEISS

Aging and the Indian Diaspora:
Cosmopolitan Families in India and Abroad
SARAH LAMB

SARAH LAMB is Associate Professor of Anthropology at Brandeis University. She is author of *White Saris and Sweet Mangoes: Aging, Gender, and Body in North India* and co-editor of *Everyday Life in South Asia* (Indiana University Press, 2002).